Intelligent Security Solutions for Cyber-Physical Systems

A cyber-physical system (CPS) is a computer system in which a mechanism is controlled or monitored by computer-based algorithms and involves transdisciplinary approaches, merging theories of cybernetics, mechatronics, design, and process science. This text mainly concentrates on offering a foundational theoretical underpinning and a comprehensive and coherent review of intelligent security solutions for cyber-physical systems.

Features:

- Provides an overview of cyber-physical systems (CPSs) along with security concepts like attack detection methods, CPS failures, and risk identification and management.
- Showcases cyber-physical systems (CPSs) security solutions, lightweight cryptographic solutions, CPS forensics, etc.
- Emphasizes machine learning methods for behavior-based intrusion detection in cyber-physical systems (CPSs), resilient machine learning for networked CPS, fog computing industrial CPS, etc.
- Elaborates classification of network abnormalities in Internet of Things–based cyber-physical systems (CPSs) using deep learning.
- Includes case studies and applications in the domain of smart grid systems, industrial control systems, smart manufacturing, social network and gaming, electric power grid and energy systems, etc.

Chapman & Hall/CRC Cyber-Physical Systems

Series Editors:

Jyotir Moy Chatterjee, Lord Buddha Education Foundation, Kathmandu, Nepal

Vishal Jain, Sharda University, Greater Noida, India

Cyber-Physical Systems: A Comprehensive Guide
By: Nonita Sharma, L K Awasthi, Monika Mangla, K P Sharma, Rohit Kumar

Introduction to the Cyber Ranges
By: Bishwajeet Pandey and Shabeer Ahmad

Security Analytics: A Data Centric Approach to Information Security
By: Mehak Khurana, Shilpa Mahajan

Security and Resilience of Cyber Physical Systems
By: Krishan Kumar, Sunny Behal, Abhinav Bhandari, Sajal Bhatia

Cyber Security Applications for Industry 4.0
By: R Sujatha, G Prakash, Noor Zaman Jhanjhi

Cyber Physical Systems: Concepts and Applications
By: Anupam Baliyan, Kuldeep Singh Kaswan, Naresh Kumar, Kamal Upreti, Ramani Kannan

Intelligent Security Solutions for Cyber-Physical Systems
By: Vandana Mohindru Sood, Yashwant Singh, Bharat Bhargava, Sushil Kumar Narang

For more information on this series please visit: https://www.routledge.com/ Chapman--HallCRC-Cyber-Physical-Systems/book-series/CHCPS?pd=published, forthcoming&pg=1&pp=12&so=pub&view=list?pd=published,forthcoming&pg= 1&pp=12&so=pub&view=list

Intelligent Security Solutions for Cyber-Physical Systems

Edited by
Vandana Mohindru Sood
Yashwant Singh
Bharat Bhargava
Sushil Kumar Narang

CRC Press
Taylor & Francis Group
Boca Raton London New York

CRC Press is an imprint of the
Taylor & Francis Group, an **informa** business

A CHAPMAN & HALL BOOK

Front cover image: metamorworks/Shutterstock

First edition published 2024
by CRC Press
2385 NW Executive Center Drive, Suite 320, Boca Raton FL 33431

and by CRC Press
4 Park Square, Milton Park, Abingdon, Oxon, OX14 4RN

CRC Press is an imprint of Taylor & Francis Group, LLC

© 2024 selection and editorial matter, Intelligent Security Solutions for Cyber-Physical Systems; individual chapters, the contributors

ISBN: 978-1-032-52152-7 (hbk)
ISBN: 978-1-032-52319-4 (pbk)
ISBN: 978-1-003-40610-5 (ebk)

DOI: 10.1201/9781003406105

Typeset in Times
by SPi Technologies India Pvt Ltd (Straive)

Contents

SECTION I   Introduction to Cyber-Physical Systems

SECTION II   Security Concepts in Cyber-Physical Systems

SECTION III   Securing Cyber-Physical Systems

SECTION IV   Machine Learning for Cyber-Physical Systems

SECTION V   Application Domains in Cyber-Physical Systems: Challenges, Trends, and Future Scope

About the Editors

Dr. Vandana Mohindru Sood is an assistant professor in the Department of Computer Science and Engineering (Artificial Intelligence) at Chitkara University Institute of Engineering & Technology, Chitkara University, Punjab, India, since 2021. She has more than 11 years of experience in teaching and research. She completed her PhD in Computer Science and Engineering from Jaypee University of Information Technology, Himachal Pradesh, India. Dr. Vandana is a renowned researcher in the areas of the Internet of Things, Wireless Sensor Networks, Security, Blockchain, Cryptography, UAV, and Machine Learning. She has published more than 30 technical research papers in leading journals and conferences from IEEE, Elsevier, Springer, etc. She has 376 citations and a H-Index of 13. She has organized international conferences and chaired various sessions during IEEE and Springer conferences. She has published 10 utility patents, 4 design patents granted, and edited 3 books.

Prof. Yashwant Singh is a professor and head of the Department of Computer Science & Information Technology at the Central University of Jammu since 2017. He completed his PhD at Himachal Pradesh University, Shimla. His research interests lie in the Internet of Things, Wireless Sensor Networks, and ICS/SCADA Cyber Security, ranging from theory to design to implementation. He has collaborated actively with researchers in several other disciplines of Computer Science, particularly Machine Learning, Electrical Engineering, and Cyber-Physical Systems. He has served on 30 International Conferences and Workshop Programs as a committee member. He currently serves as a coordinator of the Kalam Centre for Science and Technology (KCST), Computational System Security System Vertical at the Central University of Jammu established by DRDO. Yashwant has published more than 80 research articles in international journals, international conferences, and book chapters of repute. He has 1,468 citations and a H-Index of 20. He is executing a research project on IoT vulnerability worth Rs. 46.32 Lakhs sponsored by DRDO and another project on cybersecurity worth 12.19 lakhs sponsored by the National Commission for Women. He is a visiting professor at Jan Wyzykowski University, Polkowice, Poland.

Prof. Bharat Bhargava is a professor of the Department of Computer Science with a courtesy appointment in the School of Electrical & Computer Engineering at Purdue University. Professor Bhargava is conducting research on security and privacy issues in distributed systems. Professor Bhargava is a recipient of seven best paper awards at various international computer science conferences. Professor Bhargava is a Fellow of the Institute of Electrical and Electronics Engineers and the Institute of Electronics and Telecommunication Engineers. He serves on seven editorial boards of international journals. He also served on the IEEE Computer Society on Technical Achievement award and Fellow committees. Professor Bhargava is the founder of the IEEE Symposium on Reliable and Distributed Systems, IEEE Conference on Digital Library, and the ACM Conference on Information and Knowledge Management.

Dr. Sushil Kumar Narang is an associate professor and Dean in the Department of Computer Science and Engineering (Artificial Intelligence) at Chitkara University Institute of Engineering & Technology, Chitkara University, Punjab, India. He completed his Ph.D. at Panjab University, Chandigarh, India. His research on "Feature Extraction and Neural Network Classifiers for Optical Character Recognition for Good Quality Handwritten Gurmukhi and Devnagari Characters" focused on various image processing, machine as well as deep learning algorithms. His research interests lie in programming languages, ranging from theory to design to implementation, Image Processing, Data Analytics, and Machine Learning. Dr. Sushil has published technical research papers in leading journals and conferences from IEEE, Elsevier, Springer, etc. He has collaborated actively with researchers in several other disciplines of computer science, particularly machine learning on real-world use cases. He is a certified Deep Learning Engineer.

Contributors

Bibhudendra Acharya
Department of ECE
National Institute of Technology Raipur
Chhattisgarh, India

Krishnashree Achuthan
Center for Cybersecurity Systems and
    Networks
Amrita Vishwa Vidyapeetham
Kerala, India

Sangeeta Arora
KIET Group of Institutions
Delhi-NCR, India

Ankit Ashish
Department of Computer Science and
    Information Technology
Central University of Jammu
Jammu, India

Devershi Pallavi Bhatt
Department of Computer Applications
Manipal University
Jaipur, India

Moushumi Das
Chitkara University Institute of
    Engineering and Technology
Chitkara University
Punjab, India

Kamal Deep Garg
Chitkara University Institute of
    Engineering and Technology
Chitkara University
Punjab, India

Hitakshi
Chitkara University Institute of
    Engineering and Technology
Chitkara University
Punjab, India

Mohammad Reza Hosenkhan
Faculty of Information and
    Communication Technology
Universite Des Mascareignes, Mauritius

J. Jithish
Center for Cybersecurity Systems and
    Networks
Amrita Vishwa Vidyapeetham
Kerala, India

Gurleen Kaur
Department of Computer Science &
    Engineering
Chandigarh Group of Colleges
Punjab, India

Gurpreet Kaur
Department of Law
Guru Kashi University
Punjab, India

Tripat Kaur
School of Commerce and Management
GSSDGS Khalsa College
Patiala, India

Veerpal Kaur
Department of Computer Applications
Manipal University
Jaipur, India

Himanshu Khajuria
Amity Institute of Forensic Sciences
Amity University
Uttar Pradesh, India

Neha Koul
Department of Computer Science and
    Information Technology
Central University of Jammu
Jammu, India

Neerendra Kumar
Department of Computer Science and
  Information Technology
Central University of Jammu
Jammu, India

Suprava Ranjan Laha
Department of Computer Science and
  Engineering, FET-ITER
Siksha 'O' Anusandhan (Deemed to be)
  University
Odisha, India

Sheikh Imroza Manzoor
Department of Computer Science and
  Information Technology
Central University of Jammu
Jammu, India

Kapil Mehta
Department of Computer Science &
  Engineering
Chandigarh Group of Colleges
Punjab, India

Meenakshi
Dept. of Computer Science & Technology
Central University of Punjab
Bathinda, Punjab

Zeesha Mishra
Department of ECE
Chhattisgarh Swami Vivekanand
  Technical University
Chhattisgarh, India

Sushil Kumar Narang
Chitkara University Institute of
  Engineering and Technology
Chitkara University
Punjab, India

Debasish Swapnesh Kumar Nayak
Department of Computer Science and
  Engineering, FET-ITER
Siksha 'O' Anusandhan (Deemed to be)
  University
Odisha, INDIA

Biswa Prakash Nayak
Amity Institute of Forensic
  Sciences
Amity University
Uttar Pradesh, India

Binod Kumar Pattanayak
Department of Computer Science and
  Engineering, FET-ITER
Siksha 'O' Anusandhan (Deemed to be)
  University
Odisha, India

Saumendra Pattnaik
Department of Computer Science and
  Engineering, FET-ITER
Siksha 'O' Anusandhan (Deemed to be)
  University
Odisha, India

G Krishna Pranav
Department of ECE
National Institute of Technology
  Raipur
Chhattisgarh, India

Saumya Rajvanshi
Department of Computer Science &
  Engineering
Chandigarh Group of Colleges
Punjab, India

Indranath Roy
Dr. Shakuntala Misra National
  Rehabilitation University
Lucknow, U.P., India

Asadullah Safi
Dept. of Computer Science &
  Technology
Central University of Punjab
Punjab, India

Sriram Sankaran
Center for Cybersecurity Systems and
  Networks
Amrita Vishwa Vidyapeetham
Kerala, India

Aditya Sharma
Chitkara University Institute of
    Engineering and Technology
Chitkara University
Punjab, India

Zakir Ahmad Sheikh
Department of Computer Science and
    Information Technology
Central University of Jammu
Jammu, India

Chintan Singh
Amity Institute of Forensic Sciences
Amity University
Uttar Pradesh, India

Satwinder Singh
Central University of Punjab, Bathinda
Pune, India

Yashwant Singh
Department of Computer Science and
    Information Technology
Central University of Jammu
Jammu, India

Vandana Mohindru Sood
Chitkara University Institute of
    Engineering and Technology
Chitkara University
Punjab, India

Sumegh Tharewal
Symbiosis Institute of Computer Studies
    and Research (SICSR),
Symbiosis International (Deemed)
    University (SIU),
 Pune, India

Pradeep Kumar Tiwari
Dr. Vishwanath Karad MIT World Peace
    University
Pune, India

Narinder Verma
Department of Computer
    Science and Information
    Technology
Central University of Jammu
Jammu, India

Preface

The concept of cyber-physical systems (CPS) emerges as a cornerstone of contemporary technological breakthroughs in this age where the digital domain closely interleaves with the physical sphere. These systems are radically transforming industries, from smart grids to healthcare, by fusing computing and physical processes together. Yet, with great potential comes great responsibility. As CPS gets more eminent, protecting it against numerous vulnerabilities becomes both a necessity and an intellectual challenge. By going deeply into the core of CPS security, this book, *Intelligent Security Solutions for Cyber-Physical Systems*, seeks to answer this challenge and provides a thorough guide for researchers, experts, and enthusiasts alike.

Section I introduces the foundational concepts and components of CPS. This section elucidates CPS-related layers, components, models, and challenges after providing a broad overview of its design. This primer provides the necessary background for individuals who are new to the field so that the next sections can be contextualized in their proper perspective.

However, without considering the security considerations that go along with CPS, a thorough knowledge of the technology would be incomplete. The security ideas built into CPS are the emphasis of Section II, which also explores the threats and vulnerabilities inherent to these systems. This section presents a comprehensive view of the security landscape surrounding CPS, from assessing potential attack routes to simplifying security policies and risk management techniques.

The focus of Section III of the narrative is on securing the cyber-physical systems against the vulnerabilities described in Section B. Here, we explore the CPS-specific frameworks, solutions, and cryptographic safety measures. This section offers readers tools to not only prevent security breaches but also to identify them, fix them, and prevent them from transpiring again. Topics covered here range from forensics to lightweight cryptographic solutions.

But in the rapidly transforming world of technology, conventional security measures occasionally fall short. The synergy between ML and CPS security is explored in Section IV. This section explains how the power of ML may be utilized to strengthen CPS security with chapters devoted to intrusion detection, fog computing, and big data analytics. Furthermore, subjects like explainable unsupervised ML and reinforcement learning give a preview of what intelligent CPS security solutions will look like in the future.

Finally, Section V focuses on real-world CPS applications across a diversity of fields, including the possibilities of blockchain-enabled CPS and smart grids and healthcare systems. In addition to highlighting the difficulties in each field, the chapters also discuss current trends and speculate on potential future directions.

Our goal in writing this book is dual: First, to present a comprehensive analysis of CPS and the security issues that are inherently present and, second, to provide cutting-edge, intelligent solutions that can be modified and applied in a variety of contexts. This book will act as both a guide and a spark, inspiring you to break new boundaries in the development of intelligent security solutions for cyber-physical systems.

To the future, where the digital and physical realms coalesce harmoniously and securely, welcome to the world of Intelligent Security Solutions for Cyber-Physical Systems.

Editors

Section I

Introduction to Cyber-Physical Systems

1 Cyber-Physical Systems and Their Emergence in Machine Learning

Moushumi Das and Vandana Mohindru Sood

Chitkara University Institute of Engineering & Technology, Chitkara University, Punjab, India

1.1 INTRODUCTION: BACKGROUND AND DRIVING FORCES

The cyber-physical system (CPS) is a representation of an Industry 4.0 device that may combine both virtual and physical environments by delivering data processing in real time. A CPS helps any physical system to be equipped with some simulated systems such as a monitor, allowing information about the real world to be studied in the virtual world and choices to be taken to impact the course of the actual world (Duo et al. 2022).

CPS makes information integration, communication, and collaboration easier along with real-time monitoring and worldwide network optimization (Liu et al. 2022). CPSs are built as a system of computing units that communicate around their surroundings using practical inputs as well as output mechanisms. CPSs are a new type of engineering system with sophisticated processing and communication capabilities that execute specific duties within strict real-time constraints (Wu et al. 2023).

Data is frequently exchanged in real time among the many CPS components. All the necessary demands are essential for satisfying their operational demands, allowing the computer system to regulate itself and become conscious, which is especially important in real-time applications (Malik and Saleem 2022).

This is also one of the essential elements of the IIoT and will play an important part in Industry 4.0 enabling intelligent services and programs to execute precisely. They are built on the real-time interchange of various forms of data and sensitive information between cyber and physical systems. CPS development is being pursued by both academics and industry. Given CPS' immense economic potential, implementing CPS into Industry 4.0 will increase German gross value by 267 billion euros by 2025 (Chen et al. 2022).

This is an embedded system network consisting of three fundamental essential components: Sensors, aggregators, and actuators. CPS systems may also observe their environment, adapt, and manage the physical world (Wang et al. 2022a). The major components of cyber-physical systems are depicted in Figure 1.1.

Machine learning is critical for improving the capabilities of CPS by allowing them to learn from data, adapt to changing surroundings, and make intelligent

DOI: 10.1201/9781003406105-2

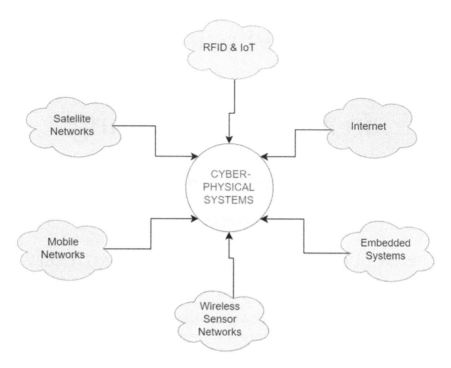

FIGURE 1.1 Components of cyber-physical systems.

judgments. Machine learning algorithms in CPS extract important insights from sensor data, historical knowledge, and real-time observations to allow autonomous decision-making (Ryalat et al. 2023).

In addition, machine learning provides predictive analytics in CPS, where models may estimate system behavior, performance, or demand based on previous data. These forecasts aid in optimizing resource allocation, energy management, and system operation scheduling, resulting in increased efficiency and cost savings. Furthermore, machine learning enables CPS to optimize control techniques. For example, reinforcement learning approaches can develop optimum control policies by exploring the environment and receiving feedback based on preset goals. This enables CPS to change control actions dynamically based on real-time circumstances, resulting in increased system stability, energy economy, and reaction times (Yu et al. 2022).

Furthermore, machine learning facilitates decision-making by evaluating massive volumes of data and finding significant patterns or insights. Machine learning algorithms may aid in decision support, risk assessment, and anomaly classification by training models on historical data and expert knowledge and helping operators and decision-makers to make educated choices in complicated CPS settings. Figure 1.2 depicts many uses of machine learning in cyber-physical systems.

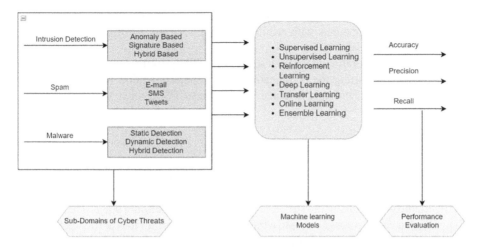

FIGURE 1.2 Machine learning-based applications in cyber-physical systems.

Data play an important part in operating CPSs, especially given that CPSs might have serious effects if choices are generated from information of poor quality. It also may jeopardize safety limitations if inaccurate data is received, time deadlines are missed, or key sensor readings are not received in real time (Rachmawati 2022).

CPSs improve interaction among intelligent manufacturing entities and cyber computer resources. Wearable sensors are often used for recognizing human activity and are a vital aspect of CPS since they are capable of directly and effectively tracking body mobility. CPSs are generated when computing, networking, and physical processes come together. Communication is used in CPSs to exchange information between objects and people. The dependability, latency, and bandwidth of these exchanges are studied. The interplay of items and calculations results in sophisticated IoT implementation (Wang et al. 2022b).

CPSs are widely utilized in the industrial, healthcare, distribution, and transportation industries, as well as in buildings. No doubt CPS is an important part of life, but it is something in need of security for priority, and for that various technologies have been introduced working on the basis of machine learning and deep learning algorithms and some of them have given satisfying results even but still, there is a lot of need for much more improvements in the coming time. A huge amount of data is being generated through CPS; in this stage, machine learning can act as a better technology for working with the data and processing it which also enables CPS to work in a dynamic environment along with intrusion detection (Patel et al. 2023).

Machine learning algorithms may modify models and adapt to changing settings by continuously learning from data, ensuring CPS stays dynamic and robust (Malikopoulos 2023). As CPS evolves, advances in machine learning will play an increasingly important role in determining the future of intelligent, linked systems. The combined application of machine learning and edge computing in CPS decreases latency and bandwidth needs, allowing important applications to make real-time decisions. The synergistic interaction between machine learning and CPS will lead to breakthrough developments with ramifications in a variety of disciplines (Lee and Kundu 2022; Lee et al. 2020).

However, incorporating machine learning into CPS presents its own set of issues. Furthermore, controlling the computational and communication needs of machine learning algorithms within a resource-constrained CPS context is crucial (Zhang et al. 2021).

1.2   LITERATURE REVIEW

Wiśniewski et al. (2022) provided a novel method for creating a Petri-net-based CPS. This recommended method shortened the time and expense of CPS prototyping by identifying faults in the structure during the early defining stage. The idea was shown with a case investigation into a traffic light intersection in real life. The system was developed, researched, constructed, and eventually confirmed within the FPGA device (Virtex-5 family).

(Amro et al. 2023). In order to exploit encoded common knowledge and make attack expression easier, a new risk assessment method supplemented with specific semantics and MITRE ATT&CK framework components has been presented. The recommended method is then shown by doing a risk analysis for a communication architecture customized for APSs. Furthermore, we present a set of measures based on graph theory for assessing the effect of the detected hazards.

NIRVANA is an innovative technique for prediction validation via uncertainty metrics (Catak et al. 2022). They first utilized prediction-time dropout-based neural networks, and the second was utilized as input for a support vector machine to forecast erroneous labels, and to construct an extremely discriminatory prediction validator model with unpredictable values.

Alohali et al. (2022) suggested a methodology that first conducts data preprocessing. Furthermore, the the fish swarm optimization-based feature selection (IFSO-FS) approach is employed for feature selection. To circumvent the local optima problem, the IFSO approach incorporates the Levy Flight (LF) notion for the searching process of the standard FSO algorithm.

Lee and Kundu (2022) proposed the 5C-CPS framework including a reference structure for DL and DT integration. It provides a complete path for developing and implementing smart manufacturing with enhanced openness, cooperation, and efficiency.

Mishra et al. (2023) proposed a generic NG-CPS framework that included all design components. The smart city was also built as an NG-CPS using the standard NG-CSP architecture. To aid network designers in networking, a cutting-edge protocol framework for smart city NG-CPS was also available.

Thus, Table 1.1 summarizes the various models and techniques presented by many authors and researchers, as well as the research gap between all of them, from which it is concluded that even after the introduction of many new technologies, certain improvements in the models are still required for much better results.

TABLE 1.1
Summary of the Related Work

References	Year	Model/Techniques Proposed	Dataset/Algorithm Used	Advantage	Research Gap
Wiśniewski et al. (2022)	2023	Petri-net-based cyber-physical system	Traffic light crossroad example	Error detection in the systems.	The absence of deadlocks needs to be checked.
Amro et al. (2023)	2023	Risk assessment approach	FMECA	The need for expert judgment was reduced	Estimation of countermeasure effectiveness.
Catak et al. (2022)	2022	NIRVANA (uNcertaInty pRediction VAlidAtor iN Ai)	Four real-world CPS datasets	Showed a negative correlation between uncertainty quantification and prediction accuracy.	Prioritization to test DL models
Alohali et al. (2022)	2022	AIMMF-IDS	IFSO algorithm	The performance was enhanced.	Intrusion detection performance is to be boosted.
Lee and Kundu (2022)	2020	Reference architecture for the integration of DL and DT	5C-CPS structure	Better efficiency	Need for improvement in the design of components.
Mishra et al. (2023)	2020	Generic NG-CPS framework	Big data (a large amount of heterogeneous, unstructured data)	Covered all the protocols stack.	Various emerging technologies can be used for better performance.

1.3 ARCHITECTURE

The following is the architecture with functions that are performed by each of the components of cyber-physical systems. Figure 1.3 depicts the architecture of cyber-physical systems (Wu et al. 2023).

a) **Sensors**: The sensors in cyber-physical systems are used to collect data in real time.
b) **Actuators**: Control commands are carried out by matching actuators in order to achieve the intended physical actions (Rai and Sahu 2020).
c) **Computing and Control Centre**: This is in charge of receiving data from sensors. The control center makes matching control choices based on the incoming data to guarantee that physical operations are carried out correctly (Olowononi et al. 2020).
d) **Communication Network**: A communication platform between the command and control center, as well as the physical system is provided by this component. The communication network transmits control signals or choices from the control center to actuators (Luo et al. 2021).

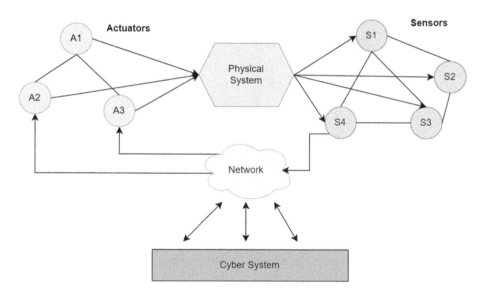

FIGURE 1.3   Architecture of cyber-physical systems.

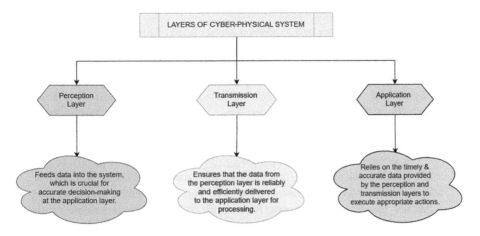

FIGURE 1.4 Various layers of cyber-physical systems.

1.3.1 DIFFERENT LAYERS OF CYBER-PHYSICAL SYSTEMS

The perception, transmission, and application layers are the three primary layers in the architecture of cyber-physical systems. Figure 1.4 is a representation of all three layers.

- **Perception Layer**
  It goes by several names, such as the identification layer and the sensing layer. To enable the monitoring, tracking, and analysis of the physical world, these technologies gather data in real time. Information on the quantity of electricity consumed, the temperature, the location, the chemistry, and the biology are some examples of the data that can be gathered depending on the type of sensor. Real-time data generated by these sensors are accessible through both wide-reaching and local network domains. It is often referred to as the sensing layer or the identifying layer. Depending on the type of sensor, data such as electrical consumption, heat, location, chemistry, and biology are also obtained, as are sound and light signals. Real-time data are generated by these sensors over large and local network domains, which the application layer aggregates and analyzes (Hussain et al. 2020).
- **Transmission Layer**
  This layer is considered to be the second layer in the cyber-physical systems (CPS) architecture. This stratum facilitates the processing and transmission of data and facilitates the transmission and exchange of data across the Internet. To handle the proliferation of devices connected to the internet, various protocols, including IPv6, are employed.

  These technologies play a crucial role in facilitating the storage, processing, and transmission of data in a networked environment. Cloud computing platforms enable users to access and utilize computer resources, such as storage and computational power, over the internet (Rathore and Park 2020).

- **Application Layer**

  This is the third layer and exhibits a higher level of interactivity compared to previous layers. The function of this process is to assess the data obtained from the data transfer layer and subsequently give instructions to physical components, including sensors and actuators. The attainment of this objective is accomplished by the utilization of intricate decision-making algorithms that rely on aggregated data. The aforementioned layer further collects and analyzes data collected by the perception layer prior to determining the requisite automated actions.

  To safeguard and preserve privacy, private data must be kept private and not released. Furthermore, this layer needs a robust multifactor authentication method to avoid unauthorized access. The magnitude of produced data has become a serious concern. As a result, safeguarding large data needs effective security systems capable of processing massive volumes of data in a fast and efficient manner (Liu et al. 2022; Liu et al. 2020).

1.3.2   COMPONENTS OF CYBER-PHYSICAL SYSTEMS

CPS components are utilized to detect information or control signals. CPS components are divided into two types given as following:

a) **Sensing Components**: These components are generally located in the perception layer which usually consists of sensors enabling the information collection which is further transferred to the aggregators. Also, the data are forwarded to the actuators that process it for guaranteeing the decision.

   The primary CPS sensor components are listed below:
   - **Sensors**: Capture and preserve real-world information using a "calibration" technique that helps in assessing the collected data to check its correctness. The sending of data from here is considered a crucial step.
   - **Aggregators**: These are generally located near the transmission layer and are in-charge of processing data received from sensors prior to issuing the corresponding decisions.
   - **Actuators**: The aggregators, as per their decisions, are responsible for ensuring the availability of information to the surrounding environment at the application level (Zhou et al. 2021).

b) **Controlling Components**: The aforementioned components are employed for the purpose of signal regulation, and they have significance in the control, monitoring, and management of signals. Their primary objective is to attain heightened levels of accuracy and safeguard against potential threats such as deliberate signal disruption, extraneous noise, and interference. Moreover, these components are employed to mitigate signal jamming, noise, and interference. The essentiality of Programmable Logic Controllers (PLCs) and Distributed Control Systems (DCSs), along with their constituent components (such as Operational Technology/Information Technology (OT/IT), Control Loop/Server, and Human–Machine Interface (HMI)/Graphical User Interface (GUI)), has emerged as a direct consequence (Tran et al. 2019).

Following that, we outline the many types of control systems utilized in CPS:

- **Programmable Logic Controllers (PLC)**: To replace the hard-wired layers, initially PLCs are used, but now, they are considered as industrial digital computers governing the production processes.
- **Distributed Control Systems (DCS)**: These are the controlling systems allowing independent controllers for dispersion across the system. The offsite surveillance and oversight approach improves the reliability of the DCS while lowering the installation cost (Leong et al. 2020).
- **Remote Terminal Units (RTU)**: The phrase "Remote Telemetry Unit" refers to microprocessor-controlled electrical equipment, MTU. They do not have any kind of control loops or control algorithms, unlike PLCs. As a result, they tend to be better for wireless communications across broader geographic telemetry zones (Dreossi et al. 2019).

1.4 MODELS OF CYBER-PHYSICAL SYSTEMS

- **Timed Actor CPS**: The functional features of behavior and accuracy, in addition to the nonfunctional characteristics of efficiency and time, are the emphasis of this paradigm. There is a theory that limits specific behavioral sets, enhancing efficiency while lowering complexity. It has a purpose and a classical modification (Jayaratne et al. 2021).
- **Event-Based CPS**: Before actuation decisions can be made in such models, an event must be identified by the appropriate CPS components. Contrarily, individual component time limits vary depending on the nondeterministic system delay brought on by the various CPS processes.
- **Lattice-Based Event Model**: Events are represented in this CPS by event type, as well as both external and internal event characteristics. In the case that these occurrences are collated, they may be used to build a spatiotemporal feature of the particular incident to recognize every observer of the event (Hu et al. 2023).
- **Hybrid-Based CPS Model**: These interactive systems are heterogeneous systems made up of discrete-state and continuous-state interactive systems. Hybrid CPS, in contrast to earlier types, connect over a network, causing delays. Additionally, hybrid CPS systems are incompatible with concurrent system simulation and do not enable hierarchical modeling. As a consequence, the limitations of hybrid system models created by CPS were examined (Latif et al. 2022).

1.5 MACHINE LEARNING IN CYBER-PHYSICAL SYSTEM

Machine learning is critical in cyber-physical systems because it enables real-time data evaluation and adaptive decision-making. Learning patterns from interconnected physical and digital components improves system efficiency, predictive maintenance, and resilience. This synergy enables CPS to evolve intelligently, successfully linking the virtual and physical worlds.

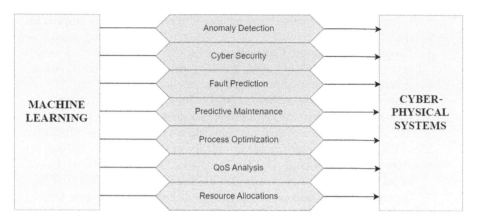

FIGURE 1.5 Various machine learning techniques.

1.5.1 MACHINE LEARNING TECHNIQUES USEFUL FOR CYBER-PHYSICAL SYSTEMS

CPS applications include driverless cars, industrial control systems, smart grids, healthcare systems, and others. Here are several machine learning approaches that are very beneficial in CPS, as represented in Figure 1.5.

- **Supervised Learning**: Anomaly detection, classification, and regression are all tasks that require supervised learning techniques in CPS. To generate predictions or choices, these algorithms learn from labeled training data. In autonomous cars, for example, supervised learning may be used to recognize things on the road and make judgments based on them.
- **Unsupervised Learning**: CPS uses unsupervised learning approaches to uncover patterns and correlations in data that lacks tagged training samples. To discover groups of similar data points, clustering methods such as k-means and hierarchical clustering can be utilized. This can be useful in discovering abnormalities in CPS or identifying anomalous behaviors.
- **Reinforcement Learning**: Reinforcement learning (RL) is a strong approach in CPS, notably for decision-making and control problems. To maximize a reward signal, RL algorithms learn through contact with the environment. RL may be utilized in CPS to develop optimum policies for tasks such as path planning, resource allocation, and scheduling (Tang et al. 2023).
- **Deep Learning**: Deep learning approaches, particularly deep neural networks, have demonstrated exceptional performance in a variety of CPS applications. Convolutional neural networks (CNNs) are often used for image and video analysis, but recurrent neural networks (RNNs) are better suited to sequential data processing applications like time series analysis or natural language processing.
- **Online Learning**: Online learning algorithms are ideal for CPS applications that use streaming data or operate in dynamic situations. As fresh data becomes available, online learning allows models to adapt and update in

real time. This is useful in scenarios requiring real-time decision-making, such as adaptive control systems or anomaly detection in quickly changing contexts (Jamal et al. 2023).

- **Ensemble Learning**: The process of merging different models to create more accurate predictions or judgments is known as ensemble learning. Ensemble approaches in CPS can improve system dependability and resilience by pooling predictions from many models or algorithms. To increase the accuracy and robustness of CPS applications, ensemble methods like Random Forests, Boosting, and Bagging can be applied.

These machine learning approaches, together with CPS developments, continue to push the frontiers of numerous disciplines. They allow for intelligent decision-making, real-time monitoring, and adaptive control, which results in more efficient, dependable, and secure cyber-physical systems (Li et al. 2020).

1.5.2 Application of Machine Learning in Cyber-Physical Systems

Cyber-physical systems (CPS) are systems that combine physical and computer components to monitor, control, and optimize physical processes in real time. Machine learning techniques might be used to analyze and learn from CPS data, which could then be used to improve performance and optimize processes. Here are some examples of CPS machine learning applications (Presekal et al. 2023):

- **Smart Grids**: Machine learning algorithms can be used to analyze data from power grid sensors and estimate real-time power demand and supply. This information might be used to optimize electricity distribution, eliminate energy waste, and reduce carbon emissions.
- **Autonomous Vehicles**: In autonomous vehicles, machine learning algorithms may be used to evaluate data from sensors and cameras, allowing them to make real-time driving decisions such as spotting obstructions, anticipating traffic patterns, and correctly altering speed and direction.
- **Industrial Monitoring**: Machine learning algorithms have the ability to improve industrial operations like production and logistics. These algorithms can analyze sensors and other data to detect equipment faults, optimize production schedules, and boost productivity (Throne and Lăzăroiu 2020).
- **Healthcare Monitoring**: Machine learning algorithms are capable of monitoring vital signs and other health metrics in real time and providing early warnings of potential health risks. This is especially true for chronic diseases like diabetes, where early detection and intervention are critical (Schneble and Thamilarasu 2019).
- **Building Automation**: Machine learning algorithms may help HVAC systems, lighting systems, and other building systems. By utilizing data from sensors and other sources, these algorithms can estimate energy demand, optimize energy usage, and improve overall building comfort and efficiency (Alsufyani et al. 2023).

- **Traffic Management**: Machine learning algorithms can be used to analyze real-time data from traffic sensors and cameras to optimize traffic flow. This can lead to fewer traffic, faster travel times, and better safety.
- **Environmental Monitoring**: Machine learning algorithms may be used to analyze data from sensors and other sources to monitor environmental aspects such as air quality, water quality, and weather patterns. This can aid in the identification of possible threats and the implementation of timely measures to protect public health and the environment (Mohindru et al. 2019).
- **Robotics**: Machine learning algorithms may assist robots in real-world scenarios such as manufacturing, logistics, and healthcare. Robots can adapt to changing situations and make judgments in real time by evaluating data from sensors and cameras, resulting in increased efficiency and production (Mohindru et al. 2020).

1.6 VARIOUS CHALLENGES FACED IN CYBER-PHYSICAL SYSTEMS

- **Privacy**: The CPS is continually collecting massive amounts of data, which most individuals are unaware of. An individual, therefore, has the right to access their own data and know what kind of information is obtained about them by those who gather data and to whom this information is transferred or sold.
- **Dependability**: Through the early implementation of fault-tolerance mechanisms, if the intelligent physical worlds (IPW) can guarantee the CPS's behavior of adaptation, the CPS will be more reliable and offer a sufficient Quality of Service (QoS). While dependability is built on the capacity to react to changing situations in order to overcome and recover from any potential interruption, whether cyber or physical (Kumar et al. 2021).
- **Resiliency**: CPS must be tough to survive accidents and violent assaults. As a result, cybersecurity risks exist in CPS's logical and physical systems. If any of the elements are unreliable, a multiview editor would be appointed to make the appropriate modifications (Rathore et al. 2021).
- **Interaction and Coordination**: These are necessary to maintain the CPS operational at all times. The aspects of the cyber world, on the other hand, are formed on sequences with no chronological significance. In addition, two key approaches to investigating and assessing this issue are explained.

REFERENCES

Alohali, Manal Abdullah, Fahd N. Al-Wesabi, Anwer Mustafa Hilal, Shalini Goel, Deepak Gupta, and Ashish Khanna. "Artificial intelligence enabled intrusion detection systems for cognitive cyber-physical systems in industry 4.0 environment." *Cognitive Neurodynamics* 16, no. 5 (2022): 1045–1057.

Alsufyani, Abdulmajeed, Youseef Alotaibi, Alaa Omran Almagrabi, Saleh Ahmed Alghamdi, and Nawal Alsufyani. "Retracted article: Optimized intelligent data management framework for a cyber-physical system for computational applications." *Complex & Intelligent Systems* 9, no. 3 (2023): 2957–2957.

Amro, Ahmed, Vasileios Gkioulos, and Sokratis Katsikas. "Assessing cyber risk in cyber-physical systems using the ATT&CK framework." *ACM Transactions on Privacy and Security* 26, no. 2 (2023): 1–33.

Catak, Ferhat Ozgur, Tao Yue, and Shaukat Ali. "Uncertainty-aware prediction validator in deep learning models for cyber-physical system data." *ACM Transactions on Software Engineering and Methodology (TOSEM)* 31, no. 4 (2022): 1–31.

Chen, Lunyuan, Shunpu Tang, Venki Balasubramanian, Junjuan Xia, Fasheng Zhou, and Lisheng Fan. "Physical-layer security based mobile edge computing for emerging cyber physical systems." *Computer Communications* 194 (2022): 180–188.

Dreossi, Tommaso, Alexandre Donzé, and Sanjit A. Seshia. "Compositional falsification of cyber-physical systems with machine learning components." *Journal of Automated Reasoning* 63 (2019): 1031–1053.

Duo, Wenli, MengChu Zhou, and Abdullah Abusorrah. "A survey of cyber attacks on cyber physical systems: Recent advances and challenges." *IEEE/CAA Journal of Automatica Sinica* 9, no. 5 (2022): 784–800.

Hu, Shiyan, Yiran Chen, Qi Zhu, and Armando Walter Colombo. "Guest editorial machine learning for resilient industrial cyber-physical systems." *IEEE Transactions on Automation Science and Engineering* 20, no. 1 (2023): 3–4.

Hussain, Bilal, Qinghe Du, Bo Sun, and Zhiqiang Han. "Deep learning-based DDoS-attack detection for cyber–physical system over 5G network." *IEEE Transactions on Industrial Informatics* 17, no. 2 (2020): 860–870.

Jamal, Alshaibi Ahmed, Al-Ani Mustafa Majid, Anton Konev, Tatiana Kosachenko, and Alexander Shelupanov. "A review on security analysis of cyber physical systems using Machine learning." *Materials Today: Proceedings* 80 (2023): 2302–2306.

Jayaratne, Dinithi, Daswin De Silva, Damminda Alahakoon, and Xinghuo Yu. "Continuous detection of concept drift in industrial cyber-physical systems using closed loop incremental machine learning." *Discover Artificial Intelligence* 1 (2021): 1–13.

Kumar, Arun, Sharad Sharma, Nitin Goyal, Aman Singh, Xiaochun Cheng, and Parminder Singh. "Secure and energy-efficient smart building architecture with emerging technology IoT." *Computer Communications* 176 (2021): 207–217.

Latif, Sohaib A., Fang B. Xian Wen, Celestine Iwendi, F. Wang Li-Li, Syed Muhammad Mohsin, Zhaoyang Han, and Shahab S. Band. "AI-empowered, blockchain and SDN integrated security architecture for IoT network of cyber physical systems." *Computer Communications* 181 (2022): 274–283.

Lee, Jay, Moslem Azamfar, Jaskaran Singh, and Shahin Siahpour. "Integration of digital twin and deep learning in cyber-physical systems: Towards smart manufacturing." *IET Collaborative Intelligent Manufacturing* 2, no. 1 (2020): 34–36.

Lee, Jay, and Pradeep Kundu. "Integrated cyber-physical systems and industrial metaverse for remote manufacturing." *Manufacturing Letters* 34 (2022): 12–15.

Leong, A. S., Ramaswamy, A., Quevedo, D. E., Karl, H., & Shi, L. (2020). Deep reinforcement learning for wireless sensor scheduling in cyber–physical systems. *Automatica*, 113, 108759.

Li, Beibei, Yuhao Wu, Jiarui Song, Rongxing Lu, Tao Li, and Liang Zhao. "DeepFed: Federated deep learning for intrusion detection in industrial cyber–physical systems." *IEEE Transactions on Industrial Informatics* 17, no. 8 (2020): 5615–5624.

Liu, Siyuan, Ashutosh Trivedi, Xiang Yin, and Majid Zamani. "Secure-by-construction synthesis of cyber-physical systems." *Annual Reviews in Control* 53 (2022): 30–50.

Liu, Teng, Bin Tian, Yunfeng Ai, and Fei-Yue Wang. "Parallel reinforcement learning-based energy efficiency improvement for a cyber-physical system." *IEEE/CAA Journal of Automatica Sinica* 7, no. 2 (2020): 617–626.

Luo, Yuan, Ya Xiao, Long Cheng, Guojun Peng, and Danfeng Yao. "Deep learning-based anomaly detection in cyber-physical systems: Progress and opportunities." *ACM Computing Surveys (CSUR)* 54, no. 5 (2021): 1–36.

Malik, Javaid Ahmad, and Muhammad Saleem. "Blockchain and cyber-physical system for security engineering in the smart industry." In Saad Motahhir and Yassine Maleh (Eds.), *Security Engineering for Embedded and Cyber-Physical Systems* (pp. 51–70). CRC Press, 2022.

Malikopoulos, Andreas A. "Separation of learning and control for cyber–physical systems." *Automatica* 151 (2023): 110912.

Mishra, Ayaskanta, Amitkumar V. Jha, Bhargav Appasani, Arun Kumar Ray, Deepak Kumar Gupta, and Abu Nasar Ghazali. "Emerging technologies and design aspects of next generation cyber physical system with a smart city application perspective." *International Journal of System Assurance Engineering and Management* 14, no. Suppl 3 (2023): 699–721.

Mohindru, Vandana, Ravindara Bhatt, and Yashwant Singh. "Reauthentication scheme for mobile wireless sensor networks." *Sustainable Computing: Informatics and Systems* 23 (2019): 158–166.

Mohindru, Vandana, Yashwant Singh, and Ravindara Bhatt. "Securing wireless sensor networks from node clone attack: a lightweight message authentication algorithm." *International Journal of Information and Computer Security* 12, no. 2–3 (2020): 217–233.

Olowononi, Felix O., Danda B. Rawat, and Chunmei Liu. "Resilient machine learning for networked cyber physical systems: A survey for machine learning security to securing machine learning for CPS." *IEEE Communications Surveys & Tutorials* 23, no. 1 (2020): 524–552.

Patel, N., Trivedi, S., and Faruqui, N. (2023, February). A novel sedentary workforce scheduling optimization algorithm using 2nd order polynomial kernel. In *2023 International Conference on Smart Computing and Application (ICSCA)* (pp. 1–7). IEEE.

Presekal, Alfan, Alexandru Ştefanov, Vetrivel S. Rajkumar, and Peter Palensky. "Attack graph model for cyber-physical power systems using hybrid deep learning." *IEEE Transactions on Smart Grid* 14, no. 10 (2023): 4007–4020.

Rachmawati, Anggi. "Analysis of machine learning systems for cyber physical systems." *International Transactions on Education Technology* 1, no. 1 (2022): 1–9.

Rai, Rahul, and Chandan K. Sahu. "Driven by data or derived through physics? a review of hybrid physics guided machine learning techniques with cyber-physical system (CPS) focus." *IEEE Access* 8 (2020): 71050–71073.

Rathore, Pramod Singh, Jyotir Moy Chatterjee, Abhishek Kumar, and Radhakrishnan Sujatha. "Energy-efficient cluster head selection through relay approach for WSN." *The Journal of Supercomputing* 77 (2021): 7649–7675.

Rathore, Shailendra, and Jong Hyuk Park. "A blockchain-based deep learning approach for cyber security in next generation industrial cyber-physical systems." *IEEE Transactions on Industrial Informatics* 17, no. 8 (2020): 5522–5532.

Ryalat, Mutaz, Hisham ElMoaqet, and Marwa AlFaouri. "Design of a smart factory based on cyber-physical systems and Internet of Things towards Industry 4.0." *Applied Sciences* 13, no. 4 (2023): 2156.

Schneble, William, and Geethapriya Thamilarasu. "Attack detection using federated learning in medical cyber-physical systems." In *Proceedings of the 28th International Conference on Computing and Communication Networks (ICCCN)* (vol. 29, pp. 1–8). 2019.

Tang, Bin, Yan Lu, Qi Li, Yueying Bai, Jie Yu, and Xu Yu. "A Diffusion Model Based on Network Intrusion Detection Method for Industrial Cyber-Physical Systems." *Sensors* 23, no. 3 (2023): 1141.

Throne, Odile, and George Lăzăroiu. "Internet of Things-enabled sustainability, industrial big data analytics, and deep learning-assisted smart process planning in cyber-physical manufacturing systems." *Economics, Management and Financial Markets* 15, no. 4 (2020): 49–58.

Tran, Hoang-Dung, Feiyang Cai, Manzanas Lopez Diego, Patrick Musau, Taylor T. Johnson, and Xenofon Koutsoukos. "Safety verification of cyber-physical systems with reinforcement learning control." *ACM Transactions on Embedded Computing Systems (TECS)* 18, no. 5s (2019): 1–22.

Wang, Baicun, Pai Zheng, Yue Yin, Albert Shih, and Lihui Wang. "Toward human-centric smart manufacturing: A human-cyber-physical systems (HCPS) perspective." *Journal of Manufacturing Systems* 63 (2022a): 471–490.

Wang, Tianteng, Xuping Wang, Yiping Jiang, Zilai Sun, Yuhu Liang, Xiangpei Hu, Hao Li, Yan Shi, Jingjun Xu, and Junhu Ruan. "Hybrid machine learning approach for evapotranspiration estimation of fruit tree in agricultural cyber-physical systems." *IEEE Transactions on Cybernetics* 53, no. 9 (2022b): 5677–5691.

Wiśniewski, Remigiusz, Marcin Wojnakowski, and Zhiwu Li. "Design and verification of petri-net-based cyber-physical systems oriented toward implementation in field-programmable gate arrays—A case study example." *Energies* 16, no. 1 (2022): 67.

Wu, Weiqiang, Chunyue Song, Jun Zhao, and Zuhua Xu. "Physics-informed gated recurrent graph attention unit network for anomaly detection in industrial cyber-physical systems." *Information Sciences* 629 (2023): 618–633.

Yu, Zhenhua, Hongxia Gao, Dan Wang, Abeer Ali Alnuaim, Muhammad Firdausi, and Almetwally M. Mostafa. "SEI2RS malware propagation model considering two infection rates in cyber–physical systems." *Physica A: Statistical Mechanics and its Applications* 597 (2022): 127207.

Zhang, Jun, Lei Pan, Qing-Long Han, Chao Chen, Sheng Wen, and Yang Xiang. "Deep learning based attack detection for cyber-physical system cybersecurity: A survey." *IEEE/CAA Journal of Automatica Sinica* 9, no. 3 (2021): 377–391.

Zhou, Junlong, Liying Li, Ahmadreza Vajdi, Xiumin Zhou, and Zebin Wu. "Temperature-constrained reliability optimization of industrial cyber-physical systems using machine learning and feedback control." *IEEE Transactions on Automation Science and Engineering* 20, no. 1 (2021): 20–31.

Section II

Security Concepts in Cyber-Physical Systems

2 A General Walkthrough of the Cyber-Physical Systems Concerning Security Threats and Safety Measures

Indranath Roy

Dr. Shakuntala Misra National Rehabilitation University, Lucknow, U.P., India

2.1 INTRODUCTION

Cyber-physical system (CPS): As the name suggests, it is a categorical integration of cyberspace and physical space. In this chapter, we will try to redefine with a proper investigation of the entire CPS and its security aspects. CPS is a generalization of advanced embedded systems, though it has some differences from trivial embedded systems. It has no resource or device constraints, better real-time operability, and full integration of physical components and software (Hatzivasilis et al. 2021). It is a product of a fusion of various engineering disciplines (industrial, aeronautical, civil, biomedical, chemical, electrical, environmental, mechanical, and, of course, computer science and engineering). The term "CPS" was first coined by Dr. Hellen Gill in 2006. CPS has a fantastic application for the next generation of sensors. In the CPS, we can find all the applications of Industry 4.0 and its different aspects for implementing the IIoT (Industrial Internet of Things) (Jazdi 2014). The leading beauty of the CPS is the ultra-automation of the functionalities. It mainly uses next-generation sensors for sensing, as that is one of the most vital aspects of implementing the system. The CPS is a general integration of various IoT devices involved in (1) sensing, (2) actuating, (3) communicating, and (4) automating. As a whole, A CPS is an intelligent system that has been jointly developed to improve human lives. The interactions between numerous physical and computational components make up the systems. From Figure 2.1, we can briefly describe how a CPS functions in the real world. We can find the usage of embedded systems in various areas, like (1) vehicles, (2) medical instruments, (3) defense systems like radars and robotics, (5) process monitoring, and (6) factory automation. Exploiting CPS makes the entire system more effective and efficient for human beings. Cyberspace can be composed

DOI: 10.1201/9781003406105-4

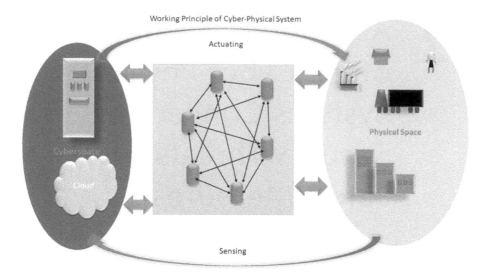

FIGURE 2.1 Brief working of CPS.

of algorithms implemented in the clouds, on servers, or anything composed of cybernetics. A physical system contains all the visible machinery or humans, and machinery includes houses, factories, automobiles, buildings, or even cameras and mobiles. The interconnecting networks contain network components (the interconnection of nodes). By detecting it through the network space, cyberspace gathers all the data and information from the physical space. Some algorithms are carried out in cyberspace using data and information from the real world. After the computation in cyberspace, the actuator performs the action. The various features of CPS are as follows.

- Outfitted with a response or feedback loop and a control system.
- Actuators have an impact on the environment, while sensors sense it.
- There are hybrid control systems for complicated tasks.

1. **Concurrency of Operation**
   - Commonly, various processes in a CPS run concurrently.
   - In runtime, processes often exchange their information to achieve the desired result.
   - The operations can be both synchronous and asynchronous modes.
2. **Reactive Computation**
   - Interaction of the system with the environment in a continuous fashion.
   - A reactive system is a system when switched on can have recreative effects on the output.
3. **Real-Time Computation**
   - The time-sensitive operations, operations like coordination and allocating resources, can be efficiently done in a CPS (Marwedel et al. 2020).
   - Time-relative computation can be significantly done by it.

4. **Safety Critical Application**
   - In these systems, there is preuse modeling that is modeled prior to development.
   - Planning can be achieved before constructing various processes that save the system from external threats.

2.2 APPLICATION OF CPS

1. Medical device applications use CPS to increase their accuracy.
   - Modern therapies like image-guided therapies are made more accessible by it.
   - Control of fluid flow or biological fluid flow analysis is made easier.
   - Evolution of intelligent operation theaters and hospitals.
2. Oil refineries
3. Water treatment plants
4. SCADA (monitoring telecoms) (Raisin et al. 2020).
5. Supply chains
6. Engineered system based on cognition and neuroscience (Brain–Machine Interfaces, etc.) (Javaid et al. 2023).
7. Transportation
   - Infrastructure-based transportation.
   - Smart vehicles.
   - Smart meters.
   - Data aggregation unit.
   - Industry
     - In a typical CPS, manufacturing systems and logistics are integrated with communication abilities, sensors, and actuators.
     - Intelligent control of the tools and the objects used.
     - Resource utilization becomes optimal by using the CPS.
     - Intelligent diagnostics and maintenance of the tools and safety and health of the machines are correctly diagnosed.
   - The end products manufactured by a CPS can be appropriately customized as per the needs of the customer.
   - Smart homes and e-commerce are revolutionized with the use of CPS. A study says that the gross value of the German economy can be boosted by 267 billion euros by 2025 using CPS.
8. Connections.
9. Conversion.
10. Cyber.
11. Cognition.
12. Configuration.

2.3 CPS SPECIALTIES

A CPS has some qualities that create a typical CPS architecture to meet the demands of Industry 4.0. However, CPS mainly comprises the IOT devices of Industry 4.0.

Cyber-physical systems are mainly built with the architecture to meet the demands of IIoT (Afrizal, Mulyanti, and Widiaty 2020).

2.4 CPS ARCHITECTURE

This architecture can be subdivided into five levels, called 5Cs.

- **The CPS establishes Connection** – Smart connections to ensure accurate data transfer among the devices. These connections are made as machines, and the processes can obtain seamless and tether-free data. As sensors play a crucial role in the fault-free functioning of the processes from the devices, those sensors are made with proper specifications.
- **Conversion** – Conversion is the central portion where the machine-friendly data is converted into human-friendly data. So, in CPS, it is made up to the mark. Because of this machine becomes self-aware.
- **Cyber** – In a typical CPS, the cyber portion becomes the decision-making and information-reading part. So, it becomes a central information hub. It gathers the system information from a fleet of machines. After gathering, it can rate individual machines from the fleet. It also can predict the future behavior of a machine from historical data. As it works with bulky data, it utilizes the clustering of data mining. Because of the cyber part of the system, only machines achieve self-comparison ability.
- **Cognition** – For the systems, appropriate cognition is giving users the information they need to understand the system comprehensively. As proper cognition is available for the system, collaborative diagnosis can be achieved for the entire system. Moreover, further, for prioritizing and optimizing purposes, decision-making can be made easy by proper cognition.
- **Configuration** – While previous-generation device configurations were made in a supervisory mode, using CPSs, self-configured devices came into function.

2.5 SECURITY ASPECTS OF CPS

As per the advancement of new technologies like CPS, new security threats emerged as the complexity of the machines evolved and their loopholes and threats also went high. Figure 2.2 describes the security of a typical cyber-physical system. The IoT protocol has vulnerabilities mainly in the four layers; the transmission layer works as the physical, network, and data link in the protocol suite. The perception layer responsible for sensing has mainly the vulnerabilities of RFID tag collision, where multiple RFID tags collide and result in ambiguous sensing in the sensors. Even in the transport layer, there are many attacks that take place. There exists an airgap (an airgap is the mechanism of completely disintegrating a computer system from the internet to protect it from malware, ransomware, etc.). The computer network layers are matched with the OSI protocol layers with the IoT protocol layers. The other layers are mainly the computation layer and the application layer. The application layer is mainly affected by the DOS attack, and several attacks are mentioned in Section 2.3.

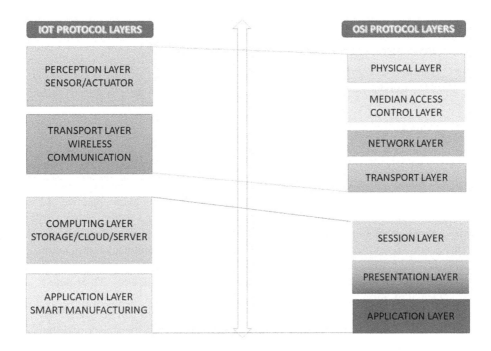

FIGURE 2.2   Layering of CPS with ISO/OSI layers.

2.6   FACTORS CONTRIBUTING TO VULNERABILITIES IN THE SECURITY OF CPS

All the machines used here are mainly heterogeneous. So, for the security personnel, there are various aspects to look after.

- CPS works with all private and sensitive data. That can be a significant loophole in the securities.
- There is accidental exposure of the systems that can lead to catastrophic effects.
- With large-scale deployments of private and sensitive data, network overhead goes very high, which can lead to network failure (Alguliyev, Imamverdiyev, and Sukhostat 2018).
- Encryption in the personal data.
- Advancements in sensing, like the use of quantum sensors, wearable sensors, and 2D/3D multisensory systems, created a better era in the world of sensing.

    All these systems are extensively used for the reliability and confidentiality of personal data. To rectify cybersecurity system security threats, sometimes the processes and measures may lead to network overhead (Hu et al. 2014).

The CPS security can be described in three layers:

- Perception or insight layer.
- Transport or communication layer.
- Prosecution layer.

2.7 PERCEPTION OR INSIGHT LAYER

The perception or insight layer is mainly devoted to sensing, so it mainly consists of devices related to sensing and related work. Insight Layer mainly consists of (1) RFID tags, (2) Sensors, (3) Actuators, (4) Aggregators, and (5) GPS. Having a physical layer is to visualize and track the physical world properly. The main objective of the insight layer is to collect the necessary data and information. As there is much verification of data available, eavesdropping attacks are possible in this and the latency of transformation can increase, as there will be integration of significant computation.

- Raising of IoT devices increases the possibility of DDoS (Distributed Denial of Service Attack)
- On occasion, the complete status of the physical system can be altered by listening in on the channels of communication between the sensor and the controller.
- Accidental exposures can sometimes result in catastrophe in the CPS.

The security threats of any CPS mainly three aspects

- Confidentiality
- Integrity
- Availability

As the threats increased, engineers devised ways to counteract the attackers.

2.8 METHODS FOR THREAT HANDLING

The first and foremost method to deal with the threats is to change the software, application, and operating system.

The following method uses modern next-generation sensors, computing, and network technologies.

We are using new computing paradigms and cyber-physical social systems.

Recent advancements of formal approaches in CPS include people-centric and scenario-based approaches. Port scan and passive reply can be made in this layer. The main concern is to ensure that confidentiality, privacy, and authentication are intact in this layer.

To avail these, we have to look after some aspects like:

1. Trust management
2. Source authentication

3. Secure data/systems
4. Data protection

(Dafflon, Moalla, and Ouzrout 2021)

Transport or Communication Layer – As the name suggests, this layer is responsible for the transition of data; this layer is also termed network layer. This layer works as an inter-connector between the insight layer and the prosecution layer. To enhance the connective devices, it uses modern protocols for stable interconnection of nodes. It uses LTE (Long-Term Evolution), Bluetooth, 4G, and IPV6. As it uses a wide range of technologies, it is vulnerable to various attacks like (1) Man in the Middle, (2) Meet in the Middle, (3) Denial of Service, (4) Distributed Denial of Service, (5) Repudiation, and (6) Replay. We have to target (1) Confidentiality, (2) Integrity, (3) Availability, and (4) Authentication. Some of the well-known processes are there for this layer, like (1) Strong Password Policy, (2) Strong Authentication, (3) Lightweight Dynamic Systematic Encryption, and (4) Secure Tunneling (Hu et al. 2014).

Prosecution layer – For further conceptual clarity, this layer can be subdivided into two layers: (1) the computing layer and (2) the application layer. The most complex algorithms are executed in this Layer. The data is sensed from the transmission or communication layer. And all the complex decision-making are done in the prosecution layer (Wang et al. 2023). The main responsibility of this layer is the bulk of data and information analysis and considering all decision-making. In this layer, the main problem for threat is at the computational level. Some of them can be stated as follows: (1) Worms, (2) Bot-nets and malware, (3) Buffer Overflow, (4) Malicious Code Injection, and (5) Trojan. This layer is responsible for upholding certain privacy, security, safety, and authentication requirements. As a security measure, there are various methodologies to make it secure from the above-mentioned threats: (1) Trust Management, (2) IDS (Intrusion Detection System) or IPS (Intrusion Prevention System), (3) Firewalls, and (4) Strong Authentication.

2.9   DEEPER ANALYSIS OF SECURITY ASPECTS AND VARIOUS VULNERABILITIES ON CPS

Concentrating Processed Data – Centering the Data Flow in All Phases

Aligned Function – This process amalgamates all the components of cyber-physical function to target the threats.

Aligned Threats – To address the aligned threats the system must be compatible with unification, accessibility, and accountability.

The above three types of threats make the system vulnerable to the following strands:

1. **Information collection** – Modern software collects confidential information by breaching into the machines by collecting personal logs and illegally using that information.
2. **Interception** – The data is made accessible to hackers to intercept or interfere with the private data.

3. **Reconnaissance** – Modern system securities like computational intelligence and industrial control systems often get access to more confidential information. We have a shortage of traditional defense systems, which opens these systems to attackers (Rushanan et al. 2014).
4. **Jamming** – It has been seen that attackers sometimes want to disrupt the ongoing activity by sending authentication signals to disrupt the ongoing operations.
5. **GPS misuse** – It is possible to track the locations of any private vehicles by tracking the GPS signals.
6. **Remote Access** – Attackers often breach a nation's CPS by using worms and Trojans for espionage, often causing a total blackout and financial losses in the industries.
7. **Exploitation in Wireless Mediums** – This type of menace requires a full knowledge of the system. This often disrupts the whole system operation and creates a loss of control.

2.10   VARIOUS TYPES OF VULNERABILITIES ASSOCIATED WITH CPS

A vulnerability can be defined as the security interlude between the nation's espionage and other passive threats. The vulnerability analyzes the nation's weakness in the CPS security aspects. The vulnerabilities of the CPS can be divided into three main categories:

- **Network Vulnerabilities** – Network (wired/wireless) can create many loopholes for the attackers, such as Denial of Service (DoS), Distributed Denial of Service (DDoS), Man in the Middle, Eavesdropping, Replay, Spoofing, Snipping, Communication Stack (Network Layer, Transport Layer, and Application Layer), Packet Manipulation, and backdoors.
- **Manifesto Vulnerabilities** – Manifesto or platform vulnerabilities happen for bugs in the entire software, hardware, or database.
- **Management Vulnerabilities** – There are sometimes loopholes in the policy and guidelines of a CPS itself that can create vulnerabilities in the system. These are the leading causes that affect the system. Apart from those, various types of vulnerabilities affect the system.
- **Presumption and Separation** – In this type, sometimes the system has been presumed and separated from the external world, which creates a loophole for the attacker.
- **Increasing Affinity** – As network surfaces increased, the risk of increasing network vulnerabilities arose. Moreover, the use of the external net or the internet has drastically increased, increasing the attackers' affinity to the system.
- **Heterogeneous Incorporation** – While building up a CPS, if any third-party component is used, the risk of security problems eventually comes up.

- **Flash Drive Usage** – USB usage can break the CPS security as the bugs can replicate quickly. The Stuxnet attack nearly destroyed Iran's nuclear program.

Moreover, homogeneous incorporation (employees inside the team) can create vulnerabilities.

2.11   CYBER ATTACKS

Recently, there has been a considerable increase in attacks on CPS. These also have been devastating effects. Some are mainly code reuse, malicious data injection, SQL injection, and many more. CPSs are prone to malicious code injection, data injection, and control flow attestation attacks (Abera et al. 2016).

- **SQL Injection** – SQL injection is a viral attack as it has been potent and effective recently. SQL injection can get administrative privileges and power to manage or shut down databases.
- **Eavesdropping** – Eavesdropping in a CPS is intruding from a sensitive database or data stream. There are two types of eavesdropping: (1) Active and (2) Passive.
   In active eavesdropping, the message is probed, scanned, or tampered with (by claiming it to be a legitimate source).
   Passive eavesdropping is listening to a CPS message transmission.
- **Phishing** – Phishing is a popular way of getting highly confidential information like the account password of the director of the CPS or the legitimate prime users of CPS. Even scientists of ISRO can be a victim of phishing, so CPS can have various types of attacks by phishing, like whaling, email phishing, and spear phishing (Duo, Zhou, and Abusorrah 2022).
- **DoS/DDoS** – DoS attacks usually target the machine which is locally infected. DDoS attacks are targeted on infected machines which are from geographically different locations. DDoS attacks are of various forms, like Smurf (Elleithy et al. 2006), Black Energy, and Ping-of-Death. So, DoS attacks are also termed Blackhole, Teardrop, etc. These attacks can affect the transmission rate of the system, which is crucial for running a system.
- **TCP SYN flood** – This system constantly does a handshake by sending syn handshaking packets to the server. This is the process by which the buffer of the cyber-physical system overflows, and it may lead to a crash of the entire system (Rushanan et al. 2014).
- **Cracking of Password** – The attacks are mainly constructed to crack the passwords of the authentic managers using Dictionary Attack, Brute-force Attack, rainbow, Birthday Attack (Evolved from hashing) (Macharia 2021), or online/offline password guessing.
- **Watering Hole Attack** – In this type of attack, first, the weakness of the entire system is found out, after which the weaker portion is attacked by the backdoor, rootkits, or zero-day exploit (Velusamy 2018).

- **Cross-site scripting** – Cross-site scripting is also abbreviated as XSS. In this, the website of the CPS is injected with the cross script of the engineers and workers. Sometimes entire session can be hijacked in this process. The XSS can sometimes get access to log keystrokes of the victim's machine (Raisin et al. 2020).
- **Malware** – Malware is a kind of main threat to the CPS. There are various types of malwares are there which create hindrances and malfunction in the working of a cyber-physical function. Those are viruses, Trojans, worms, spyware, ransomware, etc. Malware injection can severely damage the system. This malware can remain undetected and tamper with the readings of the sensors. Malware automatically propagates through the system (Marwedel et al. 2020).
- **Data Leakage** – Data leakage can be done from various sources: (1) Insider data leakage or employee leaking data. (2) Cloud data leakage – virtual machines may be spun up in other countries with little protection (Herrera Montano et al. 2022).
- **Botnet** – The word *botnet* word came from the words *robot* and *network*, which can be conceptualized by the phrase Zombie Army. Any device related to IoT (Internet of Things) can be a part of botnet. Some popular examples of botnets are Zeus, Scribi, Methbot, and Merai. Botnet attacks happen when several devices intentionally come together to exploit and harm a cyber system (Sekar et al. 2022).
- **Automatic Generation of Control Attack** – AGC controls a large area of power and tries to make sure that it is balanced. One example of someone who would use this would be a rival energy generator.

2.12 SAFETY MEASURES OF CPS VULNERABILITIES

- **General Methodologies** – Making CPS safe is not a simple aspect to deal with. So, we have to take care of various aspects to make a CPS safe. Some major aspects are integrity, confidentiality, authentication, privacy, and availability (Lozano and Vijayan 2020).
- **Taking Care of Privacy Aspects** – To target the privacy of CPS, we have to upgrade its antimalware software; antimalware includes software like antiviruses or other systems of information technologies, which are dedicated to removing the unnecessary programs that hamper the system's normal operation. IDS and IPS are the new aspects that take care of the privacy of a CPS. IDS (intrusion detection system) mainly monitors the network traffic and analyzes if there is any possibility of intrusion in the System. IPS (intrusion prevention system) not only detects malicious attempts to disrupt the stable operation of the CPS but also stops them from happening. These are achieved by terminating those sessions and dropping packets. Privacy can be altered by means of various social issues like blackmailing, phishing, and social engineering. Employees are made aware by getting trained to stop those breaching (Velusamy 2018).

- **Maintaining Confidentiality** – There is a lot of exchange of confidential information in the working of a cyber-physical system. To maintain confidentiality, plenty of lightweight cryptography algorithms have been invented. Various protocols are created to incorporate those algorithms with CPS. Various types of tools can catch the passing packets nearby, like sniffing and eavesdropping; sniffing tools are available to catch the passing packets; sniffing is similar to tapping the phone line. By sniffing, there can be information gathered for more attacks. Sniffing is also called wiretapping. Another popular attack that exploits confidentiality is a man-in-the-middle attack. It mimics the receiver's website and sends the fake website to the sender. As a result, the sender sends all the confidential information like passwords and credit card details to the attacker. Thus, all the information is exchanged. Some physical measures can be taken to counteract these attacks from happening such as document classification and garbage destruction (Kanso, Noureddine, and Exposito 2023).
- **Integrity** – Maintaining integrity in the overall CPS is the key to reviving any CPS for a long duration. One of the security measures to keep integrity intact is the advanced hashing mechanism; advanced or extensible hashing is used to increase the system's integrity as it can store multiple data using the single hash value, which can considerably increase the integrity. Auditing periodically can significantly enhance the system's integrity. Apart from these, constant maintenance of all the elements of the system brings out the possibility of perfect upgradation and integrity of the system ("Cyber-Physical Systems in Manufacturing" 2016).
- **Authenticity** – The only way to increase authentication of the system is to enhance the security of the passwords, using passwords that are away from brute force attacks. Brute force attacks only reverse engineering every possibility to crack the original one. To cope with the botnets, we can come up with a robust authentication protocol that really can keep botnets out of the cyber-physical system.
- **Availability** – Denial of Service attacks and signal jamming attacks mainly challenge the system. Various approaches like spread spectrum, IDS/IPS, firewalls, and honeypots mainly revive the system from the abovementioned threats.

2.13   SECURITY WITH MORE TECHNICAL DETAILS

Security is an essential measure of a cyber-physical system. Cyber-physical systems demand a good security measure as their application is increasing day by day and covering our day-to-day life uses like smart farms in villages, industrial control systems, government usage, and transportation. All these systems involve security aspects and maintenance; these systems incorporate operating systems for conducting a smooth operation. So, all these systems have good cyber-physical security systems for ensuring mitigation strategies and reliable operation. As the cyber-physical system came up with the fusion of the cyber world and the physical world, attack prevention can involve both control engineers and IT security engineers (Hasan et al. 2023).

The security of a typical system not only involves keeping the attackers out of the scene but also the following:

- Responding
- Understanding risks
- Detecting
- Mitigating

- To the adversaries that have partial access to the system.
  - **Prevention of Attacks** – Prevention of a system mainly deals with securing legacy systems.
  - **Securing** – Legacy systems involve maintaining the previous systems intact and also the prevention of transduction attacks which can lead to the exploitation of sensors. The sensors need to be protected from unauthorized access from external sources (Mohindru et al. 2019).
  - **Detection of Attacks** – Detection can be of several types:
    - Active Detection – This methodology involves actively detecting all the components of the system, which is the more advanced version of the embedded system (Mohindru et al. 2020).
    - Anomaly Detection – As the complexity of the cyber-physical systems increases, the need for detecting threats in those systems also increases. A lot of unsupervised learning-based algorithms have evolved to keep track of the anomalies generated by the sensors and other devices.
    - Other Types – There are also other types of detections possible which incorporate misuse detection and physics-based attack-detection (Mohindru and Singh 2018).
  - **Mitigating Attacks** – Mitigation of attacks becomes necessary when prevention and detection cannot always take place due to the high complexity of the system.

The mitigation of attack can take place while having a conservative approach toward the operation of the devices (CIRNU et al. 2018). IP theft is the unauthorized use of another's idea or work without giving them proper credit. In the application layer of the system, such kinds of vulnerabilities can take place (Kanso, Noureddine, and Exposito 2023).

REFERENCES

Abera, Tigist, N. Asokan, Lucas Davi, Jan-Erik Ekberg, Thomas Nyman, Andrew Paverd, Ahmad-Reza Sadeghi, and Gene Tsudik. 2016. "C-FLAT: Control-Flow Attestation for Embedded Systems Software." In *CCS '16*, 743–54. New York, NY, USA: Association for Computing Machinery. https://doi.org/10.1145/2976749.2978358

Afrizal, A, Budi Mulyanti, and I Widiaty. 2020. "Development of Cyber-Physical System (CPS) Implementation in Industry 4.0." *IOP Conference Series: Materials Science and Engineering* 830 (May): 042090. https://doi.org/10.1088/1757-899X/830/4/042090

Alguliyev, Rasim, Yadigar Imamverdiyev, and Lyudmila Sukhostat. 2018. "Cyber-Physical Systems and Their Security Issues." *Computers in Industry* 100: 212–23. https://doi.org/10.1016/j.compind.2018.04.017

Cirnu, Carmen Elena, Carmen Rotuna, Adrian Vevera, and Radu Boncea. 2018. "Measures to Mitigate Cybersecurity Risks and Vulnerabilities in Service-Oriented Architecture." *Studies in Informatics and Control* 27 (September): 359–68. https://doi.org/10.24846/v27i3y201811

Dafflon, Baudouin, Nejib Moalla, and Yacine Ouzrout. 2021. "The Challenges, Approaches, and Used Techniques of CPS for Manufacturing in Industry 4.0: A Literature Review." *The International Journal of Advanced Manufacturing Technology* 113 (February): 1–18. https://doi.org/10.1007/s00170-020-06572-4

Duo, Wenli, MengChu Zhou, and Abdullah Abusorrah. 2022. "A Survey of Cyber Attacks on Cyber Physical Systems: Recent Advances and Challenges." *IEEE/CAA Journal of Automatica Sinica* 9 (5): 784–800. https://doi.org/10.1109/JAS.2022.105548

Elleithy, Khaled, Drazen Blagovic, Wang Cheng, and Paul Sideleau. 2006. "Denial of Service Attack Techniques: Analysis, Implementation and Comparison." *Journal of Systemics, Cybernetics and Informatics* 3 (January): 66–71.

Hasan, Mohammad Kamrul, AKM Ahasan Habib, Zarina Shukur, Fazil Ibrahim, Shayla Islam, and Md Abdur Razzaque. 2023. "Review on Cyber-Physical and Cyber-Security System in Smart Grid: Standards, Protocols, Constraints, and Recommendations." *Journal of Network and Computer Applications* 209: 103540. https://doi.org/10.1016/j.jnca.2022.103540

Hatzivasilis, George, Konstantinos Fysarakis, Sotiris Ioannidis, Ilias Hatzakis, George Vardakis, Nikos Papadakis, and George Spanoudakis. 2021. "SPD-Safe: Secure Administration of Railway Intelligent Transportation Systems." *Electronics* 10 (January): 92. https://doi.org/10.3390/electronics10010092

Herrera Montano, Isabel, José Javier García Aranda, Juan Ramos Diaz, Sergio Molina Cardín, Isabel de la Torre Díez, and Joel J. P. C. Rodrigues. 2022. "Survey of Techniques on Data Leakage Protection and Methods to Address the Insider Threat." *Cluster Computing* 25 (6): 4289–302. https://doi.org/10.1007/s10586-022-03668-2

Hu, Wei, Dejun Mu, Jason Oberg, Baolei Mao, Mohit Tiwari, Timothy Sherwood, and Ryan Kastner. 2014. "Gate-Level Information Flow Tracking for Security Lattices." *ACM Transactions on Design Automation of Electronic Systems* 20 (November): 1–25. https://doi.org/10.1145/2676548

Javaid, Mohd, Abid Haleem, Ravi Pratap Singh, and Rajiv Suman. 2023. "An Integrated Outlook of Cyber–Physical Systems for Industry 4.0: Topical Practices, Architecture, and Applications." *Green Technologies and Sustainability* 1 (1): 100001. https://doi.org/10.1016/j.grets.2022.100001

Jazdi, Nasser. 2014. "Cyber Physical Systems in the Context of Industry 4.0." In *2014 IEEE International Conference on Automation, Quality and Testing, Robotics*, 1–4. https://doi.org/10.1109/AQTR.2014.6857843

Kanso, Houssam, Adel Noureddine, and Ernesto Exposito. 2023. "A Review of Energy Aware Cyber-Physical Systems." *Cyber-Physical Systems* 1–42. https://doi.org/10.1080/23335777.2022.2163298

Lozano, Carolina Villarreal, and Kavin Kathiresh Vijayan. 2020. "Literature Review on Cyber Physical Systems Design." *Procedia Manufacturing* 45: 295–300. https://doi.org/10.1016/j.promfg.2020.04.020

Macharia, Wahome. 2021. Cryptographic Hash Functions. *mai. de.*

Marwedel, Peter, Tulika Mitra, Martin Grimheden, and Hugo Andrade. 2020. "Survey on Education for Cyber-Physical Systems." *IEEE Design & Test* (July): 1–1. https://doi.org/10.1109/MDAT.2020.3009613

Mohindru, Vandana, Ravindara Bhatt, and Yashwant Singh. "Reauthentication Scheme for Mobile Wireless Sensor Networks." *Sustainable Computing: Informatics and Systems* 23 (2019): 158–66.

Mohindru, Vandana, and Yashwant Singh. "Node Authentication Algorithm for Securing Static Wireless Sensor Networks from Node Clone Attack." *International Journal of information and computer security* 10, no. 2-3 (2018): 129–48.

Mohindru, Vandana, Yashwant Singh, and Ravindara Bhatt. "Hybrid Cryptography Algorithm for Securing Wireless Sensor Networks from Node Clone Attack." *Recent Advances in Electrical & Electronic Engineering (Formerly Recent Patents on Electrical & Electronic Engineering)* 13, no. 2 (2020): 251–59.

Monostori, L., B. Kádár, T. Bauernhansl, S. Kondo, S. Kumara, G. Reinhart, O. Sauer, G. Schuh, W. Sihn, and K. Ueda 2016. "Cyber-Physical Systems in Manufacturing." *CIRP Annals - Manufacturing Technology* 65 (2): 621–41. https://doi.org/10.1016/j.cirp.2016.06.005

Raisin, Syarfa Najihah, Juliza Jamaludin, Farah Aina Jamal Mohamad, Nur Hazwani, and Bushra Naeem. 2020. "Cyber-Physical System (CPS) Application- A Review." November, 52–65. https://doi.org/10.26760/rekaelkomika.v1i2.52-65

Revathi, V., P. Ramya and P. Gayathri. 2018. "An Overview: Watering Hole Attack", *International Journal for Scientific Research & Development* 6 (01): 1–3.

Rushanan, Michael, Aviel D. Rubin, Denis Foo Kune, and Colleen Swanson. 2014. "SoK: Security and Privacy in Implantable Medical Devices and Body Area Networks." *2014 IEEE Symposium on Security and Privacy*, 524–39.

Sekar, S., S. Jeyalakshmi, S. Ravikumar, and D. Kavitha. 2022. "Modified Light GBM Based Classification of Malicious Users in Cooperative Cognitive Radio Networks." *Cyber-Physical Systems* 1–19. https://doi.org/10.1080/23335777.2022.2135610

Wang, Zhikang, Wu Wendi, Wu Zhengtian, and Fu Baochuan. 2023. "Microgrid Trading Mechanism Enhancement for Smart Contract Considering Reputation Values." *Cyber-Physical Systems* 1–17. https://doi.org/10.1080/23335777.2023.2175915

3 Cyber-Physical System Security Attack Detection Methods and Models

Gurleen Kaur, Kapil Mehta, and Saumya Rajvanshi

Chandigarh Group of Colleges, Punjab, India

3.1 INTRODUCTION

Cyber-physical systems (CPS) have emerged as a result of the fusion of cognitive and physical processes, transforming the way people interact with the real world. With rapid developments in internet-based technologies and applications, businesses can now effectively collaborate from anywhere in the world, enabling a fully dispersed manufacturing environment (Throne Lăzăroiu 2020). However, the magnitude and inherent variability of these systems pose significant technical challenges. To ensure their implementation, new technical techniques are necessary to define their design and manage and govern them in a scaled, effective, and secure environment (Wiśniewski et al. 2022).

CPSs combine computation, communication, and physical capabilities to interact with the physical world and people. While component failures are a common challenge, cyber-physical systems are also vulnerable to malicious attacks. The development of specialized analysis tools and monitoring systems is necessary to enforce system security and dependability. Abnormalities in the veracity of the data in a CPS can negatively impact the system's performance, which may be brought on by cyberattacks, various errors, and systemic breakdowns affecting the cyber and physical parts of the system.

Given the potential consequences of a cyberattack on CPS, researchers have been interested in the problems of security control, secure state estimation, and attack detection. An effective cyberattack could devastate a CPS, which is why integrated online monitoring is essential to detect cyberattacks. Immediate identification of cyberattacks is crucial to protect the system from protracted degradation (Catak et al. 2022).

This chapter aims to provide an in-depth analysis of the risks associated with cyberattacks on CPS and the various detection models and methods that researchers have developed to mitigate these risks. The first segment of this chapter will introduce the topic, provide the motivation for the research, and present the work history. The second portion focuses on the hazards related to cybersecurity that CPS has to contend with. The subsequent part will showcase academic research that highlights the researchers' in-depth analyses of the tactics they used to reduce hazards by applying various detection models and methodologies. The chapter will conclude with a comparison that evaluates the investigations of various study participants and highlights how their concepts and strategies may influence security by exploiting distinct features such as attacks utilizing passwords (Hussain et al. 2020).

3.2 CYBER-PHYSICAL SYSTEM SECURITY ATTACK DETECTION METHODS AND MODELS

The interrelated physical and digital systems that sustain critical infrastructure have been safeguarded by cyber-physical system (CPS) safety breach detection procedures and models (Rathore and Park 2020). CPSs, such as industrial control systems, transportation networks, and building automation systems, are platforms that combine both physical and digital components (Wu et al. 2023).

These detection methodologies and models combine an amalgam of software and hardware as their foundation methodologies that monitor and recognize potential cyberattacks on CPSs. Furthermore, they offer instantaneous updates and security measures that minimize the repercussions of a system attack (Amro et al. 2023). Intrusion prevention systems (IDS), anomaly recognition, models based on machine learning, and network-based models are a few of the frequently utilized methods and approaches for CPS security breach detection. The physical, network, and application layers of the CPS framework can all be serviced using these approaches (Dreossi et al., 2019).

Improved resilience of the system, much greater threat awareness, and more rapid response times to lessen the effects of an attack are all the pros of using CPS security attack detection methodologies and models (Schneble and Thamilarasu 2019). The successful implementation of these methods and examples might also lessen the chance of data breaches, system outages, and attacks on crucial infrastructure (Wu et al. 2023).

It is especially important not to forget that the various detection methods and algorithms might not be perfect and might have certain drawbacks. In particular, they might give rise to mistaken positives or negatives or fail to identify advanced attacks. In order to make sure that the detection methods and models are effective against novel hazards, it is essential that we periodically evaluate and update systems (Ryalat et al. 2023).

3.3 BENEFITS OF CYBER-PHYSICAL SYSTEM SECURITY ATTACK DETECTION METHODS AND MODELS

- **Early Detection**: Cyber-physical asset security attack detection methodologies and approaches are created for recognizing attacks early on, minimizing the damage they can do. Early identification lowers the overall unavailability of the system and contributes to minimizing catastrophic malfunctions.
- **Enhanced System Performance**: Cyber-physical systems' functionality may be assessed in real time with the aid of precise detection techniques

and models. Any conceivable anomalies might be automatically found and prevented by the system, which makes it more accurate and productive.

- **Abridged Risk**: The risk of an infrastructure breakdown or data breach can be lessened with the aid of cyber-physical system security breach detection methods and models. The system's overall risk has been reduced since it is capable of recognizing and preventing challenges before they threaten any real impact.
- **Customizable**: A system's distinctive safety features can be fulfilled by tailoring the attack detection techniques and designs for cyber-physical systems. The models can be tweaked to detect and prevent distinct assaults that are more prevalent across the system's scope (Liu et al. 2022).
- **Continuous Monitoring**: Cyber-Physical Platform Security Attack Diagnosis Methods and models continuously monitor the system, giving immediate recognition of any potential attacks. It enables the system to react quickly and avoid significant harm from developing.
- **Cost Effective**: By lowering the chance of system failures and data violations, firms can save money by applying cyber-physical system security intrusion detection methods and models. This might help in eliminating severe legal or monetary consequences of an infraction.
- **Enriched Compliance**: In order to ensure data privacy and system security, different sectors have legal guidelines that must be followed. Corporations might meet these criteria and enhance overall compliance by implementing crypto tangible system secure attack prevention methods and models (Duo et al. 2022).

3.4 EXAMPLES OF CYBER-PHYSICAL SYSTEM SECURITY ATTACK DETECTION METHODS AND MODELS

- **Healthcare**: Observing medical systems in real time to keep an eye for potential cyberattacks.
- **Transportation**: Detection of inconsistencies in GPS data in order to safeguard autonomous vehicles from counterattacks.
- **Energy**: Monitoring critical infrastructure in real time in order to search for potential cyberattacks on power grids.
- **Manufacturing**: Detection of aberrations in industrial control systems to stop cyberattacks on processes in production (Zhou et al., 2021).
- **Defense**: To maintain secure connections between troops and military communication systems have to recognize counterattacks.
- **Finance**: Implementing machine learning approaches to recognize fraud in financial transactions in seconds.
- **Smart homes**: Detection of counterattacks on devices in smart homes to protect residents' safety and confidentiality.
- **Agriculture**: To stop data theft or system interruptions precision farming systems must be shielded against counterattacks.
- **Aviation**: Real-time monitoring of flight control systems to prevent cyberattacks on aircraft.

- **Water supply systems**: Sensor data detects abnormalities to stop intrusions on water supply systems.
- **Telecommunications**: Identifying counterattacks on communication networks ensures a steady stream of data that is secure.
- **Autonomous systems**: Detection of cyberattacks on autonomous systems like drones and robots to prevent data theft or system disruption.
- **Critical infrastructure**: Monitoring essential facilities in real time to keep an eye for potential counterattacks on highways, electricity grids, and other essential infrastructure (Tariq et al. 2020).
- **Public safety**: Detection of digital assaults on emergency response networks alongside other systems for public safety to safeguard the safety of others in times of necessity.
- **Education**: Detection of cyberattacks on e-learning platforms and educational software to ensure the security and privacy of student data (Malik and Saleem, 2022).

3.5 RISK OF COUNTERATTACKS

Counterattacks pose significant risks to both people and corporations. It is critical for individuals and businesses to comprehend the risks involved with these attacks given the rise of the digital age has brought about in an increase in the frequency and sophistication of intrusions (Tang et al., 2023).

The risk of financial loss is one of the biggest dangers of counterattacks. Money-related data, such as credit card numbers or bank account information, may be hijacked by online criminals, which might cause individuals as well as companies to suffer large financial losses. Counterattacks can also compromise business operations, which causes revenue loss and more cleanup expenses (Chen et al. 2022).

Security at home can be significantly compromised by counterattacks as well. Counterattacks may interrupt crucial services and potentially hurt citizens if they target critical infrastructure like energy grids and transport systems. Counterattacks on government institutions have the potential to compromise highly confidential data, including secrets of national security and the personal information of residents, with extremely catastrophic results (Mishra et al. 2023).

Last but not foremost, hacks may lead to the loss of important information and intellectual property. Trade secrets, knowledge of research and development, and other highly confidential information may be stolen by noncriminals, which can have a serious strategic and economic impact on enterprises (Chen et al. 2019).

In general, counterattacks convey serious threats to both humans and enterprises. In the modern digital world, it is essential to recognize these dangers while taking action to prevent and lessen technological catastrophes.

3.6 DETECTION METHODS

- **Signature-Based Detection**: This form of detection monitors the network traffic of the system for the presence of known attack signatures, such as unique trends or traits relating to well-known counterattacks. In order to identify and prevent malicious communication, along signature-based detection systems check a database of widely recognized attack patterns (Yu et al. 2022).

- **Anomaly-Based Detection**: With such a method, the system's performance is examined in order to spot any weird activity that contrasts with the technique's ordinary conduct. Machine learning algorithms are implemented by anomaly-based detection systems to spot patterns of activity that exceed expected behavior and flag them as possible risks to security.

- **Behavior-Based Detection**: This kind of strategy requires keeping an eye on user and system activity and searching for patterns that could relate to a security breach. Machine learning algorithms are implemented by behavior-based detection systems for identifying patterns of conduct that can signal to security breach and prompt security personnel to research it (Catak et al. 2022).

- **Hybrid Detection**: In order to increase reliability and eliminate false positives, this method incorporates two or more methods for identification. To find potential security threats, hybrid detection systems blend signature-based, anomaly-based, and behavior-based identification.

- **Network Traffic Analysis**: This method involves reviewing the network traffic of the system for any anomalies or unusual activities. Machine learning algorithms are implemented by network traffic monitoring systems for identifying patterns of conduct that could be signs of a breach of security (Rachmawati, 2022).

- **Endpoint Detection and Response (EDR)**: This method involves keeping an eye on endpoints, including servers, laptops, and desktops, to look for indications of security breaches. Machine learning algorithms are implemented by EDR systems to pick up suspicious behavior and notify investigators to conduct an investigation (Jamal et al., 2023).

- **Intrusion Detection System (IDS)**: According to this methodology, the network is constantly monitoring for signals of a security breach, such as bizarre traffic flows or unauthorized access attempts. In order to identify potential security threats, IDS systems employ signature-based and detection based algorithms on anomaly (Rai and Sahu, 2020).

3.7 DETECTION ALGORITHMS

There are several emerging astrophysical system security attack detection algorithms that have not been widely adopted or used yet, including.

3.7.1 ANOMALY-BASED DETECTION ALGORITHMS

Cyber-physical systems (CPS) deploy anomaly-based detection algorithms that scan for unexpected system actions to identify potential security breaches. Creating a baseline or typical activity pattern for the CPS and contrasting it with the system's real-time performance are the fundamental ideas behind anomaly detection. Every break from the usual scenario is noted as an oddity, which may be an indication of a breach of safety or other system defect (Tran et al., 2019).

The potential of anomaly detection for recognizing previously unknown attacks is one of its most significant advantages. Anomaly recognition, as opposed to signature-based detection, can identify new and emerging threats that have not been discovered previously. This is due to the fact it isn't dependent on known attack patterns. This is crucial in CPS because it faces continuously various types of attacks (Wu et al. 2023).

However, due to their high false-positive rates, algorithms for anomaly detection are not often employed. False positives happen when normal system performance is incorrectly classified as inappropriate, triggering pointless recommendations and possibly adding to the workload of security analysts.

Researchers developed more advanced detection algorithms for anomalies that integrate data mining and other approaches to cut out false positives to address this issue. For instance, some algorithms' actions have similarities and find outliers – behaviors that differentiate from the norm – by using clustering approaches. These algorithms can decrease false positives and raise the finding system's accuracy by recognizing outliers. There are important criteria for detecting anomalies using computer programs, as displayed in Figure 3.1.

Other algorithms examine the likelihood of abnormal conduct and modify the detection threshold when needed using methods based on statistics. These algorithms can reduce the number of false positives and raise the detection system's accuracy by altering the threshold based on the probabilities of aberrant conduct (Rachmawati, 2022).

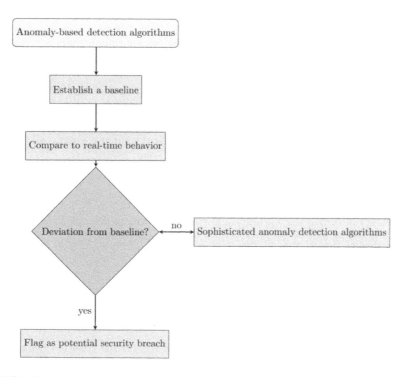

FIGURE 3.1 Anomaly-based detection algorithms.

Researchers are studying innovative approaches for anomaly identification that combine multiple state-detection techniques to meet these obstacles. In particular, hybrid algorithms combine many detection methods in order to improve the accuracy of detection (Presekal et al., 2023). In conclusion, as they are capable of recognizing previously unidentified attacks, anomaly-based detection algorithms are a crucial part of CPS security. However, the high false-positive rates of these algorithms can result in superfluous notifications and an increase in the burden for security officers. Researchers are creating more complex algorithms utilizing machine learning and other approaches to reduce false positives to address this issue of false positives. The accuracy of the detection system needs to be strengthened because, despite these advancements, algorithms for recognizing anomalies in CPS still face plenty of obstacles (Patel et al. 2023).

3.7.2 GAME-THEORETIC MODELS

An original perspective on cybersecurity threats for identification has been offered by game-theoretic models. Researchers can learn about the most effective approaches for both sides as well as the weaknesses of a cyber-physical system by simulating the interactions between attackers and defenders as a game.

In order to prevent being caught by the defender, the attacker's ideal plan of action, for example, might be to look inside the system for imperfections. On the other hand, the defender's optimal strategy of action may be casting an eye to identify any unusual behavior while reducing its impact on the performance of the system (Rachmawati, 2022).

By examining the decision-making of attackers, game-theoretic models can assist researchers in discovering faults in a system. For instance, if an attacker plays the game by regularly employing a certain method, it could be indicative of a gap in the system that the attacker is taking advantage of. In a similar vein, if the defender regularly opts for one particular technique, it may refer to a deficiency in their strategy that the attacker is taking advantage of. There are essential requirements for the game-theoretic model algorithm, which is demonstrated in Figure 3.2.

Game-theoretic models, however, pose a number of issues. Computational complexity is one of the main barriers. It can be tricky to compute the ideal responses due to the enormous amount of intriguing attack and defend techniques. The models may also be computationally expensive, which could hinder how useful they are in real-world situations (Ryalat et al. 2023).

Accurately imitating the behavioral patterns of attackers and defenders is a further issue. Game-theoretic models rely on assumptions that may not always hold true in everyday life regarding the motivations and decision-making processes of both sides. For instance, an authentic enemy can act differently than one would expect in game-theoretic modeling, causing poor or implausible planning (Olowononi et al. 2020).

Game-theoretic models continue to be a crucial tool in cybersquatting research without those challenges. They can offer crucial knowledge regarding how attackers and defenders conduct themselves as well as about an astrophysical system's limitations. Game-theoretic models may become progressively useful and efficient for identifying and avoiding counterattacks as computing power and computational

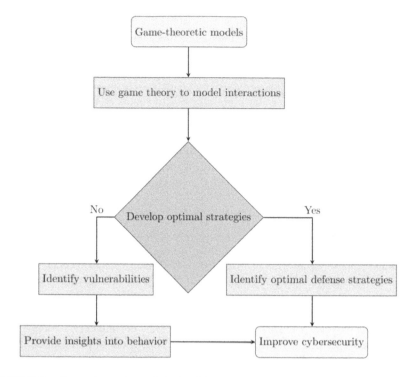

FIGURE 3.2   Game-theoretic models algorithms.

technologies advance (Alsufyani et al. 2023). There are essential necessities for machine learning–based algorithms, which are illustrated in Figure 3.3.

There are obstacles to applying game-theoretic models into execution, as well as moral dilemmas to think on. In particular, issues with confidentiality could develop if the game-theoretic model uses real-world data. Additionally, it may happen that using game-theoretic models for the development of offensive cyber weapons would go against international laws and regulations (Catak et al. 2022).

In general, game-theoretic models provide an original and advantageous technique for cybersecurity attack detection strategies.

3.7.3 MACHINE LEARNING–BASED ALGORITHMS

The capability of machine learning–based algorithms to learn patterns and adapt to new challenges is making them increasingly popular in detecting security attacks in virtual and physical systems (Wu et al. 2023). However, there are many barriers in the process of these algorithms effectively recognizing security attackers. The susceptible nature of these algorithms to hostile attacks is a significant problem. Adversarial attacks are systematic attempts to alter the system in a way that avoids the algorithm's detection. Conflicting attempts can be especially hazardous in astrophysical systems since they may result in severe repercussions (Lee et al. 2020). As an example, for improving the algorithm's power of identifying anomalies in the

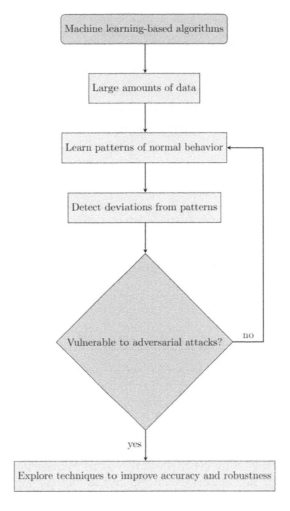

FIGURE 3.3   Algorithms based on machine learning.

system, researchers can incorporate data from several sensors or data sources (Leong et al., 2020). In order to boost the algorithm's capabilities for both detection and reaction to security attacks, the above approach might also involve employing the professional knowledge of human operatives (Wang et al. 2022a). A further approach is to utilize sophisticated machine learning models that can detect minute trends in the behavior of the system. Deep learning algorithms, for instance, can discover intricate connections and trends in big datasets, which may be helpful for recognizing small modifications in the system's performance that point to an incoming threat (Zhang et al., 2021). By making it impossible for an attacker to modify the system's configuration in a way that evades discovery, this strategy can also aid in reducing the impact of adversarial attacks (Patel et al. 2023). Algorithms that use hybrids must meet important under certain circumstances, as demonstrated in Figure 3.4.

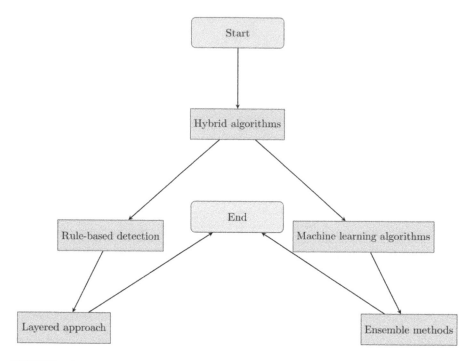

FIGURE 3.4 Hybrid algorithms.

Researchers are additionally researching the application of reinforcement learning to increase the accuracy as well as the effectiveness of algorithms based on machine learning (Alohali et al. 2022). Utilizing the feedback from its activities in an environment, an algorithm is trained through reinforcement learning. This technique may be especially helpful for cyber-physical systems, because the behaviors of the system may change instantaneously in response to multiple inputs (Amro et al. 2023). Despite all of this, more research and development is still required in order to improve the accuracy and resilience of machine learning–based algorithms (Liu et al., 2020). To detect and stop security assaults in cyber-physical systems as they grow more sophisticated, new methods and algorithms must be established and upgraded (Luo et al. 2021).

3.8 HYBRID ALGORITHMS

Due to their capacity to combine various detection techniques to increase accuracy, hybrid algorithms are becoming more and more common as a way of identifying cyber-physical system (CPS) threats (Lee and Kundu, 2022). Hybrid algorithms combine a wide range of approaches, such as rule-based, anomaly-based, and machine learning–based tactics.

Due to the fact that different procedures can be used to identify various kinds of assaults, hybrid algorithms offer a more thorough coverage of probable attack scenarios (Mohindru et al., 2019). Rule-based approaches, for instance, can be used to identify known crimes, while anomaly-based approaches can identify completely novel or unidentified attacks. Machine learning–based methods can identify convoluted attacks that would be challenging to recognize with any other method.

Hybrid algorithm execution can be difficult as it encompasses the careful consideration of the structure of the system, resource needs, and the chosen detection methods (Jayaratne et al., 2021). Using a layered approach, where various detection techniques are executed at different stages of the CPS, is an example of how to build hybrid algorithms (Mohindru and Singh, 2018). Machine learning methods, for instance, may be used at the application layer while governed by rule detection may be deployed at the network layer.

Another option is to produce an estimate by incorporating several machine learning models. This may increase the overall detection accuracy and lessen the constraints of individual models. By lowering the chance of mistaken positives or false negatives, ensemble approaches can also increase the robustness of the detection system.

However, placing hybrid algorithms into practice can be difficult and needs a lot of computer power, particularly if the methods include machine learning models. The quality and quantity of the data used for training and testing have a significant impact on how well the hybrid algorithm functions. Therefore, collecting and getting ready data are vital to check the algorithm's accuracy (Mohindru et al., 2020). Due to the ability to integrate various detection strategies to increase accuracy, hybrid algorithms are, in conclusion, expanding in acceptance as a method for identifying cyber-physical system threats. Table 3.1 is a comparative analysis of the various detection approaches.

3.9 CONCLUSION

Cyber-physical systems (CPSs) have become widespread in many different kinds of industries recently, particularly manufacturing, healthcare, and transportation. These systems are susceptible to counterattacks, which may seriously harm assets, infrastructure, and even people. To ensure the safety and stability of CPSs, it is critical to identify and mitigate counterattacks.

Numerous violence detection methodologies and models have been developed and presented in this domain. Rule-based, anomaly-based, and machine learning–based methods can be roughly separated into three different categories. Rule-based techniques leverage preestablished rules to recognize widely recognized attack patterns, whereas anomaly-based techniques look for abnormalities from typical system behaviors. Machine learning–based approaches use artificial intelligence to gain knowledge from data and uncover previously unforeseen attack movements.

While each such method has its perks and drawbacks, it must be chosen to choose the best detection technique depending on the distinctive features and peculiarities of the CPS. Rule-based techniques get closer; for instance, it may be successful for systems with well-defined attack scenarios, whereas anomaly-based strategies may be more acceptable for systems with continually changing attack patterns.

In addition to the detection methods themselves, other factors such as the availability and quality of data, the processing power and storage capacity of the system,

TABLE 3.1
Comparative Analysis

	Anomaly-Based Detection	Game-Theoretic Models	Machine Learning Based Detection	Hybrid Detection Algorithm
Type of approach	Statistical analysis	Game theory	Pattern recognition	Combination of multiple methods
Detection accuracy	Good for detecting novel attacks	Good for detecting attacks involving multiple actors	High accuracy, can learn from new data	High accuracy, can combine multiple methods
False positive rate	Can generate false positives due to detecting unusual but legitimate behavior	Can generate false positives due to the difficulty of modeling complex human behavior	Can generate false positives if the training data is not representative of the attack scenarios	Can generate false positives if the individual methods have high false positive rates
Detection time	Can detect attacks in real-time	Can detect attacks in real-time	Can detect attacks quickly after training	Can detect attacks quickly after training
Interpret-ability	Can be complicated for people to understand why a particular behavior gets designated as unacceptable.	Can be harder to truly understand how the model produces a determination.	Can interpret the model's approach to decision-making might be complex.	Could be hard for people to understand how an amalgamation of approaches reaches its culmination.
Resource requirement	Can require significant computational resources for training and detection	Can require significant computational resources for modeling complex human behavior	Can require significant computational resources for training and detection	Can require significant computational resources to combine multiple methods
Training data	Requires a large dataset of normal behavior to train the model	Requires a model of the behavior of multiple actors in the system	Requires a large dataset of normal and attack behavior to train the model	Requires a large dataset of normal and attack behavior to train the individual methods
Attack scenarios	Can detect novel attacks, but may not be able to detect attacks that resemble normal behavior	Can model complex human behavior, but may not be able to detect attacks that involve changing behavior over time.	Can detect a wide range of attack scenarios, but may struggle with novel attacks.	Can detect a wide range of attack scenarios and combine multiple methods to improve coverage

Scalability	Can be difficult to scale to large systems	Can be difficult to scale to large systems	Can be scaled to large systems with appropriate resources	Can be scaled to large systems with appropriate resources
Model complexity	Can be relatively simple models, but may require multiple models for different types of behavior	Can be complex models that require significant expertise to develop	Can be complex models that require significant expertise to develop	Can be complex models that require significant expertise to develop
Human input	May require expert knowledge to define what constitutes normal behavior	May require expert knowledge to define the game-theoretic model	May require expert knowledge to select appropriate features and algorithms	May require expert knowledge to select appropriate methods and configure parameters
Training time	Can require significant time to train the model on a large dataset of normal behavior	Can require significant time to develop and test the game-theoretic model	Can require significant time to select appropriate features and algorithms and train the model	Can require significant time to train the individual methods and configure the parameters
Adaptability	May not be adaptable to changes in the system or attack scenarios	May not be adaptable to changes in the behavior of multiple actors	Can be adaptable to	

and the cost and feasibility of implementation must be considered when selecting an attack detection method. Overall, ensuring the security of a CPS is a complex and ongoing challenge, and effective attack-detection methods are critical in mitigating the risk of cyberattacks. While no single detection method is perfect, selecting an appropriate method based on the specific characteristics of a CPS can significantly improve the system's security posture.

REFERENCES

Alohali, Manal Abdullah, Fahd N. Al-Wesabi, Anwer Mustafa Hilal, Shalini Goel, Deepak Gupta, and Ashish Khanna. "Artificial intelligence enabled intrusion detection systems for cognitive cyber-physical systems in industry 4.0 environment." *Cognitive Neurodynamics* 16, no. 5 (2022): 1045–1057.

Alsufyani, Abdulmajeed, Youseef Alotaibi, Alaa Omran Almagrabi, Saleh Ahmed Alghamdi, and Nawal Alsufyani. "Retracted article: Optimized intelligent data management framework for a cyber-physical system for computational applications." *Complex & Intelligent Systems* 9, no. 3 (2023): 2957–2957.

Amro, Ahmed, Vasileios Gkioulos, and Sokratis Katsikas. "Assessing cyber risk in cyber-physical systems using the ATT&CK framework." *ACM Transactions on Privacy and Security* 26, no. 2 (2023): 1–33.

Catak, Ferhat Ozgur, Tao Yue, and Shaukat Ali. "Uncertainty-aware prediction validator in deep learning models for cyber-physical system data." *ACM Transactions on Software Engineering and Methodology (TOSEM)* 31, no. 4 (2022): 1–31.

Chen, Lunyuan, Shunpu Tang, Venki Balasubramanian, Junjuan Xia, Fasheng Zhou, and Lisheng Fan. "Physical-layer security based mobile edge computing for emerging cyber physical systems." *Computer Communications* 194 (2022): 180–188.

Chen, Yuqi, Christopher M. Poskitt, Jun Sun, Sridhar Adepu, and Fan Zhang. "Learning-guided network fuzzing for testing cyber-physical system defences." In *2019 34th IEEE/ACM International Conference on Automated Software Engineering (ASE)*, pp. 962–973. IEEE, 2019.

Dreossi, Tommaso, Alexandre Donzé, and Sanjit A. Seshia. "Compositional falsification of cyber-physical systems with machine learning components." *Journal of Automated Reasoning* 63 (2019): 1031–1053.

Duo, Wenli, MengChu Zhou, and Abdullah Abusorrah. "A survey of cyber attacks on cyber physical systems: Recent advances and challenges." *IEEE/CAA Journal of Automatica Sinica* 9, no. 5 (2022): 784–800.

Hussain, Bilal, Qinghe Du, Bo Sun, and Zhiqiang Han. "Deep learning-based DDoS-attack detection for cyber–physical system over 5G network." *IEEE Transactions on Industrial Informatics* 17, no. 2 (2020): 860–870.

Jamal, Alshaibi Ahmed, Al-Ani Mustafa Majid, Anton Konev, Tatiana Kosachenko, and Alexander Shelupanov. "A review on security analysis of cyber physical systems using machine learning." *Materials Today: Proceedings* 80 (2023): 2302–2306.

Jayaratne, Dinithi, Daswin De Silva, Damminda Alahakoon, and Xinghuo Yu. "Continuous detection of concept drift in industrial cyber-physical systems using closed loop incremental machine learning." *Discover Artificial Intelligence* 1 (2021): 1–13.

Lee, Jay, Moslem Azamfar, Jaskaran Singh, and Shahin Siahpour. "Integration of digital twin and deep learning in cyber-physical systems: Towards smart manufacturing." *IET Collaborative Intelligent Manufacturing* 2, no. 1 (2020): 3–36.

Lee, Jay, and Pradeep Kundu. "Integrated cyber-physical systems and industrial metaverse for remote manufacturing." *Manufacturing Letters* 34 (2022): 12–15.

Leong, A. S., Ramaswamy, A., Quevedo, D. E., Karl, H., & Shi, L. "Deep reinforcement learning for wireless sensor scheduling in cyber–physical systems." *Automatica* 113, (2020): 108759.

Li, Beibei, Yuhao Wu, Jiarui Song, Rongxing Lu, Tao Li, and Liang Zhao. "DeepFed: Federated deep learning for intrusion detection in industrial cyber–physical systems." *IEEE Transactions on Industrial Informatics* 17, no. 8 (2020): 5615–5624.

Liu, Siyuan, Ashutosh Trivedi, Xiang Yin, and Majid Zamani. "Secure-by-construction synthesis of cyber-physical systems." *Annual Reviews in Control* 53 (2022): 30–50.

Liu, Teng, Bin Tian, Yunfeng Ai, and Fei-Yue Wang. "Parallel reinforcement learning-based energy efficiency improvement for a cyber-physical system." *IEEE/CAA Journal of Automatica Sinica* 7, no. 2 (2020): 617–626.

Luo, Yuan, Ya Xiao, Long Cheng, Guojun Peng, and Danfeng Yao. "Deep learning-based anomaly detection in cyber-physical systems: Progress and opportunities." *ACM Computing Surveys (CSUR)* 54, no. 5 (2021): 1–36.

Malik, Javaid Ahmad, and Muhammad Saleem. "Blockchain and cyber-physical system for security engineering in the smart industry." In *Security Engineering for Embedded and Cyber-Physical Systems*, pp. 51–70. CRC press, Boca Raton, 2022.

Mishra, Ayaskanta, Amitkumar V. Jha, Bhargav Appasani, Arun Kumar Ray, Deepak Kumar Gupta, and Abu Nasar Ghazali. "Emerging technologies and design aspects of next generation cyber physical system with a smart city application perspective." *International Journal of System Assurance Engineering and Management* 14, no. Suppl 3 (2023): 699–721.

Mohindru, Vandana, Ravindara Bhatt, and Yashwant Singh. "Reauthentication scheme for mobile wireless sensor networks." *Sustainable Computing: Informatics and Systems* 23 (2019): 158–166.

Mohindru, Vandana, and Yashwant Singh. "Node authentication algorithm for securing static wireless sensor networks from node clone attack." *International Journal of information and computer security* 10, no. 2–3 (2018): 129–148.

Mohindru, Vandana, Yashwant Singh, and Ravindara Bhatt. "Securing wireless sensor networks from node clone attack: a lightweight message authentication algorithm." *International Journal of Information and Computer Security* 12, no. 2–3 (2020): 217–233.

Olowononi, Felix O., Danda B. Rawat, and Chunmei Liu. "Resilient machine learning for networked cyber physical systems: A survey for machine learning security to securing machine learning for CPS." *IEEE Communications Surveys & Tutorials* 23, no. 1 (2020): 524–552.

Patel, N., Trivedi, S., & Faruqui, N. (2023, February). A Novel Sedentary Workforce Scheduling Optimization Algorithm using 2nd Order Polynomial Kernel. In 2023 *International Conference on Smart Computing and Application (ICSCA)* (pp. 1–7). IEEE.

Presekal, Alfan, Alexandru Ştefanov, Vetrivel S. Rajkumar, and Peter Palensky. "Attack graph model for cyber-physical power systems using hybrid deep learning." *IEEE Transactions on Smart Grid* 14, no. 5 (2023): 4007–4020.

Rachmawati, Anggi. "Analysis of machine learning systems for cyber physical systems." *International Transactions on Education Technology* 1, no. 1 (2022): 1–9.

Rai, Rahul, and Chandan K. Sahu. "Driven by data or derived through physics? a review of hybrid physics guided machine learning techniques with cyber-physical system (cps) focus." *IEEE Access* 8 (2020): 71050–71073.

Rathore, Shailendra, and Jong Hyuk Park. "A blockchain-based deep learning approach for cyber security in next generation industrial cyber-physical systems." *IEEE Transactions on Industrial Informatics* 17, no. 8 (2020): 5522–5532.

Ryalat, Mutaz, Hisham ElMoaqet, and Marwa AlFaouri. "Design of a smart factory based on cyber-physical systems and Internet of Things towards Industry 4.0." *Applied Sciences* 13, no. 4 (2023): 2156.

Schneble, William, and Geethapriya Thamilarasu. "Attack detection using federated learning in medical cyber-physical systems." In *Proceedings or the 28th International Conference on Computing and Communication Networks(ICCCN)*, vol. 29, pp. 1–8. 2019.

Tang, Bin, Yan Lu, Qi Li, Yueying Bai, Jie Yu, and Xu Yu. "A diffusion model based on network intrusion detection method for industrial cyber-physical systems." *Sensors* 23, no. 3 (2023): 1141.

Tariq, Muhammad, Mansoor Ali, Faisal Naeem, and H. Vincent Poor. "Vulnerability assessment of 6G-enabled smart grid cyber–physical systems." *IEEE internet of things journal* 8, no. 7 (2020): 5468–5475.

Throne, Odile, and George Lăzăroiu. "Internet of Things-enabled sustainability, industrial big data analytics, and deep learning-assisted smart process planning in cyber-physical manufacturing systems." *Economics, Management and Financial Markets* 15, no. 4 (2020): 49–58.

Tran, Hoang-Dung, Feiyang Cai, Manzanas Lopez Diego, Patrick Musau, Taylor T. Johnson, and Xenofon Koutsoukos. "Safety verification of cyber-physical systems with reinforcement learning control." *ACM Transactions on Embedded Computing Systems (TECS)* 18, no. 5s (2019): 1–22.

Wang, Baicun, Pai Zheng, Yue Yin, Albert Shih, and Lihui Wang. "Toward human-centric smart manufacturing: A human-cyber-physical systems (HCPS) perspective." *Journal of Manufacturing Systems* 63 (2022a): 471–490.

Wang, Tianteng, Xuping Wang, Yiping Jiang, Zilai Sun, Yuhu Liang, Xiangpei Hu, Hao Li, Yan Shi, Jingjun Xu, and Junhu Ruan. "Hybrid machine learning approach for evapotranspiration estimation of fruit tree in agricultural cyber-physical systems." *IEEE Transactions on Cybernetics* 53, no. 9 (2022b): 5677–5691.

Wiśniewski, Remigiusz, Marcin Wojnakowski, and Zhiwu Li. "Design and verification of petri-net-based cyber-physical systems oriented toward implementation in field-programmable gate arrays—A case study example." *Energies* 16, no. 1 (2022): 67.

Wu, Weiqiang, Chunyue Song, Jun Zhao, and Zuhua Xu. "Physics-informed gated recurrent graph attention unit network for anomaly detection in industrial cyber-physical systems." *Information Sciences* 629 (2023): 618–633.

Yu, Zhenhua, Hongxia Gao, Dan Wang, Abeer Ali Alnuaim, Muhammad Firdausi, and Almetwally M. Mostafa. "SEI2RS malware propagation model considering two infection rates in cyber–physical systems." *Physica A: Statistical Mechanics and its Applications* 597 (2022): 127207.

Zhang, Jun, Lei Pan, Qing-Long Han, Chao Chen, Sheng Wen, and Yang Xiang. "Deep learning based attack detection for cyber-physical system cybersecurity: A survey." *IEEE/ CAA Journal of Automatica Sinica* 9, no. 3 (2021): 377–391.

Zhou, Junlong, Liying Li, Ahmadreza Vajdi, Xiumin Zhou, and Zebin Wu. "Temperature-constrained reliability optimization of industrial cyber-physical systems using machine learning and feedback control." *IEEE Transactions on Automation Science and Engineering* 20, no. 1 (2021): 20–31.

Section III

Securing Cyber-Physical Systems

4 Lightweight Cryptographic Algorithms for Cyber-Physical Systems

Sheikh Imroza Manzoor and Yashwant Singh

Central University of Jammu, Jammu, India

4.1 INTRODUCTION

A CPS is a type of complex engineering system that integrates physical and computational components to create an intelligent, automated system that can interact with the physical world in real time (Habib and Chukwuemeka 2022; Yaacoub et al. 2020; Lv et al. 2021; Sheikh et al. 2022). CPS integrates digital elements (algorithms, software, communication networks) with physical components such as sensors and actuators. CPSs are used for many different applications, including smart manufacturing, autonomous vehicles, smart grid systems, and healthcare systems. These are designed to provide real-time monitoring, control, and optimization of physical processes using sophisticated software algorithms and machine learning techniques. CPSs can be roughly divided into three groups autonomous CPS (Guiochet, Machin, and Waeselynck 2017), networked CPS (Stefan Schupp et al. 2015), and industrial automation and control systems (Kriaa et al. 2015). CPSs are critical to many industries because they offer improved efficiency, accuracy, and safety compared to traditional systems. They also offer new opportunities for creativity in a variety of fields. However, they also pose significant challenges, such as security risks, data privacy concerns, and the need for specialized skills and expertise to design, develop, and maintain these systems.

Lightweight cryptography is a relatively new phrase that describes a method of data security that makes better use of fewer resources while maintaining the same or better throughput, conservatism, and power efficiency. There are two types of lightweight cryptographic algorithms, symmetric and asymmetric, just like regular cryptographic algorithms (Vennela 2021). Lightweight symmetric block ciphers are often used in widespread figuring. Symmetric ciphers include both block ciphers and stream ciphers. They are made to be used with electrical gadgets, and their lightweight is not strictly regulated. Any design for lightweight cryptography needs to take into account not just safety and efficiency, but also cost and performance (Shah and Engineer 2019). While it is simple to optimize any one of these three key design goals, it is extremely challenging to optimize for all three at once.

DOI: 10.1201/9781003406105-7

4.2   SECURING THE CPS

The security of CPS (Wu, Sun, and Chen 2016) is critical, as these systems can be vulnerable to cyberattacks that could compromise safety, cause physical damage, or disrupt critical infrastructure (Karimipour et al. 2020). Attacks on CPS can originate from a wide variety of places, such as malicious participants, hackers, or even unintentional human errors. When it comes to securing CPS, one of the challenges is finding a solution to the dilemma of combining digital and physical components. Because it might be challenging to replace or repair the CPS's physical components, the system itself is susceptible to being attacked (Yaacoub et al. 2020). Additionally, many CPSs are designed to operate in real time, which means that security measures must be implemented without causing delays or disruptions to the system (Bolbot et al. 2019).

CPS can be protected from these threats by implementing a number of different security mechanisms, some of which are illustrated in Figure 6.1 (Yaacoub et al. 2020; Bolbot et al. 2019).

    i. **Access Control Mechanisms**: Using authentication and authorization methods, one can place restrictions on who can access the CPS and its various components. Users' identities can be validated by utilizing a range of authentication approaches, such as passwords, biometrics, and two-factor authentication, among others. Passwords are the most common form of authentication. Users should only have access to the resources they actually need, and this can be achieved through the use of authorization techniques to restrict the resources to which they have access.

   ii. **Network Security Measures**: Protecting a network against unauthorized access and attacks is possible through the implementation of network security mechanisms such as firewalls, intrusion detection systems, and other protective measures.

  iii. **Encryption**: The encryption of sensitive information and signals with the purpose of protecting them from being intercepted or accessed without authorization.

  iv. **Physical Security**: To safeguard the physical components of CPS systems from being stolen, damaged, or tampered, some physical security measures must be established such as access control mechanisms, video surveillance, and alarms.

   v. **Continuous monitoring of CPS**: Keeping track of the CPS on a regular basis for any security flaws and abnormalities, and acting swiftly in response to any occurrences that are discovered.

  vi. **Regular updates and patches**: Ensuring every aspect of the CPS's hardware, software, and firmware are kept up-to-date and updated on a regular basis in order to address any known security flaws or weaknesses in the system.

 vii. **Security Testing**: Perform regular security inspections and evaluations on the CPS in order to discover and repair any potential vulnerabilities in a timely manner, before those vulnerabilities may be exploited.

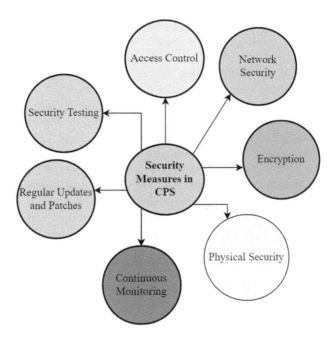

FIGURE 4.1 Security measures in cyber-physical systems.

CPS can be better safeguarded against cyberattacks by taking these measures. Because of this, these essential systems will be guaranteed to be risk-free as well as reliable. Figure 4.1 depicts the security measures in cyber-physical systems.

4.3 LIGHTWEIGHT CRYPTOGRAPHY

The concept of lightweight cryptography has undergone certain changes as a direct result of the rising utilization of devices in CPSs that have restricted resources. According to NIST, conventional cryptographic algorithms such as AES and RSA were designed to function properly on desktop PCs and servers since these types of devices have a lot of processing power and memory (NIST 2017). However, the same algorithms might not be appropriate for application in CPS, because the devices in those systems might only have a limited amount of computing power, memory, and energy.

The development of cryptographic algorithms that are effective while consuming a small number of resources is the primary emphasis of lightweight cryptography. This consists of algorithms with lower computational complexity, smaller key sizes, and smaller block sizes. The objective is to give a high level of protection while at the same time having as little of an effect as possible on the resources available on the device (Thakor, Razzaque, and Khandaker 2021).

From the start, there has been a rise in the demand for encrypted communication between devices in the Internet of Things (IoT) because there has been a growth in the number of connected devices. Second, the proliferation of wireless communication technologies such as Bluetooth and Zigbee has resulted in the emergence of a new set of challenges with regard to the protection of sensitive information. Third, the integration of cyber-physical systems with critical infrastructure, such as healthcare and transportation, has increased the need of putting in place stringent procedures to protect against potential security breaches.

In cyber-physical systems, the need for lightweight cryptography has arisen as a result of a number of issues, which has led to its widespread adoption. To begin, an increase in the number of connected devices in the Internet of Things has led to a larger need for encrypted communication between those devices. This demand has led to an increase in the number of encrypted communication options. Second, the proliferation of wireless communication technologies such as Bluetooth and Zigbee has resulted in the emergence of a new set of challenges with regard to the protection of sensitive information. Third, the integration of cyber-physical systems with critical infrastructure, such as healthcare and transportation, has increased the need of putting in place stringent procedures to protect against potential security breaches.

4.4 APPLICATIONS OF LIGHTWEIGHT CRYPTOGRAPHY

Lightweight cryptography offers a wide range of potential applications in a variety of contexts, as it is both effective and resource-friendly. Figure 6.2 depicts some common applications of lightweight cryptography. All of these applications are briefly discussed below.

i.   **IoT**: Lightweight cryptography, which can be used to encrypt communications between devices and other components of IoT systems, is required because the number of devices connected to the Internet of Things continues to expand. The fact that lightweight cryptographic algorithms are optimized for devices with minimal memory and low power consumption makes them a desirable option for Internet of Things applications (Thakor, Razzaque, and Khandaker 2021).

ii. **Wireless Sensor Networks (WSN)**: WSN nodes, which are limited in computational aspects and energy resources, can employ lightweight cryptography to protect communications. For secure and efficient WSN communication, lightweight cryptographic methods are optimized.

iii. **Smart Cards**: Lightweight cryptographic techniques can safeguard smartcard-reader interactions, preventing unauthorized access. Figure 4.2 represents the applications of lightweight cryptographic algorithms.

iv. **Embedded Systems**: Embedded systems have several uses, such as in the automotive industry, factories, and hospitals. By using lightweight cryptographic algorithms, we can ensure that all parts of these systems can communicate securely with one another.

v.   **Cloud Computing**: The use of cloud computing as a method for storing and processing data is quickly becoming one of the most common choices. A very basic encryption method can be used to encrypt the transmission of sensitive data between cloud servers and client devices. This helps to protect the data from unauthorized access and retain the confidentiality of the data.

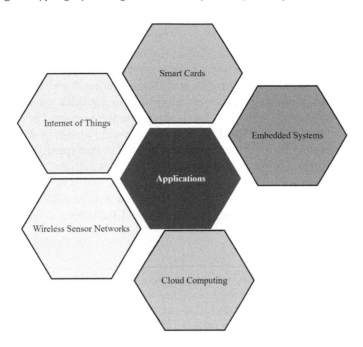

FIGURE 4.2   Applications of lightweight cryptographic algorithms.

4.5   LIGHTWEIGHT CRYPTOGRAPHIC ALGORITHMS FOR CPS

Cryptographic algorithms are used to secure communication and data transfer in CPS. In CPS, lightweight cryptographic algorithms are preferred because they use less memory and don't need as much processing power. In this section, we will look at some of the most popular lightweight cryptographic algorithms used in CPS. A summary of some of the existing algorithms is shown in Table 4.1.

4.5.1   GENERALIZED TRIANGLE-BASED SECURITY ALGORITHM (G-TBSA)

The G-TBSA, created by Ahmed et al., is used in wireless sensor networks with low-power Wi-Fi (Ahmed et al. 2019). G-TBSA comprises two parts: A way to encrypt data that uses few resources and a way to make keys quickly. The key generation process is the most important part of the algorithm because it uses fewer resources to make the keys. This makes the algorithm less complicated and uses less energy. The proposed mechanism was based on a triangle that didn't have a right angle, and the output signal was used instead of figuring out how much time had passed. The G-TBSA is better at using energy than other algorithms. But this method only works for devices with sensors (Ahmed et al. 2019).

4.5.2 Modified PRESENT

Chatterjee and Chakraborty made a new, lightweight PRESENT cipher called Modified PRESENT (Chatterjee and Chakraborty 2020). The original PRESENT cipher has been modified by having its encryption shortened and its key register altered. The value of the key register is encrypted using a delta value function of TEA (Tiny encryption algorithm), before being put to the register. The supplementary layer permits a drop in PRESENT rounds from a minimum of 31 to just 25. The algorithm can do its job better if the key register is encrypted. The suggested algorithm shows that it is the best by looking at different software parameters like N-gram, nonhomogeneity, frequency distribution graph, and histogram. This algorithm performs better than others while looking at gate value. But it hasn't been tested to see how much power it uses (Chatterjee and Chakraborty 2020).

4.5.3 PRESENT

PRESENT is a block cipher that was made to be used in RFID tags and other lightweight applications where computing resources and power consumption are limited. Bogdanov et al. created it in 2007 (Bogdanov et al. 2007). The cipher has a block size of 64 bits and supports key sizes of 80 and 128 bits. It uses a Feistel network structure with 31 rounds. The round function consists of a combination of bit-level permutations, substitution boxes, and a key mixing operation. The top-level algorithm description is shown in Figure 4.3. One of the best things about PRESENT is that it is simple, which makes it fast and small in terms of code size. It can also protect against attacks like differential and linear cryptanalysis (Rolfes et al. 2008). However, one of the limitations of PRESENT is its relatively small block size, which may not provide sufficient security against brute force attacks if the key size is not large enough.

4.5.4 SIMON

The US National Security Agency (NSA) created a family of lightweight block ciphers called SIMON. SIMON can utilize keys that are 64 bits, 96 bits, or 128 bits in size, and it can employ either a 32-bit or a 64-bit block size. It is built to run very quickly and has a minimal amount of code because those are the design goals. Because of this, it is an excellent option for use in settings that have restricted access to resources, such as those found in cyber-physical systems. SIMON makes use of a Feistel network topology with a round function that incorporates logical AND, and OR operations, bitwise XOR, and circular bit shifts. The key scheduling is also highly effective, which enables the round keys to be made fast and with minimal usage of memory (Rashidi 2020). One potential disadvantage of SIMON is that it has not yet been subjected to as much analysis and scrutiny as some other ciphers, like AES. However, it has been studied and analyzed by cryptographers and has been shown to have good security properties. Overall, SIMON could be a good choice for a cyber-physical system that needs a lightweight cryptographic cipher. This is especially true if code size and speed are important.

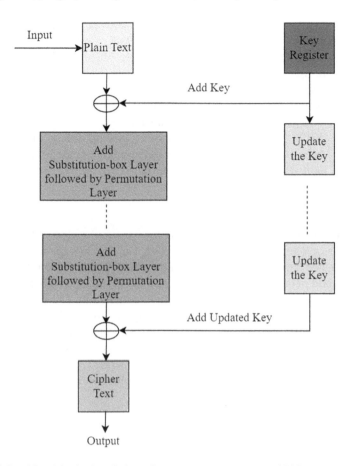

FIGURE 4.3 Algorithmic description of present (Bogdanov et al. 2007).

4.5.5 MODIFIED BLOCK CIPHER TECHNIQUE (MBCT)

The MBCT was made by Chaudhary and Chatterjee in 2020. It uses the XOR and Expansion functions and one Matrix Rotation. During the encryption process, the most important thing that changes is how the Expansion and Round key generation function works. The key is 256 bits long, and in this process, a 256-bit piece of plain text was used. This algorithm has 32 rounds, and it takes less time than AES, DES, or SIMON to secure and decrypt (Chaudhary and Chatterjee 2020).

4.5.6 TEA

In 1994, researchers David Wheeler and Roger Needham of Cambridge's Computer Laboratory created TEA (Tiny Encryption Algorithm) (Kataoka et al. 2016). It is a lightweight cryptographic algorithm that is designed to provide fast and secure encryption for small data blocks. TEA encrypts and decrypts 64-bit data bits with a

128-bit key (Kataoka et al. 2016). Using a Feistel network topology, the algorithm splits the data block in half and applies the same key to each half. The algorithm encrypts and decrypts data using a total of 64 rounds. When it comes to speed, code size, and ease of use, TEA is incomparable (Banik et al. 2017). It finds widespread application in resource-constrained and embedded systems where performance is paramount. However, it has been demonstrated that TEA has several vulnerabilities, especially in its key scheduling, that can render it susceptible to specific assaults (Banik et al. 2017). Therefore, safe variants of the algorithm, like XTEA and XXTEA, have been created to counteract these flaws (Guo et al. 2011). Table 4.1 is a summary of lightweight cryptographic algorithms.

4.5.7   GIFT

GIFT was created to offer robust security on low-powered gadgets like those found in the Internet of Things. Key sizes of 128, 192, and 256 bits are supported by the cipher, which uses a 64-bit block size (Mohindru et al. 2020b). The GIFT algorithm employs a hybrid network architecture based on the Feistel and SPN topologies and a configurable permutation inspired by the Gimli permutation. The authors also present a thorough security analysis of GIFT, proving the protocol's invulnerability to attacks like differential and linear cryptanalysis. GIFT is a lightweight block cipher that features faster encryption and decryption times, less memory requirements, and a smaller code size. Additionally, the authors demonstrate GIFT's efficient portability across a variety of platforms, from microcontrollers to FPGAs (Mohindru and Singh 2018).

4.5.8   LED

LED is a block cipher that can function in low-resource settings, making it ideal for RFID tags and wireless sensor networks. Researchers at the French Orange Labs submitted it to the NIST lightweight cryptography competition after developing it. LED is a 64-bit block cipher that supports keys of lengths 80, 128, and 192 bits. The plaintext has been encrypted with a Feistel network that consists of 32 rounds. The process of rounding makes use of a linear diffusion layer, an operation called a sub-byte, and an action called a mix-column. The sub-byte operation is a byte replacement process that is bound by the S-box and uses 8 bits. In the Galois Field (GF), the operation that is equivalent to matrix multiplication is referred to as the mix column operation. The diffusion layer undergoes a linear transformation while the bits that make up the state are being changed. Because of its very small memory footprint and code size, LED is an excellent choice for low-power devices. In addition to this, it offers robust protection against differential as well as linear cryptanalysis (Mohindru et al. 2020a). It is not recommended for use in applications that require high levels of security because of its relatively small block size and short key length.

TABLE 4.1

Summary of Lightweight Cryptographic Algorithms

Name of Algorithm	Block Size (bits)	Key size (bits)	No. of Rounds	Cipher Type	Techniques used	Advantages
G-TBSA (Ahmed et al. 2019)	—	—	—	—	TBSA, non-right-angle triangle	It consumes less amount of energy and is suitable for Wireless Sensor Networks (WSN).
Modified PRESENT (Chatterjee and Chakraborty 2020)	64	80	25	SPN, FN	PRESENT, TEA, S-box layer, and P-box layer	In terms of gate value, this method performs better than others.
PRESENT (A. et al. 2007)	64	80, 128	31	FN	S-box layer, P-box layer, and add a round key	The PRESENT cipher is a very secure, fast, easy-to-use, and flexible encryption algorithm that works well in environments with limited resources, like IoT devices.
SIMON (Rashidi 2020)	32, 64	64, 96, 128		FN	Logical AND, and OR operations, bitwise XoR, and Circular Shift	SIMON is a viable option for use in systems that demand low-overhead cryptographic algorithms without sacrificing security.
MBCT (Chaudhary and Chatterjee 2020)	256	256	32	Block cipher	Matrix location, XOR, Expansion function	When compared to AES, DES, and SIMON, it takes less time to encrypt and decrypt.

(Continued)

TABLE 4.1 (Continued)

Name of Algorithm	Block Size (bits)	Key size (bits)	No. of Rounds	Cipher Type	Techniques used	Advantages
TEA (Kataoka et al. 2016)	64	128	64	FN	Key Expansion, Data block splitting, Bitwise XoR, Right Shift, Left Shift.	TEA is a lightweight algorithm that requires minimal memory and processing power, making it well suited for use in embedded systems and other low-resource environments.
GIFT (Banik et al. 2017)	64	128, 192, 256	40 (for 128-bit), 48 (for 192 bits), 56 (for 256 bits)	Hybrid (SPN, FN)	Initialization, SubCells, PermBits, AddRoundKey, Key Schedule, and Round Constants	GIFT's efficient portability across platforms means it may be used in a broad variety of contexts, from embedded microcontrollers to field-programmable gate arrays.
LED (Guo et al. 2011)	64	80, 128, 192	32	FN	Add Round Key, Add Constants, SubCells, ShiftRow, MixColumnsSerial	LED is a secure and efficient block cipher that works well in low-resource settings. It's a viable option for many uses thanks to its speed, key length versatility, and general availability.

Note: FN: Feistel Network, SPN: Substitution-Permutation Network.

4.6 SUMMARY

Small computing devices (RFID tags, sensor nodes, smart cards, etc.) are gaining widespread adoption and are increasingly used in a variety of applications. The miniaturization of devices and the adoption of using small devices instead of desktops have raised many security and privacy issues. Therefore, applying conventional cryptographic methods to these small devices is a challenging task as these are resource constrained and require more power. Thus, lightweight cryptography is utilized to overcome such challenges. In this chapter, an overview of CPS, the requirements of securing a CPS, lightweight cryptography, and its applications have been discussed. In addition to this, an analysis of existing lightweight cryptographic techniques is presented. It has been found that while choosing a lightweight cryptographic algorithm for a CPS, it is important to think carefully about the specific needs of that CPS to make sure it provides the right level of security and speed.

REFERENCES

Ahmed, Sharif Faisal, Md Rahimul Islam, Tushar Deb Nath, Bilkis Jamal Ferdosi, and A. S.M. Touhidul Hasan. 2019. "G-TBSA: A Generalized Lightweight Security Algorithm for IoT." *2019 4th International Conference on Electrical Information and Communication Technology, EICT 2019*, December: 20–22. https://doi.org/10.1109/EICT48899.2019.9068848

Banik, Subhadeep, Sumit Kumar Pandey, Thomas Peyrin, Yu Sasaki, Siang Meng Sim, and Yosuke Todo. 2017. "GIFT: A Small Present: Towards Reaching the Limit of Lightweight Encryption." *Lecture Notes in Computer Science (Including Subseries Lecture Notes in Artificial Intelligence and Lecture Notes in Bioinformatics)* 10529 LNCS: 321–45. https://doi.org/10.1007/978-3-319-66787-4_16

Bogdanov, A., L.R. Knudsen, G. Leander, C. Paar, A. Poschmann, M.J.B. Robshaw, Y. Seurin, and C. Vikkelsoe 2007. "Present:An Ultra-Lightweight Block Cipher." In *Springer*, 450–66. Springer. https://doi.org/10.1163/15709256-12341242

Bolbot, Victor, Gerasimos Theotokatos, Luminita Manuela Bujorianu, Evangelos Boulougouris, and Dracos Vassalos. 2019. "Vulnerabilities and Safety Assurance Methods in Cyber-Physical Systems: A Comprehensive Review." *Reliability Engineering and System Safety* 182 (March 2018): 179–93. https://doi.org/10.1016/j.ress.2018.09.004

Chatterjee, Runa, and Rajdeep Chakraborty. 2020. "A Modified Lightweight PRESENT Cipher For IoT Security." In *2020 International Conference on Computer Science, Engineering and Applications (ICCSEA)*. IEEE. https://doi.org/10.1109/ICCSEA49143.2020.9132950

Chaudhary, Ravi Raushan Kumar, and Kakali Chatterjee. 2020. "An Efficient Lightweight Cryptographic Technique for Iot Based E-Healthcare System." *2020 7th International Conference on Signal Processing and Integrated Networks, SPIN 2020*, 991–95. https://doi.org/10.1109/SPIN48934.2020.9071421

Guiochet, Jérémie, Mathilde Machin, and Hélène Waeselynck. 2017. "Safety-Critical Advanced Robots: A Survey." *Robotics and Autonomous Systems* 94: 43–52. https://doi.org/10.1016/j.robot.2017.04.004

Guo, Jian, Thomas Peyrin, Axel Poschmann, and Matt Robshaw. 2011. "The LED Block Cipher." *Lecture Notes in Computer Science (Including Subseries Lecture Notes in Artificial Intelligence and Lecture Notes in Bioinformatics)* 6917 LNCS: 326–41. https://doi.org/10.1007/978-3-642-23951-9_22

Habib, Maki K., and Chukwuemeka Chimsom I. 2022. "CPS: Role, Characteristics, Architectures and Future Potentials." *Procedia Computer Science* 200: 1347–58. https://doi.org/10.1016/j.procs.2022.01.336

Karimipour, Hadis, Pirathayini Srikantha, Hany Farag, and Jin Wei-Kocsis. 2020. *Security of Cyber-Physical Systems Vulnerability and Impact. Security of Cyber-Physical Systems.* Springer Cham.

Kataoka, Hiroki, Atsuhiro Sawada, Dilawaer Duolikun, Tomoya Enokido, and Makoto Takizawa. 2016. "Energy-Aware Server Selection Algorithms in a Scalable Cluster." *Proceedings - International Conference on Advanced Information Networking and Applications, AINA* 2016 May (March 2021): 565–72. https://doi.org/10.1109/AINA.2016.154

Kriaa, Siwar, Ludovic Pietre-Cambacedes, Marc Bouissou, and Yoran Halgand. 2015. "A Survey of Approaches Combining Safety and Security for Industrial Control Systems." *Reliability Engineering and System Safety* 139: 156–78. https://doi.org/10.1016/j.ress.2015.02.008

Lv, Zhihan, Dongliang Chen, Ranran Lou, and Ammar Alazab. 2021. "Artificial Intelligence for Securing Industrial-Based Cyber–Physical Systems." *Future Generation Computer Systems* 117: 291–98. https://doi.org/10.1016/j.future.2020.12.001

Mohindru, Vandana, and Yashwant Singh. "Node Authentication Algorithm for Securing Static Wireless Sensor Networks from Node Clone Attack." *International Journal of information and computer security* 10, no. 2–3 (2018): 129–48.

Mohindru, Vandana, Yashwant Singh, and Ravindara Bhatt. "Hybrid Cryptography Algorithm for Securing Wireless Sensor Networks from Node Clone Attack." *Recent Advances in Electrical & Electronic Engineering (Formerly Recent Patents on Electrical & Electronic Engineering)* 13, no. 2 (2020a): 251–59.

Mohindru, Vandana, Yashwant Singh, and Ravindara Bhatt. "Securing wireless sensor networks from node clone attack: A lightweight message authentication algorithm." *International Journal of Information and Computer Security* 12, no. 2–3 (2020b): 217–33.

NIST. 2017. "Report on Lightweight Cryptography March 2017 Final Publication. https://doi.org/10.6028/NIST.IR.8114 (Which Links to • Information on Other NIST Cybersecurity Publications A." *Nist* 8114 (March).

Rashidi, Bahram. 2020. "Flexible Structures of Lightweight Block Ciphers Present, Simon and Led." *IET Circuits, Devices and Systems* 14 (3): 369–80. https://doi.org/10.1049/iet-cds.2019.0363

Rolfes, Carsten, Axel Poschmann, Gregor Leander, and Christof Paar. 2008. "Ultra-Lightweight Implementations for Smart Devices - Security for 1000 Gate Equivalents." *Lecture Notes in Computer Science (Including Subseries Lecture Notes in Artificial Intelligence and Lecture Notes in Bioinformatics)* 5189 LNCS: 89–103. https://doi.org/10.1007/978-3-540-85893-5_7

Shah, Ankit, and Margi Engineer. 2019. *A Survey of Lightweight Cryptographic Algorithms for IoT-Based Applications. Advances in Intelligent Systems and Computing* Vol. 851. Springer Singapore. https://doi.org/10.1007/978-981-13-2414-7_27

Sheikh, Zakir Ahmad, Yashwant Singh, Pradeep Kumar Singh, and Kayhan Zrar Ghafoor. 2022. "Intelligent and Secure Framework for Critical Infrastructure (CPS): Current Trends, Challenges, and Future Scope." *Computer Communications* 193 (July): 302–31. https://doi.org/10.1016/j.comcom.2022.07.007

Stefan Schupp, B, Erika Abrah, Xin Chen, and Ibtissem Ben Makhlouf. 2015. "Cyber Physical Systems. Design, Modeling, and Evaluation". *5th International Workshop, CyPhy 2015,* Amsterdam, The Netherlands, October 8, 2015, Proceedings 9361 (611115): 8–24. https://doi.org/10.1007/978-3-319-25141-7

Thakor, Vishal A., Mohammad Abdur Razzaque, and Muhammad R.A. Khandaker. 2021. "Lightweight Cryptography Algorithms for Resource-Constrained IoT Devices: A Review, Comparison and Research Opportunities." *IEEE Access* 9 (January): 28177–93. https://doi.org/10.1109/ACCESS.2021.3052867

Vennela, Vasireddy. 2021. "Lightweight Cryptography Algorithms for IOT Devices." *International Journal for Research in Applied Science and Engineering Technology* 9 (VI): 1678–83. https://doi.org/10.22214/ijraset.2021.35358

Wu, Guangyu, Jian Sun, and Jie Chen. 2016. "A Survey on the Security of Cyber-Physical Systems." *Control Theory and Technology* 14 (1): 2–10. https://doi.org/10.1007/s11768-016-5123-9

Yaacoub, Jean Paul A., Ola Salman, Hassan N. Noura, Nesrine Kaaniche, Ali Chehab, and Mohamad Malli. 2020. "Cyber-Physical Systems Security: Limitations, Issues and Future Trends." *Microprocessors and Microsystems* 77. https://doi.org/10.1016/j.micpro.2020.103201

5 Lightweight Cryptographic Solutions for Resource-constrained Devices in Cyber-Physical Systems

G Krishna Pranav

National Institute of Technology Raipur, Department of ECE, Chhattisgarh, India

Zeesha Mishra

Chhattisgarh Swami Vivekanand Technical University, Department of ECE, Chhattisgarh, India

Bibhudendra Acharya

National Institute of Technology Raipur, Department of ECE, Chhattisgarh, India

5.1 INTRODUCTION

Multimedia studies have found a home in information technology, which is rapidly growing as a field. Growing demand for smartphone technology has pushed scientists to create more advanced hardware features and apps. Online banking, shopping, social network browsing, and a plethora of other programs that rely on exceptional security have become deeply embedded in modern life. The internet, a global system that links trillions of devices, has been a boon to today's youth. As a result of the internet, our lives have become much easier and better. It's no secret that the internet is increasingly used by smart gadgets. Smart locks, smart televisions, smartphones, smart PCs, etc. are becoming increasingly commonplace as the internet spreads throughout the world and into people's homes. Cyber-physical systems (CPS) and other recent technological advances rely largely on online connectivity. Computer systems in which techniques are used to manage or regulate physical systems are known as cyber-physical systems (CPS) or intelligent systems. The computer units in a CPS network collaborate with one another and the outside environment via a feedback mechanism of actuators and sensing devices. Cyber-physical systems are networks that consist of both computer and physical parts. Often referred to as a 'Computing System of the Future'. Cyber-physical systems have been nicknamed 'the next industrial revolution' due to their impact on people's day-to-day lives, including where they choose to live, work,

DOI: 10.1201/9781003406105-8

socialize, and travel, whereas IoT is the subset of CPS. Cyber-physical systems (CPS) provide a more advanced integration and coordination of physical and computer components, while the Internet of Things (IoT) aims to link everyday things to the web. In its early stages, the internet was an attempt to bridge geographical distances by connecting people through video conferencing and social networking sites; this concept is also referred to as the 'Internet of People'. The Internet of Things (IoT) (Laghari et al. 2021) is the next step in the development of technology as it shifts its focus from humans to inanimate objects. For the purposes of this definition, 'things' refer to any internet-enabled item or gadget that runs a certain piece of software or contains a certain set of circuit components. In addition to having sensors, these devices are also capable of communicating with others of their kind. These include smartphones, smart air conditioners, smart washing machines, and smart autos. Increases in the use of low-resource devices and wireless networks like cyber-physical Systems (CPS) (Yaacoub et al. 2020), wireless sensor nodes (WSN) (Landaluce et al. 2020), smart cards, radiofrequency identification (RFID) (Gupta et al. 2022a), and the Internet of Things (IoT) (Shafique et al. 2020) have led to a corresponding rise in the importance of ensuring the safety of these systems and the data they transmit. The Internet of Things is user-friendly, saves time and effort, and reduces human error.

As a result, CPS has attracted the attention of academics and the corporate world. Because of the ability of the Internet of Things devices to communicate with one another and share data, it is used in nearly every industry, from farming and medicine to cars and home appliances to RF ID and smart cards (Pradhan et al. 2021). Therefore, almost every sector makes use of our personal data attacks against systems and decentralized networks may have increased as a result of technical progress. Due to this, there is a pressing requirement to ensure confidentiality. That's why protecting our information is crucial to avoiding identity theft, privacy breaches, and other hassles. For safety reasons, we must use cryptography.

5.2 METHODOLOGY

This chapter's main contribution is an explanation of what cryptography is and how lightweight cryptography works, followed by the shadow block cipher's algorithm and the unrolled architecture of shadow cipher's hardware implementation. Lastly, a table contrasting the properties of this architecture with those of other ciphers on a variety of platforms. The tool which is used for this operation is Xilinx 14.7 ISE, and the software used is Verilog.

5.3 CHAPTER ORGANIZATION

Here we will explain how the chapter is broken up into its numerous sections and the content that goes into each. Introduction to cryptography covers topics including symmetric and asymmetric cryptography, block and stream ciphers, and various block cipher algorithms in Section 5.4. The importance of lightweight cryptography is discussed in Section 5.5, and the concept itself, along with its introduction and primitives, is covered in Section 5.6. Several architecture models are defined in Section 5.7. Alternate hardware is discussed in Section 5.8. There is a discussion of the many performance metrics that can be applied to cipher analysis. The shadow cipher algorithm, together with encryption and decryption, is presented in Section 5.9. It is discussed how unrolled architecture is implemented in hardware in Section 5.10. In Section 5.11, we see how the proposed unrolled architecture performs in contrast to other ciphers and what those results look like across different platforms. To wrap out the chapter, we have Section 5.12.

5.4   RELATED WORK

Cyber-physical systems are expanding into every field of our lives with the help of the rapid advancement of IoT. But securing the data while transmitting through nodes is an issue. Cryptography is a tool that is used for secure communication by the process of encryption and decryption. Since we face issues with resource constraint applications it fails to an extent. Lightweight cryptography is developed in response to the need for secure yet resource-constrained applications. The widely used AES and DES cryptographic block ciphers both provide top-notch security on a global scale. Then, new, lighter algorithms were developed to succeed these older ciphers. To improve their efficiency, the complexity of several ciphers has been stripped down to create 'lightweight' variants (Dhanda et al. 2020). We have block and stream ciphers based on the input intake. The lightweight block ciphers are optimized for speed on both software and hardware platforms. They include SLIM (Aboushosha et al. 2020), CHASKEY (Dwivedi 2020), IVLBC (Huang et al. 2022), DULBC (Yang et al. 2022a), SCENERY (Feng and Li 2022), GIFT (Banik et al. 2020), SPECK-R (Sleem and Couturier 2021), PRESENT (Bharathi and Parvatham 2022), SIMON (Niveda et al. 2022), LED (Al-Shatari et al. 2022), LORCA (Noura et al. 2022), ACT (Shahana and Jithendra 2020), LCB (Roy et al. 2021), LBC (Ramadan et al. 2021) and FUTURE (Gupta et al. 2022b) etc. The lightweight stream ciphers take a stream of input bits at a time as input which constitutes ciphers like FRUIT 80 (Yang et al. 2022b), LIZARD (Li, Liu and Lin, 2020), EXPRESSO (Kumisbek et al. 2021), SLEPX (Shah et al. 2020), etc. The block ciphers are easier to operate than stream ciphers. The various architectures of the above lightweight ciphers are made for better speed, high throughput, low area, and better frequency. The architectures can be round-based, pipelined, unrolled, and serial-based depending upon the requirement.

5.5   PRELIMINARIES

There are various hardware implementations that are observed in various ciphers in recent years. As per Mishra, Mishra, and Acharya (2021), we have seen that the pipelined and serial architecture of Secure IoT (SIT) which consumes less hardware resources is useful in high-frequency, low-area requirements and leads to a reduction in the cost incurred on hardware. According to Mhaouch et al. (2020), we observe round-based and 4-bit serial architecture for the Piccolo cipher which has less area and high use of resource. According to El Hadj Youssef et al. (2020), we observed the 32-bit data path architectures of LED 64/128, Simon 64/128, and Simeck 64/128 which achieved good performance and less cost. In July 2021, we saw a new cipher BRISI which is a combination of bright and Simon ciphers and its implementations as per Kiran Kumar (2021). In September 2021 (Abbas et al. 2021), we found a resource-shared structure that optimized the area of the mCrypton cipher as well as better frequency. According to Singh et al. (2021) three architectures are proposed for the Klien cipher which increased the security vastly. According to Mishra et al. (2021), four architectures, i.e., TEA, XTEA, XXTEA, and hybrid model, are implemented, with the first three using the pipelined method to increase the frequency and the fourth for area improvement. According to Damodharan et al. (2023), the key schedule architecture and a hardware accelerator are proposed for the PRESENT cipher, which boosted their throughput and reduced their latency. As we have the PRINCE cipher (Kumar et al. 2023) that proposed a serial, round-based, and unrolled pipelined architecture for high throughput, low latency, and low area application, our current work is an extension to the Shadow cipher which was proposed by Guo et al. (2021) in which we proposed an unrolled architecture.

5.6 INTRODUCTION TO CRYPTOGRAPHY

Data transmission and storage can be done with cryptography in a highly private and secure manner. In modern cryptography, a key is used to transform otherwise readable information into indecipherable nonsense. At the verified receiver, the same data is decrypted using the same key or a different key. Ciphers are used for this purpose. A cipher is a set of instructions for turning plaintext into an encrypted form. It can be used for both encrypting and decrypting data. The two main steps of cryptography are encrypting and decrypting. To encrypt a communication means to transform it into a coded structure, and to decode it means to restore it to its original form. It allows us to send secret information across potentially shady networks without worrying about anyone but the intended recipient gaining access to it. Cryptographic methods are depicted in Figure 5.1 and grouped into the two categories of symmetric key and asymmetric key cryptography. Stream ciphers and block ciphers are two subcategories of symmetric-key encryption (Marqas et al. 2020).

5.6.1 CLASSIFICATION OF CRYPTOGRAPHY

A) Asymmetric Cryptography
   Public-key cryptography, which is a subset of asymmetric cryptography, is another name for this kind of encryption. Both the sender and the recipient utilize their own unique keys for encryption and decryption during the whole end-to-end communication.

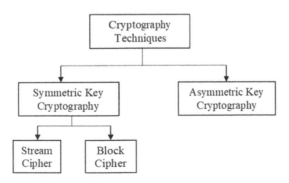

FIGURE 5.1   Types of cryptographic techniques.

Public key cryptography is another name for this. Asymmetric key cryptography, whereby separate keys are used for encryption and decoding, as shown in Figure 5.2.

B) Symmetric Cryptography

All parties involved in end-to-end communication utilize the same secret key for encryption and decryption in a symmetric cryptographic system. The term 'secret key cryptography' describes this practice. In symmetric key cryptography, as seen in Figure 5.3, both the sender and the recipient share the same key for both the encryption and decryption processes.

5.6.2 DIFFERENT TYPES OF CIPHERS

* Block Ciphers and Stream Ciphers
  Block ciphers and stream ciphers are examples of symmetric key ciphers. The plaintext is transformed into ciphertext using one of two block ciphers or a stream cipher. The major distinction between block ciphers and stream ciphers is that the former uses the plain text in blocks, while the latter uses the whole message at once. When using a stream cipher, the plain text is

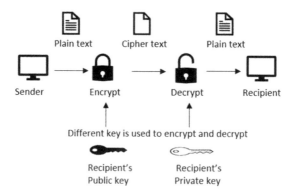

FIGURE 5.2   Asymmetric key cryptography.

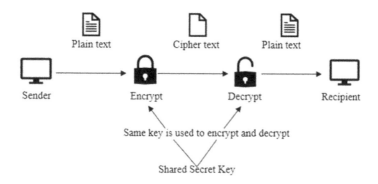

FIGURE 5.3   Symmetric key cryptography.

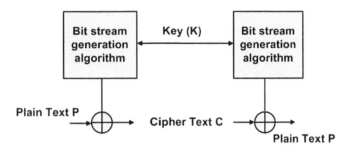

FIGURE 5.4 Block representation of stream cipher.

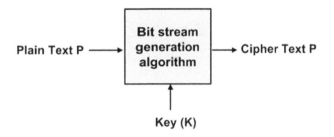

FIGURE 5.5 Block representation of block cipher.

transformed into ciphertext one byte at a time. Figures 5.4 and 5.5 depict the block representations of block and stream ciphers (Jiao et al. 2020).

5.6.3 DESIGN TECHNIQUES OF BLOCK CIPHERS

Lightweight block cipher performance is highly dependent on key size and the number of rounds. More rounds and a larger key size make the cipher more secure. The round functions of various ciphers vary. Substitution permutation network (SPN) ciphers, Feistel structures, and ARX operation-based ciphers are the three main categories of lightweight block ciphers based on their underlying cryptographic primitives. Lightweight block ciphers must be designed in accordance with mathematical modeling features like confusion and diffusion. Using methods like confusion and dispersion, cryptographers may make their ciphers more secure. What follows is a detailed description of the construction of several lightweight encryption types.

A) Feistel ciphers

The encryption and decryption processes of a Feistel network are almost similar; the only variation is the sequencing of the structure's keys, making Feistel ciphers easy to crack. Lightweight Feistel network block cryptography is shown in Figure 5.6. The input plaintext in a Feistel-based network is split into two parts: L and R. When many rounds of applying various operations to the L and R halves of the cipher, the desired ciphertext is finally revealed after the L and R halves are exchanged. In a Feistel network, round

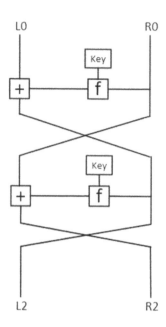

FIGURE 5.6   Feistel structure.

functions cannot be inverted. Feistel-based networks need twice as many
rounds as SPN-based networks because only half of the input is encrypted
in each round.

B) Substitution-Permutation Network

An additional type of block cipher is the substitution and permutation network cipher (SPN cipher). which uses P-boxes and S-boxes, to generate
cipher output from ordinary input. These boxes add layers of uncertainty
and diffusion to the underlying cryptographic method, making the cipher
more secure. The SPN-based structure is used in the Advanced Encryption
Standard (AES) (Heron 2009). The substitution permutation network of a
lightweight block cipher is shown in Figure 5.7. The key and plain text are
the input, and after being processed by the S-box and the P-box for a few
iterations, we get the final encrypted text.

5.7   NEED OF LIGHTWEIGHT CRYPTOGRAPHY FOR CYBER-
PHYSICAL SYSTEMS (CPS)

The aforementioned cryptographic methods may be categorized according to the size
of the key, the number of bits on which the operation is done, and the number of
rounds. Encryption algorithms vary in efficiency based on factors such as their level
of security, cost, size, and energy consumption. Data is encrypted in such a way
that it is both difficult but not impossible to crack the encryption techniques during
transmission. Data transmission, however, needs more power than was calculated.
There is a demand for low-cost and low-hardware-complexity encryption algorithms

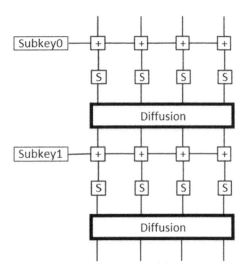

FIGURE 5.7   SPN structure.

as the trend of device integration into a single platform continues to grow in popularity. Resource-constant hardware implementation is critical. Because of the size of the device, it is crucial that the hardware implementation of an encryption system has low power consumption and a small footprint (consisting of an encryption system). Recently, there has been a big uptick in interest in apps that make do with less resources. Lightweight cryptography is a subfield of encryption designed for low-power gadgets. As an example, RFID tags may be used for detection purposes. RFID tags can only function properly in a safe setting. Lightweight cryptographic algorithms are used in a variety of applications ranging from smart home gadgets and retail to healthcare.

5.8   LIGHTWEIGHT CRYPTOGRAPHY

It is crucial to study and prioritize lightweight cryptography (LWC) while developing modern ciphers. As the name suggests, this section is in charge of devising strategies for situations when resources are limited. The minimum necessary requirements for establishing the restricted use of resources include the lack of computational power, minimization of size or space, low power use, and lower code size. As a result, the basic requirements that stem from traditional cryptographic approaches are called to as lightweight. The hardware to handle security issues outlined by lightweight algorithms is becoming more important in contexts with limited resources. As a result, making effective use of cryptographic methods is a primary concern in this domain.

5.8.1   Introduction to Lightweight Cryptography

Lightweight cryptography (LWC) is an important area to study and prioritize while creating new ciphers. The challenge of working with little available resources falls on this department's shoulders. Low processing capabilities, small size or area, low power consumption, and short code length are all examples of the lowest potential conditions for achieving constrained resource use. Therefore, 'lightweight' describes these primary needs that derive from conventional cryptography methods (McKay et al. 2016). The demand for tools that can address the security concerns raised by low-overhead algorithms working in a scarce resource setting is growing. As a result, the proper use of cryptographic techniques is a central focus of this study.

This emerging area of research merges the disciplines of electronics engineering, computer science, and cryptography. Designers and researchers in the subject of lightweight cryptography are focused on finding a happy medium between cost, security, and performance. While pursuing such a course of action, it is impossible to give primacy to any one of the aforementioned parameters without having an impact on the others. Data volume and implementation details are the primary drivers of cost. Security relies on a number of parameters, including key size and algorithm complexity. High levels of security and privacy are provided by algorithms with large key sizes and a large number of rounds.

However, the costs and risks associated with fast algorithm execution are substantial. As an added downside, the algorithm will be slower and more vulnerable on cheaper hardware. Lightweight designers also aim to provide a fair degree of security in constrained systems, thus there has been a lot of focus in recent years on learning how to do so while minimizing the resources used. Data integrity, authentication, and secrecy are all examples of security services that help define this market.

5.8.2 Trade-offs of Lightweight Cryptography

The development of lightweight cryptographic primitives in recent years has improved performance compared to traditional algorithms. According to Singh et al. (2021), lightweight cryptography relies on three different kinds of primitives: Stream ciphers, block ciphers, and hash functions. These primitives not only mandate limitations on the interceptor's potential but also are often anticipated for a wide variety of uses. These differences set lightweight primitives apart from the norm in algorithm design. Furthermore, with symmetric keys, the attacker's access to information may be limited. For contexts with limited resources, this style of cryptography aims to employ the best possible implementation to strike a balance between price, security, and performance.

A) Lightweight block ciphers

Various design decisions make lightweight block ciphers quicker than typical encryption techniques. Few Lightweight block ciphers are LLLWBC (Zhang et al. 2023), SAND (Chen et al. 2022), CSL (Lamkuche and Pramod 2020), μ2 (Yeoh et al. 2020), PIPO (Kim et al. 2021), DABC (Chen et al. 2023), PRIPRESENT (Girija et al. 2021), M-XXTEA (Ragab et al. 2021), LRBC (Biswas et al. 2020), BORON (Salunke et al. 2021), KOREAN (Jang et al. 2020), SIT (Mishra and Acharya 2021) RBFK (Rana et al. 2023), PRINCE (Kumar et al. 2023), CHAM (Roh et al. 2020). The primitives of lightweight block ciphers are as follows-

- **Short block length**:
  The lightweight cipher's input message length dictates the amount and kind of information that may be encrypted. These ciphers use 64-bit blocks instead of 128- or 256-bit blocks. During encryption execution, small block sizes remove the need to store components. Instead of providing a performance increase, smaller blocks may allow for a more efficient one known as Plaintext.
- **Short length of key**:
  Lightweight block ciphers are optimized for constrained devices that require a moderate level of security. Because of the lower memory requirements at the intermediate stages of cipher algorithms, a key of size 80 bits is projected to offer sufficient security for such devices. Brute force, algebraic threats, and the related keys can recover a key under 80 bits.
- **Easy Round function and Key generation**:
  The round function's data is remarkably close to that of classic block ciphers in cryptography despite the round function's simplicity. To boost security, a simple round function with extra iterations can be utilized.

  Key scheduling techniques determine cryptographic security. Complex key scheduling takes time, storage, and processing resources. As a result, almost all lightweight block ciphers use key algorithms that are either constructed on the fly or used directly. By using this, you may save space and battery while increasing performance and speed.
- **Small-scale implementations**:
  Some compact block ciphers employ the same basic building blocks for both encryption and decryption techniques. This strategy has the potential to lower implementation costs. For some programs with minimal resources, only activating the encryption process may be required. As a result, using only the essential blocks during development may result in resource constraints as compared to using all of the blocks.

B) Lightweight Stream Ciphers

To decrypt a binary message, a stream cipher uses the binary message and a stream of digital keys created by a pseudo-random number generator. Separate adjustments are made to each bit or byte of the incoming data stream. Simple stream ciphers like VHFO (Zhao et al. 2020), A4 (Mohandas et al. 2020), DRACO (Hamann et al. 2023), and LESCA (Noura et al. 2023) making use of primitives that might be helpful in certain contexts, have been produced in plenty. Autocorrelation, linear complexity, and unpredictable duration are three crucial design considerations that affect the safety of stream ciphers. For the sake of creating a lightweight stream cipher design, just the most important design features are selected.

- **Pseudorandom number generator**:
  To generate random numbers, use a pseudo-random number generator. Pseudorandom number generators contribute significantly to encryption's central role in meeting a wide range of security needs. This takes advantage of the capability to generate a stream of bits that, after a

considerable amount of time, is predictable. In general, cryptanalysis becomes increasingly difficult as repetition time increases. Most lightweight stream ciphers employ either a Linear Feedback Shift Register (LFSR) or a Non-linear Feedback Shift Register (NFSR) to generate bit streams because of their simplicity and widespread availability.

- **Short length of the internal state**:
  In resource-constrained applications, the duration of the inner state determines the amount of extra area required. It was decided to create a new stream cipher with a less stringent interior requirement in order to do this. Sprout stream cipher, although being built with a smaller internal capacity, has been shown to be susceptible. So, a new idea is proposed to improve cipher safety. The plan is to employ the key not just during configuration but also while creating the keystream. However, the brief lifespan of the internal state makes the stream cipher vulnerable.

C) Lightweight Hash Functions

Hash functions take a message of unknown input size and produce a message of fixed length, called a hash code or message digest. It is a function of the message and initialization vector IV but does not utilize a key. Since a conventional hash function appears to consume more power and have a larger processing state, it is inappropriate for devices with low resources. We have lightweight hash functions for limited-resource applications. RM-70 (Widhiara et al. 2023) and HVH (Huang et al. 2021) are a few examples of lightweight hash functions.

- **Small hash code**:
  Hash code that is just the right size can be used for some tasks. Both the hardware price and the internal state size are lowered as a result. But for algorithms that must prevent collisions, the enormous size of the hash code provides an extra layer of safety.

- **Small block size**:
  Implementations for serial hash structure functions are very small. Minimizing the basic data size is essential for achieving a lightweight hash function. However, doing so may make the bad performance worse and even cause the length of the hash code to go down. To make it easier to figure out a code, attacks should be made less complicated.

- **Simple compression function**:
  In a simple compression function, the output of the previous function is added to the next message block before it is processed for a certain number of rounds. Because there are more rounds and they are more complicated, there is an extra area overhead. It also causes more power to be used and takes longer to process. Hash function methods can be used in situations with limited resources by taking advantage of the simple way the compression algorithm works.

- **Fewer input blocks**:
  The compression function uses a small number of round functions to process the data over and over again. A hash function divides the message into chunks of a certain size and number. Algorithms are able to

'fill in the blanks' if the number of bits in the last block is less than the total number of bits in each block. The last block has extra bits that make it harder for the attacker to do their job. Hash algorithms that aren't as heavy can work with fewer input blocks.

5.9 DIFFERENT ARCHITECTURE STRATEGIES FOR HARDWARE IMPLEMENTATION

The needs of the application should dictate the architecture approach selected. Different designs prioritize different goals, such as low footprint and high throughput. The following are a few examples of commonly used architectures that meet the criteria.

5.9.1 PIPELINED ARCHITECTURE

Various applications like RF-ID tags and smart cards which have high throughput demand might benefit from a pipelined/parallel design. The design path can be compressed in a pipelined architecture by inserting a register at the very center of the essential path. The necessary path length is decreased when a register is inserted in the midst of the path. The critical route determines the architecture's operating frequency; a shorter critical path results in a faster clock rate. By using a loop unrolled design method in a parallel architecture, numerous rounds of encryption may be accomplished in a single cycle, therefore reducing latency and increasing throughput. Due to this architecture, there is an increase in area and consumption as register count increases, there is always a trade-off between size, power, and efficiency.

5.9.2 ROUND-BASED ARCHITECTURE

One round of encryption in a round-based architecture takes place in a single clock cycle. A larger number of clock cycles are needed in a round-based design if, for instance, the shadow cipher requires a total of 16 rounds to acquire the final ciphertext for 32-bit input which utilizes a 64-bit key and similarly it takes 32 rounds in case of 64-bit input with a 128-bit key. Both latency and throughput of the design grew as a result, unlike pipelined/parallel architecture. However, round-based design has lower space and energy needs than pipelined architecture does since there are fewer registers needed. Where space and electricity are at a premium, a circular design is the way to go.

5.9.3 SERIALIZED ARCHITECTURE

There is a primary focus on minimizing both space and power usage in this serial design. This layout requires less room and energy than conventional round-based layouts. For this, we reduce the design's data route, which results in a higher throughput and lower latency since fewer encryption operations need to be completed in a single clock cycle. This architecture works well when neither latency nor throughput requirements are very stringent. When implementing lightweight ciphers, there is always a trade-off between space, power, and performance. A lightweight cipher's layout is selected based on the situation's demands. There were devices that needed plenty of bandwidth and almost no lag time and others that needed to be compact and efficient. Therefore, it is conditional upon the need.

5.9.4 LOOP UNROLLED ARCHITECTURE

As a loop transformation technique, loop unrolling architectures can be used to speed up a program's execution. Due to the lack of loop control instruction, iterations can be reduced or eliminated, resulting in a noticeable increase in speed (Mohindru et al. 2019). Designing in this way is the primary compiler technique that enables high levels of parallelism on reconfigurable architectures. This tactic helps with making buildings more energy efficient. Due to this implementation, the architecture consumes less power per bit. This layout is known as an unfolded implementation as well.

5.10   DIFFERENT HARDWARE METRICS OF PERFORMANCE FOR CIPHER ANALYSIS

Various parameters are evaluating lightweight block ciphers. Hardware implementation dominates IOT lightweight block cipher design (Mohindru et al. 2020a). Therefore, suggested implementations are solely evaluated using hardware metrics (Lara-Nino et al., 2017). Evaluations of several metrics are achieved in FPGA parameters, which include:

(A) **Area**:
In considering block ciphers for hardware implementation, the area is a significant issue. It is calculated in terms of slice and flipflop count and Look Up Tables. Few FPGA technologies measure this parameter by a count of logic components. Changing FPGA families and devices affects the block cipher's area. The circuit realization methodologies also impact the block cipher's area. There are a variety of circuit realization approaches utilized for cipher implementation. Some implementations make use of serial architectures, while others use parallel implementation. Typically, the area determines the implementation cost.

(B) **Speed or Throughput**:
A throughput is measured in bits of output generated per unit time by the algorithm. It is a measurement of the number of actions conducted to achieve a predetermined outcome during a certain time period. Throughput is the primary determinant of cipher speed. In IoT applications, solutions with higher throughput are seen as superior. The increase in the frequency of the clock boosts throughput. Throughput for block ciphers is determined by Equation (5.1):

$$\text{Throughput} = \frac{\text{Blocksize} * \text{Frequency}}{\text{Latency}} \tag{5.1}$$

(C) **Latency**:

Latency is the amount of time between introducing input data into a cipher and receiving the appropriate output data. In cryptographic techniques, the time taken to encrypt the plaintext is the measure of delay. As the clock pulse count reduces, the latency also gets minimized, which boosts the performance of block ciphers.

5.11 SHADOW CIPHER ALGORITHM AND WORKING

Shadow is a lightweight block cipher proposed by Guo et al. (2021) that uses a hybrid of the generalized Feistel structure and ARX operations to construct ciphertext by first splitting the input into four separate branches before applying the encryption algorithm to each one. There are 2 distinct variants. For an input block of 32 bits with a 64-bit key size, which iterates for 16 rounds, i.e., RN of 16, creates 32 bits of encrypted ciphertext as output which is termed Shadow-32, etc. Likewise, Shadow-64 refers to a 64-bit input that uses a 128-bit key and has a round number (RN) of 32.

5.11.1 ENCRYPTION ALGORITHM

The plain text block (32-bit or 64-bit) to be encrypted is first divided into four equal parts. A primary key (64-bit or 128-bit) is taken and made to perform operations like AND, Rotation, and XOR (ARX) to generate the ciphertext after a few rounds

---

ALGORITHM: SHADOW

Input: Plaintext – 32-bit, Primary key – 64-bit
Output: Ciphertext – 32-bit

1. (L0, L1, R0, R1)←Plain text
2. for i=1 to RN do
3. state0 = (L0≪1 & L0≪7) $\oplus$ L1 $\oplus$ L0≪2 $\oplus$ key0;
4. state1 = (R0≪1 & R0≪7) $\oplus$ R1 $\oplus$ R0≪2 $\oplus$ key1;
5. L0' = state1;
6. L1' = (state0≪1 & state0≪7) $\oplus$ L0 $\oplus$ state0≪2 $\oplus$ key2;
7. R0' = state0;
8. R1' = (state1≪1& state1≪7) $\oplus$ R0 $\oplus$ state1≪2 $\oplus$ key3;
9. end for
10. Ciphertext ← (L0', L1', R0', R1');
11. Return Ciphertext;

As shown in Figure 5.8, the input text is divided into two equal portions that can be denoted as L for the left half and R for the right half, which in turn was parted equally into L0, L1 and R0, and R1. The operations are performed which is as follows.

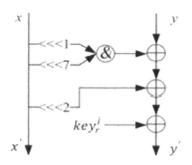

FIGURE 5.8   Two-branch round function (Guo et al. 2021).

The operation begins with an AND operation performed on 1-bit left-shifted L0 and 7-bit left-shifted L0. The result is then XORed with L1, 2-bit left-shifted L0 and the key. This is what happened with the left half. The similar operation is performed on the right half as well replacing L0 with R0 and L1 with R1, which results in the formation of State0 and State1. This is the round function. During each iteration while encrypting, the two-branch round function is called four times. This above process is iterated for RN rounds. The four outputs which are generated are concatenated to obtain the final ciphertext. The notations used in the algorithm and in Figure 5.8 are elaborated in Table 5.1.

5.11.2   KEY GENERATION

For a 32-bit input text block, we use 64-bit as the primary key. K, the primary key is generally a collection of 64 1-bit keys convoluted which can be described as k0 ‖ k1 ‖ k2 ...... k62 ‖ k63. We basically have two generators that help us produce us the final key. The operations performed are add round constant, NX module, and permutation.

TABLE 5.1
Notation for Encryption Operation

Notation	Meaning
L0, L1	Left half of Plaintext
R0, R1	Right half of Plaintext
$\oplus$	XOR Operation
<<<	Left Shift Operation
&	AND Operation
State0, State1	State
L0', L1'	Left half of Ciphertext
R0', R1'	Right half of Ciphertext

5.11.3 ADD ROUND CONSTANT

The input 5 bits k3 ∥ k4 ∥ k5 ∥ k6 ∥ k7 are XORed with 5-bit round constants c0 ∥ c1 ∥ c2 ∥ c3 ∥ c4 to generate k3' ∥ k4' ∥ k5' ∥ k6' ∥ k7'. The following operation is performed.

$$k3' = k3 \oplus c0; \; k4' = k4 \oplus c1; \; k5' = k5 \oplus c2; \; k6' = k6 \oplus c3; \; k7' = k7 \oplus c4;$$

5.11.4 NX MODULE

This module is used for subkey generation. For Shadow-32 cipher, the 8 bits, k56 ∥ k57 ∥ k58 … ∥ k62 ∥ k63 undergo the NX module operation. The AND and XOR operations are performed to generate k56' ∥ k57' ∥ k58' … ∥ k62' ∥ k63'. The following operation is performed.

$$k'56 = k56 \,\&\, [k56 \wedge k62]; \; k'57 = k57 \,\&\, [k57 \wedge k63];$$
$$k'58 = k58 \,\&\, [k58 \wedge k56 \wedge k62]; k'59 = k59 \,\&\, [k59 \wedge k57 \wedge k63];$$
$$k'60 = k60 \,\&\, [k60 \wedge k58 \wedge k56 \wedge k62];$$
$$k'61 = k61 \,\&\, [k61 \wedge k59 \wedge k57 \wedge k63];$$
$$k'62 = k62 \,\&\, [k62 \oplus k61 \oplus k58 \oplus k56 \oplus k62];$$
$$k'63 = k63 \,\&\, [k63 \wedge k62 \wedge k59 \wedge k57 \wedge k63];$$

5.11.5 PERMUTATION

The processed 64-bit key for Shadow-32, after passing through the add round constant and NX modules, is sent to perform permutation to generate a final 64-bit key. This permutation process involves the replacement of k3, k4, k5, k6, and k7 with k3', k4', k5', k6', and k7' basically replacing the former bits with the ones that have undergone Add Round constant module. The bits k56, k57, k58 … k62, k63 are replaced with bits that went through NX module, k56', k57', k58' … k62', k63'. This key is then right shifted by 48 bits, to generate the key for the next round of key generation. The upper 32 bits are used to create subkey, key0, key1, key2, key3 in each round. The shifting of nibbles of keys is performed to increase the security and reduce the redundancy, such that the chance of decoding the key is as complex as possible.

5.11.6 DECRYPTION ALGORITHM

IoT nodes are equipped with an encryption circuit that transmits collected data of ciphertext. Thereafter, the data to be decrypted will be collected, transmitted, and stored on the client side to guarantee their privacy. The round keys are really reversed, and the shadow encryption technique mentioned here is specifically designed to allow the decryption procedure matching the encryption procedure consistently.

5.12 HARDWARE IMPLEMENTATION OF UNROLLED ARCHITECTURE

The maximum number of rounds of the cipher may be unrolled using this implementation. The execution speed of a system may be optimized with the use of a loop-unrolling architecture, which is a transformational approach for dealing with loops. By omitting the necessary loop control instruction, iterations are either eliminated or drastically reduced, resulting in a noticeable boost in performance. The key compiler approach that lets reconfigurable systems reach high levels of parallelism is based on this concept. A more energy-efficient design may be achieved using this method. This implementation results in the architecture using less energy per data bit. This architecture, also known as an unfolded implementation, allows for the full realization of round functions in one cycle of clock, without using a register (Mohindru et al. 2020b). For any round function, all sub-keys are accessible at the same tick of time. As latency decreases with this implementation, we require less energy to execute a block. As a result, although unrolled architecture increases system latency and area in terms of the count of Look Up Tables and slices, it decreases the clock cycles for encrypting.

5.12.1 PROPOSED UNROLLED-BASED ARCHITECTURE OF SHADOW CIPHER

This loop unroll design was developed with the goal of reducing latency. The whole encoding procedure takes place inside a single clock cycle. By skipping over loop control instructions, loop unrolling speeds up the encryption process. Figure 5.9 depicts the final output being created using an unrolled for loop design. However, the increased throughput comes at the price of more space. Its primary purpose is to allow for rapid data transfer.

Table 5.2 represents the different parameters of unrolled architecture like LUT count, Flipflops, Maximum Frequency, and throughput on different boards which can be observed as follows.

Throughputs of 1291.400 Mbps, 2264.776 Mbps, and 844.521 Mbps, are achieved on Virtex 5, Virtex 7, and Spartan 6 platforms, respectively.

TABLE 5.2

Hardware performance of Unrolled-Based Architecture of Shadow (32-bit)

Parameter/Device	Virtex-5	Virtex-7	Spartan-6
Look Up Table	230	249	365
Flipflop	100	100	107
Max Frequency (MHz)	362.753	636.173	237.225
Cycle	9	9	9
Throughput (Mbps)	1291.400	2264.776	844.521

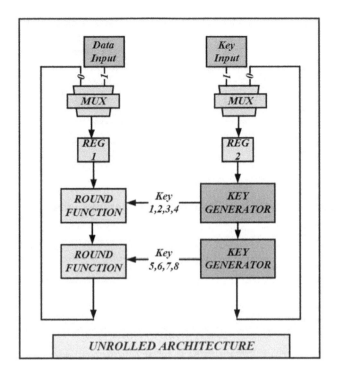

FIGURE 5.9   The proposed loop unrolled architecture block diagram of 32-bit shadow cipher.

5.13   SIMULATION RESULTS OF PROPOSED UNROLLED ARCHITECTURE OF SHADOW CIPHER

Tables 5.3 and 5.4 show different parameters across different ciphers and their comparison across the Virtex-5 platform. We can clearly observe high throughput and high frequency compared to the rest of the ciphers across various FPGA platforms.

TABLE 5.3
Throughput of Different Ciphers

Algorithm	Throughput (Mbps)	Device
LEA-192 (Lee et al. 2014)	996	Virtex-5
LEA-256 (Lee et al. 2014)	505	Virtex-5
PRESENT 80 (Lara et al. 2017)	260.96	Virtex-5
LILLIPUT [SP] (Singh et al. 2019)	684.06	Virtex-5
LILLIPUT [FP] (Singh et al. 2019)	490.35	Virtex-5
PICCOLO [UR] (Ramu et al. 2020)	691.54	Virtex-5
PICCOLO [RB] (Ramu et al. 2020)	613.26	Virtex-5
Shadow 64/128 (Guo et al. 2021)	743.038	Virtex-5
SIT [S] (Mishra and Acharya 2020)	290.750	Virtex-5

(Continued)

TABLE 5.3   (Continued)

Algorithm	Throughput (Mbps)	Device
SIMON 64/128 (Beaulieu et al. 2015)	870	Virtex-5
PRINCE (Kumar et al. 2023)	346.554	Virtex-5
RECTANGLE ^{RB} (Srivastava et al. 2019)	517.454	Virtex-5
RECTANGLE ^S (Srivastava et al. 2019)	206.107	Virtex-5
Shadow 64/128 *[Our work]	**1291.400**	**Virtex-5**

TABLE 5.4
Throughput and Utilization of Resources of Different Ciphers

Algorithm	Slice Count	LUT	Throughput (Mbps)	Device
LEA 128/128 [Lee et al. 2014]	392	249	205.450	Virtex-5
PRESENT ^{RB} (Hanley & ONeill 2012)	88	283	316.120	Virtex-5
PRESENT ^S (Hanley & ONeill 2012)	72	237	61.190	Virtex-5
PRESENT 128(Lara-Nino et al. 2017)	73	239	203.190	Virtex-5
Shadow 64/128 [Guo et al. 2021]	199	227	743.038	Virtex-5
Shadow 64/128 *[Our Work]	**100**	**249**	**1291.400**	**Virtex-5**

Where SP - Sub Pipeline, FP - Full Pipeline, UR - Unrolled, RB - Round Based, S - Serial

5.14 CONCLUSION

Given the widespread use of IoT nodes across industries, it is crucial to improve the safety and efficiency of cyber-physical systems. Private information sent across a sensor network is easy to intercept, and data manipulation is a major concern. Shadow, the new encryption being developed for this project, is based on the Feistel structure and also makes use of ARX operations. Existing lightweight algorithms based on ARX will be improved upon to the point where they can be used securely. When faced with the problem that half of the input text remains unchanged after the first round, as was proposed with the ARX operation, Shadow provides a solution. Implementation of Shadow's unrolled hardware architecture is a part of this effort. Optimized frequency and throughput were achieved with the suggested designs; a table of values is supplied for easy comparison to other ciphers and the FPGA implementation on different platforms.

REFERENCES

Abbas, Yasir Amer, Ahmed Salah Hameed, Safa Hazim Alwan, and Maryam Adnan Fadel. "Efficient hardware implementation for lightweight mCrypton algorithm using FPGA." *Indonesian Journal of Electrical Engineering and Computer Science* 23, no. 3 (2021): 164–1680.

Aboushosha, Bassam, Rabie A. Ramadan, Ashutosh Dhar Dwivedi, Ayman El-Sayed, and Mohamed M. Dessouky. "SLIM: A lightweight block cipher for internet of health things." *IEEE Access* 8 (2020): 203747–203757.

Al-Shatari, Mohammed, Fawnizu Azmadi Hussin, Azrina Abd Aziz, Mohd Saufy Rohmad, and Xuan-Tu Tran. "Composite Lightweight Authenticated Encryption Based on LED Block Cipher and Photon Hash Function for IoT Devices." In *2022 IEEE 15th International Symposium on Embedded Multicore/Many-core Systems-on-Chip (MCSoC)*, pp. 134–139. IEEE, 2022.

Banik, Subhadeep, Avik Chakraborti, Akiko Inoue, Tetsu Iwata, Kazuhiko Minematsu, Mridul Nandi, Thomas Peyrin, Yu Sasaki, Siang Meng Sim, and Yosuke Todo. "Gift-cofb." *Cryptology ePrint Archive* (2020): 1–30.

Beaulieu, Ray, Douglas Shors, Jason Smith, Stefan Treatman-Clark, Bryan Weeks, and Louis Wingers. "Simon and speck: Block ciphers for the internet of things." *Cryptology ePrint Archive* (2015): 1–15.

Bharathi, R., and N. Parvatham. "Light-weight present block cipher model for IoT security on FPGA." *Intelligent Automation & Soft Computing* 33, no. 1 (2022): 35–49.

Biswas, A., A. Majumdar, S. Nath, A. Dutta, and K. L. Baishnab. "LRBC: a lightweight block cipher design for resource constrained IoT devices." *Journal of Ambient Intelligence and Humanized Computing* 14 (2020): 5773–5787.

Chen, Shiyao, Yanhong Fan, Ling Sun, Yong Fu, Haibo Zhou, Yongqing Li, Meiqin Wang, Weijia Wang, and Chun Guo. "Sand: an AND-RX Feistel lightweight block cipher supporting S-box-based security evaluations." *Designs, Codes and Cryptography* (2022): 1–44.

Chen, Wen, Lang Li, and Ying Guo. "DABC: A dynamic ARX-based lightweight block cipher with high diffusion." *KSII Transactions on Internet & Information Systems* 17, no. 1 (2023): 165–184.

Damodharan, Jamunarani, Emalda Roslin Susai Michael, and Nasir Shaikh-Husin. "High throughput present cipher hardware architecture for the medical IoT applications." *Cryptography* 7, no. 1 (2023): 6.

Dhanda, Sumit Singh, Brahmjit Singh, and Poonam Jindal. "Lightweight cryptography: A solution to secure IoT." *Wireless Personal Communications* 112 (2020): 1947–1980.

Dwivedi, Ashutosh Dhar. "Security analysis of lightweight IoT cipher: Chaskey." *Cryptography* 4, no. 3 (2020): 22.

Feng, Jingya, and Lang Li. "Scenery: a lightweight block cipher based on Feistel structure." *Frontiers of Computer Science* 16, no. 3 (2022): 163813.

Girija, M., P. Manickam, and M. Ramaswami. "PriPresent: An embedded prime LightWeight block cipher for smart devices." *Peer-to-Peer Networking and Applications* 14 (2021): 2462–2472.

Guo, Ying, Lang Li, and Botao Liu. "Shadow: A lightweight block cipher for IoT nodes." *IEEE Internet of Things Journal* 8, no. 16 (2021): 13014–13023.

Gupta, Ankita, Afshan Asad, Laxmi Meena, and Rohit Anand. "IoT and RFID-based smart card system integrated with health care, electricity, QR and banking sectors." In *Artificial Intelligence on Medical Data: Proceedings of International Symposium, ISCMM 2021*, pp. 253–265. Singapore: Springer Nature Singapore, 2022a.

Gupta, Kishan Chand, Sumit Kumar Pandey, and Susanta Samanta. "Future: A Lightweight Block Cipher Using an Optimal Diffusion Matrix." In *Progress in Cryptology-AFRICACRYPT 2022: 13th International Conference on Cryptology in Africa, AFRICACRYPT 2022*, Fes, Morocco, July 18–20, 2022, *Proceedings*, pp. 28–52. Cham: Springer Nature Switzerland, 2022b.

Hamann, Matthias, Alexander Moch, Matthias Krause, and Vasily Mikhalev. "The Draco Stream Cipher." (2023).

Hanley, Neil, and Maire ONeill. "Hardware comparison of the ISO/IEC 29192-2 block ciphers." In *2012 IEEE computer society annual symposium on VLSI*, Amherst, MA, USA, pp. 57–62. IEEE, 2012. 10.1109/ISVLSI.2012.25

Heron, Simon. "Advanced encryption standard (AES)." *Network Security* 2009, no. 12 (2009): 8–12.

Huang, Xiantong, Lang Li, and Jinling Yang. "IVLBC: An Involutive Lightweight Block Cipher for Internet of Things." *IEEE Systems Journal* 17, no. 2 (2022): 3192–3203.

Huang, Yuhua, Shen Li, Wanlin Sun, Xuejun Dai, and Wei Zhu. "HVH: A lightweight hash function based on dual pseudo-random transformation." In *Security, Privacy, and Anonymity in Computation, Communication, and Storage: Spaccs 2020 International Workshops*, Nanjing, China, December 18–20, 2020, *Proceedings 13*, pp. 492–505. Springer International Publishing, 2021.

Jang, Kyoungbae, Seungju Choi, Hyeokdong Kwon, Hyunji Kim, Jaehoon Park, and Hwajeong Seo. "Grover on Korean block ciphers." *Applied Sciences* 10, no. 18 (2020): 6407.

Jiao, Lin, Yonglin Hao, and Dengguo Feng. "Stream cipher designs: a review." *Science China Information Sciences* 63 (2020): 1–25.

Kim, Hangi, Yongjin Jeon, Giyoon Kim, Jongsung Kim, Bo-Yeon Sim, Dong-Guk Han, Hwajeong Seo et al. "PIPO: A lightweight block cipher with efficient higher-order masking software implementations." In *Information Security and Cryptology–ICISC 2020: 23rd International Conference*, Seoul, South Korea, December 2–4, 2020, *Proceedings 23*, pp. 99–122. Springer International Publishing, 2021.

Kiran Kumar, V.G. "Design and implementation of novel BRISI lightweight cipher for resource constrained devices." *Microprocessors and Microsystems* 84 (2021): 104267.

Kumar, Abhiram, Pulkit Singh, K. Abhimanyu Kumar Patro, and Bibhudendra Acharya. "High-throughput and area-efficient architectures for image encryption using Prince cipher." *Integration* 90 (2023): 224–235.

Kumisbek, Gani, N. Nalla Anandakumar, and Mohammad Hashmi. "FPGA implementations of Espresso stream cipher." In *2021 28th IEEE International Conference on Electronics, Circuits, and Systems (ICECS)*, pp. 1–6. IEEE, 2021.

Laghari, Asif Ali, Kaishan Wu, Rashid Ali Laghari, Mureed Ali, and Abdullah Ayub Khan. "A review and state of art of Internet of Things (IoT)." *Archives of Computational Methods in Engineering* 29 (2021): 1–19.

Lamkuche, Hemraj Shobharam, and Dhanya Pramod. "CSL: FPGA implementation of lightweight block cipher for power-constrained devices." *International Journal of Information and Computer Security* 12, no. 2–3 (2020): 349–377.

Landaluce, Hugo, Laura Arjona, Asier Perallos, Francisco Falcone, Ignacio Angulo, and Florian Muralter. "A review of IoT sensing applications and challenges using RFID and wireless sensor networks." *Sensors* 20, no. 9 (2020): 2495.

Lara-Nino, Carlos Andres, Arturo Diaz-Perez, and Miguel Morales-Sandoval. "Lightweight hardware architectures for the present cipher in FPGA." *IEEE Transactions on Circuits and Systems I: Regular Papers* 64, no. 9 (2017): 2544–2555.

Lee, Donggeon, Dong-Chan Kim, Daesung Kwon, and Howon Kim. "Efficient hardware implementation of the lightweight block encryption algorithm LEA." *Sensors* 14, no. 1 (2014): 975–994.

Li, Bohan, Meicheng Liu, and Dongdai Lin. "FPGA implementations of grain v1, mickey 2.0, trivium, lizard and plantlet." *Microprocessors and Microsystems* 78 (2020): 103210.

Marqas, Ridwan B., Saman M. Almufti, and Rasheed Rebar Ihsan. "Comparing Symmetric and Asymmetric cryptography in message encryption and decryption by using AES and RSA algorithms." *Xi'an Jianzhu Keji Daxue Xuebao/Journal of Xi'an University of Architecture & Technology* 12, no. 3 (2020): 3110–3116.

McKay, Kerry, Lawrence Bassham, Meltem Sönmez Turan, and Nicky Mouha. *Report on lightweight cryptography*. No. NIST Internal or Interagency Report (NISTIR) 8114 (Draft). National Institute of Standards and Technology, 2016.

Mhaouch, Ayoub, Wajdi Elhamzi, and Mohamed Atri. "Lightweight hardware architectures for the piccolo block cipher in FPGA." In *2020 5th International Conference on Advanced Technologies for Signal and Image Processing (ATSIP)*, pp. 1–4. IEEE, 2020.

Mishra, Zeesha, and Bibhudendra Acharya. "High throughput and low area architectures of secure IoT algorithm for medical image encryption." *Journal of Information Security and Applications* 53 (2020): 102533.

Mishra, Zeesha, and Bibhudendra Acharya. "High throughput novel architectures of TEA family for high speed IoT and RFID applications." *Journal of Information Security and Applications* 61 (2021): 102906.

Mishra, Zeesha, Shubham Mishra, and Bibhudendra Acharya. "High throughput novel architecture of SIT cipher for IoT application." In *Nanoelectronics, Circuits and Communication Systems: Proceeding of NCCS 2019*, pp. 267–276. Springer Singapore, 2021.

Mohandas, Nair Arun, Adinath Swathi, R. Abhijith, Ajmal Nazar, and Greeshma Sharath. "A4: A lightweight stream cipher." In *2020 5th International Conference on Communication and Electronics Systems (ICCES)*, pp. 573–577. IEEE, 2020.

Mohindru, Vandana, Ravindara Bhatt, and Yashwant Singh. "Reauthentication scheme for mobile wireless sensor networks." *Sustainable Computing: Informatics and Systems* 23 (2019): 158–166.

Mohindru, Vandana, Yashwant Singh, and Ravindara Bhatt. "Hybrid cryptography algorithm for securing wireless sensor networks from node clone attack." *Recent Advances in Electrical & Electronic Engineering (Formerly Recent Patents on Electrical & Electronic Engineering)* 13, no. 2 (2020a): 251–259.

Mohindru, Vandana, Yashwant Singh, and Ravindara Bhatt. "Securing wireless sensor networks from node clone attack: a lightweight message authentication algorithm." *International Journal of Information and Computer Security* 12, no. 2–3 (2020b): 217–233.

Niveda, S., A. Siva Sakthi, S. Srinitha, V. Kiruthika, and R. Shanmugapriya. "A Novel Simon Light Weight Block Cipher Implementation in FPGA." In *Pervasive Computing and Social Networking: Proceedings of ICPCSN 2021*, pp. 159–170. Springer Singapore, 2022.

Noura, Hassan N., Ola Salman, Raphaël Couturier, and Ali Chehab. "LoRCA: Lightweight round block and stream cipher algorithms for IoV systems." *Vehicular Communications* 34 (2022): 100416.

Noura, Hassan, Ola Salman, Raphaël Couturier, and Ali Chehab. "LESCA: LightwEight Stream Cipher Algorithm for emerging systems." *Ad Hoc Networks* 138 (2023): 102999.

Pradhan, Bikash, Saugat Bhattacharyya, and Kunal Pal. "IoT-based applications in healthcare devices." *Journal of healthcare engineering* 2021 (2021): 1–18.

Ragab, Ahmed Ab M., Ahmed Madani, A. M. Wahdan, and Gamal M.I. Selim. "Design, analysis, and implementation of a new lightweight block cipher for protecting IoT smart devices." *Journal of Ambient Intelligence and Humanized Computing* 14, no. 2 (2021): 1–18.

Ramadan, Rabie A., Bassam W. Aboshosha, Kusum Yadav, Ibrahim M. Alseadoon, Munawar J. Kashout, and Mohamed Elhoseny. "LBC-IoT: Lightweight block cipher for IoT constraint devices." *Computers, Materials & Continua* 67, no. 3 (2021): 3563–3579.

Ramu, Gandu, Zeesha Mishra, Pulkit Singh, and Bibhuendra Acharya. "Performance optimised architectures of Piccolo block cipher for low resource IoT applications." *International Journal of High Performance Systems Architecture* 9, no. 1 (2020): 49–57.

Rana, Sohel, M. Mondal, and Joarder Kamruzzaman. "RBFK cipher: a randomized butterfly architecture-based lightweight block cipher for IoT devices in the edge computing environment." *Cybersecurity* 6, no. 1 (2023): 1–19.

Roh, Dongyoung, Bonwook Koo, Younghoon Jung, Il Woong Jeong, Dong-Geon Lee, Daesung Kwon, and Woo-Hwan Kim. "Revised version of block cipher CHAM." In *Information Security and Cryptology–ICISC 2019: 22nd International Conference, Seoul, South Korea, December 4–6, 2019, Revised Selected Papers 22*, pp. 1–19. Springer International Publishing, 2020.

Roy, Siddhartha, Saptarshi Roy, Arpita Biswas, and Krishna Lal Baishnab. "LCB: Light Cipher Block An Ultrafast Lightweight Block Cipher For Resource Constrained IOT Security Applications." *KSII Transactions on Internet & Information Systems* 15, no. 11 (2021): 4122–4144.

Salunke, Mahendra Balkrishna, Parikshit Narendra Mahalle, and Gitanjali Rahul Shinde. "Ultra-Lightweight Block Cipher in Medical Internet of Things for Secure Machine-to-Machine Communication Using FPGA." *Revista Geintec-Gestao Inovacao E Tecnologias* 11, no. 4 (2021): 236–251.

Shafique, Kinza, Bilal A. Khawaja, Farah Sabir, Sameer Qazi, and Muhammad Mustaqim. "Internet of things (IoT) for next-generation smart systems: A review of current challenges, future trends and prospects for emerging 5G-IoT scenarios." *IEEE Access* 8 (2020): 23022–23040.

Shah, Rizwan Ali, Mamoona N. Asghar, Saima Abdullah, Nadia Kanwal, and Martin Fleury. "SLEPX: An efficient lightweight cipher for visual protection of scalable HEVC extension." *IEEE Access* 8 (2020): 187784–187807.

Shahana, T Kassim, and K.B. Jithendra "ACT: An Ultra Light Weight Block Cipher For Internet of Things." *International Journal of Computing and Digital Systems* 9, no. 5 (2020): 921–929.

Shrivastava, Nivedita, and Bibhudendra Acharya. "FPGA Implementation of Rectangle Block Cipher Architectures.". *International Journal of Innovative Technology and Exploring Engineering*, ISSN: 2278-3075 (Online), 8, no. 10 (August 2019): 2382–2391.

Singh, Pulkit, Bibhudendra Acharya, and Rahul Kumar Chaurasiya. "Pipelined architectures of LILLIPUT block cipher for RFID logistic applications." In *2019 International Conference on Computing, Communication, and Intelligent Systems (ICCCIS)*, pp. 452–457. IEEE, 2019.

Singh, Pulkit, Bibhudendra Acharya, and Rahul Kumar Chaurasiya. "Lightweight cryptographic algorithms for resource-constrained IoT devices and sensor networks." In *Security and Privacy Issues in IoT Devices and Sensor Networks*, pp. 153–185. Academic Press, 2021.

Sleem, Lama, and Raphaël Couturier. "Speck-R: An ultra light-weight cryptographic scheme for Internet of Things." *Multimedia Tools and Applications* 80 (2021): 17067–17102.

Widhiara, Benardi, Yusuf Kurniawan, and Bety Hayat Susanti. "RM70: A Lightweight Hash Function." *IAENG International Journal of Applied Mathematics* 53, no. 1 (2023): 94–102.

Yaacoub, Jean-Paul A., Ola Salman, Hassan N. Noura, Nesrine Kaaniche, Ali Chehab, and Mohamad Malli. "Cyber-physical systems security: Limitations, issues and future trends." *Microprocessors and microsystems* 77 (2020): 103201.

Yang, Gangqiang, Zhengyuan Shi, Cheng Chen, Hailiang Xiong, Honggang Hu, Zhiguo Wan, Keke Gai, and Meikang Qiu. "Work-in-progress: Towards a smaller than grain stream cipher: optimized fpga implementations of fruit-80." In *2022 International Conference on Compilers, Architecture, and Synthesis for Embedded Systems (CASES)*, pp. 19–20. IEEE, 2022a.

Yang, Jinling, Lang Li, Ying Guo, and Xiantong Huang. "DULBC: A dynamic ultra-lightweight block cipher with high-throughput." *Integration* 87 (2022b): 221–230.

Yeoh, Wei-Zhu, Je Sen Teh, and Mohd Ilyas Sobirin Bin Mohd Sazali. "µ2: A lightweight block cipher." In *Computational Science and Technology: 6th ICCST 2019*, Kota Kinabalu, Malaysia, 29–30 August 2019, pp. 281–290. Springer Singapore, 2020.

El Hadj Youssef, Wajih, Ali Abdelli, Fethi Dridi, and Mohsen Machhout. "Hardware implementation of secure lightweight cryptographic designs for IoT applications." *Security and Communication Networks* 2020 (2020): 1–13.

Zhang, Lei, Ruichen Wu, Yuhan Zhang, Yafei Zheng, and Wenling Wu. "LLLWBC: A new low-latency light-weight block cipher." In *International Conference on Information Security and Cryptology*, pp. 23–42. Cham: Springer, 2023.

Zhao, Huifang, Fang Yang, Yuxiang Cui, Rui Yang, Dafeng Pan, and Liang Zhao. "Design of a new lightweight stream cipher VHFO algorithm." In *2020 3rd International Conference on Advanced Electronic Materials, Computers and Software Engineering (AEMCSE)*, pp. 379–382. IEEE, 2020.

6 Performance Analysis of Machine Learning Classifiers for Detection of Phishing Websites

Asadullah Safi
Central University of Punjab, Punjab, India

Satwinder Singh
Central University of Punjab, Bathinda, Punjab, India

Gurpreet Kaur
Guru Kashi University, Punjab, India

Meenakshi
Central University of Punjab, Punjab, India

Tripat Kaur
GSSDGS Khalsa College, Punjab, India

6.1 INTRODUCTION

Phishing attacks, as referenced by Paliath et al. (2020), Nakamura and Dobashi (2019), and Zabihimayvan and Doran (2019), encompass manipulative tactics employed by cybercriminals to illicitly acquire personal information from the internet user, such as information about credit card, usernames, passwords, and more (Ramana et al., 2021; Faris and Yazid, 2021). These attacks also serve as a means to disseminate malware within networks (Gupta et al., 2021). Unauthorized access to sensitive user data can occur through the targeting of IoT devices, commonly referred to as cyber-physical systems (CPS) in current times. Perpetrators employ diverse methods, including malware installation, device tampering, or exploiting vulnerabilities by sharing phishing URLs, to extract additional confidential information from targeted organizations. Spoofing, malware-based phishing, DNS-based phishing, data theft, email/spam, web-based delivery, and phone phishing merely represent a few

DOI: 10.1201/9781003406105-9

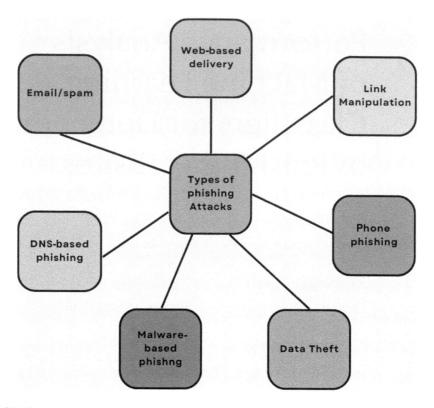

FIGURE 6.1 Types of phishing attacks.

of the phishing attacks shown in Figure 6.1 (Kathrine et al., 2019). Phishing attacks make use of a wide range of communication channels, including social media, email, instant messaging, and QR codes (Geng et al., 2018). They also take many various shapes. Attackers commonly use tricks or fear to get users to log into fraudulent websites and unintentionally disclose their credentials by posing as reputable banks, credit card agencies, or well-known e-commerce websites. A user may, for instance, be forwarded to a website that substantially looks similar to the website of the real bank after receiving an instant message warning them of a problem with their bank account. The user types their credentials into the fields given without realizing that they are unintentionally falling into the attackers' trap. The data are subsequently used by criminals to enter the user's genuine accounts without authorization (Liu et al., 2021). According to the Internet Crime Complaint Centre (IC3) report on an alarming spike in suspected Internet crimes, the FBI received 791,790 complaints in 2020, an increase of more than 300,000 over the previous year (FBI, 2020). Only a few methods have been proposed in the literature to recognize phishing websites, including lists-based, visual similarity, heuristic, machine learning (Somesha et al., 2020; Nakamura and Dobashi, 2019), and deep learning (Basit et al., 2020).

The rest of the chapter is organized as follows: Section 6.2 reviews earlier research in the area to give an overview of the relevant work. The proposed strategy is fully described in Section 6.3. Section 6.4 gives the implementation procedure and the analysis of the outcomes. The work is finally brought to a close in Section 6.5 with a summary of the results and suggestions for further research.

6.2 RELATED WORK

To identify and stop phishing attempts, there are several anti-phishing approaches. Safi and Singh (2023) have also published an extensive literature review in the current field of study following the systematic review technique used by Singh and Beniwal (2022), Singh and Kaur (2018), and Kaur and Singh (2021). Further, following the suggested classification in Safi and Singh (2023), this chapter's literature is classified into five categories as shown in Figure 6.2.

6.2.1 HEURISTIC TECHNIQUE

By examining particular characteristics that set phishing websites apart from authentic websites, the heuristic technique is used to identify them. This method collects information from a wide range of sources, including URLs, text content, DNS information, digital certificates, and website traffic. This strategy's effectiveness hinges on the thoughtful choice of features, training data, and classification algorithms. In particular, Jain and Gupta (2017) point out that the heuristic technique has the benefit of being able to identify zero-hour phishing attempts.

Babagoli et al. (2018) proposed a nonlinear regression method to assess the reliability of websites. SVM metaheuristic techniques and harmony search were implemented by the researchers to train the system. For the assessment, 11,000 web pages from the UCI dataset were used. In response, the accuracy rate of the harmony search algorithm was 94.13% for training operations and 92.80% for testing operations.

According to Rao et al. (2019), CatchPhish is a program that predicts the validity of URLs without requiring real website visits. For training and testing, the authors used the random forest (RF) classifier. Three sources provided the information for their model: PhishTank for phishing samples, Common Crawl, and Alexa for legitimate URLs. The proposed model's accuracy of 94.26% was quite high.

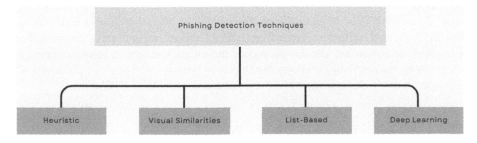

FIGURE 6.2   Techniques for identifying phishing websites.

6.2.2   Visual Similarity Technique

The aforementioned method compares legitimate and suspect websites based on a variety of visual attributes. These methods contrast malicious websites with trustworthy ones while taking into account things like CSS, text layout, source code, website logos, screenshots, and other graphical elements. However, these methods rely on comparing suspicious web pages to previously visited or saved ones, rendering them ineffective in detecting zero-hour phishing attacks (Jain and Gupta, 2017).

Liu and Fu (2020) introduced SPWalk, a feature-learning system without supervision for identifying phishing websites. In SPWalk collection of phishing and genuine web pages are able to be identified by looking for similar property nodes. The authors gathered 0.5 million phishing URL samples from OpenPhish and PhishTank and one million valid URLs from Alexa and Dmoz. The study demonstrates the superior performance of SPWalk compared to other phishing detection techniques, particularly in terms of precision, with an accuracy rate exceeding 95%.

In order to distinguish between authentic and fraudulent websites, Barlow et al. (2020) suggested a technique that visualizes scraped HTML files as 2D pictures and uses TensorFlow to analyze them using its training modules. 250 pictures, each 128 pixels in size representing real and fraudulent sites, were applied to train the TensorFlow algorithm. The study's phishing dataset had 25 samples drawn from PayPal, ABSA, Bank of America, DHL Tracking, and Microsoft Login, among other places. Binary visualization and neural networks were used to give the system a detection accuracy of 94.16% overall.

In order to identify brand logos on 'zero-hour' phishing websites, Bozkir and Aydos (2020) created a method that applies computer vision techniques in an object detection approach. To create scale-invariant outlines of target brand logos, the system uses the attributes of a Histogram of Oriented Gradients. A max-margin loss-equipped SVM algorithm was applied to handle the few training pictures and lessen false positives. Data was gathered by the writers from websites like PhishTank and PhishBank. According to experimental findings, the system's ideal setup resulted in the precision, recall, and F1 scores of 93.50%, 77.94%, and 85.02%, respectively.

A search engine-based method was proposed by Jain et al. (2020) that employed TF-IDF to find pertinent phrases from a website to include in the search query. The dataset included phishing sites from OpenPhish and PhishTank as well as reliable websites from Alexa. After being tested on 200 websites, including 100 legitimate and 100 phishing sites, the system has an accuracy of 89.0%.

Alsariera et al. (2020) introduced four meta-learner models, namely, 'AdaBoost-Extra Tree (ABET)', 'Bagging-Extra Tree (BET)', 'Rotation Forest-Extra Tree (RoFBET)', and 'LogitBoost-Extra Tree (LBET)', which were created utilizing the extra-tree base algorithm. The dataset used in their work had 11,055 instances and 30 independent characteristics and was developed by Mohammad et al. In the result, a detection accuracy of more than 97.5% was attained using the LBET model.

6.2.3   List-Based Technique

Popular web browsers like Internet Explorer, Mozilla Firefox, and Google Chrome utilize list-based algorithms to spot phishing websites. These methods may be categorized into two groups: whitelisting and blacklisting. Whitelisting involves maintaining a record of trusted URLs that the browser can approach, allowing web-page downloads only if the URL is present in the whitelist. Conversely, blacklisting involves maintaining a database of known phishing or fraudulent URLs, preventing the browser from downloading webpages from these sources. However, list-based techniques have significant limitations. Minor alterations in the URL can evade these methods, and regular updates are required to include new phishing URLs (Yang et al., 2021).

Maroofi et al. (2020) presented a domain reputation technique that examines the life cycle of domains and their associated characteristics to detect phishing websites. The researchers collected data from various sources, including OpenPhish, PhishTank, APWG, and URLhaus. The system utilizes a set of 38 features that are difficult to circumvent. In the study, two methods, namely Logistic Regression and Random Forest, were employed. The RM achieved an impressive accuracy of 97.0% for phishing detection.

6.2.4 Machine Learning–based Techniques

The capability of ML techniques to recognize phishing websites has received a lot of attention recently. In order to represent phishing URLs and associated websites, Sindhu et al. (2020) gathered a variety of data, such as URL details, website archi-tecture, and JavaScript features. They attained a remarkable accuracy of over 99% by training ML classifiers on these parameters, revealing the potency of ML as a very reliable tool for identifying phishing websites (Alkawaz et al. 2021).

Shirazi et al. (2018) concentrated on examining phishing websites' domain names. They used seven characteristics from the URLs and page contents of websites and assessed how well ML classifiers like SVM, DT, NB, KNN, and GBM performed. The GBM classifier scored the greatest accuracy of 97.00% using genuine samples from Alexa and phishing samples from PhishTank and OpenPhish, demonstrating its superiority in this situation.

Hannousse and Yahiouche (2021) introduced a method for developing replicable and scalable datasets for the detection of phishing websites. They obtained the infor-mation from many sources, including Yandex, Alexa, PhishTank, and OpenPhish, and chose 87 well-known attributes. They used hybrid features in conjunction with the RF classifier to reach an excellent accuracy score of 96.61% when applying ML techniques including SVM, DT, NB, LR, and RF.

Rashid et al. (2020) introduced an effective machine learning–based anti-phishing technique. Through their experiments, they demonstrated that their approach, com-bined with the SVM classifier, outperformed others by accurately classifying 95.66% of phishing and legitimate sites. The dataset used in this research was gathered from Alexa and the Common Crawl archive.

Basit et al. (2020) introduced an ensemble technique for the detection of online phishing attacks. They selected three ML classifiers (ANN, KNN, and DT) to be used in conjunction with the RF classifier. Their dataset, sourced from the UCI database, consisted of 11,055 samples of phishing and legitimate URLs with 30 features. The combination of KNN and RF classifiers achieved an accuracy of 97.33% in detecting phishing attacks, as demonstrated by their experimental results.

With the aid of seven distinct categorization techniques and characteristics based on natural language processing (NLP), Sahingoz et al. (2019) created a real-time anti-phishing system. They employed the NB, RF, KNN, Adaboost, K-star, SMO, and DT algorithms in their research. The RF algorithm fared the best, detecting phishing URLs with a 97.98% accuracy rate using solely NLP-based features, according to experimental data and comparisons.

Abedin et al. (2020) conducted research involving three Machine Learning algorithms, namely KNN, LR, and RF, to predict the phishing status of websites. The classifiers were trained using URL-based features, specifically targeting Zero-Day attacks. The study's dataset, which included 32 characteristics and 11,504 occurrences, was gathered from Kaggle. 97.0% accuracy, 99.0% recall, and 97.0% F1 score were displayed by the random forest classifier.

Saha et al. (2020) used machine learning techniques like RF and DT to create a model for recognizing phishing websites. The dataset utilized in their study, which was acquired from Kaggle, has 32 features. Feature selection techniques like Principal Component Analysis (PCA) were used in the proposed model to assess the dataset's characteristics. The Random Forest classifier had the greatest accuracy overall, at 97.0%.

Mao et al. (2018) introduced a 'learning-based aggregation analysis mechanism' to improve phishing website detection using ML approaches. They collected phishing websites from PhishTank and employed SVM and DT classifiers. Both classifiers achieved accuracies of over 93.0% according to the experimental results.

Sindhu et al. (2020) implemented improved RF classification, SVM classification, and NN with backpropagation classification methods for detecting phishing websites. Their dataset, sourced from UCI, consisted of 11,055 URLs, with 6,157 phishing URLs and 4,898 valid URLs. The accuracies obtained by the mentioned classifiers were 97.36%, 97.45%, and 97.25%, respectively.

Sánchez-Paniagua et al. (2020) conducted research on phishing URL classification utilizing ML models. They collected valid URLs from the Top Million Quantcast and verified phishing URLs from PhishTank. Five Machine Learning classifiers, including RF, KNN, SVM, NB, and LR, were utilized. With an accuracy percentage of 94.59%, RF classified the phishing URLs with the highest degree of accuracy.

Geyik et al. (2021) developed a system called 'Detection of Phishing Websites from URLs by using Classification Techniques on WEKA'. They utilized four machine learning classification algorithms: RF, DT, LR, and NB. The data these researchers utilized in their research was gathered from a variety of sources, including Common Crawl, Alexa, and PhishTank for the phishing sites and PhishTank for genuine websites. The RF classifier in this study had the highest accuracy (83.0%).

Korkmaz et al. (2020) proposed an ML-based phishing detection system using eight distinct ML algorithms, including LR, DT, SVM, NB, XGB, RF, ANN, and KNN. They used three datasets, including real URLs gathered from the Alexa and Common Crawl databases and phishing websites gathered from PhishTank. When used on Dataset 1, the RF classifier attained the best accuracy of 94.59%.

Patil et al. (2018) introduced a hybrid method for phishing detection, in which the system combines the whitelist and blacklist, visual similarity, and heuristics techniques. They used the DT, LR, and RF classifiers from machine learning. A total of 9,076 test websites were used in the investigation, and the RF classifier had the greatest accuracy (96.58%).

Palaniappan et al. (2020) worked on research aimed at distinguishing between phishing and legitimate domains. The authors used lexical characteristics, blacklists, DNS data, and web-based features. They collected a list of 20,000 domains from DNS-BH, PhishTank, Alexa, and Reputation Blacklist. The accuracy achieved using the LR classification algorithm was approximately 60.00%.

Shirazi et al. (2020) suggested an Adversarial Autoencoder (AAE) method to create samples that mimicked phishing websites and test them against models tuned using real-world data. For training, they employed various six ML classifiers, including Decision Tree, GBM, KNN, RF, and SVM. The authors utilized publicly accessible datasets from Mendeley and the UCI Machine Learning library. The maximum accuracy was attained by the GBM classifier, 95.47% (Zhu et al. 2020).

For phishing detection systems, Chiew et al. (2019) presented the Hybrid Ensemble Feature Selection (HEFS) architecture. Along with 5,000 genuine sites from Common Crawl and Alexa, they also gathered 5,000 phishing sites from PhishTank and OpenPhish. ML classifiers from the RF, SVM, NB, C4.5, JRip, and PART families were used in their experimental design. The RF classifier had the best accuracy, coming in at 96.17%.

Parekh et al. (2018) worked on a research method for phishing website detection utilizing URL features and the RF algorithm. Their system consisted of three phases: parsing, heuristic data classification, and performance analysis. A total of 31 distinct URL characteristics were used in the dataset, which was obtained from PhishTank. A level of accuracy of about 95.0% was attained by the RF classifier.

Bai (2020) proposed a system that analyzed the structural features of phishing website URLs, extracting 12 different features. They gathered 3,547 phishing websites from PhishTank and 3,511 genuine sites from the Dmoz directory. Four Machine Learning algorithms, LR, SVM, NB, and DT, were employed. The LR algorithm achieved an accuracy of 95.12%, which was the optimal solution.

Muhammad and Shahid (2019) introduced a URL-based phishing detection method that used ML classifiers such as NB, Iterative Dichotomiser-3, KNN, DT, and RF. The UCI Machine Learning Repository is where they got the phishing dataset. When they used Genetic Algorithms (GAs) for feature selection, they discovered that the detection accuracy had risen. The greatest accuracy of 94.99% was attained by combining ID3 with Yet Another Generating Genetic Algorithm (YAGGA).

Jain and Gupta (2018) suggested a system called PHISH-SAFE, a machine learning–based anti-phishing solution that focuses on exploiting 14 characteristics retrieved from URLs to detect phishing and non-phishing websites. More than 33,000 valid and phishing URLs from PhishTank were used to train their algorithm. The study findings demonstrate that the SVM classifier had an accuracy of 91.28% in identifying phishing websites. SVM and NB classifiers were used for training.

Ortiz Garces et al. (2019) worked on research for analyzing anomalous behavior associated with phishing web attacks and explored the potential of machine learning techniques in addressing this issue. They performed their analysis using contaminated datasets and Python tools to develop ML models for the detection of phishing attacks based on specific URL characteristics. The authors utilized a dataset shared through Kaggle for their research and employed LR and NN classifiers in the system for classification purposes.

6.2.5   DEEP LEARNING

In fact, recent advancements in Deep Learning approaches have outperformed traditional ML techniques in the identification of phishing websites. Here are a few significant studies in this area: Basit et al. (2020) explored the use of Deep Learning algorithms, including Deep Neural Networks, RNN, Feed-forward Deep Neural Networks, Limited Boltzmann Machines, CNN, Deep Auto-Encoders, and Deep Belief Networks for phishing detection.

Korkmaz et al. (2021) developed an anti-phishing system using a CNN with n-gram characteristics taken from URLs. Their study focused on a High-Risk URL dataset from PhishTank and achieved a maximum accuracy rate of 88.90% using 70 specified characters. The system was able to classify URLs as authentic or phishing in approximately 0.008 seconds.

Sirigineedi et al. (2020) worked on a real-time phishing detection system that utilized lexical and host-based attributes, URL characteristics, natural language processing, and host-based properties. They employed various ML algorithms, including K-NN, LR, SVM, Gradient Boosting, AdaBoost, and RM classifiers. They also utilized a Neural Network as part of their Deep Learning approach. The system achieved a phishing URL detection rate of 96.60% using the Neural Network.

A deep learning-based end-to-end automated system for classifying phishing websites known as HTMLPhish was created by Opara et al. (2020). They used CNNs to examine the textual contents of HTML pages in order to understand the semantic relationships present therein. While legal URLs come from Alexa.com's top 500,000 domains, phishing URLs were acquired through continuous PhishTank monitoring. The research employed a dataset of more than 50,000 HTML documents, and their accuracy rate was higher than 93.00%.

Saha et al. (2020) presented a data-driven anti-phishing system using a DL approach, specifically a multilayer perceptron (feed-forward neural network). They used a dataset taken from Kaggle, which contained data from 10,000 web pages with 10 attributes. The study got an accuracy of 95.00% during the training phase and 93.00% during testing.

6.3   PROPOSED APPROACH

The objective of the work is to create a machine learning–based phishing website detection system that quickly and effectively determines if a URL is legitimate or phishing. The entire process consists of the following steps:

1. Phishing Websites Dataset: The researchers utilized a dataset called 'Phishing Websites Dataset' (Vrbančič et al., 2020), which consists of a collection of genuine and phishing website URLs, totaling 88,647 URLs.
2. Data Preprocessing: The data undergoes preprocessing, which typically involves cleaning and preparing the dataset for further analysis and modeling.
3. Data Balancing: To address any class imbalance issues, the researchers employed the SMOTE (Synthetic Minority Over-sampling Technique).

This technique employs synthetic samples of the minority class (phishing websites) to balance the dataset.

4. Feature Extraction: Relevant features are extracted from the URLs. These attributes are likely designed to capture characteristics and patterns that differentiate phishing websites from legitimate ones.

5. Train-Test Split: Datasets for training and testing are created from the preprocessed and feature-extracted data. The testing dataset is applied to assess the performance of the trained models whereas the training dataset is utilized to train the ML algorithms.

6. Training ML Algorithms: Different ML algorithms such as DT, LR, RF, and SVM are trained using the training dataset. The choice of algorithms may vary depending on the research.

7. Evaluation of Trained Models: The trained Machine Learning models are evaluated using the testing dataset. Performance evaluation measures, including accuracy, precision, recall, and F1 score, are typically measured to demonstrate how well the models classify URLs as phishing or legitimate.

8. Comparative Analysis: The various ML algorithms utilized in the research are compared using the performance evaluation criteria. This investigation helps in finding the algorithm(s) that successfully detect phishing websites.

Overall, this research aims to develop an efficient phishing website detection system by leveraging Machine Learning algorithms and URL features. By following these steps, the researchers can build and evaluate models to identify phishing URLs accurately and efficiently.

The flow chart of the present methodology is demonstrated in Figure 6.3.

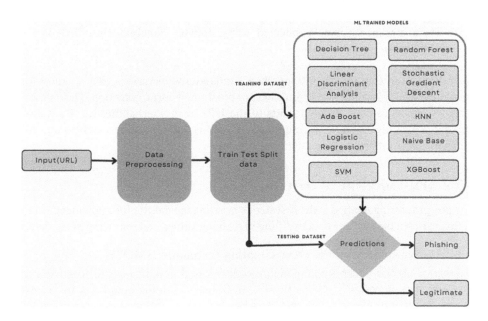

FIGURE 6.3 The architecture diagram of the proposed work.

6.3.1 Dataset

A total of 88,647 instances made up the dataset used in this study (Vrbančič et al., 2020), with 30,647 samples representing phishing URLs and 58,000 samples representing genuine URLs. The dataset consists of 111 features (excluding the target phishing attribute) that are used to classify the instances as either legitimate (0) or phishing (1).

The dataset is prepared by processing it to make sure the data is in the right format. The A training set with 70% of the dataset and a testing set with the remaining 30% make up the pre-processed dataset after that.

The dataset's attributes can be categorized into six larger groups:

- Features from the Whole URL: These attributes capture information from the complete URL string.
- Features from the Domain Name: These attributes are derived from the domain name present in the URL.
- Attributes from the URL Directory: These features are constructed based on the URL directory.
- Features from the URL File: These attributes are derived from the URL file.
- Features from the URL Parameter: These features capture information from the URL parameters.
- Features from URL External Metrics and Resolving: These characteristics are based on measurements for URL resolution and third-party services, including the Google search index.
- The list of confirmed phishing URLs, consisting of 30,647 instances, was obtained from the PhishTank website. Additionally, 58,000 legitimate web-page URLs were retrieved from the Alexa rankings website.
- The experiments were conducted using Jupyter Notebook installed on Windows 10.

Overall, this research utilizes a comprehensive dataset with various URL features to develop and test classification approaches for phishing website detection. The dataset includes attributes from different parts of the URL and external metrics. By training and evaluating machine learning models on this dataset, the researchers aim to achieve effective phishing detection.

6.3.2 Pre-Processing of Data

The pre-processing method is the first step in creating the dataset for implementation. In this part, we cleaned the data by filling in missing values and removing noisy data.

6.3.2.1 Synthetic Minority Over-sampling Technique (SMOTE)

Oversampling and undersampling are procedures used in data analysis to modify a dataset's class distribution. When there is an imbalance in the number of instances among the various classes, with one class being underrepresented in comparison to the other, they are used.

Oversampling is a strategy used to raise the minority class's (the underrepresented class) representation to match that of the dominant class. This is accomplished by creating synthetic samples that closely mimic the minority class instances that already exist. The SMOTE, a well-liked oversampling method, generates synthetic samples by randomly selecting characteristics from instances in the minority class.

In the case of the dataset used in this work, the class distribution was imbalanced, with the phishing class (class 1) having fewer samples compared to the legitimate class (class 0). To address this imbalance, the researchers applied the SMOTE technique. As a result, the number of samples in the phishing class increased to 88,161, matching the number of instances in the legitimate class, which also remained at 88,161 samples.

By applying oversampling through SMOTE, the researchers ensured a balanced representation of both classes in the dataset, which can help train machine learning models and improve classification algorithms' accuracy for the detection of phishing websites.

6.3.3 FEATURE EXTRACTION

The dataset contains 111 different features excluding the target phishing attribute, and those features are such as based on the URL properties, URL resolving metrics, and external services as shown in Figure 6.4 (Vrbančič et al. (2020)).

Based on the study by Vrbancic et al. (2020), the attributes of the mentioned dataset can be grouped into six categories presented as follows:

- Dataset features based on the whole URL.
- Dataset features derived from domain URL.
- Dataset features taken from the URL directory.
- Dataset features collected from the URL file name.
- Dataset features taken from URL parameters.
- Dataset features derived from external services and resolving URLs.

6.4 PERFORMANCE EVALUATION

The proposed research work has been implemented in Jupyter Notebook installed on Windows 10 (64-bit). The Phishing Website dataset (Vrbančič et al. (2020)) used in this work contains 88,647 phishing and legitimate website instances. The 10 different ML classifier algorithms used to analyze the dataset are compared on accuracy, precision, recall, and F1 measures.

FIGURE 6.4   Separation of the whole URL string into sub-strings (Vrbančič et al. 2020).

6.4.1 EXPERIMENTAL RESULTS

The summary of the classification report of all ML classifiers used in the work is presented in Table 6.1 and shown graphically in Figure 6.5. It shows that the RF classifier produced the highest results with an accuracy of 97.53%, precision of 97.06%, recall of 97.94%, and F1 score of 97.50%, respectively. The second highest results were produced by the XGBoost Classifier, giving an accuracy of 97.45%, a precision of 97.30%, a recall of 97.54%, and an F1 score of 97.42%. The third best result was produced by the DT classifier, giving an accuracy of 95.96%, a precision of 96.01%, a recall of 95.85%, and an F1 score of 95.93%. The lowest scores in the classification report were produced by the SVM classifier, it gives an accuracy of 75.74%, a precision of 70.12%, a recall of 78.63%, and an F1 score of 74.13%, respectively. This result confirms that using URL-based features by applying an RF classifier can accurately capture phishing websites.

The results of Table 6.1 are produced with the default values of parameters for the mentioned machine learning classifiers.

Table 6.2 presents the results of Machine learning classifiers applying some tuning parameters. Compared to the results in Table 6.1, produced with the default values of parameters for the machine learning classifiers, it shows that when we add parameter N_estimators and set its value to 120 to the RM classifier, the accuracy of the classifier increased with 0.03%.

On adding the parameter Max_Depth with the value 20 to the Decision tree classifier the accuracy increased with 0.025%. The results for some of the classifiers are mentioned in Table 6.2.

6.4.2 COMPARATIVE ANALYSIS

Based on the provided information, it is stated that the proposed approach in the study produced the top accuracy among the existing anti-phishing systems compared (Mohindru et al. 2019). The accuracy score of the proposed approach was reported to be 0.9756 (97.56%).

TABLE 6.1
Classification Report

Classifier	Accuracy	Precision	Recall	F1 score
Random Forest	0.9753	0.9706	0.9794	0.975
XG Boost	0.9745	0.973	0.9754	0.9742
Decision Tree	0.9596	0.9601	0.9585	0.9593
Stochastic Gradient Descent	0.9128	0.8469	0.9739	0.906
Linear Discriminant Analysis	0.9128	0.8469	0.9739	0.906
Ada Boost	0.9899	0.8823	0.9324	0.9067
K-Nearest Neighbor	0.9016	0.8845	0.9141	0.8991
Logistic Regression	0.8894	0.9332	0.8566	0.8932
Naive Bayes	0.8209	0.9484	0.7539	0.84
Support Vector Machine	0.7574	0.7012	0.7863	0.7413

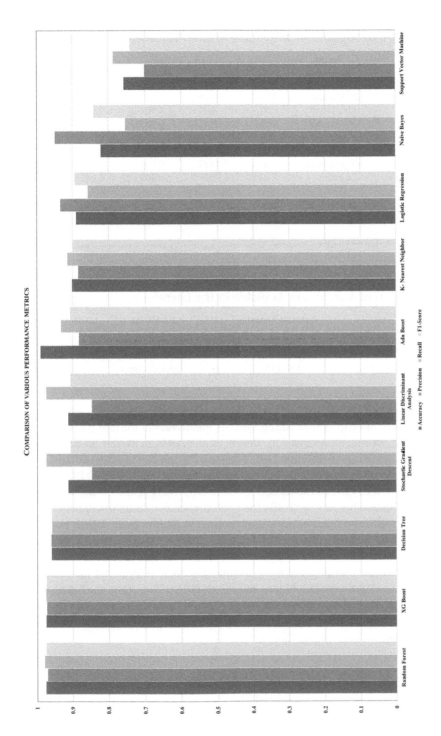

FIGURE 6.5   Comparison of various performance metrics.

TABLE 6.2

Machine Learning Algorithms with Some of Their Parameters

Classifier	Turing Parameter	Value	Accuracy	Precision	Recall	F1 Score
Random Forest	N_Estimator	120	0.9756	0.9707	0.9799	0.9753
Decision Tree	Max Depth	20	0.9621	0.9614	0.9621	0.9617
Decision Tree	Min_sample_ split	20	0.9605	0.9632	0.9574	0.9603
K- Nearest Neighbor	n_neighbor	3	0.9016	0.8845	0.9141	0.8991
Ada Boost	N_estimator	120	0.9527	0.949	0.9553	0.9521
Ada Boost Support Vector Machine	Learning Rate	0.9	0.9527	0.949	0.9553	0.9521
	Gamma	scale	0.7574	0.7012	0.7863	0.7413

TABLE 6.3

Result of Different Approaches Available in the Literature

Approach	Number Features	Classifier	Accuracy(%)
Chiew et al. (2019)	Full 48	Random Forest	0.9617
Parekh et al. (2018)	8 out of 31	Random Forest	0.9500
Our proposed approach	Full 111	Random Forest	0.9756

The accuracy of other anti-phishing systems mentioned in the comparison is also provided. The approach presented by Chiew et al. (2019) achieved an accuracy of 0.9617 (96.17%) using 48 different URL features. Parekh et al. (2018) utilized 8 out of 31 features in their dataset and obtained an accuracy score of 0.9500 (95.00%).

Comparative analysis, as mentioned in Table 6.3, likely includes additional performance evaluation metrics or results for a comprehensive comparison between the proposed approach and other existing approaches (Mohindru et al. 2020). However, without access to the specific details of Table 6.3, it is not possible to provide further information on the comparative analysis conducted in the study.

It is emphasized that a good anti-phishing approach should not misclassify a phishing URL as legitimate (Mohindru and Singh 2018). Therefore, the higher accuracy rate achieved by the proposed approach (0.9756 or 97.56%) suggests its effectiveness in accurately detecting phishing websites and differentiating them from legitimate ones.

6.5   CONCLUSION AND FUTURE WORK

In this research work, we considered the problem of performance analysis of ML classifiers for the detection of phishing websites. To identify the phishing attacks over the cyber-physical system, a study finds a Phishing Websites Dataset

(Vrbančič et al. (2020)) that contains 111 interesting URL features excluding the target phishing attribute to predict the malicious URL. Experimental results show that the current work achieves good accuracy for phishing website URL detection by using 10 different Machine Learning Algorithms (RF, XGBoost, DT, SGD, SVM, AdaBoost, LDA, KNN, LR, and NB). Among them, the RF classifier achieved the highest accuracy of 97.53% with its default values and 97.56% when parameter N_ estimators were set to 120. Precision was 97.06%, recall 97.94, and F1 score of 97.50%, respectively, for this study. The SVM Classifier achieved the least score among the classifiers; it achieved an accuracy score of 75.74%, whereas the precision, recall, and F1 scores are 70.12%, 78.63%, and 74.13%, respectively.

In the future, the study proposes to work on phishing website detection for cyber-physical systems using a hybrid approach based on four different approaches including heuristic, visual similarity, list-based, and machine learning. Additionally, efforts will also be made to develop an IoT-based browser add-on that alerts users when they are visiting phishing sites.

REFERENCES

Abedin, Noor Faisal, Rosemary Bawm, Tawsif Sarwar, Mohammed Saifuddin, Mohammd Azizur Rahman, and Sohrab Hossain(2020). "Phishing Attack Detection Using Machine Learning Classification Techniques." *2020 3rd International Conference on Intelligent Sustainable Systems (ICISS)*, December 3, 2020. https://doi.org/10.1109/iciss49785.2020.9315895

Alkawaz, Mohammed Hazim, Stephanie Joanne Steven, Asif Iqbal Hajamydeen, and Rusyaizila Ramli (2021). "A Comprehensive Survey on Identification and Analysis of Phishing Website Based on Machine Learning Methods." *2021 IEEE 11th IEEE Symposium on Computer Applications & Industrial Electronics (ISCAIE)*, April 3, 2021. https://doi.org/10.1109/iscaie51753.2021.9431794

Alsariera, Yazan Ahmad, Victor Elijah Adeyemo, Abdullateef Oluwagbemiga Balogun, and Ammar Kareem Alazzawi(2020). "AI Meta-Learners and Extra-Trees Algorithm for the Detection of Phishing Websites." *IEEE Access* 8 (2020): 142532–42. https://doi.org/10.1109/access.2020.3013699

Babagoli, Mehdi, Mohammad Pourmahmood Aghababa, and Vahid Solouk (2018). "Heuristic Nonlinear Regression Strategy for Detecting Phishing Websites." *Soft Computing* 23, no. 12 (February 20, 2018): 4315–27. https://doi.org/10.1007/s00500-018-3084-2

Bai, Weiheng (2020). "Phishing Website Detection Based on Machine Learning Algorithm." *2020 International Conference on Computing and Data Science (CDS)*, August 2020. https://doi.org/10.1109/cds49703.2020.00064

Barlow, Luke, Gueltoum Bendiab, Stavros Shiaeles, and Nick Savage (2020). "A Novel Approach to Detect Phishing Attacks Using Binary Visualisation and Machine Learning." *2020 IEEE World Congress on Services (Services)*, October 2020. https://doi.org/10.1109/services48979.2020.00046

Basit, Abdul, Maham Zafar, Abdul Rehman Javed, and Zunera Jalil (2020). "A Novel Ensemble Machine Learning Method to Detect Phishing Attack." *2020 IEEE 23rd International Multitopic Conference (INMIC)*, November 5, 2020. https://doi.org/10.1109/inmic50486.2020.9318210

Basit, Abdul, Maham Zafar, Xuan Liu, Abdul Rehman Javed, Zunera Jalil, and Kashif Kifayat (2020). "A Comprehensive Survey of AI-Enabled Phishing Attacks Detection Techniques." *Telecommunication Systems* 76, no. 1 (October 23, 2020): 139–54. https://doi.org/10.1007/s11235-020-00733-2

Bozkir, Ahmet Selman, and Murat Aydos (2020). "LogoSENSE: A Companion HOG Based Logo Detection Scheme for Phishing Web Page and E-Mail Brand Recognition." *Computers & Security* 95 (August 2020): 101855. https://doi.org/10.1016/j.cose.2020.101855

Chiew, Kang Leng, Choon Lin Tan, KokSheik Wong, Kelvin S.C. Yong, and Wei King Tiong(2019). "A New Hybrid Ensemble Feature Selection Framework for Machine Learning-Based Phishing Detection System." *Information Sciences* 484 (May 2019): 153–66. https://doi.org/10.1016/j.ins.2019.01.064

Faris, Humam, and Setiadi Yazid(2021). "Phishing Web Page Detection Methods: URL and HTML Features Detection." *2020 IEEE International Conference on Internet of Things and Intelligence System (IoTaIS)*, January 27, 2021. https://doi.org/10.1109/iotais50849.2021.9359694

FBI. (2020). "FBI Releases the Internet Crime Complaint Center 2020 Internet Crime Report, Including COVID-19 Scam Statistics." www.fbi.gov. Accessed June 9, 2022. https://www.fbi.gov/news/pressrel/press-releases/fbi-releases-the-internet-crime-complaint-center-2020-internet-crime-report-including-covid-19-scam-statistics

Geng, Guang-Gang, Zhi-Wei Yan, Yu Zeng, and Xiao-Bo Jin. (2018). "RRPhish: Anti-Phishing via Mining Brand Resources Request." *2018 IEEE International Conference on Consumer Electronics (ICCE)*, January 2018. https://doi.org/10.1109/icce.2018.8326085

Geyik, Buket, Kubra Erensoy, and Emre Kocyigit (2021). "Detection of Phishing Websites from URLs by Using Classification Techniques on WEKA." *2021 6th International Conference on Inventive Computation Technologies (ICICT)*, January 20, 2021. https://doi.org/10.1109/icict50816.2021.9358642

Gupta, Brij B., Krishna Yadav, Imran Razzak, Konstantinos Psannis, Arcangelo Castiglione, and Xiaojun Chang(2021). "A Novel Approach for Phishing URLs Detection Using Lexical Based Machine Learning in a Real-Time Environment." *Computer Communications* 175 (July 2021): 47–57. https://doi.org/10.1016/j.comcom.2021.04.023

Hannousse, Abdelhakim, and Salima Yahiouche(2021). "Towards Benchmark Datasets for Machine Learning Based Website Phishing Detection: An Experimental Study." *Engineering Applications of Artificial Intelligence* 104 (September 2021): 104347. https://doi.org/10.1016/j.engappai.2021.104347

Jain, Ankit Kumar, and Gupta, B. B. (2017). "Two-Level Authentication Approach to Protect from Phishing Attacks in Real Time." *Journal of Ambient Intelligence and Humanized Computing* 9, no. 6 (November 8, 2017): 1783–96. https://doi.org/10.1007/s12652-017-0616-z

Jain, Ankit Kumar, and B. B. Gupta(2018). "PHISH-SAFE: URL Features-Based Phishing Detection System Using Machine Learning." *Advances in Intelligent Systems and Computing*, 2018, 467–74. https://doi.org/10.1007/978-981-10-8536-9_44

Jain, Ankit Kumar, Sakshi Parashar, Palak Katare, and Isha Sharma(2020). "PhishSKaPe: A Content Based Approach to Escape Phishing Attacks." *Procedia Computer Science* 171 (2020): 1102–9. https://doi.org/10.1016/j.procs.2020.04.118

Kathrine, G., Jaspher Willsie, Paradise Mercy Praise, A. Amrutha Rose, and Eligious C Kalaivani (2019). "Variants of Phishing Attacks and Their Detection Techniques." *2019 3rd International Conference on Trends in Electronics and Informatics (ICOEI)*, April 2019. https://doi.org/10.1109/icoei.2019.8862697

Kaur, Dilshad, and Satwinder Singh. "A Systematic Literature Review on Extraction of Parallel Corpora from Comparable Corpora." *Journal of Computer Science* 17, no. 10 (October 1, 2021): 924–52. https://doi.org/10.3844/jcssp.2021.924.952

Korkmaz, Mehmet, Emre Kocyigit, Ozgur Koray Sahingoz, and Banu Diri (2021). "Phishing Web Page Detection Using N-Gram Features Extracted From URLs." *2021 3rd International Congress on Human-Computer Interaction, Optimization and Robotic Applications (HORA)*, June 11, 2021. https://doi.org/10.1109/hora52670.2021.9461378

Korkmaz, Mehmet, Ozgur Koray Sahingoz, and Banu Diri (2020). "Detection of Phishing Websites by Using Machine Learning-Based URL Analysis." *2020 11th International Conference on Computing, Communication and Networking Technologies (ICCCNT)*, July 2020. https://doi.org/10.1109/icccnt49239.2020.9225561

Liu, Dong-Jie, Guang-Gang Geng, Xiao-Bo Jin, and Wei Wang(2021). "An Efficient Multistage Phishing Website Detection Model Based on the CASE Feature Framework: Aiming at the Real Web Environment." *Computers & Security* 110 (November 2021): 102421. https://doi.org/10.1016/j.cose.2021.102421

Liu, Xiuwen, and Jianming Fu (2020). "SPWalk: Similar Property Oriented Feature Learning for Phishing Detection." *IEEE Access* 8 (2020): 87031–45. https://doi.org/10.1109/access.2020.2992381

Mao, Jian, Jingdong Bian, Wenqian Tian, Shishi Zhu, Tao Wei, Aili Li, and Zhenkai Liang (2018). "Detecting Phishing Websites via Aggregation Analysis of Page Layouts." *Procedia Computer Science* 129 (2018): 224–30. https://doi.org/10.1016/j.procs.2018.03.053

Maroofi, Sourena, Maciej Korczynski, Cristian Hesselman, Benoit Ampeau, and Andrzej Duda (2020). "COMAR: Classification of Compromised versus Maliciously Registered Domains." *2020 IEEE European Symposium on Security and Privacy (EuroS&P)*, September 2020. https://doi.org/10.1109/eurosp48549.2020.00045

Mohindru, Vandana, Ravindara Bhatt, and Yashwant Singh. (2019). "Reauthentication scheme for mobile wireless sensor networks." *Sustainable Computing: Informatics and Systems* 23 (2019): 158–166.

Mohindru, Vandana, and Yashwant Singh (2018). "Node authentication algorithm for securing static wireless sensor networks from node clone attack." *International Journal of information and computer security* 10, no. 2–3 (2018): 129–48.

Mohindru, Vandana, Yashwant Singh, and Ravindara Bhatt (2020). "Hybrid cryptography algorithm for securing wireless sensor networks from Node Clone Attack." *Recent Advances in Electrical & Electronic Engineering (Formerly Recent Patents on Electrical & Electronic Engineering)* 13, no. 2 (2020): 251–59.

Muhammad, Taseer Suleman, and Mahmood Awan Shahid (2019). "Optimization of URL-Based Phishing Websites Detection through Genetic Algorithms." *Automatic Control and Computer Sciences* 53, no. 4 (July 2019): 333–41. https://doi.org/10.3103/s01464 11619040102

Nakamura, Akihito, and Fuma Dobashi.(2019) "Proactive Phishing Sites Detection." *IEEE/ WIC/ACM International Conference on Web Intelligence*, October 14, 2019. https://doi.org/10.1145/3350546.3352565

Opara, Chidimma, Bo Wei, and Yingke Chen (2020). "HTMLPhish: Enabling Phishing Web Page Detection by Applying Deep Learning Techniques on HTML Analysis." *2020 International Joint Conference on Neural Networks (IJCNN)*, July 2020. https://doi.org/10.1109/ijcnn48605.2020.9207707

Ortiz Garces, Ivan, Maria Fernada Cazares, and Roberto Omar Andrade (2019). "Detection of Phishing Attacks with Machine Learning Techniques in Cognitive Security Architecture." *2019 International Conference on Computational Science and Computational Intelligence (CSCI)*, December 2019. https://doi.org/10.1109/csci49370.2019.00071

Palaniappan, Gopinath, Sangeetha S, Balaji Rajendran, Sanjay, Shubham Goyal, and Bindhumadhava, B. S. (2020). "Malicious Domain Detection Using Machine Learning On Domain Name Features, Host-Based Features and Web-Based Features." *Procedia Computer Science* 171 (2020): 654–61. https://doi.org/10.1016/j.procs.2020.04.071

Paliath, Suhail, Mohammad Abu Qbeitah, and Monther Aldwairi (2020) "PhishOut: Effective Phishing Detection Using Selected Features." *2020 27th International Conference on Telecommunications (ICT)*, October 5, 2020. https://doi.org/10.1109/ict49546.2020.9239589

Parekh, Shraddha, Dhwanil Parikh, Srushti Kotak, and Smita Sankhe (2018). "A New Method for Detection of Phishing Websites: URL Detection." *2018 Second International Conference on Inventive Communication and Computational Technologies (ICICCT)*, April 2018. https://doi.org/10.1109/icicct.2018.8473085

Patil, Vaibhav, Pritesh Thakkar, Chirag Shah, Tushar Bhat, and S. P. Godse (2018). "Detection and Prevention of Phishing Websites Using Machine Learning Approach." *2018 Fourth International Conference on Computing Communication Control and Automation (ICCUBEA)*, August 2018. https://doi.org/10.1109/iccubea.2018.8697412

Ramana, A. V., K. Lakshmana Rao, and Routhu Srinivasa Rao (2021). "Stop-Phish: An Intelligent Phishing Detection Method Using Feature Selection Ensemble." *Social Network Analysis and Mining* 11, no. 1 (October 30, 2021). https://doi.org/10.1007/s13278-021-00829-w

Rao, Routhu Srinivasa, Tatti Vaishnavi, and Alwyn Roshan Pais (2019). "CatchPhish: Detection of Phishing Websites by Inspecting URLs." *Journal of Ambient Intelligence and Humanized Computing* 11, no. 2 (May 10, 2019): 813–25. https://doi.org/10.1007/s12652-019-01311-4

Rashid, Junaid, Toqeer Mahmood, Muhammad Wasif Nisar, and Tahira Nazir (2020). "Phishing Detection Using Machine Learning Technique." *2020 First International Conference of Smart Systems and Emerging Technologies (SMARTTECH)*, November 2020. https://doi.org/10.1109/smart-tech49988.2020.00026

Safi, Asadullah, and Satwinder Singh. "A Systematic Literature Review on Phishing Website Detection Techniques." *Journal of King Saud University - Computer and Information Sciences* 35, no. 2 (February 2023): 590–611. https://doi.org/10.1016/j.jksuci.2023.01.004

Saha, Ishita, Dhiman Sarma, Rana Joyti Chakma, Mohammad Nazmul Alam, Asma Sultana, and Sohrab Hossain (2020). "Phishing Attacks Detection Using Deep Learning Approach." *2020 Third International Conference on Smart Systems and Inventive Technology (ICSSIT)*, August 2020. https://doi.org/10.1109/icssit48917.2020.9214132

Sahingoz, Ozgur Koray, Ebubekir Buber, Onder Demir, and Banu Diri (2019). "Machine Learning Based Phishing Detection from URLs." *Expert Systems with Applications* 117 (March 2019): 345–57. https://doi.org/10.1016/j.eswa.2018.09.029

Sánchez-Paniagua, M., E. Fidalgo, V. González-Castro, and E. Alegre (2020). "Impact of Current Phishing Strategies in Machine Learning Models for Phishing Detection." *13th International Conference on Computational Intelligence in Security for Information Systems (CISIS 2020)*, August 28, 2020, 87–96. https://doi.org/10.1007/978-3-030-57805-3_9

Shirazi, Hossein, Bruhadeshwar Bezawada, and Indrakshi Ray (2018). "'Know Thy Domain Name.'" *Proceedings of the 23nd ACM on Symposium on Access Control Models and Technologies*, June 7, 2018. https://doi.org/10.1145/3205977.3205992

Shirazi, Hossein, Shashika R. Muramudalige, Indrakshi Ray, and Anura P. Jayasumana (2020). "Improved Phishing Detection Algorithms Using Adversarial Autoencoder Synthesized Data." *2020 IEEE 45th Conference on Local Computer Networks (LCN)*, November 16, 2020. https://doi.org/10.1109/lcn48667.2020.9314775

Sindhu, Smita, Sunil Parameshwar Patil, Arya Sreevalsan, Faiz Rahman, and A. N. Saritha (2020). "Phishing Detection Using Random Forest, SVM and Neural Network with Backpropagation." *2020 International Conference on Smart Technologies in Computing, Electrical and Electronics (ICSTCEE)*, October 9, 2020. https://doi.org/10.1109/icstcee49637.2020.9277256

Singh, Satwinder, and Himanshu Beniwal (2022). "A Survey on Near-Human Conversational Agents." *Journal of King Saud University - Computer and Information Sciences* 34, no. 10 (November 2022): 8852–66. https://doi.org/10.1016/j.jksuci.2021.10.013

Singh, Satwinder, and Sharanpreet Kaur (2018). "A Systematic Literature Review: Refactoring for Disclosing Code Smells in Object Oriented Software." *Ain Shams Engineering Journal* 9, no. 4 (December 2018): 2129–51. https://doi.org/10.1016/j.asej.2017.03.002

Sirigineedi, Surya Srikar, Jayesh Soni, and Himanshu Upadhyay (2020). "Learning-Based Models to Detect Runtime Phishing Activities Using URLs." *Proceedings of the 2020 the 4th International Conference on Compute and Data Analysis*, March 9, 2020. https://doi.org/10.1145/3388142.3388170

Somesha, M., Alwyn Roshan Pais, Routhu Srinivasa Rao, and Vikram Singh Rathour (2020). "Efficient Deep Learning Techniques for the Detection of Phishing Websites." *Sādhanā* 45, no. 1 (June 27, 2020). https://doi.org/10.1007/s12046-020-01392-4

Vrbančič, Grega, Iztok Fister, and Vili Podgorelec (2020). "Datasets for Phishing Websites Detection." *Data in Brief* 33 (December 2020): 106438. https://doi.org/10.1016/j.dib.2020.106438

Yang, Liqun, Jiawei Zhang, Xiaozhe Wang, Zhi Li, Zhoujun Li, and Yueying He (2021). "An Improved ELM-Based and Data Preprocessing Integrated Approach for Phishing Detection Considering Comprehensive Features." *Expert Systems with Applications* 165 (March 2021): 113863. https://doi.org/10.1016/j.eswa.2020.113863

Zabihimayvan, Mahdieh, and Derek Doran (2019). "Fuzzy Rough Set Feature Selection to Enhance Phishing Attack Detection." *2019 IEEE International Conference on Fuzzy Systems (FUZZ-IEEE)*, June 2019. https://doi.org/10.1109/fuzz-ieee.2019.8858884

Zhu, Erzhou, Yinyin Ju, Zhile Chen, Feng Liu, and Xianyong Fang (2020). "DTOF-ANN: An Artificial Neural Network Phishing Detection Model Based on Decision Tree and Optimal Features." *Applied Soft Computing* 95 (October 2020): 106505. https://doi.org/10.1016/j.asoc.2020.106505

7 Cybersecurity Issues and Artificial Intelligence– Based Solutions in Cyber-Physical Systems

Narinder Verma, Neerendra Kumar,
Zakir Ahmad Sheikh, Neha Koul, and
Ankit Ashish
Central University of Jammu, Jammu, India

7.1 INTRODUCTION

Cyber-physical systems (CPSs) are computer-based systems that interact with the physical world to perform a variety of tasks. As computing and communication continue to evolve rapidly, CPSs play an increasingly important role in many types of critical infrastructure such as energy, transportation, and health (Khalil et al. 2023; Wu, Song, and Moon 2019; Al-Mhiqani et al. 2019). The CPSs have become ubiquitous in modern society, from autonomous vehicles to smart home appliances. Figure 7.1 illustrates CPS applications for a wide range of domains (Sakhnini et al. 2020; Kumar and Chatterjee 2023). The capacity to remotely monitor a patient's health is another benefit of integrating CPS into medical devices (Kocabas, Soyata, and Aktas 2016). The implementation of CPS has revolutionized technological interactions; however, it also represents distinct challenges in the domains of security, privacy, and safety (Tan et al. 2023). Connecting CPSs to the internet exposes the devices susceptible to cyberattacks. The Stuxnet attack, in which malicious software was supplied through USB and used to compromise Iran's nuclear power plants, is a well-known real-world example (Ahmed and Zhou 2020). Therefore, there is an urgent requirement to protect such CPSs from potential threats.

7.1.1 ARCHITECTURE

The architecture of CPSs can be categorized into multiple layers (Alguliyev, Imamverdiyev, and Sukhostat 2018; Singh, Yadav, and Chuarasia 2020; C. Kumar, Marston, and Sen 2020; Duo et al. 2022). Figure 7.2 illustrates the general architecture of CPSs.

The physical layer is composed of actuators and sensor components that are connected via either wireless or wired networks. The physical layer facilitates the

DOI: 10.1201/9781003406105-10

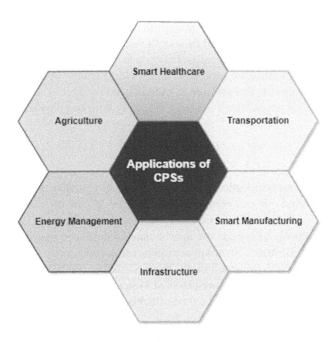

FIGURE 7.1 Cyber-physical systems applications in different domains.

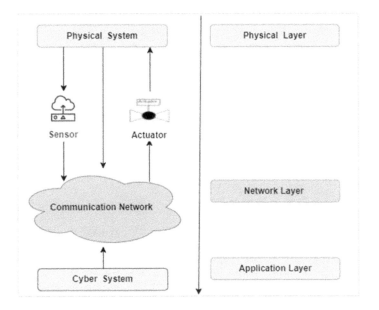

FIGURE 7.2 General architecture of CPSs.

connection of devices to the internet through the utilization of various communication protocols, including ZigBee and Bluetooth (Singh, Yadav, and Chuarasia 2020).
Network layers facilitate communication between the physical and application layers
using different communication protocols. Information from physical and network
layers is stored, analyzed, and updated in the application layer. This layer provides
the user interface for applications to interact directly with the physical components
of the system.

7.1.2 PROTOCOLS IN CPS

CPS protocols are communication protocols that are specifically designed to facilitate between the physical and computational components of the system (Yaacoub
et al. 2020). To ensure smooth functioning and cooperation among various system
elements, the protocols allow for the interchange of data, commands, and control
signals. Figure 7.3 illustrates the main communication protocols used in CPSs such
as MODBUS and DNP3 (Yaacoub et al. 2020; Sheikh et al. 2022). CPS protocols
are critical to the operation of cyber-physical systems, but they can also introduce
vulnerabilities that can be exploited by the attacker. Humayed et al. 2017 assert that
because MODBUS lacks basic security methods like authentication, authorization,
and encryption, it is vulnerable to eavesdropping and fake data injection attacks.
Apart from buffer overflow, the DNP3 protocol is affected by the same vulnerabilities (Sheikh et al. 2022).

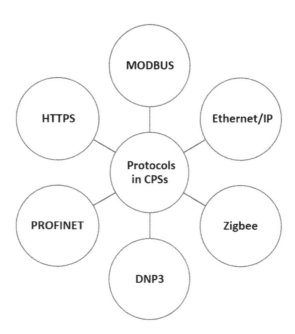

FIGURE 7.3 Protocols in CPS.

7.2 VULNERABILITIES IN CPSS

CPSs are complex systems that integrate physical and computational components. CPSs are susceptible to a wide range of vulnerabilities that can compromise security and functionality (Duo et al. 2022).

Figure 7.4 represents the classification of various cyberattacks on CPSs that can affect the three main properties – confidentiality, integrity, and availability – of a secure CPS (Alguliyev, Imamverdiyev, and Sukhostat 2018; Sheikh et al. 2022; Rouzbahani et al. 2020; Al-Mhiqani et al. 2018).

Data from a wide range of sources were quantitatively analyzed and presented in Figure 7.5 (Al-Mhiqani et al. 2018). The statistical analysis presents the most frequently occurring vulnerabilities in CPSs.

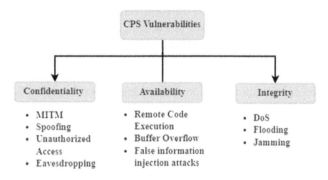

FIGURE 7.4 Vulnerabilities in CPSs.

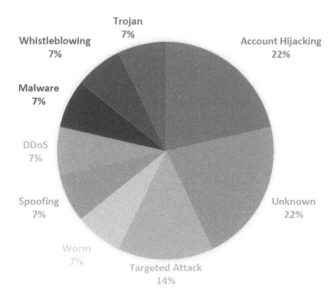

FIGURE 7.5 Most frequently occurring vulnerabilities in CPSs.

7.2.1 CPS Real Attacks

CPSs are vulnerable to a wide variety of different kinds of cyberattacks. Examples of actual attacks against CPSs that had a significant effect on vital infrastructure are presented in Table 7.1 (C. Kumar, Marston, and Sen 2020; Karnouskos 2011; Mallick 2019). Stuxnet in 2010 was one of the most famous CPS cyberattacks in history. Stuxnet was a worm that was designed to target industrial control systems (ICS) used in nuclear facilities. Stuxnet targeted the Siemens SCADA systems used in the Iranian nuclear program, causing significant damage to centrifuges used for uranium enrichment (Karnouskos 2011).

7.3 EXISTING CPS SECURITY SYSTEM

Different researchers have presented different security solutions to overcome the security problems in CPSs as depicted in Table 7.2. He et al. (2020) proposed classification models for identifying communication cyberattacks on Connected and Autonomous Vehicles (CAVs). A CAV cybersecurity framework based on Unified Modeling Language is proposed to classify CAV vulnerabilities. The experiment generates a novel CAV communication cyberattack dataset based on the thoroughly examined dataset KDD99. The decision tree model outperforms Naïve Bayes after analyzing the results. Dutta and Kant (2020) proposed a Naive Bayes classifier model for generating actionable threat intelligence by utilizing artificial intelligence and machine learning techniques. For an experiment, data from the Kaggle ('Kaggle: Your Machine Learning and Data Science Community' n.d.) online platform, which included the most recent CVE entries and a malware dataset, is utilized. The model under consideration attains an accuracy level of 96.6% in identifying instances of cyberattacks. Ghanem and Jantan in 2020 introduced a hybrid approach utilizing the ABC algorithm and MBO for categorizing network traffic as either malicious or nonmalicious. The experiment employs an ANN machine learning model to analyze three distinct benchmark datasets: UNSW-NB15, ISCX 2012, and KDD Cup 99. The performance is evaluated with existing techniques. The proposed method achieves an accuracy of 90.89% with KDD Cup 99, 98.25%, for ISCX 2012 and 96.41% for the UNSW-NB15 dataset. The performance evaluated is considerably higher than existing techniques.

$$s = \frac{t_p + t_n}{t_p + t_n + f_p + f_n} \tag{7.1}$$

$$fpr = \frac{f_p}{f_p + t_n} \tag{7.2}$$

$$tpr = \frac{t_p}{t_p + f_n} \tag{7.3}$$

$$f_1 = \frac{2 * pre * tpr}{pre + tpr} \tag{7.4}$$

TABLE 7.1
Past Attacks on CPSs

Year	Country	Attack Name	Attack Method	Target Sector	Impact
2010	Iran	Stuxnet	Trojan, Worm	Nuclear power plant	Disruption in power plant readings
2012	Egypt	Maritime transport Sector	DDoS	Government transport	Delay in services
2013	Saudi Arab	Saudi Arabian Defence Ministry System Breached	Hijacking	Military system	Sensitive data exposure
2013	USA	Physical breach on Georgia Water Treatment Plant	Unauthorized access	Water treatment Plant	Disruption in services
2015	UAE	Trojan Laziok attack	Malware	Government energy sector	Sensitive data extraction
2016	Ukraine	Ukraine attack	Malware	Power disruption network	Malware causes crash in smart power grid
2019	India	Kudankulam Power Plant	DTrack malware	Nuclear power plant	Temporary stoppage of plant

$$\text{Precision} = \frac{t_p}{t_p + f_p} \tag{7.5}$$

where s = accuracy, t_n = true negative, tpr = true positive rate, t_p = true positive, fpr = false-positive rate.

In this study, researchers proposed a CNN ML-based technique for identifying intrusion detection in a network (Khan et al. 2019). The model can automatically extract the useful aspects of penetration samples, allowing for precise classification. Experiments carried out using the KDD99 datasets demonstrated that the proposed method considerably improved the accuracy of intrusion detection. ScaleMalNet is a framework that is designed to detect, identify, and categorize zero-day malware at scale (Vinayakumar et al. 2019). Using static analysis, dynamic analysis, and image processing approaches, this work examined the comparison of conventional machine learning algorithms with deep learning architectures for malware detection. This research found that deep learning–based approaches surpassed traditional machine learning algorithms when compared to both publicly available benchmark datasets and privately obtained datasets. The identification of software vulnerabilities was proposed to be examined via a machine learning–based method by Lee et al. (2019). The framework models assembly code effectively by utilizing Instruction2vec and educates itself on the characteristics of software vulnerability code by utilizing Text-CNN. The experiment demonstrated that our system can identify software vulnerabilities even in the absence of patterns or rules.

TABLE 7.2

Existing Work for CPS Security

Year	Reference	Security Mechanism	Technique	Attack	Description	Performance	Limitation
2022	Meleshko et al. (2022)	Combination of machine learning and visualization techniques.	Anomaly and attack detection	Different classes of attacks	Machine learning and visualization-assisted strategy for anomaly and attack detection in a wireless sensor network-based water treatment system.	Accuracy values above 95% for different ML models.	The presented solution is not scalable for other cyberattacks.
2023	A. Kumar and Chatterjee (2023)	Blockchain-based framework	Prevention	Manipulation of data, data falsification, and *DOS attacks.	Framework to overcome data security and privacy challenges in medical cyber-physical system	Latency time <46–50%, Throughput >44–50%.	The absence of device authentication consideration in the MCPS module is the main drawback of the study.
2020	He et al. (2020)	Decision tree and Naïve Bayes	Detection	*DOS, U2R, R2L, and PROBE	Framework to identify vulnerabilities in Connected and Autonomous Vehicle	Accuracy = 99.7%	Unable to detect unknown attacks
2020	Dutta and Kant (2020)	Naïve Bayes classifier	Detection	*DOS and other threats	Naïve Bayes classifier model for generating actionable threat intelligence by utilizing artificial intelligence and machine learning technique	Accuracy = 96.6%	Unable to detect unknown attacks

Year	Author	Method/Algorithm	Task	Attacks	Description	Results	Limitations
2020	Ghanem and Jantan (2020)	*ANN-based hybrid algorithm	Detection	Various attacks	ABC and MBO-based hybrid technique for classification of malicious and nonmalicious traffic in the network using different datasets.	Accuracy = 98.25%	An optimal feature selection approach needsto be considered.
2020	Rouzbahani et al. (2020)	Various ML algorithms for categorizing threats of cyber-physical systems.	Detection	False data injection, malicious traffic	Researchers deployed ML classifiers to determine if the smart grid readings were legitimate or tampered with by different IEEE power systems.	SVM presents the highest classification accuracy of 90.58%.	Unknown threats are not considered.
2019	Khan et al. (2019)	Deep learning–based CNN Model	Detection	DOS[a], U2R, R2L, PROBE	A method is presented that uses both the CNN and softmax algorithms. The results of the evaluations indicate that the model improves the efficiency and precision of human intrusion detection systems.	Accuracy = 99.23%	Validation of the proposed model's accuracy on alternative datasets needs to be considered.
2019	Vinayakumar et al. (2019)	Deep learning–based Hybrid ScaleMalNet framework	Detect, classify, and categorizeattacks	Zero-day malware	The proposed framework can be scaled to analyze multiple malware threats in real time.	Accuracy = 99.23%	The robustness of the proposed architecture is not discussed.
2019	Lee et al. (2019)	CNN	Identification of software vulnerabilities	Various attacks	The framework models assembly code to identify vulnerability code by utilizing Text-CNN even without patterns or rules.	91.11%	N.A

(Continued)

TABLE 7.2 (Continued)

Year	Reference	Security Mechanism	Technique	Attack	Description	Performance	Limitation
2019	Geris and Karimipour (2019)	Decision tree classifier	Anomaly detection	False data injection, malicious traffic	Decision tree classifier method for detecting malicious threats in smart grid CPSs.	Detection rate = 97%	The proposed model cannot be generalized for other cyberattacks.
2019	Wu, Song, and Moon (2019)	Anomaly detection and random forests	Detection	Man-in-the-middle	To detect malicious attacks on cyber manufacturing system physical data.	Accuracy = 96.1%	Detection of cyberattacks on more types of data.
2017	Goh et al. (2017)	Unsupervised ML technique recurrent neural network	Attack detection	Programmable logic controller attacks	An attack scenario has been created for anomaly detection in CPS using an RNN method based on behavioral technique	N.A	The proposed model is restricted only to particular types of cyberattack.
2016	Kocabas, Soyata, and Aktas (2016)	Blockchain-based AES technique for medical cyber-physical systems	Prevention	Various attacks	Secure encryption techniques are employed for secure data sharing and computation of medical data.	Encryption and decryption time < 1 sec	High-end computation resources are required.

[a] DoS = Denial of Service, CPADF = Consumption pattern-based anomaly detection framework, U2R = User-to-Root, R2L = Remote-to-Local, DoS = Denial of Service, AES = Advanced Encryption Standard, CNN = Convolutional Neural Network, ANN = Artificial Neural Networks, SVM = Support Vector Machine, ABC = Artificial Bee Colony algorithm, MBO = Monarch Butterfly optimization, Acc = Accuracy.

Meleshko et al. (2022) proposed a methodology that employs visualization techniques to facilitate the identification of anomalies and attacks in a water treatment system. The proposed method relies on a wireless sensor network. The proposed method's standout characteristic is that it combines machine learning with visualization. The simulation modeled five forms of system sensor attacks and combinations of attacks. Attack detection classifiers and visualization component efficiency were tested using the data sets.

To address the data security and privacy issues that arise in a medical cyber-physical system, a framework based on blockchain technology has been suggested (A. Kumar and Chatterjee 2023). Based on the computed outcomes, there is a reduction of 46–50% in the mean latency time and an increase of 44–50% in the throughput. A microgrid system is used as a case study to illustrate the study's proposed technique for applying STRIDE to cyber-physical systems (Khalil et al. 2023). Based on an attack taxonomy presented, the technique offers a methodical approach to eliciting potential threats. The study also demonstrates how, in the context of a cyber-physical system, one may catalog assets, construct a data flow diagram, establish trust boundaries, and evaluate threats (Khalil et al. 2023). An unsupervised learning strategy, recurrent neural network along with the cumulative sum technique, is the focus of research by Goh et al. (2017) for finding CPS anomalies in a water treatment facility. A secure water treatment testbed (SWaT) was used to obtain the complicated dataset used in the studies. Experimental results demonstrate that the suggested method is effective in detecting most of the assaults created by the research team, while also exhibiting low levels of false positives. In this study, researchers deploy ML classifiers to determine if the smart grid readings were legitimate or tampered with (Rouzbahani et al. 2020). Classification accuracy is evaluated using a Support Vector Machine (SVM), K-Nearest Neighbor (KNN), and Naive Bayesian (NB) classifier. For evaluation, different IEEE power systems datasets, i.e., IEEE bus systems 14-bus and 118-bus, are used. The classification accuracy, F1 score, and precision are calculated with equations 1 to 5. The results of the case study demonstrate the use of several ML algorithms for categorizing threats to cyber-physical systems. SVM presents the highest classification accuracy of 90.58%. Using a feature grouping and linear correlation coefficient (FGLCC) algorithm, this research (Geris and Karimipour 2019) suggests a method for detecting malicious threats in smart grid CPSs. The proposed method makes use of a decision tree classifier. The proposed method was used to validate the system's performance on an IEEE 39-bus system. The results indicate a 97% detection rate and 96% accuracy compared to other methods currently available in the literature, along with a low false-positive rate of 1.65%.

7.4   CHALLENGES IN CPS CYBERSECURITY

Securing CPS poses several unique cybersecurity challenges. The highly integrated nature of CPS makes it possible for widely used applications in the current industry but also makes it vulnerable to cyber threats (Duo et al. 2022). By studying current trends, some security challenges are identified as shown in Figure 7.6. As technology is accelerating, cyberattackers use advanced attacks (Al-Mhiqani et al. 2019; Gupta et al. 2020). One such example is that CPSs can be attacked randomly with DoS and

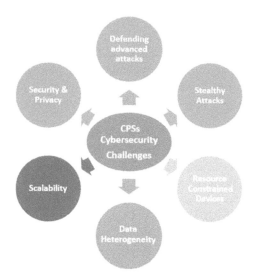

FIGURE 7.6   CPSs cybersecurity challenges.

integrity assaults to avoid detection (Zhang et al. 2021). The increase in the number of IOT sensor devices has presented additional challenges in the areas of privacy and scalability (Mohindru et al. 2021). Handling users' private and sensitive information and the scalability of security solutions is also one of the issues in CPSs.

The heterogeneity of data refers to the fact that these systems collect and process data from various sources and in different formats (Mohindru et al. 2020). This heterogeneity can pose significant challenges for CPS applications, particularly in terms of data integration, management, and analysis (Mohindru et al. 2019).

7.5   CONCLUSION

Cyber-physical systems are vulnerable to various cyber threats, which can have severe consequences on the safety, reliability, and performance of the system. In this study, the CPS architecture, protocols, and past attacks on CPSs are presented. Further, some common vulnerabilities of CPS and potential solutions presented in the literature to mitigate cyberattacks are studied. Moreover, the research presented here seeks to identify the security-related concerns concerning CPSs. Several cyber-physical attacks have been compared and analyzed based on several characteristics. Zero-day attacks and other challenges nevertheless constitute significant threats to CPS security. Future work will consider designing an intrusion-detection framework that can overcome the performance of existing techniques in various CPSs.

REFERENCES

Ahmed, Chuadhry Mujeeb, and Jianying Zhou. 2020. "Challenges and Opportunities in Cyberphysical Systems Security: A Physics-Based Perspective." *IEEE Security and Privacy* 18 (6): 14–22. https://doi.org/10.1109/MSEC.2020.3002851

Alguliyev, Rasim, Yadigar Imamverdiyev, and Lyudmila Sukhostat. 2018. "Cyber-Physical Systems and Their Security Issues." *Computers in Industry* 100 (September): 212–23. https://doi.org/10.1016/J.COMPIND.2018.04.017

Al-Mhiqani, Mohammed Nasser, Rabiah Ahmad, Zaheera Zainal Abidin, Nabeel Salih Ali, and Karrar Hameed Abdulkareem. 2019. "Review of Cyber Attacks Classifications and Threats Analysis in Cyber-Physical Systems." *International Journal of Internet Technology and Secured Transactions* 9 (3): 282–98. https://doi.org/10.1504/IJITST.2019.101827

Al-Mhiqani, Mohammed Nasser, Rabiah Ahmad, Warusia Yassin, Aslinda Hassan, Zaheera Zainal Abidin, Nabeel Salih Ali, and Karrar Hameed Abdulkareem. 2018. "Cyber-Security Incidents: A Review Cases in Cyber-Physical Systems." *International Journal of Advanced Computer Science and Applications* 9 (1): 499–508. https://doi.org/10.14569/IJACSA.2018.090169

Duo, Wenli, MengChu Zhou, Abdullah Abusorrah, Wenli Duo, MengChu Zhou, and Abdullah Abusorrah. 2022. "A Survey of Cyber Attacks on Cyber Physical Systems: Recent Advances and Challenges." *IEEE/CAA Journal of Automatica Sinica* 9(5): 784–800. https://doi.org/10.1109/JAS.2022.105548

Dutta, Abir, and Shri Kant. 2020. "An Overview of Cyber Threat Intelligence Platform and Role of Artificial Intelligence and Machine Learning." *Lecture Notes in Computer Science (Including Subseries Lecture Notes in Artificial Intelligence and Lecture Notes in Bioinformatics)* 12553 LNCS: 81–86. https://doi.org/10.1007/978-3-030-65610-2_5/COVER

Geris, Sandra, and Hadis Karimipour. 2019. "Joint State Estimation and Cyber-Attack Detection Based on Feature Grouping." *Proceedings of 2019 the 7th International Conference on Smart Energy Grid Engineering, SEGE 2019*, August, 26–30. https://doi.org/10.1109/SEGE.2019.8859926

Ghanem, Waheed A.H.M., and Aman Jantan. 2020. "Training a Neural Network for Cyberattack Classification Applications Using Hybridization of an Artificial Bee Colony and Monarch Butterfly Optimization." *Neural Processing Letters* 51 (1): 905–46. https://doi.org/10.1007/S11063-019-10120-X/TABLES/16

Goh, Jonathan, Sridhar Adepu, Marcus Tan, and Zi Shan Lee. 2017. "Anomaly Detection in Cyber Physical Systems Using Recurrent Neural Networks." *Proceedings of IEEE International Symposium on High Assurance Systems Engineering*, April, 140–5. https://doi.org/10.1109/HASE.2017.36

Gupta, Rajesh, Sudeep Tanwar, Fadi Al-Turjman, Prit Italiya, Ali Nauman, and Sung Won Kim. 2020. "Smart Contract Privacy Protection Using AI in Cyber-Physical Systems: Tools, Techniques and Challenges." *IEEE Access* 8: 24746–72. https://doi.org/10.1109/ACCESS.2020.2970576

He, Qiyi, Xiaolin Meng, Rong Qu, and Ruijie Xi. 2020. "Machine Learning-Based Detection for Cyber Security Attacks on Connected and Autonomous Vehicles." *Mathematics* 8(8): 1311. https://doi.org/10.3390/MATH8081311

Humayed, Abdulmalik, Jingqiang Lin, Fengjun Li, and Bo Luo. 2017. "Cyber-Physical Systems Security - A Survey." *IEEE Internet of Things Journal* 4 (6): 1802–31. https://doi.org/10.1109/JIOT.2017.2703172

"Kaggle: Your Machine Learning and Data Science Community." n.d. Accessed April 8, 2023. https://www.kaggle.com/

Karnouskos, Stamatis. 2011. "Stuxnet Worm Impact on Industrial Cyber-Physical System Security." *IECON Proceedings (Industrial Electronics Conference)*, 4490–94. https://doi.org/10.1109/IECON.2011.6120048

Khalil, Shaymaa Mamdouh, Hayretdin Bahsi, Henry Ochieng' Dola, Tarmo Korõtko, Kieran McLaughlin, and Vahur Kotkas. 2023. "Threat Modeling of Cyber-Physical Systems - A Case Study of a Microgrid System." *Computers & Security* 124 (January): 102950. https://doi.org/10.1016/J.COSE.2022.102950

Khan, Riaz Ullah, Xiaosong Zhang, Mamoun Alazab, and Rajesh Kumar. 2019. "An Improved Convolutional Neural Network Model for Intrusion Detection in Networks." *Proceedings - 2019 Cybersecurity and Cyberforensics Conference, CCC 2019*, May, 74–77. https://doi.org/10.1109/CCC.2019.000-6

Kocabas, Ovunc, Tolga Soyata, and Mehmet K. Aktas. 2016. "Emerging Security Mechanisms for Medical Cyber Physical Systems." *IEEE/ACM Transactions on Computational Biology and Bioinformatics* 13 (3): 401–16. https://doi.org/10.1109/TCBB.2016.2520933

Kumar, Ashish, and Kakali Chatterjee. 2023. "A Lightweight Blockchain-Based Framework for Medical Cyber-Physical System." *Journal of Supercomputing*, March, 1–29. https://doi.org/10.1007/S11227-023-05133-2/TABLES/3

Kumar, Chetan, Sean Marston, and Ravi Sen. 2020. "Cyber-Physical Systems (CPS) Security: State of the Art and Research Opportunities for Information Systems Academics." *Communications of the Association for Information Systems* 47 (1): 36. https://doi.org/10.17705/1CAIS.04731

Lee, Yongjun, Hyun Kwon, Sang Hoon Choi, Seung Ho Lim, Sung Hoon Baek, and Ki Woong Park. 2019. "Instruction2vec: Efficient Preprocessor of Assembly Code to Detect Software Weakness with CNN." *Applied Sciences* 9 (19): 4086. https://doi.org/10.3390/APP9194086

Mallick, P. 2019. "Cyber Attack on Kudankulam Nuclear Power Plant – A Wake Up Call," no. September. https://www.researchgate.net/publication/344336074_Cyber_Attack_on_Kudankulam_Nuclear_Power_Plant_-_A_Wake_Up_Call

Meleshko, Alexey, Anton Shulepov, Vasily Desnitsky, Evgenia Novikova, and Igor Kotenko. 2022. "Visualization Assisted Approach to Anomaly and Attack Detection in Water Treatment Systems." *Water* 14 (15): 2342. https://doi.org/10.3390/W14152342

Mohindru, Vandana, Ravindara Bhatt, and Yashwant Singh. "Reauthentication Scheme for Mobile Wireless Sensor Networks." *Sustainable Computing: Informatics and Systems* 23 (2019): 158–66.

Mohindru, Vandana, Yashwant Singh, and Ravindara Bhatt. "Hybrid Cryptography Algorithm for Securing Wireless Sensor Networks from Node Clone Attack." *Recent Advances in Electrical & Electronic Engineering (Formerly Recent Patents on Electrical & Electronic Engineering)* 13, no. 2 (2020): 251–9.

Mohindru, Vandana, Sunidhi Vashishth, and Deepak Bathija. 2021. "Internet of Things (IoT) for healthcare systems: A comprehensive survey." *Recent Innovations in Computing: Proceedings of ICRIC* 1 (2022): 213–9.

Rouzbahani, Hossein Mohammadi, Hadis Karimipour, Abolfazl Rahimnejad, Ali Dehghantanha, and Gautam Srivastava. 2020. "Anomaly Detection in Cyber-Physical Systems Using Machine Learning." *Handbook of Big Data Privacy*, March, 219–35. https://doi.org/10.1007/978-3-030-38557-6_10

Sakhnini, Jacob, Hadis Karimipour, Ali Dehghantanha, and Reza M. Parizi. 2020. "AI and Security of Critical Infrastructure." *Handbook of Big Data Privacy*, March, 7–36. https://doi.org/10.1007/978-3-030-38557-6_2/COVER

Sheikh, Zakir Ahmad, Yashwant Singh, Pradeep Kumar Singh, and Kayhan Zrar Ghafoor. 2022. "Intelligent and Secure Framework for Critical Infrastructure (CPS): Current Trends, Challenges, and Future Scope." *Computer Communications* 193 (September): 302–31. https://doi.org/10.1016/J.COMCOM.2022.07.007

Singh, Sunil, Neha Yadav, and Pawan Kumar Chuarasia. 2020. "A Review on Cyber Physical System Attacks: Issues and Challenges." *Proceedings of the 2020 IEEE International Conference on Communication and Signal Processing, ICCSP 2020*, July, 1133–38. https://doi.org/10.1109/ICCSP48568.2020.9182452

Tan, Yawen, Pindi Weng, Bo Chen, and Li Yu. 2023. "Nonlinear Fusion Estimation for False Data Injection Attack Signals in Cyber-Physical Systems." *Science China Information Sciences* 66 (7): 1–2. https://doi.org/10.1007/S11432-021-3428-Y/METRICS

Vinayakumar, R., Mamoun Alazab, K. P. Soman, Prabaharan Poornachandran, and Sitalakshmi Venkatraman. 2019. "Robust Intelligent Malware Detection Using Deep Learning." *IEEE Access* 7: 46717–38. https://doi.org/10.1109/ACCESS.2019.2906934

Wu, Mingtao, Zhengyi Song, and Young B. Moon. 2019. "Detecting Cyber-Physical Attacks in CyberManufacturing Systems with Machine Learning Methods." *Journal of Intelligent Manufacturing* 30 (3): 1111–23. https://doi.org/10.1007/S10845-017-1315-5/TABLES/4

Yaacoub, Jean Paul A., Ola Salman, Hassan N. Noura, Nesrine Kaaniche, Ali Chehab, and Mohamad Malli. 2020. "Cyber-Physical Systems Security: Limitations, Issues and Future Trends." *Microprocessors and Microsystems* 77 (September): 103201. https://doi.org/10.1016/J.MICPRO.2020.103201

Zhang, Dan, Qing Guo Wang, Gang Feng, Yang Shi, and Athanasios V. Vasilakos. 2021. "A Survey on Attack Detection, Estimation and Control of Industrial Cyber–Physical Systems." *ISA Transactions* 116 (October): 1–16. https://doi.org/10.1016/J.ISATRA.2021.01.036

Section IV

Machine Learning for Cyber-Physical Systems

8 A Machine Learning–Based Smart Framework for Intrusion Detection in Cyber-Physical Systems

Hitakshi and Vandana Mohindru Sood

Chitkara University Institute of Engineering & Technology, Chitkara University, Punjab, India

Kapil Mehta and Gurleen Kaur

Chandigarh Group of Colleges, Punjab, India

8.1 INTRODUCTION

Cyber-physical systems (CPS) are rapidly developing as an innovative and interdisciplinary field that combines the power of computation with physical components. These integrated systems have an extraordinary ability to sense, analyze, and respond to their immediate physical surroundings (Zia et al. 2019) By linking the digital and physical domains, CPSs have the potential to transform various industries, including transportation, healthcare, manufacturing, and energy management (Qu et al. 2019).

CPS seamlessly integrates software, hardware, and physical processes, ushering forth a new era of intelligent systems (Zia et al. 2019). Through advancements in sensors, actuators, communication networks, and embedded systems, CPS creates integrated ecosystems that interact with their surroundings in real time. This combination of physical systems and computational intelligence provides CPS with improved management, automation, and decision-making capabilities.

CPS offers a wide range of uses. In transportation, CPS paves the way for autonomous vehicles, intelligent traffic management, and efficient logistics. In healthcare, CPS enables remote patient monitoring, wearable devices, and personalized medicine. In industrial settings, CPS facilitates smart manufacturing, predictive maintenance, and energy-efficient operations (Zhang et al. 2018). However, designing and implementing CPS present unique challenges. Ensuring reliability, security, privacy, and interoperability is a critical consideration in CPS development (Hoque et al. 2020).

DOI: 10.1201/9781003406105-12

In order to develop secure and dependable CPS solutions, scientists and technicians are actively investigating rigorous methodology, standards, and cutting-edge approaches.

Improvements in artificial intelligence, machine learning, and edge computing hold great potential for the future of CPS (Hossain et al. 2018). These scientific advances enable autonomous systems, smart cities, and seamless Internet of Things (IoT) integration, significantly enhancing CPS's potential (Moin et al. 2022). CPS has the potential to restructure sectors, optimize resource use, and improve the standard of living for people and society as they continue to develop (Hoque et al. 2020).

The risk of cyberthreats and invasions is growing more serious as CPS becomes more complex and interdependent (Hossain et al. 2018). As a result, researchers and practitioners are focusing on how machine learning techniques might be used to create smart frameworks for CPS's intrusion detection system (IDS, Fernandes et al. 2020).

Smarter architectures for intrusion detection in CPS that are based on machine learning leverage the power of cutting-edge algorithms to find and stop potential security breaches. To analyze huge amounts of data gathered from sensors, actuators, and network devices integrated into CPS, these frameworks make use of machine learning models (Virdis et al. 2019).

Machine learning algorithms can efficiently identify and highlight suspicious activity suggestive of future intrusions or security breaches by identifying anomalies and patterns within this data (Jamal et al. 2023).

There are various benefits to using machine learning for intrusion detection. As a result of ongoing learning and updating of its detection skills, it enables CPS to dynamically respond to changing cyber threats and shifting settings (Zhang et al. 2018). Large and complex data sets are processed expertly by machine learning models, enabling in-the-moment analysis and reaction to any security incidents.

Machine learning–based intrusion detection systems also have the appealing advantage of being able to recognize previously unknown or unique attack patterns (Khan et al. 2018).

A number of crucial steps must be taken in order to develop a machine learning–based smart framework for intrusion detection in CPS. These include gathering and preparing data, extracting features, training models, and deploying trained models inside the CPS environment. It is essential to continuously monitor and assess the model's performance to guarantee its efficacy and adaptability throughout time (Madani et al. 2022).

Organizations are given the ability to increase the security and resilience of their systems through the integration of machine learning–based intrusion detection frameworks within CPS (Almajed et al. 2022). These frameworks are essential for quickly seeing and responding to suspected intrusions or abnormalities, which reduces the effect of cyberattacks on CPS infrastructure and prevents potential harm or interruptions (Hoque et al. 2020).

The usefulness of the intrusion detection system in detecting disruptions and guaranteeing network security is well known. By achieving a balance between high detection accuracy and low false-positive rates, traffic reliability can be increased (Hawawreh et al. 2018).

To handle the complexity of vast data, machine learning (ML) algorithms play a pivotal role in delivering robust solutions. These ML techniques swiftly predict information patterns and perform consecutive numerical analyses to provide consistent and reliable decisions. Notably, various ML techniques, including Decision Trees (DT), K-Nearest-Neighbors (KNN), Support Vector Machine (SVM), Random Forest (RF), Naive Bayes (NB), Multi-Layered Perceptions (MLP), Artificial Neural Networks (ANN), and other algorithms, have been effectively applied for detecting malicious activities within networks (Chkirbene et al. 2020).

In one particular study (Yang et al. 2019), the authors proposed a neural network classifier leveraging the Levenberg–Marquardt (LM) algorithm and the Backpropagation (BP) algorithm for anomaly detection in the KDD CUP 99 dataset. The results demonstrated remarkable efficiency, with the proposed method achieving a detection rate of 93.31% and a false alarm rate of only 1.34% under the LM–BP algorithm. This success highlights the potential of using ML-based techniques in IDS to bolster network security and ensure prompt detection of anomalous activities (Sharma and Shandilya 2023).

Overall, the combination of powerful IDS capabilities and the strategic application of ML algorithms offers a promising approach to safeguarding network infrastructures from potential intrusions and threats (Akintade et al. 2023). The continuous advancement and optimization of ML techniques hold the key to further improving intrusion detection accuracy and efficiency in modern network environments.

This chapter delves into the concept of leveraging machine learning for developing smart frameworks dedicated to intrusion detection within CPS. It explores the underlying principles, techniques, challenges, and potential benefits associated with such frameworks. By embracing intrusion detection solutions driven by machine learning, CPSs can fortify their defenses against a wide array of cyber threats, safeguard critical infrastructure, and ensure the secure operation of interconnected systems in today's digitized landscape. Through a comprehensive understanding of these machine learning–driven intrusion detection frameworks, organizations can proactively navigate the complex cybersecurity landscape and protect the integrity of their cyber-physical systems (Sahin and Muheidat 2022).

8.2 RELATED WORKS

Here are some of the benefits and drawbacks of various machine learning models, taking into account the previously mentioned conditions. Table 8.1 is about the various related work done by the researchers till now.

Table 8.2 mentions some of the accuracies of various machine learning models applied in intrusion detection of CPS and gives us a clear picture of what kind of algorithm works better for the same.

8.3 CYBER-PHYSICAL SYSTEM (CPS)

In a cyber-physical system, sensors are tasked with acquiring data from the physical environment. On the other hand, actuators are responsible for effecting changes and controlling the physical aspects of the system. The CPS relies on communication

TABLE 8.1
Related Work

References	Model	Advantage	Disadvantage
Crescitelli et al. (2008)	Decision Tree	Easy to interpret and handle both numerical and categorical data. Suitable for real-time decision-making.	Prone to overfitting when the tree depth becomes excessive, limiting generalization.
Crescitelli et al. (2008)	Random Forest	Combines multiple decision trees, reducing overfitting and improving accuracy. Effective for handling high-dimensional CPS data.	Computationally more expensive compared to individual decision trees.
Crescitelli et al. (2008)	Support Vector Machine (SVM)	Can handle complex decision boundaries, suitable for classifying nonlinear CPS data.	Requires extensive parameter tuning and may be memory intensive for large CPS datasets.
Crescitelli et al. (2008)	Neural Network	Can model complex relationships and learn intricate patterns in CPS data, suitable for applications like anomaly detection and predictive maintenance.	Require significant amounts of data and computational resources for training.
Umer et al. (2022)	Gradient Boosting Machine (GBM)	High predictive accuracy and the ability to handle heterogeneous CPS data effectively.	Prone to overfitting if not tuned properly.
Umer et al. (2022)	Long Short-Term Memory (LSTM) Networks	Particularly effective for sequential CPS data, such as time series sensor readings, due to their ability to maintain the memory of past information.	Computationally expensive and requires careful hyperparameter tuning.
Umer et al. (2022)	Gaussian Mixture Models (GMM)	Suitable for unsupervised learning in CPS, enabling anomaly detection and clustering of CPS data.	Assumes that CPS data is generated from a mixture of Gaussian distributions, which may not always hold true.
Crescitelli et al. (2008)	K-Nearest Neighbors (KNN)	Simple and easy to implement for CPS datasets with low dimensionality and small sizes.	Computationally expensive for large CPS datasets, as distance calculations increase with data size.
Crescitelli et al. (2008)	Reinforcement Learning Models	Suitable for CPS scenarios where an agent interacts with the environment, enabling autonomous decision-making and control.	Requires extensive exploration and learning time, which can be a limitation in time-critical CPS applications.

TABLE 8.2
Accuracy of Different Algorithms

Models	Accuracy	References
Neural Network	99.2%	Umer et al. (2022)
Support Vector Machine (SVM)	98.7%	Umer et al. (2022)
GBM	98.5%	Umer et al. (2022)
Decision Tree	97.8%	Umer et al. (2022)
Random Forest	96.28%	Do Xuan et al. (2020)

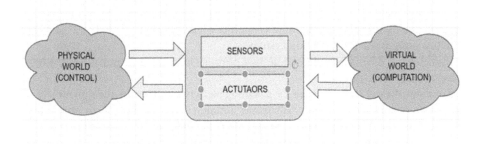

FIGURE 8.1   Classic CPS architecture.

networks to establish connections between sensors, actuators, and other CPS components (Kumar and Kumar 2019). Computational resources play a pivotal role in processing the vast amount of sensor data and orchestrating the precise control of actuators. Figure 8.1 depicts a classic CPS architecture.

Various CPS architectures are commonly employed to design complex systems with different requirements. The following are some of the most popular CPS architectures:

- **Layered Architecture**: In CPS, the layered architecture is the framework that is most frequently employed (Hoque et al. 2020). It is made up of three unique layers: The sensing layer, which is in charge of gathering data from the physical environment; the processing layer, where data is processed and analyzed; and the actuating layer, which is in charge of regulating and modifying the physical environment.
- **Architectural Hierarchy**: The CPS design is made more difficult by the hierarchical architecture. It has several levels, each of which is responsible for particular functions and duties (Hoque et al. 2020). These layers have a hierarchical structure, with each layer building on the features of the levels below it.
- **Distributed design**: In a distributed design, different nodes house the CPS components (Zhang et al. 2021). This architecture enables a better fault tolerance and a more decentralized approach to system design.

- **Cloud-Based Architecture**: The CPS components are hosted in the cloud in a cloud-based architecture (Zhang et al. 2021). This architecture offers scalable and flexible solutions by utilizing cloud computing capabilities, making it appropriate for CPS applications with various computational demands.

The best CPS architecture to use will rely on the particular requirements and restrictions of the system being designed. Each of these CPS designs offers advantages and disadvantages.

8.4 INTRUSION DETECTION

By attaining a combination of high detection accuracy and low false-positive rates, the intrusion detection system is well acclaimed for its efficiency in spotting interruptions and assuring network traffic reliability (Hawawreh et al. 2018). Figure 8.2 depicts a basic intrusion detection system.

In the realm of intrusion detection, two primary architectures prevail: Signature-based and anomaly-based.

Signature-based IDSs operate by scanning network traffic for recognizable patterns of known attack signatures. Whenever a match is found, the IDS promptly triggers an alarm, alerting the security personnel to the presence of a known threat.

Conversely, anomaly-based IDSs take a different approach, where they continuously assess the ongoing system activity against a baseline of normal behavior. If the current activity substantially deviates from this established baseline, the IDS immediately raises an alarm, indicating a potential intrusion or abnormal behavior that merits investigation (Mohindru et al. 2020).

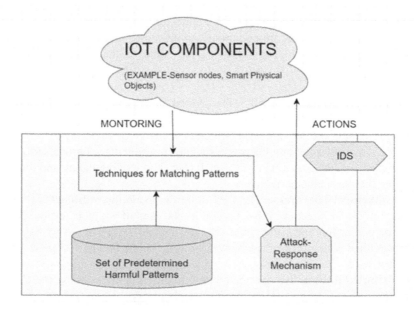

FIGURE 8.2 Basic intrusion detection system.

The efficacy of signature-based IDSs is better than that of anomaly-based IDSs, which makes them ideal for quick detection and reaction to established assault patterns. The vulnerability of signature-based IDSs to evasion by attackers using fresh or previously unidentified attack signatures, however, is a serious drawback. Any innovative assault without a corresponding signature can go undetected in these systems since they rely on preset patterns to identify threats, leaving the system open to possible dangers (Mohindru et al. 2019).

On the other hand, Anomaly-based IDSs adopt a more sophisticated approach by continuously monitoring and comparing the ongoing system activity against a baseline of normal behavior. This makes them resilient against new and previously unseen attacks since they don't rely on predefined signatures (Ebere et al. 2021). However, this advantage comes with a trade-off, as anomaly-based IDSs are more prone to generating false alarms. The complexity of distinguishing genuine anomalies from benign deviations in behavior can result in a higher rate of false positives, potentially leading to alert fatigue and decreased efficiency in threat response (Hossain et al. 2018).

Regarding intrusion detection architectures, there are several common types:

- **Host-based IDSs**: These IDSs focus on monitoring individual hosts (servers and workstations) for indications of malicious activities or potential security breaches (Alam and Khan 2021). They provide a granular level of monitoring, making them suitable for protecting critical assets residing on specific hosts.
- **Network-based IDSs**: These IDSs concentrate on monitoring network traffic for signs of malicious behavior. They are often deployed at strategic points within the network infrastructure, such as gateways or switches, to scrutinize incoming and outgoing traffic for threats affecting the entire network (Alam and Khan 2021).
- **Hierarchical IDSs**: Combining the strengths of host-based and network-based IDSs, hierarchical IDSs offer a comprehensive security view of the system. By integrating both types of IDSs, organizations can achieve a multilayered defense strategy, where network-based IDSs protect the network perimeter, while host-based IDSs focus on safeguarding critical internal assets.

Selecting the most appropriate intrusion detection architecture hinges on the specific application and security requirements of the organization. For instance, a host-based IDS might be implemented to protect a high-value server, while a network-based IDS might be employed to safeguard the overall network and its gateways. Careful consideration of the system's components, potential threats, and desired level of coverage is vital in determining the optimal intrusion detection approach.

8.5 MACHINE LEARNING

Machine learning is a subset of artificial intelligence that encompasses the development and application of algorithms and statistical models enabling computer systems to learn from data, identify patterns, and make decisions without explicit programming. The core concept behind machine learning is to utilize data-driven approaches, where algorithms extract meaningful insights from examples and experiences, allowing them to adapt and improve their performance over time (Mitchell 1997).

Machine learning has emerged as a powerful tool with numerous applications across various domains, such as computer vision, natural language processing, data mining, robotics, and more. Its success heavily relies on robust data collection, suitable algorithm selection, and efficient model evaluation and optimization. Figure 8.3 shows a classic neural network depiction of a machine learning algorithm.

Machine learning encompasses a diverse array of models, each possessing unique characteristics and applications to tackle various problem domains. Following are several commonly utilized types of machine learning models along with their respective applications:

a) **Supervised Learning Models**: In supervised learning, algorithms are trained on labeled data, with each input example paired with its corresponding target output.

The algorithms learn how to transform inputs into outputs and make predictions on new, unanticipated data based on the patterns uncovered in the training data.
- Linear Regression: Employed for regression problems, it predicts continuous numeric values based on input variables.
- Logistic Regression: Applied to binary classification problems, it estimates the probability of an instance belonging to a particular class.

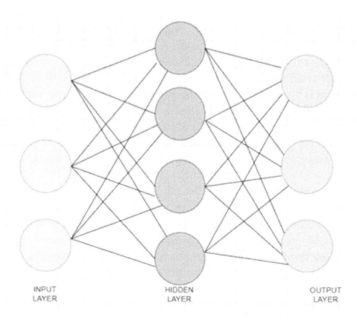

FIGURE 8.3   Neural network.

- Decision Trees: Nonlinear models that partition data using a hierarchical series of decisions, applicable to both regression and classification tasks.
- Random Forest: Ensemble models that amalgamate multiple decision trees to improve prediction accuracy and handle complex data.
- Support Vector Machines (SVM): Effective for both linear and nonlinear classification problems by creating decision boundaries between classes (Hastie et al. 2009).

b) Unsupervised Learning Models: Unsupervised learning involves training algorithms on unlabeled data, seeking to discover inherent structures, patterns, or groupings within the data. These algorithms aim to find representations that best capture the data's underlying characteristics.

- K-means Clustering: Organizes similar data points into clusters based on their proximity or similarity (Hastie et al. 2009).
- Hierarchical Clustering: Divides data into a hierarchical tree-like structure of nested clusters, relying on similarities for grouping.
- Gaussian Mixture Models (GMM): Probability-based models that assume data points are generated from a mixture of Gaussian distributions.
- Principal Component Analysis (PCA): Diminishes data dimensionality while retaining crucial features for subsequent analysis.

c) Neural Networks:

- Feedforward Neural Networks: Comprising interconnected layers of nodes (neurons), these networks process information in a unidirectional flow. They excel in complex tasks such as image recognition and natural language processing.
- Convolutional Neural Networks (CNNs): Specifically designed for visual data analysis, CNNs exhibit exceptional performance in image classification and object detection.
- Recurrent Neural Networks (RNNs): Proficient in sequential data analysis, RNNs maintain an internal memory to process data with temporal dependencies, commonly utilized in speech recognition and natural language processing.
- Long Short-Term Memory (LSTM): A variant of RNN that addresses the vanishing gradient problem, making it well-suited for tasks requiring the modeling of longer-term dependencies (Bishop 2006).

d) Reinforcement Learning Models: In reinforcement learning, algorithms interact with an environment and receive feedback in the form of rewards or penalties based on their actions. The goal is to learn optimal strategies that maximize the cumulative reward over time (Sutton and Barto 2018).

- Q-Learning: A value-based model that learns through exploration and exploitation to maximize cumulative rewards in a given environment.
- Deep Q-Networks (DQNs): Combining reinforcement learning with deep neural networks, DQNs handle complex environments and high-dimensional state spaces.
- Policy Gradient Methods: Directly learns policies by optimizing the expected cumulative reward, suitable for continuous action spaces.

e) Semi-Supervised Learning Models: This approach combines elements of both supervised and unsupervised learning. It leverages a mix of labeled and unlabeled data during training, enabling the algorithm to benefit from the labeled data while also exploring the patterns within the unlabeled data.

Integrating aspects of supervised and unsupervised learning, these models leverage limited labeled data alongside a larger pool of unlabeled data to enhance overall performance (Goodfellow et al. 2016).

While these examples provide a glimpse into the realm of machine learning models, it's important to note that numerous variations and hybrid models exist. The selection of a specific model depends on factors such as the problem's nature, the availability of labeled data, the complexity of the data, and the desired task or output to be accomplished. The versatility of machine learning offers a vast landscape of possibilities for solving real-world challenges across a wide range of domains.

8.6 MACHINE LEARNING–BASED FRAMEWORK FOR INTRUSION DETECTION IN CPS

A machine learning–based smart framework for intrusion detection in cyber-physical systems (CPS) encompasses a comprehensive architecture that harmonizes various components to detect and mitigate potential security breaches. This architecture integrates data collection, preprocessing, feature extraction, model training, real-time monitoring, and adaptive feedback loops to enable effective intrusion detection within CPS. Let's explore each component in detail:

- **Data gathering**: The CPS environment is made up of sensors, actuators, and network devices that gather a variety of data about system behavior, network activity, and environmental parameters. These gadgets record real-time data that is crucial for intrusion detection, such as sensor readings, network packet data, and system logs.
- **Preprocessing**: To make the raw data from the CPS collection appropriate for analysis, preprocessing is applied to the data. Data cleaning, normalization, feature scaling, and handling missing values are all preprocessing approaches. This step ensures that the data is properly prepared for subsequent analysis and model training.
- **Feature Extraction**: To capture meaningful patterns and characteristics, relevant features are extracted from the preprocessed data. Feature extraction techniques may involve statistical analysis, time-series analysis, frequency domain analysis, or domain-specific feature engineering. This process enhances the representation of the data, enabling the subsequent machine learning algorithms to detect intrusions effectively.
- **Model Training**: Machine learning algorithms are applied to train intrusion detection models using labeled data. Supervised learning techniques, such as decision trees, support vector machines, or neural networks, are commonly employed in this stage. The data is split into training and validation

sets, and model parameters are optimized to achieve the best performance. Evaluation metrics such as accuracy, precision, recall, and F1 score are utilized to assess the model's effectiveness.

- **Intrusion deployment**: Following model training, the machine learning–based intrusion detection system is implemented for real-time intrusion detection. The model operates by continuously analyzing incoming data, encompassing network traffic and system logs, in order to swiftly identify potential intrusions or anomalies within the cyber-physical system (CPS) environment. The model's dynamic analysis ensures timely responses to any security threats that may arise (Mezzour et al. 2021). Depending on the specific use case, the model exhibits the capability to classify network traffic as either malicious or benign, thereby distinguishing between normal and suspicious activities (Gümüşbaş et al. 2020). Moreover, in the event of detected anomalies within the CPS, the model can generate timely alerts, promptly notifying relevant stakeholders for swift action and mitigation.

- **Model Deployment**: To carry out real-time monitoring and detection, the trained intrusion detection model is deployed into the CPS environment. The model can be disseminated across multiple CPS components or given centrally, depending on the CPS design. To detect anomalies and potential intrusions, the model continuously examines incoming data from sensors, network traffic, and system records.

- **Real-time Tracking and Warning**: The installed model continuously analyses the CPS environment for any unusual or suspicious activity. When an anomaly or potential intrusion is discovered, the system sends alerts or messages to the appropriate stakeholders, such as system administrators or security staff. These notifications provide timely responses and allow for rapid mitigation of found dangers.

- **Model Evaluation and Updating**: The performance measures of the intrusion detection model's accuracy, precision, recall, and overall efficacy are checked and updated on a regular basis. The outcomes of the study assisted in updating and improving the model by exposing any potential shortcomings or limitations. To respond to changing threats, modifications in CPS behavior, or the advent of new attack vectors, models may need to be retrained.

- **Feedback Loop**: The intrusion detection system includes a feedback loop mechanism that makes use of data from identified occurrences, erroneous positive results, or fresh attack patterns. The feedback is used to improve the intrusion detection model's capabilities, accuracy, and ability to respond to new cyber threats. The intrusion detection architecture is kept current and effective by the process of continual learning.

By following this comprehensive architecture, a machine learning–based smart framework for intrusion detection in CPS can effectively identify and mitigate potential security breaches. This framework safeguards the integrity and resilience of interconnected CPS infrastructures, bolstering the security measures required to protect critical systems in the face of evolving cyber threats.

8.7 KEY FACTORS TO CONSIDER

In the realm of machine learning model selection, several crucial considerations arise, impacting the choice of the most appropriate model for a given application. These considerations include data availability, computational resources, and accuracy requirements.

- **Data Availability**: The quantity and quality of available data significantly influence the choice of machine learning models. Complex models, such as neural networks, often demand large datasets for effective training and generalization. In scenarios where data is limited or sparse, opting for a simpler model might yield more reliable results. Simpler models are good options for contexts with limited resources since they can perform satisfactorily with less datasets.
- **Computational Resources**: Machine learning models can have high computational needs, especially for more intricate structures like deep neural networks. Such models might require a lot of computing power and memory to train and deploy (Bakirtzis et al 2020). It makes sense to favor simpler models with lower computational cost when available computational resources are limited. With less complexity, efficient algorithms can nevertheless produce acceptable outcomes without taxing the resources at hand.
- **Accuracy Requirements**: One of the most important factors affecting the complexity of the model is the needed level of accuracy for a particular application. High accuracy demands frequently call for the deployment of more complex models that can accurately depict complex patterns and relationships in the data (Bakirtzis et al 2020). Complex models are better suited to handle complex tasks and produce superior accuracy, such as ensemble approaches or deep learning architectures. On the other hand, less sophisticated models' simplicity and speed may be advantageous for applications with less demanding accuracy requirements (Alom, M. Z., et al. 2019).

In conclusion, choosing a machine learning model involves striking a delicate balance between the need for accuracy, the availability of data, and the processing resources.

For applications with abundant data and substantial computational capabilities, sophisticated models like neural networks can be advantageous. However, in scenarios with limited data, constrained resources, or moderate accuracy demands, simpler models can be more practical and still deliver reliable results. By thoughtfully assessing these technical factors, practitioners can make well-informed decisions in choosing the most suitable machine learning model for their specific use case.

8.8 CONCLUSION

The application of machine learning for intrusion detection in cyber-physical systems (CPS) offers huge potential to increase networked system security and robustness. Through the application of advanced algorithms, machine learning–based smart frameworks can effectively evaluate data obtained from CPS sensors, actuators, and network devices, allowing the identification and mitigation of any security breaches. These frameworks' advantages include their capacity to react to evolving threats, undertake real-time analysis, and recognize previously unreported attack patterns.

CPS's ability to identify intrusions can be improved by employing a range of machine learning methods, including as supervised learning, unsupervised learning, neural networks, and reinforcement learning. These models, which include deep neural networks and Q-learning as well as decision trees and linear regression, are intended to accommodate a wide range of CPS scenarios and system requirements.

Collecting data, preprocessing, extracting features, model training, and real-time monitoring are just a few of the time-consuming steps involved in developing and deploying machine learning–based smart frameworks for intrusion detection in CPS. The framework's effectiveness and adaptability are ensured over time by continuous evaluation, model updates, and feedback systems that keep up with emerging cyber threats and changes in CPS behavior.

Beyond the detection of intrusions, machine learning has implications for CPS. Intelligent decision-making, automation, and optimization of CPS operations can assist the transportation, healthcare, manufacturing, and energy management industries. As CPS evolves and becomes more interconnected, the necessity for dependable and secure machine learning–based solutions grows. Lastly, sophisticated frameworks based on machine learning for CPS intrusion detection show tremendous potential for preserving the integrity and security of connected systems. CPS can proactively detect and mitigate security breaches by leveraging the power of cutting-edge algorithms and data analysis, ensuring the reliable and safe operation of critical infrastructure. Continuous research and advancements in machine learning techniques, as well as ongoing efforts to address challenges related to reliability, privacy, and interoperability, will improve the effectiveness of machine learning in CPS intrusion detection, propelling the development of intelligent and secure cyber-physical systems.

REFERENCES

Akintade, Sesan, Seongtae Kim, and Kaushik Roy. "Explaining Machine Learning-Based Feature Selection of IDS for IoT and CPS Devices." In *IFIP International Conference on Artificial Intelligence Applications and Innovations*, pp. 69–80. Springer Nature Switzerland, 2023.

Alam, A., and Khan, M. K. "Intrusion Detection Techniques for Network Security: A Comprehensive Survey." *In Proceedings of the International Conference on Computational Intelligence*, pp. 389–397. Springer, Singapore, 2021.

Almajed, Rasha, Amer Ibrahim, Abedallah Zaid Abualkishik, Nahia Mourad, and Faris A. Almansour. "Using Machine Learning Algorithm for Detection of Cyber-Attacks in Cyber Physical Systems." *Periodicals of Engineering and Natural Sciences* 10, no. 3 (2022): 261–275.

Alom, M. Z., et al. "A state-of-the-art Survey on Deep Learning Theory and Architectures." *Electronics* 8, no. 3 (2019): 292.

Bakirtzis, Georgios, Garrett Ward, Christopher Deloglos, Carl Elks, Barry Horowitz, and Cody Fleming. "Fundamental challenges of cyber-physical systems security modeling." In *2020 50th Annual IEEE-IFIP International Conference on Dependable Systems and Networks-Supplemental Volume (DSN-S)*, pp. 33–36. IEEE, 2020.

Bishop, C. M. *Pattern Recognition and Machine Learning*. Springer, 2006.

Chkirbene, Z., Erbad, A., Hamila, R., Mohamed, A., Guizani, M., and Hamdi, M. "TIDCS: A Dynamic Intrusion Detection and Classification System Based Feature Selection." *IEEE Access* 8 (2020): 95864–95877.

Crescitelli, A., M. Consales, A. Cutolo, A. Cusano, M. Penza, P. Aversa, and M. Giordano. "Novel Sensitive Nanocoatings Based on SWCNT Composites for Advanced Fiber Optic Chemo-Sensors." In *Sensors, 2008 IEEE*, pp. 965–968. IEEE, 2008.

Do Xuan, Cho, Hoa Dinh Nguyen, and Victor Nikolaevich Tisenko. "Malicious URL Detection Based on Machine Learning." *International Journal of Advanced Computer Science and Applications* 11, no. 1 (2020). DOI:10.14569/ijacsa.2020.0110119

Ebere, Ohuabunwa Augustine, Icheke Led, Ukaegbu ThankGod Ekene, Dilibe Godson Chijioke, and Kadiri Ramotu Ochuwa. "A Comprehensive Review of Intrusion Detection System Approach and Technique." *International Journal of Advances in Engineering and Management (IJAEM)* 3, no. 12 (2021): 70–81.

Fernandes, E., Soares, L., and Viegas, V. "A Survey on Machine Learning Approaches for Intrusion Detection Systems." *Journal of Information Security and Applications* 50 (2020): 102421.

Goodfellow, I., Bengio, Y., and Courville, A. *Deep Learning*. MIT Press, 2016.

Gümüşbas, D., Yıldırım, T., Genovese, A., & Scotti, F. "A comprehensive survey of databases and deep learning methods for cybersecurity and intrusion detection systems." *IEEE Systems Journal*, 15, no. 2 (2020): 1717–1731.

Hastie, T., Tibshirani, R., and Friedman, J. H. *The Elements of Statistical Learning: Data Mining, Inference, and Prediction*. Springer Science & Business Media, 2009.

Hawawreh, M. A., Moustafa, N., and Sitnikova, E. "Identification of malicious activities in industrial internet of things based on deep learning models." *Journal of Information Security and Applications* 41 (2018): 1–11.

Hoque, K. A., Kim, H. J., Kim, J. B., and Moon, Y. S. "Machine Learning in Cyber Physical Systems: A Survey." *ACM Computing Surveys* 53, no. 3 (2020).

Hossain, M. S., Hasan, M. M., Almogren, A., Alkhalifa, M. A., and Alelaiwi, A. "Machine Learning-Based Intrusion Detection Systems for Critical Infrastructures in Cyber Physical Systems." *IEEE Access* 6 (2018): 39629–39648.

Jamal, Alshaibi Ahmed, Al-Ani Mustafa Majid, Anton Konev, Tatiana Kosachenko, and Alexander Shelupanov. "A Review on Security Analysis of Cyber Physical Systems using Machine learning." *Materials Today: Proceedings* 80 (2023): 2302–2306.

Khan, N., Hayat, S., Gani, A., and Ghani, A. "A Survey of Machine Learning Techniques for Malware Detection." *Information Sciences* 467 (2018): 445–464.

Kumar, Gurpreet, and Rajeev Kumar. "A Survey on Planar Ultra-Wideband Antennas with Band Notch Characteristics: Principle, Design, and Applications." *AEU-International Journal of Electronics and Communications* 109 (2019): 76–98.

Madani, Hafidi Mohamed, Meriem Djezzar, Hemam Mounir, Ahmed Seghir Zianou, and Moufida Maimour. "Semantic Models and Machine Learning Approach in CPS: A Survey." In *SIoT-2022: International Workshop on Semantic IoT, Co-located with the KGSWC-2022*, November 21–23, 2022, Madrid, Spain, pp. 130–149.

Mezzour, G., and Erritali, M. "A Survey of Intrusion Detection Techniques." *International Journal of Communication Networks and Information Security (IJCNIS)* 13, no. 1 (2021): 26–35.

Mitchell, T. M. *Machine Learning*. McGraw-Hill, 1997.

Mohindru, Vandana, Ravindara Bhatt, and Yashwant Singh. "Reauthentication Scheme for Mobile Wireless Sensor Networks." *Sustainable Computing: Informatics and Systems* 23 (2019): 158–166.

Mohindru, Vandana, Yashwant Singh, and Ravindara Bhatt. "Securing Wireless Sensor Networks from Node Clone Attack: A Lightweight Message Authentication Algorithm." *International Journal of Information and Computer Security* 12, no. 2–3 (2020): 217–233.

Moin, Armin, Moharram Challenger, Atta Badii, and Stephan Günnemann. "A Model-Driven Approach to Machine Learning and Software Modeling for the IoT: Generating Full Source Code for Smart Internet of Things (IoT) Services and Cyber-Physical Systems (CPS)." *Software and Systems Modeling* 21, no. 3 (2022): 987–1014.

Qu, Y., Zhu, M., Xu, X., Tang, Y., Zhang, Y., and Li, H. "Deep Learning for Industrial Big Data Analytics in Cyber-Physical Systems." *IEEE Transactions on Industrial Informatics* 15, no. 5 (2019): 3197–3206.

Sahin, Muammer Eren, and Fadi Muheidat. "The Security Concerns on Cyber-Physical Systems and Potential Risks Analysis Using Machine Learning." *Procedia Computer Science* 201 (2022): 527–534.

Sharma, Durgesh M., and Shishir Kumar Shandilya. "Attack Detection Based on Machine Learning Techniques to Safe and Secure for CPS—A Review." In *International Conference on IoT, Intelligent Computing and Security: Select Proceedings of IICS 2021*, pp. 273–286. Singapore: Springer Nature Singapore, 2023.

Sutton, Richard S., and Andrew G. Barto. *Reinforcement Learning: An introduction*. MIT press, 2018.

Umer, Muhammad, Saima Sadiq, Hanen Karamti, Reemah M. Alhebshi, Khaled Alnowaiser, Ala'Abdulmajid Eshmawi, Houbing Song, and Imran Ashraf. "Deep Learning-Based Intrusion Detection Methods in Cyber-Physical Systems: Challenges and Future Trends." *Electronics* 11, no. 20 (2022): 3326.

Virdis, A., Fiorucci, F., Sangiovanni-Vincentelli, A. L., and Lovera, M. "Machine Learning for Cyber-Physical Systems: A Survey." *Proceedings of the IEEE* 107, no. 3 (2019): 508–522.

Yang, A., Zhuansun, Y., Liu, C., Li, J., and Zhang, C. "Design of Intrusion Detection System for Internet of Things Based on Improved BP Neural Network." *IEEE Access* 7 (2019): 106043–106052.

Zhang, Xiaoran, Kantilal Pitambar Rane, Ismail Kakaravada, and Mohammad Shabaz. "Research on Vibration Monitoring and Fault Diagnosis of Rotating Machinery Based on Internet of Things Technology." *Nonlinear Engineering* 10, no. 1 (2021): 245–254.

Zhang, Y., Xiao, Y., Li, C., Li, F., Chen, J., and Huang, F. "A Survey of Intrusion Detection Systems: Techniques and Challenges for Cyber-Physical Systems." *Future Generation Computer Systems* 78 (2018): 1055–1068.

Zia, M. A., Abbasi, A., Tariq, S., and Raza, M. A. "Machine Learning-Based Intrusion Detection Techniques for Cyber Physical Systems: A Review." *IEEE Access* 7 (2019): 22832–22845.

9 Machine Learning Techniques for Real-Time Concept Drift Detection in Industrial Cyber-Physical Systems

Sangeeta Arora
KIET Group of Institutions, India

Sushil Kumar Narang
Chitkara University Institute of Engineering & Technology,
Chitkara University, Punjab India

9.1 INTRODUCTION

Transportation, electricity grids, healthcare, and manufacturing are just a few of the important infrastructure systems that currently depend on cyber-physical systems (CPS). Greater efficiency, precision, and comfort are provided by these systems' seamless integration of physical and computational components. To regulate and continuously monitor physical processes, CPS makes use of sophisticated hardware, software, sensor networks, and communication protocols. These systems generate vast amounts of data that need to be processed and looked at right away in order to maintain their dependability and safety.

CPS is prone to variations over time, including adjustments to the fundamental statistical properties of the data or modifications to the physical process, known as concept drift, which is a key issue in CPS. Concept drift can be triggered by a number of activities, including sensor failure, changes in the environment, or deterioration of the components, among others. If it is not identified and dealt with right away, it could result in incorrect predictions or even system breakdowns.

Concept drift detection in real time is essential for keeping CPS trustworthy and safe. In numerous fields, including CPS, machine learning algorithms have been shown to be successful in spotting and adjusting to concept drift. Machine learning algorithms can be drilled on historical data to find patterns and interactions between variables, and then used to quickly identify and act upon concept drift.

Several machine learning strategies are suggested and assessed in this chapter for the real-time identification of concept drift in industrial CPS. The proposed

DOI: 10.1201/9781003406105-13

techniques are based on the machine temperature system failure dataset from the Numenta Anomaly Benchmark, which is a time-series dataset that includes temperature data from sensors monitoring an internal component of an industrial machine. The dataset includes anomalies that occur due to planned shutdown, system degradation, and catastrophic failure.

Several methods for detecting idea drift in real time have been developed in this study using preprocessed data, including statistical techniques and machine learning algorithms. These techniques' performance is assessed using a variety of criteria and contrasts them with current state-of-the-art methods. In this study, findings demonstrated that the suggested strategies are very accurate and have minimal false alarm rates when it comes to detecting concept drift in real time.

The remaining chapter are structured as follows. A summary of related research on concept drift detection in CPS is provided in Section 9.2. The machine temperature system failure dataset and the preprocessing procedures used are described in Section 9.3 of this chapter. Section 9.4 presents the proposed statistical methods for concept drift detection. Section 9.5 presents machine learning techniques for concept drift.

9.2 LITERATURE REVIEW

In their paper Gonçalves Jr. et al. (2014) conduct a comparative analysis utilizing concept drift detectors and algorithms that can detect variations in data distribution for streaming environments. The authors evaluated the performance through different concept drift detectors using benchmark datasets and provided recommendations for selecting appropriate detectors based on the data stream's characteristics. A technique (Wang and Abraham 2015) is proposed for detecting idea deviations in real-time data using the correlation between consecutive instances in the stream. Their approach used a correlation-based technique to monitor the variation in the data stream and detect the drift points. The potential (Monostori et al. 2016) of CPSs is discussed to transform manufacturing. The paper included a general overview of numerous CPS components, including sensors, actuators, and control systems, and highlighted how those components might be incorporated into the production process to increase productivity and minimize errors.

The security issues (Alguliyev et al. 2018; Alguliyev et al. 2019) that CPSs encounter were of the primary focus. The former paper, published in *Computers in Industry*, provides a more detailed discussion of the security issues faced by CPSs, including attacks on sensor networks, controllers, and actuators. The latter paper provided an overview of various security issues in CPSs and suggests some potential solutions. In this paper (Xu and Duan 2019), Industry 4.0-related big data applications in cyber-physical systems (CPSs) are discussed. This paper discusses how CPSs produce many kinds of big data, including sensor data and production data, and how this data can be used to enhance the functionality of CPSs and the manufacturing process. The compositional falsification (Dreossi et al. 2019) of CPSs with machine learning components was covered. It provided a technique for confirming the security of CPSs with machine learning components, which can be problematic due to the complexity of modeling their behavior. The authors provided a case study utilizing a self-driving car to illustrate their methodology.

A novel method (Yang, et al. 2019) has been developed for approach for concept drift detection in the nonstationary, with the context of incremental learning. Their approach used a nearest-neighbor method and clustering to recognize drift and adjust, achieving improved performance in real-world datasets. A machine learning–based approach is used for detecting concept drifts in predictive maintenance (Zenisek, Holzinger and Affenzeller 2019). Their method used a random forest classifier and clustering to detect drifts and adjust the model, accordingly, achieving improved predictive performance. A comparison of various ensemble-based approaches exercised for concept drift recognition was done (de Barros and de Carvalho Santos, 2019). They evaluated the performance of different ensemble classifiers and concluded that a hybrid approach that combines different ensemble methods can achieve better results. A methodology (Lin et al., 2019) is presented for concept drift recognition in nonstationary learning contexts an ensemble learning-based strategy for the identification of concept drift and adaptation in industrial IoT data with big class imbalance. Their method used offline classifiers and a dynamic ensemble learning strategy to achieve high accuracy in drift detection and adjusting to data stream changes.

A learning guarantee method (de Mello et al., 2019) is proposed for unsupervised concept drift detection in data streams. Their approach used binary classification problem formulation and statistical analysis to provide guarantees on the detection accuracy of the drift points, achieving high accuracy in real-world datasets. An overview (Yaacoub et al. 2020) is provided of the security challenges faced by CPSs and discusses potential solutions. The paper highlights the limitations and issues with existing security measures in CPSs and suggests some future trends in CPS security, such as blockchain technology and machine learning–based security solutions. The challenges (Pereira and Thomas 2020) were discussed in using machine learning in safety-critical cyber-physical systems. The authors highlight the importance of addressing issues related to data quality, explainability, and model uncertainty, and provide recommendations for future research.

A deep learning approach (Rathore and Park 2020) based on blockchain for industrial cyber-physical system security was put forth. Deep learning algorithms were utilized by the authors to analyze the data and find abnormalities while blockchain was employed to store and manage data gathered from industrial systems. Using machine learning (Mohammadi Rouzbahani et al. 2020), a method is proposed for identifying anomalies in cyber-physical systems. In order to find anomalies in sensor data gathered from industrial systems, the authors employed an unsupervised machine learning approach. They then tested the implementation's effectiveness using real-world datasets. The use of deep learning (Luo et al. 2021) algorithm-based anomaly identification in cyber-physical systems (CPSs) was covered. Convolutional or recurrent neural networks, autoencoders, and other deep learning methods that can be employed for anomaly detection in CPSs were all given a general review in the paper. The authors also covered some of the opportunities and difficulties associated with implementing deep learning in CPSs. A lightweight framework (Yang and Shami, 2021) for IoT data streams to detect and respond to idea drift was introduced. By identifying drifts and modifying the model in real time, their solution used a sliding window technique and statistical analysis to increase accuracy in IoT applications.

ElStream (Abbasi et al., 2021) is a concept drift detection approach for dynamic social large data stream learning that was proposed. To detect drifts and achieve high accuracy in social media data streams, their solution utilized three different base learner types along with an ensemble learning strategy. Machine learning approaches (Jamal et al. 2021) have been used in the security analysis of cyber-physical systems. The authors gave a summary of the state of the art in this area and discussed the advantages and disadvantages of machine learning–based approaches to assuring the security of cyber-physical systems. AlZubi et al. 2021 proposed a cyber-physical system and machine learning–based approach for detecting cyber-attacks in health-care systems. The authors implemented a system that analyzes network traffic and extracts features using machine learning techniques to identify and classify attacks. Sharma and Guleria (2022) present Intelligent vulnerability detection using machine learning techniques in CPSs. The paper reviewed various machine learning techniques that can be used for CPS security, including artificial neural networks, decision trees, and support vector machines.

A hybrid approach (Garg et al. 2022) for balancing cyber-physical security in cloud-based smart businesses was presented. To identify and stop cyberattacks on industrial systems installed in the cloud, the authors used encryption, machine learning, and hardware-based security measures. The security of cyber-physical systems (Zaguia et al. 2022) was examined by utilizing machine learning and deep learning methods. The writers outlined the state of the field's research at the time and pointed out major obstacles and unanswered concerns. An extensive literature study (Agrahari and Singh, 2022) of concept drift detection in data stream mining was carried out. They studied and evaluated numerous methods put forward in the literature while providing an overview of the state-of-the-art at the time. For multilabel data streams (Gulcan and Can, 2023), an unsupervised concept drift detection approach is introduced. Their method, which demonstrated great accuracy in detecting drifts in multilabel datasets, used a clustering-based strategy to identify drifts in the data stream. Table 9.1 displays the methods utilized by several authors.

9.3   PROBLEM AND RELATED DATASET

The machine_temperature_system_failure dataset from the Numenta Anomaly Benchmark (NAB) contains temperature readings from a machine in one complete year from 2 December 2013, at 21:15 until 19 February 2014, at 15:25. It was created to evaluate anomaly detection algorithms on streaming data. The data was collected using multiple sensors placed throughout the machine and measured the temperature of its components, such as motors, pumps, and fans. The dataset includes temperature readings taken every 5 minutes, resulting in a total of approximately 31,536 readings. The anomalies are categorized into five different types, including 'cooldowns', 'startup failures', 'power supply failures', 'corrupted sensors', and 'sensor swapped'. The dataset is useful for studying anomaly detection and time series analysis in the context of machinery and temperature control systems. The objective of the dataset is to recognize anomalies in the temperature readings that may point to an imminent system failure. This dataset is one of the many publicly accessible datasets in the

TABLE 9.1

Summary of the Review of Literature

Paper No	Authors	Year	ML Methods	Key Points
1	Gonçalves Jr, P. M. et al.	2014	Various concept drift detectors	A comparative study of ten concept drift detection algorithms, applied to ten different datasets, using performance metrics and runtime analysis.
2	Wang, H. and Abraham, Z.	2015	Decision tree-based	Proposed a decision tree-based approach for identifying idea drift in streaming data and contrasted it with other techniques.
3	Monostori, L. et al.	2016	N/A	Overview of cyber-physical systems (CPS) in manufacturing, discussing various aspects such as architecture, key technologies, and applications.
4	Alguliyev, R. et al.	2018	N/A	Discusses the security challenges of CPSs, identifies different threats, and proposes various solutions such as access control, cryptography, and intrusion detection systems.
5	Alguliyev, R. et al.	2019	N/A	Discusses the security challenges of CPSs, proposes solutions such as access control, cryptography, and intrusion detection systems, and evaluates their effectiveness using a case study.
6	Xu, L. D. and Duan, L.	2019	N/A	A review of big data and machine learning techniques focused on Industry 4.0 for CPSs.
7	Dreossi, T. et al.	2019	Falsification method	Proposed a compositional falsification method based on the notion of robustness, for CPSs with machine learning components, and demonstrated its effectiveness using several case studies.
8	Yang, Z. et al.	2019	Decision tree-based	Proposed a methodology for recognizing concept drift in nonstationary environments based on a decision tree, which combines multiple trees and uses a sliding window to adapt the changes in the data.
9	Zenisek, J. et al.	2019	Ensemble methods	Proposed a machine learning–based approach to detect concept drift in predictive maintenance of machinery, using an ensemble of online classifiers, and evaluated its effectiveness using several datasets.
10	de Barros and de Carvalho Santos	2019	Ensemble methods	Based on performance metrics and runtime analysis, an overview and comparison of different ensemble-based techniques to detect concept drift in streaming data.
11	Lin, C. C. et al.	2019	Ensemble methods	Proposed a method to detect concept drift using an ensemble learning method in imbalanced industrial IoT data, using offline classifiers, and evaluated its effectiveness using a real-world dataset.

#	Author	Year	Keyword	Description
12	de Mello, R. F. et al.	2019	Unsupervised learning	Proposed a technique to identify concept drift in data streams utilizing an unsupervised learning-based method that uses the notion of density, and derived theoretical guarantees for its effectiveness.
13	Yaacoub, J. P. A. et al.	2020	N/A	Discussed limitations and challenges in securing cyber-physical systems and identified future research trends.
14	Pereira, A. and Thomas, C.	2020	N/A	Explores safety-critical cyber-physical systems and identifies the challenges of applying machine learning.
15	Rathore and Park	2020	Deep learning using Blockchain	Proposed a method for next-generation industrial-grade cyber-physical systems' cyber-security that is built on blockchain-based deep learning.
16	Mohammadi Rouzbahani, H. et al.	2020	Anomaly detection using machine learning	Reviews anomaly detection in cyber-physical systems using machine learning
17	Luo, Y. et al.	2021	Anomaly detection	Surveys the progress and opportunities for anomaly detection using deep learning for in cyber-physical systems.
18	Yang, L. and Shami, A.	2021	Lightweight concept drift identification	Concept drift detection and adaption framework for IoT data streams is proposed as a lightweight solution.
19	Abbasi, A. et al.	2021	Ensemble learning approach	An ensemble learning-based method for concept drift detection in dynamic, social, and large data stream learning.
20	Jamal, A. A. et al.	2021	Machine learning for security analysis	Analyze the security in cyber-physical systems using machine learning
21	AlZubi, A. A. et al.	2021	Machine learning for cyber-attack detection	Proposed a machine learning approach for cyber-attack identification in healthcare utilizing cyber-physical system techniques.
22	Sharma, S. and Guleria, K.	2022	Machine learning for vulnerability detection	Proposed using machine learning approaches for cyber-physical system vulnerability identification that is intelligent.
23	Garg, D. et al.	2022	Hybrid technique for cyber-physical security	Proposed a hybrid method for cloud-based smart industries' cyber-physical security.
24	Zaguia, A. et al.	2022	Machine and deep learning analysis	Analysis of cyber-physical system security using machine and deep learning techniques
25	Agrahari and Singh	2022	Concept drift identification	Concept drift recognition in data stream mining is reviewed in the literature.
26	Gulcan, E. B. and Can, F.	2023	Unsupervised concept drift detection	Proposed a technique for multilabel data streams to identify unsupervised concept drift.

NAB, which is designed to deliver a standardized benchmark for assessing anomaly detection algorithms and techniques.

The dataset from the Numenta Anomaly Benchmark contains time-series data, and over time, the temperature measurements may change owing to many parameters such as seasonality, changes in operating circumstances, or equipment deterioration. As a result, the notion of concept drift detection is significant in this dataset. Therefore, the dataset may exhibit concept drift, which is the phenomenon where the underlying concept or data distribution in a machine learning system changes over time, leading to a decrease in its performance. Detecting concept drift in this dataset is essential to ensure the accuracy and reliability of any anomaly detection system developed from this data. The size of this dataset is also considerable, with temperature readings taken every five minutes over the course of a year, which makes it suitable for training and testing machine learning models. Additionally, since it is a real-world dataset from an industrial setting, it has the potential to reflect the complexity and challenges of real-world problems and can be used to test the efficacy of various anomaly detection techniques. Figure 9.1 depicts all the temperature readings over all days. Two points in the chart have been marked which show some anomalous behavior, and the same has been evaluated through experiments in the following sections.

9.4 STATISTICAL METHODS FOR CONCEPT DRIFT DETECTION (CDD)

The Seasonal Decomposition of Time Series (STL) is performed over the whole set of data to study the trend, seasonal, and residual components through their visualization.

Figure 9.2 suggests that there is no specific trend, but the seasonal component does have some unusual patterns (somewhere clearly visible). But there are certainly some extreme values in the residuals which indicate that there are unusual or anomalous observations in the data that the model is not accounting for. In this paper, SARIMAX, an extension of the ARIMA model, usually known as Seasonal Autoregressive Integrated Moving Average with exogenous regressors, is implemented which is a time-series model. It allows for the modeling of both trend and seasonal components, as well as incorporating exogenous variables (Mohindru et al. 2019).

The coefficients of the ARIMA (2, 1, 2) model indicate that the first autoregressive term (ar.L1) has a significant positive effect on the dependent variable, while the second autoregressive term (ar.L2) has a nonsignificant effect (Kumar et al. 2021). The first moving average term (ma.L1) has a significant negative effect on the dependent variable, while the second moving average term (ma.L2) has a significant positive effect (Mohindru et al. 2020).

The Ljung–Box statistic tests for residual autocorrelation, and in this case, the statistic has a value of 0.00, demonstrating that the residuals have no detectable autocorrelation. With a statistical value of 465835.82 and a p-value of 0.00, the Jarque–Bera statistic in this case indicates that the residuals are not normally distributed, indicating that there may be some nonrandom patterns in the data that the model is

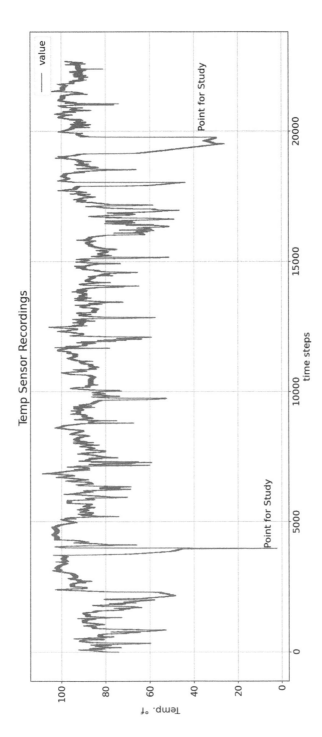

FIGURE 9.1   Temperature sensor readings.

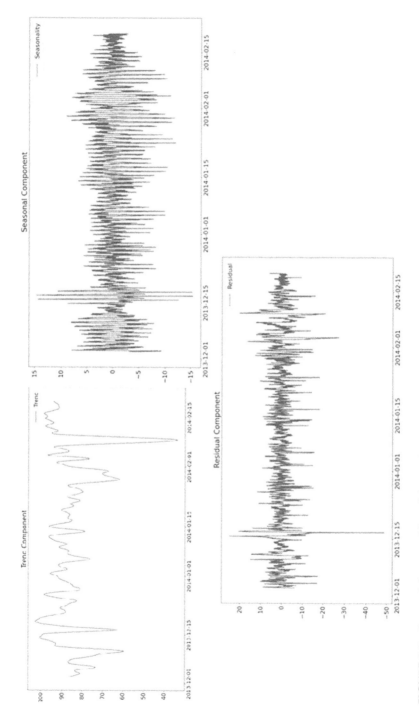

FIGURE 9.2 Seasonal decomposition of time series (STL).

missing (Rathore et al. 2021). There may be some concept drift in the data that is causing these nonrandom patterns, but further investigation would be needed to confirm this.

9.5   MACHINE LEARNING TECHNIQUES FOR CDD

To analyze more about the data pattern, the Isolation Forest algorithm, which is an unsupervised machine learning algorithm used for outlier detection, was applied. The algorithm works by constructing a random forest and isolating instances in the dataset by recursively partitioning them until each instance is in its leaf node. The process is based on the principle that anomalies are more easily isolated than normal points and that isolation occurs faster. The instances that require fewer splits to be isolated are considered more anomalous than those that require more splits.

The algorithm operates as follows:

1. Select a random subset of data points from the dataset and create a new node containing these points.
2. Select a random feature and a random split point on that feature.
3. Partition the data points based on whether they fall on the left or right side of the split.
4. Repeat steps 1–3 until all data points are isolated in their leaf nodes.
5. Determine the anomaly score for each point based on the number of splits required to isolate it. The fewer the splits, the more anomalous the point is considered.

Isolation Forest has several advantages over other outlier detection algorithms. It is efficient, can handle high-dimensional data, and does not require the assumption of a specific data distribution. The implementation resulted in 227 observations in the dataset that have been identified as outliers by the isolation forest algorithm. These outliers are assigned a value of −1, while the inliers or normal observations are assigned a value of 1. The majority of the observations (22,456 out of 22,683) are identified as inliers by the isolation forest algorithm. One-Class SVM was implemented to validate the isolation forest algorithm's output. One-Class Support Vector Machines (OCSVM) is a class of SVM algorithms that is employed for unsupervised anomaly detection. OCSVM is particularly useful when the anomalous data points are not known a priori, which is often the case in real-world anomaly detection problems. It is also computationally efficient and can handle large datasets.

The goal of OCSVM always remains to find a boundary that encloses the normal data points and to classify any data point outside of that boundary as an anomaly. In order to do this, the algorithm first transforms the input data into a high-dimensional feature space, after which it searches for a hypersphere that contains the vast majority of the data points. Any data points that fall outside of that hypersphere are classified as anomalies. The OCSVM implementation on our dataset also resulted in 223 possible anomalies which establish the interpretation of the Isolation Forest algorithm in Figure 9.3.

The Random Forest Algorithm is implemented and applied for anomaly detection. In this approach, the Random Forest model is trained on the training data, and the

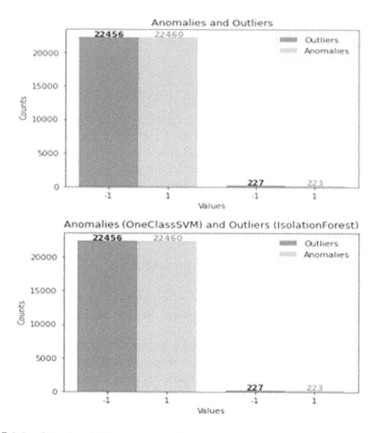

FIGURE 9.3 One-class SVM versus isolation forest.

trained model is then used to detect anomalies in the test data. The basic idea behind using Random Forest for anomaly detection is that normal data points tend to cluster together, while anomalies are isolated and far away from the cluster. Random Forest can capture these differences and effectively classify anomalies.

The steps involved in using Random Forest for anomaly detection are as follows:

1. Train a Random Forest model on the normal data.
2. Use the trained model for the prediction of labels of the test data.
3. Classify the data points as anomalies or normal based on the predicted labels and the threshold.

The random forest regressor is trained with the max depth = 3 and plots the predicted values which are shown in Figure 9.4.

The predicted values using random forest and real values are visualized, after the comparison, shown in Figure 9.5.

After this, to find concept drift in the signal, k-means is implemented to find the centroid for the signal. Then the values that are farther from it which are indicators of the concept drift can be looked for.

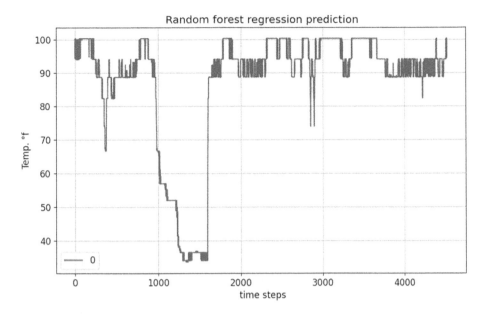

FIGURE 9.4   Random forest regressor predicted values.

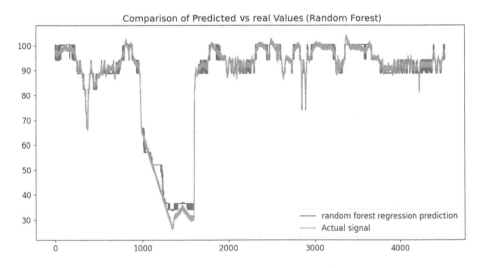

FIGURE 9.5   Comparison of predicted versus real values.

The steps to implement this approach are:

1. Preprocess the data and extract relevant features.
2. Choose the initial number of clusters (k) for k-means ($k = 1$ in our case)
3. Fit the k-means model to the data and get the cluster centroids.
4. Calculate the distance of each data point to the nearest centroid.
5. Identify the data points that have the longest distance from their nearest centroid as anomalies.

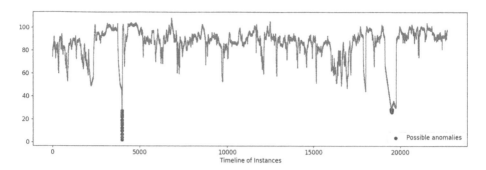

FIGURE 9.6   Possible anomalies showing concept drift.

The above approach implemented and evaluated its performance using cross-validation. The r2-score is a statistical measure that demonstrates the proportion of a dependent variable's variance that can be accounted for by one or more independent variables in a regression model. It is employed as a performance statistic to assess how well a regression model performs. When the model's R2 value is 1, it precisely describes the data; when it's 0, it doesn't account for any of the data's variability. It is cross-validated in five splits and received r2 scores as [0.96804982, 0.96644086, 0.96558059, 0.96577368, 0.96939427].

The mean squared error resulted as 5.862568267547376 and the center of the signal was found to be 85.92649821. Now it was time to look for the readings that have the longest distance from it. Figure 9.6 displays that there are two possible anomalies in the signal which are perfect indicators of concept drift in the signal.

9.6   CONCLUSION

Concept drift is the process by which a data stream's statistical characteristics vary over time. Concept drift detection is crucial for monitoring and maintaining system performance and security in the context of industrial cyber-physical systems (ICPS), which integrate physical processes and computational systems. It's crucial to remember that the selection of idea drift detection methodology depends on the individual ICPS characteristics and the type of data being tracked. For industrial cyber-physical systems to successfully detect and adjust to concept drift, a mix of approaches and ongoing monitoring may be necessary.

The machine temperature system failure dataset from the Numenta Anomaly Benchmark, which is a time-series dataset with temperature data from sensors monitoring an internal component of an industrial machine, is the foundation for the suggested solutions. Anomalies resulting from the scheduled shutdown, system deterioration, and catastrophic failure are included in the dataset.

In this study, several statistical and machine learning strategies are implemented and tested in for real-time idea drift detection in industrial CPS. A version of the ARIMA time-series algorithm dubbed as SARIMAX, is used in this study. It enables the modeling of exogenous factors as well as trend and seasonal components. The dependent variable is significantly impacted negatively by the first moving average term (ma.L1) and significantly positively by the second moving average term (ma.L2). The Ljung–Box statistic measures residual autocorrelation; in this instance, the statistic has a value of 0.00, signifying that the residuals do not exhibit any discernible autocorrelation. The Jarque–Bera measure is used to determine if the residuals show normal distribution or not. In this case, the statistic's value is 465835.82 and its p-value is 0.00, indicating that the residuals are not normally distributed and that there may be some nonrandom patterns in the data that the model is missing. These nonrandom patterns could be the result of idea drift in the data, but additional research is required to validate this.

In this chapter, various machine learning algorithms are implemented to the data; i.e., Isolation Forest, One-Class Support Vector Machines, Random Forest, and k-means are used. The implementation produced 227 observations in the dataset that the isolation forest method has classified as outliers. The normal or inlier observations are given a value of 1, while the outliers are given a value of −1. The isolation forest method identifies 22,456 of the observations (out of 22,683) as inliers. The OCSVM is then used to validate the isolation forest's output. Additionally, OCSVM implementation on our dataset produced 223 potential anomalies, which helped to clarify how the Isolation Forest technique should be interpreted. The result of OCSVM is very close to Isolation Forest. Random forest is applied to detect anomalies because anomalies are not clustered. The result of the Random Forest is compared with real values, which are also very close to actual values. In the end, k-means is implemented for cross-validation. In this case, the centroid is calculated and then the anomalies are identified based on the longer distance. In the result, two possible signal anomalies were found, indicating the concept drift in the signal.

REFERENCES

Abbasi, A., Javed, A. R., Chakraborty, C., Nebhen, J., Zehra, W., and Jalil, Z. (2021). ElStream: An ensemble learning approach for concept drift detection in dynamic social big data stream learning. *IEEE Access*, 9, 66408–66419.

Agrahari, S., and Singh, A. K. (2022). Concept drift detection in data stream mining: A literature review. *Journal of King Saud University-Computer and Information Sciences*, 34(10), 9523–9540.

Alguliyev, R., Imamverdiyev, Y. Dsouza, J., Elezabeth, L., Mishra, V. P., and Jain, R. (2019, February). Security in cyber-physical systems. In *2019 Amity International Conference on Artificial Intelligence (AICAI)* (pp. 840–844). IEEE.

Alguliyev, R., Imamverdiyev, Y., and Sukhostat, L. (2018). Cyber-physical systems and their security issues. *Computers in Industry*, 100, 212–223.

AlZubi, A. A., Al-Maitah, M., and Alarifi, A. (2021). Cyber-attack detection in healthcare using cyber-physical system and machine learning techniques. *Soft Computing*, 25(18), 12319–12332.

de Barros, R. S. M., and de Carvalho Santos, S. G. T. (2019). An overview and comprehensive comparison of ensembles for concept drift. *Information Fusion*, 52, 213–244.

de Mello, R. F., Vaz, Y., Grossi, C. H., and Bifet, A. (2019). On learning guarantees to unsupervised concept drift detection on data streams. *Expert Systems with Applications*, 117, 90–102.

Dreossi, T., Donzé, A., and Seshia, S. A. (2019). Compositional falsification of cyber-physical systems with machine learning components. *Journal of Automated Reasoning*, 63, 1031–1053.

Garg, D., Rani, S., Herencsar, N., Verma, S., Wozniak, M., and Ijaz, M. F. (2022). Hybrid technique for cyber-physical security in cloud-based smart industries. *Sensors*, 22(12), 4630.

Gonçalves Jr, P. M., de Carvalho Santos, S. G., Barros, R. S., and Vieira, D. C. (2014). A comparative study on concept drift detectors. *Expert Systems with Applications*, 41(18), 8144–8156.

Gulcan, E. B., and Can, F. (2023). Unsupervised concept drift detection for multi-label data streams. *Artificial Intelligence Review*, 56(3), 2401–2434.

Jamal, A. A., Majid, A. A. M., Konev, A., Kosachenko, T., and Shelupanov, A. (2021). A review on security analysis of cyber physical systems using Machine learning. *Materials Today: Proceedings*, 80, 2302–2306.

Kumar, Arun, Sharma, Sharad, Goyal, Nitin, Singh, Aman, Cheng, Xiaochun, and Singh, Parminder. (2021). Secure and energy-efficient smart building architecture with emerging technology IoT. *Computer Communications* 176, 207–217.

Lin, C. C., Deng, D. J., Kuo, C. H., and Chen, L. (2019). Concept drift detection and adaption in big imbalance industrial IoT data using an ensemble learning method of offline classifiers. *IEEE Access*, 7, 56198–56207.

Luo, Y., Xiao, Y., Cheng, L., Peng, G., and Yao, D. (2021). Deep learning-based anomaly detection in cyber-physical systems: Progress and opportunities. *ACM Computing Surveys (CSUR)*, 54(5), 1–36.

Mohammadi Rouzbahani, H., Karimipour, H., Rahimnejad, A., Dehghantanha, A., and Srivastava, G. (2020). Anomaly detection in cyber-physical systems using machine learning. *Handbook of Big Data Privacy*, 219–235. Springer, Cham

Mohindru, Vandana, Bhatt, Ravindara, and Singh, Yashwant. (2019). Reauthentication scheme for mobile wireless sensor networks. *Sustainable Computing: Informatics and Systems* 23, 158–166.

Mohindru, Vandana, Singh, Yashwant, and Bhatt, Ravindara. (2020). Securing wireless sensor networks from node clone attack: A lightweight message authentication algorithm. *International Journal of Information and Computer Security* 12, no. 2–3, 217–233.

Monostori, L., Kádár, B., Bauernhansl, T., Kondoh, S., Kumara, S., Reinhart, G., ... and Ueda, K. (2016). Cyber-physical systems in manufacturing. *Cirp Annals*, 65(2), 621–641.

Pereira, A., and Thomas, C. (2020). Challenges of machine learning applied to safety-critical cyber-physical systems. *Machine Learning and Knowledge Extraction*, 2(4), 579–602.

Rathore, Pramod Singh, Chatterjee, Jyotir Moy, Kumar, Abhishek, and Sujatha, Radhakrishnan. (2021). Energy-efficient cluster head selection through relay approach for WSN. *The Journal of Supercomputing* 77, 7649–7675.

Rathore, S., and Park, J. H. (2020). A blockchain-based deep learning approach for cyber security in next generation industrial cyber-physical systems. *IEEE Transactions on Industrial Informatics*, 17(8), 5522–5532.

Sharma, S., and Guleria, K. (2022, October). Machine Learning Techniques for Intelligent Vulnerability Detection in Cyber-Physical Systems. In *2022 International Conference on Data Analytics for Business and Industry (ICDABI)* (pp. 200–204). IEEE.

Wang, H., and Abraham, Z. (2015, July). Concept drift detection for streaming data. In *2015 International Joint Conference on Neural Networks (IJCNN)* (pp. 1–9). IEEE.

Xu, L. D., and Duan, L. (2019). Big data for cyber-physical systems in industry 4.0: A survey. *Enterprise Information Systems*, 13(2), 148–169.

Yaacoub, J. P. A., Salman, O., Noura, H. N., Kaaniche, N., Chehab, A., and Malli, M. (2020). Cyber-physical systems security: Limitations, issues and future trends. *Microprocessors and microsystems*, 77, 103201.

Yang, L., and Shami, A. (2021). A lightweight concept drift detection and adaptation framework for IoT data streams. *IEEE Internet of Things Magazine*, 4(2), 96–101.

Yang, Z., Al-Dahidi, S., Baraldi, P., Zio, E., and Montelatici, L. (2019). A novel concept drift detection method for incremental learning in nonstationary environments. *IEEE Transactions on Neural Networks and Learning Systems*, 31(1), 309–320.

Zaguia, A., Rani, S., and Bashir, A. K. (2022, July). Analysis of Machine Learning and Deep Learning in Cyber-Physical System Security. In *Proceedings of International Conference on Computing and Communication Networks: ICCCN 2021* (pp. 355–363). Springer Nature Singapore.

Zenisek, J., Holzinger, F., and Affenzeller, M. (2019). Machine learning based concept drift detection for predictive maintenance. *Computers & Industrial Engineering*, 137, 106031.

10 A Hybrid Machine Learning Approach for Intrusion Detection in Cyber-Physical Manufacturing Systems

J. Jithish, Sriram Sankaran, and Krishnashree Achuthan

Center for Cybersecurity Systems and Networks, Amrita Vishwa Vidyapeetham, India

10.1 INTRODUCTION

In recent times, Industry 4.0 has emerged, which involves the seamless integration of physical and digital technologies such as the Internet of Things (IoT), cloud computing, and artificial intelligence to enhance the quality of products and operational efficiency. (Preuveneers and Ilie-Zudor, 2017; Darwish and Hassanien, 2018; Prabha and Sankaran, 2019). This integration has been made possible due to advancements in M2M communications, wireless sensor networks, and cloud computing, leading to the development of cyber-physical systems (CPS) (Jithish and Sankaran, 2021). These systems are crucial for the digital transformation of manufacturing industries, as they replace many decision-making and control functions. However, as cyber threats targeting CPSs increase, they pose a risk to the reliability and safety of industrial systems (Nair et al. 2022).

Our proposal is to use a self-organizing map (SOM) as an anomaly-based intrusion detection system in CPMS (Sakkari and Zaied, 2020). Compared to other machine learning techniques, SOMs have demonstrated superior performance in detecting intrusion attempts (Li et al. 2020). The topological properties of SOMs allow them to cluster complex multidimensional data effectively, making them widely used in security applications (Yao et al., 2018, Ying and Pingfan, 1999, Wang et al. 2012, Jithish and Sankaran, 2017). Previous studies have shown that SOM-based techniques exhibit better performance with shorter training time and higher detection rates for real-time systems (Feyereisl and Aickelin, 2009, Chen et al. 2021). We enhance the SOM architecture's performance by including an additional Kernel Principal Component Analysis stage, which improves the speed and classification accuracy of our proposed IDS. To detect intrusions, we use the SOM by feeding it

DOI: 10.1201/9781003406105-14

with real-time data from the system and detecting anomalies by analyzing the data points with the clusters in the preceding SOM. We use a simulated model of a continuous stirred tank reactor (CSTR) in MATLAB as our testbed for CPS.

10.1.1 NOVELTY OF THE PROPOSED APPROACH

Our approach has three key novel elements:

 (i) Using KPCA for both dimensionality reduction and enhancing class separability of industrial data,
 (ii) employing an SOM algorithm to further reduce data dimensionality and improve class separation, and
(iii) applying the SOM algorithm for intrusion detection using the quantization error metric.

10.2 RELATED WORK

10.2.1 TRADITIONAL SOM-BASED TECHNIQUES

SOM has gained popularity as an intrusion detection technique, as demonstrated by Ables et al. (2022). Min et al. utilized SOM to create an intrusion detection system that operates in real time. Wilson and Obimbo (2011) applied SOM to network intrusion detection in computer networks, and Barletta et al. (2020) used it for intrusion detection in vehicular networks. However, the traditional SOM approach is computationally demanding and unsuitable for online detection. Therefore, several modified versions of SOM have been developed to address these limitations.

10.2.2 HIERARCHICAL SOM (HSOM)-BASED TECHNIQUES

Huang et al. (2017) have utilized this method to propose an intrusion detection technique for Visual Sensor Networks, which involves learning traffic patterns. They extract the optimal feature set based on a traffic model and use HSOM to detect intrusions. Alsulaiman et al. (2009) have proposed a method that enhances the accuracy of Hierarchical SOMs by incorporating additional layers and utilizing a performance-based ranking method. Kayacik et al. (2007) have suggested an intrusion detection system based on Hierarchical SOM with two layers. Their study indicates that the performance of HSOM is contingent on the combination of different features and HSOM layers. Lichodzijewski et al. (2002) have employed hierarchical SOM for intrusion detection in computer networks. Their approach uses real-time system data with minimal expert knowledge.

10.2.3 GROWING HIERARCHICAL SOM (GHSOM)-BASED TECHNIQUES

Salem and Buehler (2013) made modifications to the topology and weight initialization of GHSOM, while Mansour et al. (2010) used GHSOM to develop a Network Intrusion Detection System (NIDS) that can uncover attack vectors through clustering.

TABLE 10.1

SOM-Based Anomaly Detection Techniques

Reference	Approach	Application	Domain
Concetti et al. (2023)	SOM	Anomaly Detection	Oil and Gas Industry
Licen et al. (2020)	SOM	Anomaly Detection	Manufacturing Industries
Yin et al. (2017)	Improved SOM	Intrusion Detection	Mobile Devices
Li et al. (2020)	SOM	Outlier Detection	Outlier Detection
Karami (2018)	Modified SOM	Intrusion Detection	Computer Networks.
Venskus et al. (2019)	SOM	Anomaly Detection.	Maritime Sensors
Toshpulatov and Zincir-Heywood (2021)	HSOM	Anomaly Detection.	Smart Meter
Merainani et al. (2018)	Singular Value Decomposition (SVD), and SOM	Fault Detection	Manufacturing Industry
Angulo-Saucedo et al. (2022)	Unsupervised SOM	Damage Classification	Structural Health Monitoring

Ippoliti and Zhou (2010) proposed architectural improvements to GHSOM, such as enhanced training, normalization of inputs, and adaptive thresholds to improve its accuracy in detecting intrusions. Vasighi and Amini (2017) introduced a batch learning strategy to enhance the clustering ability and computation time of GHSOM, which resulted in the creation of a new architecture called Direct Batch Growing SOM (DBGSOM), which can improve intrusion detection rates.

10.2.4 HYBRID SOM-BASED TECHNIQUES

McElwee and Cannady (2016) employ discretization, data deduplication, and filtering during the input stage to enhance performance before using the SOM stage. Almi'ani et al. (2018) utilize a combination of k-means clustering and SOM to detect network intrusions, while Landress (2016) uses a blend of k-means clustering, decision trees, and SOM to lower false positive rates for intrusion detection. However, hybrid SOM techniques have the drawback of being overly sensitive, which results in a low detection rate (Landauer et al., 2020). Table 10.1 presents SOM-based anomaly detection techniques.

10.3 BACKGROUND

10.3.1 KERNEL PRINCIPAL COMPONENT ANALYSIS (KPCA)

Kernel Principal Component Analysis (KPCA) is a nonlinear variant of PCA. Instead of directly analyzing the original data in feature space R_n, KPCA uses a nonlinear function ϕ to map the data x_i to a higher-dimensional feature space F.

The mapping can be described mathematically as in Equation 10.1

$$\phi : \{R\}^n \rightarrow \{F\}, x_i \rightarrow \phi(x_i) \tag{10.1}$$

The eigenvector P of the covariance matrix in the new feature space F can be expressed as in Equation 10.2

$$P = \sum_{i=1}^{n} \alpha_i \phi(x_i) \tag{10.2}$$

where in Equation 10.3

$$\phi(x_i) = \phi(x_i) - \frac{1}{n} \sum_{k=1}^{n} \phi(x_k) \tag{10.3}$$

and the coefficient α_i are the elements of the vector α. The corresponding kernel of KPCA $K_{ij} = \phi(x_i)\phi(x_j)$ is described by the expression in Equation 10.4.

$$K_{ij} = \frac{1}{n} \sum_{k=1}^{n} K_{ik} - \frac{1}{n} \sum_{k=1}^{n} K_{kj} + \frac{1}{n^2} \sum_{k,l=1}^{n} K_{k,l} \tag{10.4}$$

10.3.2 Self-Organizing Map (SOM)

The process of how a Self-Organizing Map (SOM) neural network learns can be explained as follows: Suppose we have a random input vector X that has m dimensions; then, X can be represented by Equation 10.5.

$$X = \left[x_1 x_2 x_3 x_4 \dots x_n \right]^T \tag{10.5}$$

If the output layer of the Self-Organizing Map (SOM) contains 1 neurons, then the weight vector W_j of neuron j in the output layer can be computed using Equation 10.6.

$$W_j = \left[w_{j1} w_{j2} w_{j3} \dots w_{jm} \right]^T \tag{10.6}$$

The weight update equation of the synaptic weights of the excited neuron at the output layer is described as in Equation 10.7:

$$W_j(n+1) = W_j(n) + \eta(n) N_{j,R(x)}(n)(X - W_j(n)) \tag{10.7}$$

10.3.3 CONTINUOUS STIRRED TANK REACTOR (CSTR)

The CSTR is a conventional model of a reactor that is commonly employed in chemical engineering for liquid-phase and multiphase chemical reactions (depicted in Figure 10.1). The dynamics of the CSTR, which generates a chemical compound B from compound A via a nonisothermal irreversible adiabatic reaction, are explained by the subsequent Equations 10.8–10.11.

$$\frac{\partial X_A}{\partial t} = \frac{R}{U}\left(X_{A_0} - X_A\right) - K_0 e^{\left(\frac{-E}{kT}\right)} X_A \tag{10.8}$$

$$\frac{\partial T}{\partial t} = \frac{R}{U}\left(T_0 - T\right) + \frac{(-\Delta H)}{\rho C_p} e^{\frac{-E}{kT}} X_A - \frac{q}{U\rho C_p} \tag{10.9}$$

$$q = VA\left(T - T_j\right) \tag{10.10}$$

$$q = \frac{aR_c^{b+1}}{R_c + \dfrac{aR_c^b}{2\rho_c C_{pc}}} \tag{10.11}$$

In the above set of equations, X_A is the concentration of chemical A, K_0 is the constant of reaction rate, E represents the activation energy, T denotes the temperature of the inlet stream, R and R_c are the rates of flow of reactant and coolant, respectively, U is the volume of the reactor, T_i and T_j represent the temperatures of the exit stream and cooling fluid, respectively, ΔH is the net heat change of the reaction, C_p and ρ are the heat capacity and density of reactants, V is the coefficient of heat transfer, A is the area of heat transfer, and a, b are reaction specific parameters (Mohindru et al., 2022). The concentration (X_A) and outlet temperature (T) are regulated using a proportional-integral-derivative (PID) controller by adjusting the reactant flow rate (R) and coolant flow rate (R_c) respectively. Figure 10.1 displays a continuous stirred tank reactor.

10.4 CPS SIMULATION ENVIRONMENT

Our CSTR model, as shown in Figure 10.2, is created using the *TrueTime* simulator (Cervin and Årzén 2009). *TrueTime* is a testbed based on MATLAB/Simulink that facilitates the modeling and simulation of cyber-physical systems (CPSs) (Mohindru et al., 2019). By considering various parameters such as network bandwidth, CPU speed, and network delays, the *TrueTime* toolbox enables the simulation of CPSs.

10.4.1 DATASET GENERATION

To obtain datasets for our simulated CSTR model, we adjust the set points of the PID controller that regulates the chemical concentration and reactor temperature in a

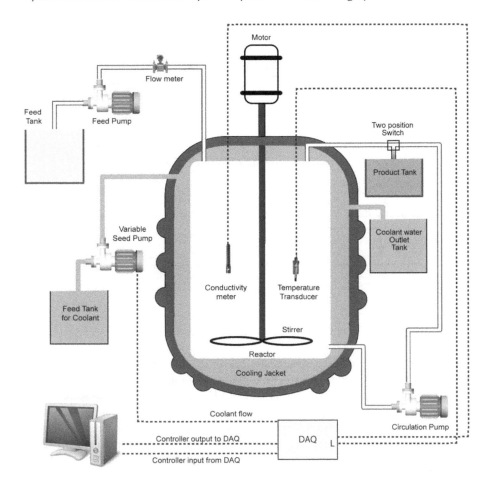

FIGURE 10.1   Continuous stirred tank reactor (CSTR).

stepwise fashion. We train the proposed KPCA+SOM model using the data prior to intrusion attack attempts.

10.4.2 DECEPTION ATTACKS

Deception attacks involve the tampering of crucial system data, resulting in the loss of data packet integrity. By introducing false data into the network, the adversary can disrupt CPS operations. Mathematically, deception attacks can be defined as follows in Equation 10.12.

$$\hat{R}[k] = R[k], k < \varepsilon\eta, k \geq \varepsilon \tag{10.12}$$

In the above expression, $R[k]$ denotes the sensor output, $R[k]$ is the legitimate sensor value at time k, ε denotes the attack time instance, and η denote the tampered sensor

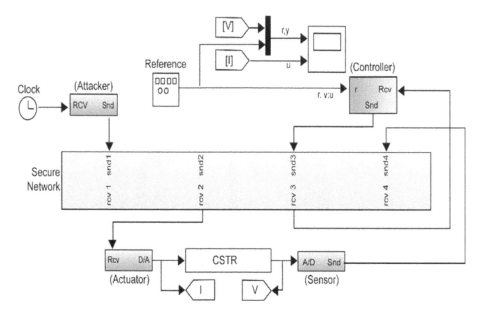

FIGURE 10.2 Modeling of CSTR process using *TrueTime* testbed.

value. In our case, the attacker manipulates sensor readings corresponding to coolant flow rate (R_c), feed-flow rate (R), reactor outlet temperature (T), temperatures of exit stream (T_i) and cooling fluid (T_j), heat-change (ΔH) chemical concentration (X_A), and pressure at reactor core (P) and exit stream (P_i) at random time instances. The data matrix, in this case, consists of 5,000 rows and nine columns, and rows represent testing instances, whereas the columns represent feature vectors (Mohindru et al., 2020).

10.5 PROPOSED APPROACH

In our approach, the input data we are working with is generated by the simulated CSTR model.

10.5.1 INTRUSION DETECTION

The intrusion detection technique proposed for cyber-physical manufacturing systems follows the following set of procedures:

- Data Normalization: To ensure that no feature dominates the classification process, we adjust the dataset features to the same scale.
- KPCA: Next, the normalized data undergoes KPCA, which retains the principal components contributing to 90% of the total variance. We apply the Gaussian kernel for the KPCA stage.

10.5.2 Intrusion Detection Using Quantization Error (QE)

To calculate the QE of a SOM, we measure the average distance between sample vectors in SOM clusters and the centroid of each corresponding cluster. In our scenario, we employ the Minimum Quantization Error (MQE) as an indicator to detect anomalies. To use the MQE, we establish a threshold, which is the maximum acceptable deviation for a data point. Data points exhibiting a deviation greater than this threshold are considered anomalous. This can be expressed mathematically as in Equation 10.3:

$$D_i = \left\| x_i - C_c \right\| \qquad (10.13)$$

where D_i is the MQE, C_c is the cluster centroid, x_i is the test data, and T_D is the threshold of detection.

10.5.3 Detection Threshold

The detection threshold, T_D, the probability distribution of the distance vector between the cluster centroid and the test data sample, is analyzed. The 99.73 percentile, also known as the three-sigma rule, is utilized to differentiate the normal and abnormal data samples. Any distances that are smaller than the threshold value indicate that the data instances correspond to normal behavior. Therefore, data instances falling into these regions are considered anomalous.

10.6 RESULTS AND DISCUSSION

We evaluate various methods for identifying unusual events in a dataset to determine the optimal number of features for detecting intrusion attempts. We compare techniques such as PCA+SOM, SOM+K-Means, one-class SVM, local outlier factor (LOF), and artificial neural networks (ANN) to achieve this.

Figure 10.3 presents a comparison of various intrusion detection techniques based on the number of features used. Table 10.2 provides details of the sensitivity, specificity, and accuracy measures for different algorithms with respect to the number of features. From Table 10.2 and Figure 10.3, it can be concluded that KPCA+SOM performs the best in terms of accuracy, sensitivity, and overall performance. Other techniques use the recursive elimination algorithm to select the top four features, except for KPCA+SOM and PCA+SOM, which employ cumulative percentage variance for dimensionality reduction. The proposed KPCA+SOM method achieves a significantly higher maximum accuracy of 95.05% compared to other approaches (as described in Table 10.2). The ROC curve in Figure 10.4 confirms our observation that KPCA+SOM has the highest AUC (Area Under the Curve) value among all the techniques.

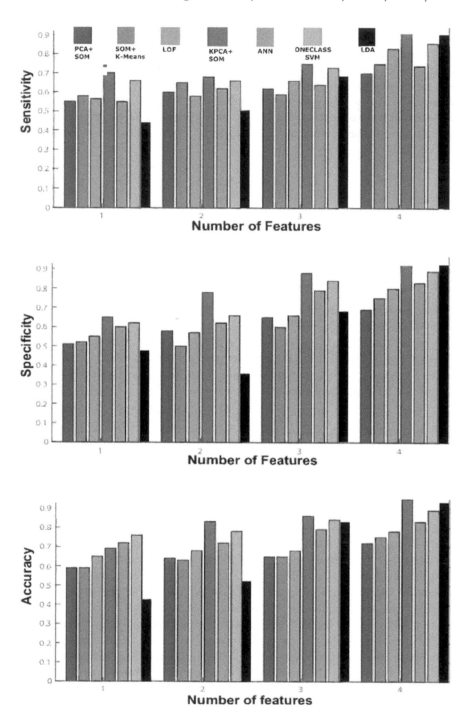

FIGURE 10.3   Sensitivity, specificity, and accuracy of different techniques.

TABLE 10.2

Performance Comparison of Techniques with 95% Confidence Interval

Technique	N	Sensitivity	Specificity	Accuracy
PCA+SOM	1	.55 ± .03	.52 ± .04	.59 ± .05
	2	.57 ± .02	.56 ± .03	.64 ± .01
	3	.58 ± .06	.64 ± .02	.65 ± .04
	4	.69 ± .04	.65 ± .04	.72 ± .05
SOM+K-Means	1	.57 ± .01	.53 ± .04	.59 ± .06
	2	.64 ± .07	.49 ± .04	.63 ± .05
	3	.56 ± .05	.59 ± .04	.65 ± .04
	4	.67 ± .03	.72 ± .02	.75 ± .07
LOF	1	.54 ± .04	.59 ± .04	.63 ± .04
	2	.54 ± .07	.61 ± .05	.67 ± .07
	3	.63 ± .01	.76 ± .05	.67 ± .09
	4	.75 ± .04	.82 ± .04	.78 ± .08
ANN	1	.54 ± .03	.61 ± .02	.72 ± .04
	2	.61 ± .02	.63 ± .08	.71 ± .04
	3	.63 ± .06	.82 ± .05	.81 ± .05
	4	.67 ± .03	.85 ± .03	.83 ± .02
One-Class SVM	1	.67 ± .03	.61 ± .02	.76 ± .05
	2	.66 ± .05	.63 ± .08	.77 ± .06
	3	.72 ± .02	.82 ± .05	.84 ± .05
	4	.84 ± .02	.85 ± .07	.87 ± .05
KPCA+ SOM	1	.69 ± .01	.63 ± .07	.69 ± .04
	2	.67 ± .02	.75 ± .07	.83 ± .07
	3	.75 ± .04	.86 ± .07	.86 ± .07
	4	.93 ± .05	.90 ± .08	.95 ± .05
LDA	1	.44 ± .05	.45 ± .03	.43 ± .06
	2	.52 ± .04	.35 ± .04	.47 ± .03
	3	.67 ± .06	.65 ± .05	.74 ± .03
	4	.81 ± .02	.79 ± .08	.81 ± .04

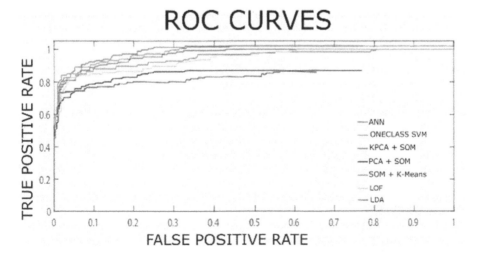

FIGURE 10.4 ROC curves of different techniques.

10.7 CONCLUSION

The chapter discussed the use of Kernel Principal Component Analysis (KPCA) and Self-Organizing Maps (SOMs) as a means of intrusion detection in cyber-physical manufacturing systems (CPMS). The dataset used in this study was generated by simulating a continuous stirred tank reactor (CSTR). The proposed approach was based on detecting deviations in system process variables from established behavior and using KPCA to model the data from the CSTR, followed by applying the SOM algorithm to detect anomalous system behavior. The goal of using KPCA was to enhance the classification performance of the SOM. To evaluate the effectiveness of this hybrid approach, the accuracy, sensitivity, and specificity were compared to those of several related methods. The results indicated that the proposed hybrid approach was successful in detecting intrusions and achieved higher accuracy for anomaly detection than traditional approaches.

REFERENCES

Ables, Jesse, Thomas Kirby, William Anderson, Sudip Mittal, Shahram Rahimi, Ioana Banicescu, and Maria Seale. "Creating an Explainable Intrusion Detection System Using Self Organizing Maps." arXiv preprint arXiv:2207.07465 (2022).

Almi'ani, Muder, Alia Abu Ghazleh, Amer Al-Rahayfeh, and Abdul Razaque. "Intelligent Intrusion Detection System Using Clustered Self-Organized Map." In *2018 Fifth International Conference on Software Defined Systems (SDS)*, pp. 138–144. IEEE, 2018. https://doi.org/10.1109/sds.2018.8370435

Alsulaiman, Mansour M., Aasem N. Alyahya, Raed A. Alkharboush, and Nasser S. Alghafis. "Intrusion Detection System Using Self-Organizing Maps." In *2009 Third International Conference on Network and System Security*, pp. 397–402. IEEE, 2009. https://doi.org/10.1109/nss.2009.62

Angulo-Saucedo, Gilbert A., Jersson X. Leon-Medina, Wilman Alonso Pineda-Muñoz, Miguel Angel Torres-Arredondo, and Diego A. Tibaduiza. 2022. "Damage Classification Using Supervised Self-Organizing Maps in Structural Health Monitoring" *Sensors* 22, no. 4: 1484. https://doi.org/10.3390/s22041484

Barletta, Vita Santa, Danilo Caivano, Antonella Nannavecchia, and Michele Scalera. 2020. "Intrusion Detection for in-Vehicle Communication Networks: An Unsupervised Kohonen SOM Approach" *Future Internet* 12, no. 7: 119. https://doi.org/10.3390/fi12070119

Cervin, Anton, and Karl-Erik Årzén. "TrueTime." *Computational Analysis, Synthesis, & Design Dynamic Systems* (November 24, 2009): 145–176. https://doi.org/10.1201/9781420067859-c6

Chen, Yang, Nami Ashizawa, Chai Kiat Yeo, Naoto Yanai, and Seanglidet Yean. "Multi-Scale Self-Organizing Map Assisted Deep Autoencoding Gaussian Mixture Model for Unsupervised Intrusion Detection." *Knowledge-Based Systems* 224 (July 2021): 107086. https://doi.org/10.1016/j.knosys.2021.107086

Concetti, Lorenzo, Giovanni Mazzuto, Filippo Emanuele Ciarapica, and Maurizio Bevilacqua. "An Unsupervised Anomaly Detection Based on Self-Organizing Map for the Oil and Gas Sector" *Applied Sciences* 13, no. 6 (2023): 3725. https://doi.org/10.3390/app13063725

Darwish, Ashraf, and Aboul Ella Hassanien. "Cyber Physical Systems Design, Methodology, and Integration: The Current Status and Future Outlook." *Journal of Ambient Intelligence and Humanized Computing* 9, no. 5 (2018): 1541–1556.

Feyereisl, Jan, and Uwe Aickelin. "Self-Organizing Maps in Computer Security." In Ronald D. Hopkins et al. (Eds.), *Computer Security: Intrusion, Detection and Prevention*, (2009): 1–30. https://papers.ssrn.com/sol3/papers.cfm?abstract_id=2827928

Huang, Kaixing, Qi Zhang, Chunjie Zhou, Naixue Xiong, and Yuanqing Qin. "An Efficient Intrusion Detection Approach for Visual Sensor Networks Based on Traffic Pattern Learning." *IEEE Transactions on Systems, Man, and Cybernetics: Systems* 47, no. 10 (2017): 2704–2713. https://doi.org/10.1109/tsmc.2017.2698457

Ippoliti, Dennis, and Xiaobo Zhou. "An Adaptive Growing Hierarchical Self-Organizing Map for Network Intrusion Detection." In *2010 Proceedings of 19th International Conference on Computer Communications and Networks*, pp. 1–7. IEEE, 2010. https://doi.org/10.1109/icccn.2010.5560165

Jithish, J., and Sankaran, S. (2017). "A Hybrid Adaptive Rule based System for Smart Home Energy Prediction." In *Joint Proceedings of the 3rd Modelling Symposium (ModSym), Developmental Aspects of Intelligent Adaptive Systems (DIAS), and Educational Data Mining Practices in Indian Academia (EDUDM) co-located with 10th Innovations in Software Engineering (ISEC 2017)*, Jaipur, India, February 5, 2017, pp. 1–6.

Jithish, J., & Sankaran, S. A Game-Theoretic Approach for Ensuring Trustworthiness in Cyber-Physical Systems with Applications to Multiloop UAV Control. *Transactions on Emerging Telecommunications Technologies* 32, no. 5 (2021): e4042.

Karami, Amin. "An Anomaly-Based Intrusion Detection System in Presence of Benign Outliers with Visualization Capabilities." *Expert Systems with Applications* 108 (2018): 36–36. https://doi.org/10.1016/j.eswa.2018.04.038

Kayacik, H. Gunes, A. Nur Zincir-Heywood, and Malcolm I. Heywood. "A Hierarchical SOM-Based Intrusion Detection System." *Engineering applications of artificial intelligence* 20, no. 4 (2007): 439–451. https://doi.org/10.1016/j.engappai.2006.09.005

Landauer, Max, Florian Skopik, Markus Wurzenberger, Wolfgang Hotwagner, and Andreas Rauber. "Visualizing Syscalls Using Self-Organizing Maps for System Intrusion Detection." *Proceedings of the 6th International Conference on Information Systems Security and Privacy*, 2020. https://doi.org/10.5220/0008918703490360

Landress, Angela Denise. "A Hybrid Approach to Reducing the False Positive Rate in Unsupervised Machine Learning Intrusion Detection." In *SoutheastCon 2016*, pp. 1–6. IEEE, 2016. https://doi.org/10.1109/secon.2016.7506773

Li, Menglu, Rasha Kashef, and Ahmed Ibrahim. "Multi-Level Clustering-Based Outlier's Detection (MCOD) Using Self-Organizing Maps." *Big Data and Cognitive Computing* 4, no. 4 (2020): 24. https://doi.org/10.3390/bdcc4040024

Li, Min, and Wang Dongliang. "Anormaly Intrusion Detection Based on SOM." In *2009 WASE International Conference on Information Engineering*, vol. 1, pp. 40–43. IEEE, 2009. https://doi.org/10.1109/ijcnn.2003.1223682

Licen, Sabina, Alessia Di Gilio, Jolanda Palmisani, Stefania Petraccone, Gianluigi de Gennaro, and Pierluigi Barbieri. "Pattern Recognition and Anomaly Detection by Self-Organizing Maps in a Multi Month E-nose Survey at an Industrial Site" *Sensors* 20, no. 7 (2020): 1887. https://doi.org/10.3390/s2007188

Lichodzijewski, Peter, A. Nur Zincir-Heywood, and Malcolm I. Heywood. "Dynamic Intrusion Detection Using Self-Organizing Maps." In *The 14th Annual Canadian Information Technology Security Symposium (CITSS)*, 2002. https://doi.org/10.1109/ijcnn.2002.1007776

Mansour, Nashat, Maya I. Chehab, and Ahmad Faour. "Filtering Intrusion Detection Alarms." *Cluster Computing* 13, no. 1 (2010): 19–29. https://doi.org/10.1007/s10586-009-0096-9

McElwee, Steven, and James Cannady. "Improving the Performance of Self-Organizing Maps for Intrusion Detection." In *SoutheastCon 2016*, pp. 1–6. IEEE, 2016. https://doi.org/10.1109/secon.2016.7506766

Merainani, Boualem, Chemseddine Rahmoune, Djamel Benazzouz, and Belkacem Ould-Bouamama. "A Novel Gearbox Fault Feature Extraction and Classification Using

Hilbert Empirical Wavelet Transform, Singular Value Decomposition, and SOM Neural Network." *Journal of Vibration and Control* 24, no. 12 (2018): 2512–2531. https://doi.org/10.1177/1077546316688991

Mohindru, Vandana, Ravindara Bhatt, and Yashwant Singh. "Reauthentication Scheme for Mobile Wireless Sensor Networks." *Sustainable Computing: Informatics and Systems* 23 (2019): 158–166.

Mohindru, Vandana, Yashwant Singh, and Ravindara Bhatt. "Securing Wireless Sensor Networks from Node Clone Attack: A Lightweight Message Authentication Algorithm." *International Journal of Information and Computer Security* 12, no. 2–3 (2020): 217–233.

Mohindru, Vandana, Sunidhi Vashishth, and Deepak Bathija. "Internet of Things (IoT) for Healthcare Systems: A Comprehensive Survey." *Recent Innovations in Computing: Proceedings of ICRIC 2021* 1 (2022): 213–229.

Nair, Manish, Tommaso Cappello, Shuping Dang, Vaia Kalokidou, and Mark A. Beach. "RF Fingerprinting of LoRa Transmitters Using Machine Learning with Self-Organizing Maps for Cyber Intrusion Detection." In *2022 IEEE/MTT-S International Microwave Symposium-IMS 2022*, pp. 491–494. IEEE, 2022.

Prabha, R., and Sankaran, S. "An Experimental Platform for Security of Cyber Physical Systems." In *2019 IEEE International Symposium on Smart Electronic Systems (iSES) (Formerly iNiS)*, pp. 123–128, December 2019, IEEE.

Preuveneers, Davy, and Elisabeth Ilie-Zudor. "The Intelligent Industry of the Future: A Survey on Emerging Trends, Research Challenges and Opportunities in Industry 4.0." *Journal of Ambient Intelligence and Smart Environments* 9, no. 3 (2017): 287–298. https://doi.org/10.3233/ais-170432

Sakkari, Mohamed, and Mourad Zaied. "A Convolutional Deep Self-Organizing Map Feature Extraction for Machine Learning." *Multimedia Tools and Applications* 79, no. 27–28 (March 24, 2020): 19451–19470. https://doi.org/10.1007/s11042-020-08822-9

Salem, Maher, and Ulrich Buehler. "An enhanced GHSOM for IDS." In *2013 IEEE International Conference on Systems, Man, and Cybernetics*, pp. 1138–1143, 2013, IEEE. https://doi.org/10.1109/smc.2013.198

Toshpulatov, M., and N. Zincir-Heywood, "Anomaly Detection on Smart Meters Using Hierarchical Self Organizing Maps." In *2021 IEEE Canadian Conference on Electrical and Computer Engineering (CCECE)*, ON, Canada, 2021, pp. 1–6. https://doi.org/10.1109/CCECE53047.2021.9569097

Vasighi, Mahdi, and Homa Amini. "A Directed Batch Growing Approach to Enhance the Topology Preservation of Self-Organizing Map." *Applied Soft Computing* 55 (2017): 424–435.

Wang, Qian, Cheng Wang, Zhen-yuan Feng, and Jin-feng Ye. "Review of K-Means Clustering Algorithm." *Electronic Design Engineering* 20, no. 7 (2012): 21–24. http://en.cnki.com.cn/Article_en/CJFDTotal-GWDZ201207009.htm

Wilson, Ryan, and Charlie Obimbo. "Self-Organizing Feature Maps for User-to-Root and Remote-to-Local Network Intrusion Detection on the KDD Cup 1999 Dataset." In *2011 World Congress on Internet Security (WorldCIS-2011)*, pp. 42–47, 2011, IEEE. https://doi.org/10.1109/worldcis17046.2011.5749879

Yao, X. Q., G. Tang, and X. Hu. "Method for Recognizing Mechanical Status of Container Crane Motor Based on SOM Neural Network." In *IOP Conference Series: Materials Science and Engineering*, vol. 435, p. 12009. 2018. (15) https://doi.org/10.1088/1757-899x/435/1/012009

Yin, Chunyong, Sun Zhang, and Kwang-jun Kim. "Mobile Anomaly Detection Based on Improved Self-Organizing Maps." *Mobile Information Systems* 2017 (2017). https://doi.org/10.1155/2017/5674086

Ying, Wu, and Yan Pingfan. "A Study on Structural Adapting Self Organizing Neural Network." *Acta Electronica Sinica* 7 (1999). http://en.cnki.com.cn/Article_en/CJFDTotalDZXU907.013.htm

11 Machine Learning–Based Early Diagnosis of Unstable Cyber-Physical Systems

Saumya Rajvanshi, Gurleen Kaur, and Kapil Mehta

Chandigarh Group of Colleges, India

11.1 INTRODUCTION

Cyber-physical systems (CPS) have emerged as a significant technological advancement that integrates physical and cyber automation in real time. The CPS network connects the physical and cyber worlds, allowing for real-time communication, remote control, and management of mechanical objects. However, the integration of physical and cyber worlds presents new challenges and vulnerabilities, making safety and privacy the primary concerns for CPSs.

Machine learning (ML) technologies have been employed to enhance CPS security. Anomaly detection using ML-based methodologies is crucial for maintaining CPS security (Kim and Park 2021). Live/captured data from the cyber-physical system is compared with forecasted producing systems based on reference datasets available during training. We classify semi-supervised learning-based techniques, clustering algorithms, semi-supervised learning, and reinforcement learning into four classes.

The physical system, network, and software applications compose the three layers of the CPS system that we discuss in this chapter. From the viewpoints of the physical system, network, and computation system, we analyze the taxonomy of attacks that are cyber-physical for each layer and assess prior research on identifying cyber-physical breaches using standard machine learning (ML) methodologies (Jadidi et al. 2022).

Virtual security threats to CPSs must be examined carefully to ensure the safety of these systems. The development of effective security measures for CPSs is imperative to ensure the continued safe operation of these systems. The findings and recommendations of this chapter can be used as a foundation for future research and development in CPS security.

DOI: 10.1201/9781003406105-15

11.2 UNDERSTANDING UNSTABLE CYBER-PHYSICAL SYSTEMS AND THEIR CONSEQUENCES

Unstable cyber-physical systems (CPS) are systems that experience unexpected or unpredictable behavior due to disruptions or disturbances in the physical or cyber world. These disruptions can be caused by natural phenomena such as earthquakes or human-made events like cyber-attacks. The consequences of unstable CPS can be severe, ranging from equipment damage and financial loss to injury or loss of life (Yu 2021).

Unstable CPS can happen for a wide range of reasons, involving software faults, hardware issues interruptions in networks, and intrusions. It proves difficult to recognize and deal with destabilization issues in CPS as a result of its intricate structure, and it includes cyber and physical systems interacting in real time (Ashibani and Mahmoud 2017).

In vital infrastructure systems, which include electric power lines, transit systems, and healthcare facilities, the impacts of an unstable CPS can be devastating. For instance, an insecure electricity grid could end up resulting in blackouts, which can cause serious disruptions to society and the economy. Similar to the previous illustration, a volatile healthcare sector can cause disruptions in health services that damage or kill sufferers.

A crucial aspect of ensuring that there is no threat to the operation of CPS is the detection and management of unstable CPS. For uncovering unstable CPS, conventional methods including fault-tree analysis and rule-based systems have been submitted for d their application. However, the amount of detail and variation of CPS are beyond the limits of traditional approaches (Junejo and Goh 2016).

The use of algorithms for machine learning (ML) has evolved into an attractive option for detecting and managing unstable CPS. Large volumes of data generated by CPS can be utilized to teach ML systems to find anomalous patterns that typical methods would overlook. Real-time ML-based diagnosis offers the early evaluation and reduction of issues associated with instability.

It is critical to learn about unstable CPS and its impact to create efficient testing and preventive approaches. There will be an increased danger of instability and distractions as CPS becomes more integrated and sophisticated look. Therefore, it is necessary to create precise and effective methods for identifying and preventing unstable CPS to ensure the secure and secure operation of CPS (Tyagi and Sreenath 2021).

11.2.1 IMPORTANCE OF EARLY DIAGNOSIS

Initial identification is necessary in unstable cyber-physical systems (CPS) because it assists in avoiding security breaches that may harm the physical system and the people who use it. The worth of early diagnosis has been demonstrated by the points that follow:

- **Prevention of network crashes**: Quick identification of prospective problems could reveal them before they escalate into serious challenges that can result in system descriptions and downtime.

- **Improved network accuracy**: Initial identification aids in discovering potential vulnerabilities in the system, letting the start of remedial measures and mitigating system episodes of breakdowns.
- **Effort and resource savings**: System improvements take minimal time as well as less cash when they get detected early. Also, it saves costs on major immediate repairs.
- **Limiting damages**: Rapid diagnosis can minimize harm to the human body's physical system and guard against jeopardy.
- **Improving platform efficacy**: By highlighting trouble spots, early testing assists the entire system in operating more.
- **Strengthening privacy**: Rapid diagnosis helps spot potential dangers before they can cause any kind of damage.
- **Minimizing litigation challenges**: Corrective action can be useful in averting legal challenges that may evolve as a result of system failures.
- **Ensuring platform longevity**: By recognizing and solving any issue that is likely to result in premature failure, early diagnosis can extend the existence of the system as a whole.
- **Lowering software delay**: Network time off, which may outcome in significant financial losses for organizations, can be minimized via diagnosing problems early on (Kayan et al. 2022).

11.3 MACHINE LEARNING'S (ML) FUNCTION IN CPS SECURITY

Cyber-physical system (CPS) security is greatly enhanced by machine learning (ML). CPSs become more complicated and harder to keep safe as they combine physical components with cyber intelligence. These systems' overall security can be boosted by machine learning (ML) methods that could help in recognizing threats and inconsistencies (Raza et al. 2022).

Numerous ML-based techniques, which include intrusion detection, malware recognition, and finding anomalies, have been used for better CPS security. These approaches are successful in discovering cyber-physical leaps in large-scale, complex CPSs when normal security measures might not be appropriate.

Methods that use machine learning have perks for CPS security; nonetheless, there are still issues that still have to be tackled. Particularly, selecting and gathering source sources can be a challenging and tedious procedure. In addition, the setting up of ML-based strategies in large-scale CPSs may be heavy on resources and demanding analytically.

In general, ML-based methodologies are essential for the security of CPSs, primarily when it relates to anomaly detection. The implementation of methods based on machine learning will continue to be required as CPSs become more widely used and convoluted for their confidentiality and security. Whilst there are challenges when taking these tactics into execution, what benefits they offer in terms of identifying cyber-physical dangers make them a significant tool in CPS management.

11.3.1 Types of Datasets Used for Training Machine Learning Models

There are various types of datasets used for activity machine erudition models, reckon:

- **Labeled Datasets**: Each data point in these datasets has been previously granted labels or tags discovering its class or genre. For instruction, approved machine learning models need to be identified in training data.
- **Unlabeled Datasets**: Every data point in those datasets doesn't currently have a label or tag allocated to it. On data sets without labels, unsupervised machine learning algorithms can be developed.
- **Time-Series Datasets**: Every data point in these datasets has a unique time fingerprint due to their temporal-dependent structure. On timing-series databases, methods of machine learning for time-varying data can be picked up.
- **Image Datasets**: These collections of data include visuals or graphics. Machine learning algorithms for visual recognition can be obtained through image samples.
- **Text Datasets**: These collections of data incorporate text-based data like communications, files, or entries on social media platforms. Text datasets are suitable for training algorithms using machine learning to handle natural languages.
- **Audio Datasets**: These datasets include musical data such as music, sound effects, and voice. Machine learning methods for speech identifying and processing sounds can be educated on aural files.
- **Graph Datasets**: These datasets display information as visualizations, with any node suggesting a point of information and each edge suggesting the associations between the points in the data. On graph historical data, methods of machine learning based on colonies can be learned (Zhang et al. 2021).

By its area, the method for machine learning being used, and the data in conjunction, the proper dataset type ought to have been determined.

11.3.2 Early Diagnosis with Machine Learning Algorithms

- **Decision Trees**: Regression and classification analysis often employs decision trees. They are easy to comprehend because they are basic and intuitive. Decision trees can be deployed to categorize various CPS responses and discover the root cause of the problem.
- **Artificial Neural Networks (ANNs)**: ANNs' propensity to learn from data is what makes them a popular tool for CPS diagnosis. Classification, regression, and grouping tasks can be achieved with ANNs. ANNs are used frequently to model and forecast CPS movement.
- **Support Vector Machines (SVMs)**: SVMs have been widely used in regression and classification analyses. SVMs are recognized for having a high degree of accuracy and for being capable of managing complex data sets. SVMs can be employed for determining various CPS patterns (Jadidi et al. 2022).

- **Random Forests**: A compilation of decision trees, randomly generated forests. For regression and classification analysis, they are used frequently. It has become apparent that Random Forests can handle enormous data sets and can deliver exceptional precision. CPS diagnosis can be accomplished via random forest algorithms.
- **K-Nearest Neighbor (KNN)**: KNN is a simplistic and efficient methodology used in both regression and classification experiments. It runs by discovering the k-nearest companions to the given data point and is based on the similarity idea. KNN might be used to diagnose CPS.
- **Clustering**: To find a collection of similar information points, strategies for clustering have been used. By discovering clusters of CPS conduct clustering can be implemented for identifying CPS.
- **Principal Component Analysis (PCA)**: Its dimensionality-reduction procedure is known as PCA. By decreasing the number of different factors that need to be analyzed, PCA can be used for CPS assessment.
- **Long Short-Term Memory (LSTM) Networks**: Time-series evaluation is one application for LSTM networks, a subset of ANN. It is simple to detect time-dependent CPS action via networks of LSTM (Zhang et al. 2021).
- **Convolutional Neural Networks (CNNs)**: CNNs, a subset of ANN, are widely used in the broadcasting and image processing industries. CNNs can be used to evaluate the patterns of behavior of image-based CPS.
- **Reinforcement Learning**: Reinforcement learning is an instance of an ML algorithm that happens when an agent picks up knowledge concerning its surroundings by making mistakes. By streamlining the decision-making process, reinforcement learning can be employed to diagnose CPS activity (Mohammadi et al. 2020).

11.3.3 CASE STUDIES ON MACHINE LEARNING–BASED EARLY DIAGNOSIS OF UNSTABLE CPS

- **Case Study 1**: Detect HVAC System Issues Early. The heating and ventilation system is a vital component of a building's structures, and a breakdown can cause serious disruptions to normal operations. The early warning indications of an HVAC system breakdown were identified in this case study using a machine learning algorithm. The algorithm was trained on prior information on HVAC equipment operation and was able to conduct real-time anomaly detection. This stopped a complete breakdown of the system and permitted its regular consumption, saving the business a lot of expense and inconvenience.
- **Case Study 2**: Early Detection of Power Grid Degradation. Power grids are important pieces of facilities that need to be closely examined for any indicators of instability or collapse. In this case study, a machine learning system was employed to detect a possible power grid failure in its infancy. The software program was able to identify problems in the electrical nature grid's performance in real time after being taught previous data. This avoided blackouts and other major problems by enabling the system

operators to take corrective action before the complete breakdown trans-
pired (Olowononi et al. 2020).

- **Case Study 3**: Autonomous Vehicle Problems Early Identification. Integrated
cyber-physical systems have to exist for autonomous vehicles to perform
their tasks safely and efficiently. In this case study, an algorithm that uses
machine learning is being used to identify potential problems with autonomous vehicles. The program was able to identify anomalies in real time after
having been taught on historical performance data of the vehicle. This eliminated accidents and maintained the safety of passengers and other road users
by enabling the vehicle to be mended before a complete breakdown arose.

- **Case Study 4**: Detecting Industrial Equipment Failure Early. The efficient
running of manufacturing plants and other industrial facilities relies on the
equipment used in their operations. In this case study, a malfunction early
in the process was identified using an algorithm made up of machine learning. The application was able to detect anomalies in real time after being
educated on the past performance of the equipment data. This prevented
downtime and guaranteed the company's effective operation when the
equipment could be restored before it was altogether damaged (Rouzbahani
et al., 2020).

- **Case Study 5**: Detecting Medical Instrument Failure Early. The safe and
successful therapy of patients in hospitals and other health facilities depends
on the availability of medical devices. In this case study, a machine learning
algorithm was put to use to identify prospective medical equipment failure
at its earliest stages. The application was able to spot anomalies in real time
after being trained on past performance of the equipment data. This reduced
patient harm and protected the facility's ability to offer outstanding care by
allowing the technology to be fixed before it altogether degraded.

11.4   THREE-LAYER CPS SYSTEM

Cyber-physical systems (CPS) blend technology with the physical environment by
combining interlinked physical and cyber components that operate in real time. Safety
and privacy are the top challenges for CPSs because these systems make use of many
cyber-physical systems and sophisticated characteristics that are prone to various
risks and attacks. The key component of sustaining security is anomaly detection. We
suggest a three-layer CPS system for using machine learning to perform early exami-
nations of unstable cyber-physical systems to navigate these difficulties as shown in
Figure 11.1 (Ahmed et al. 2021).

11.4.1   Physical System Layer

The bodily layer, also known as the first layer of the CPS system, contains the system's physical elements, notably its sensors, actuators, and controllers. These elements generate data that are sent to the network layer as a consequence of their
interactions with the physical environment. Data from the physical layer is gathered
and examined by the physical layer it is sent to the network layer for extra processing.

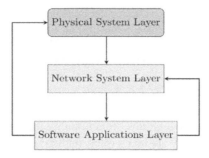

FIGURE 11.1   Three-layer CPS system.

The physical layer is at risk from cyber-physical invasions such as sensor or actuator attacks which can make the system's physical components behave strangely or malfunction. Anomaly recognition methods based on machine learning are used to identify such attacks. Those methods study the sensor data and compare it to the physiological technique's predicted function to spot any unusual events or discrepancies (Khojasteh et al. 2020).

In a nutshell, the physical layer is a crucial part of the CPS system and is in charge of acquiring, analyzing, and passing on data from the physical world to the network layer. Cyber-physical attacks can be made against it, and machine learning–based variance detection techniques can be recycled to find threats. To stop and lessen the adverse consequences of attacks, the real-world system's buildings are equally significant.

11.4.2   Network System Layer

Between the physical and cyber portions of the CPS, reliable and secure communication can be guaranteed by the network layer. It includes the infrastructure needed to handle the transfer of information and control messages, enabling the remote control of physical things. A variety of technologies, including cable and wireless communications, are included at the network layer to enable constant interaction between the physical and digital worlds (Bokovnya and Begishev 2022).

However, the addition of so many CPSs and smart features in a network might lead to security threats and vulnerabilities. The risks involved might be internal or external and might involve denial-of-service attacks, data breaches, and malicious attacks on the network infrastructure. Security measures including antivirus programs, intrusion detection systems, and encryption technologies are used in the complex layer to mitigate these threats.

The network layer of CPSs might benefit from improved safety thanks to machine learning (ML). Examples of ML algorithms can examine network data to find unusual activity that might point to a possible security breach. These algorithms are capable of recognizing patterns and deviations in network traffic using past data, and when found may immediately warn security staff of potential risks.

Overall, the key component of CPSs that permits real-time communication between physical and cyber components is the networked layer. To protect the security and privacy of the CPS, it also offers several security issues that must be resolved. Security based on machine learning can be quite effective in decreasing these risks to safety (Diaz-Rozo et al. 2017).

11.4.3 Software Applications Layer

The top layer of the three-layer CPS system, known as the software applications layer, is in charge of creating high-level functionality that enables the CPS to carry out specific functions. To carry out many roles, including the monitoring and control of physical systems, data processing, and analysis, this layer interacts with both the structure of the system layer and the network layer.

Machine learning–based techniques can be used in the software applications layer to find abnormalities and identify any CPS instability. These algorithms are capable of examining data gathered from the linkage layer and the physical system layer to spot any unforeseen behavior that might be a sign of a cyber-physical intrusion (Pan et al. 2017).

Some common applications of machine learning in the software applications layer include fault detection and diagnosis, predictive maintenance, and anomaly detection. For instance, machine learning algorithms can be trained to detect early warning signs of an impending failure in a physical component of the CPS, enabling timely maintenance and preventing system downtime.

Overall, the software applications layer plays a crucial role in the functioning of CPSs, and machine learning–based approaches can significantly enhance the security and reliability of these systems (Nazarenko and Safdar 2019).

11.4.4 Taxonomy of Cyber-Physical Outbreaks on Each Layer

The physical layer, network layer, and software layer are all included in the taxonomy of cyber-physical attacks on each layer of the CPS system.

Physical Layer Attacks: The physical layer of the CPS system includes the physical objects and devices that interact with the cyber world. Attacks on this layer can cause physical damage to the devices or the environment. Some common types of attacks on this layer include:

- Tampering with sensors: Attackers may modify the sensor readings to cause false alarms or hide their activities.
- Denial-of-service (DoS) attacks: Attackers may overload the physical system with excessive requests, leading to system failure.
- Physical destruction: Attackers may physically damage the devices or infrastructure, leading to system failure or even harm to people.

Network Layer Attacks: The network layer of the CPS system connects the physical layer with the software application layer. Attacks on this layer can compromise the network infrastructure, leading to data theft, system failure, or other malicious activities. Some common types of attacks on this layer include:

- Man-in-the-middle (MITM) attacks allow for the theft of information or system-level adjustment by allowing attackers to intercept and alter communication between both the hardware and the software layers.
- Eavesdropping: Attackers intercept and listen to the communication between the physical and software layers, allowing them to steal sensitive data (Mozaffari et al. 2020).
- Network flooding: Attackers send a large volume of network traffic to overload the network infrastructure, causing system failure (Dibaji et al. 2019).

Software Application Layer Attacks: The software programming and algorithms that regulate the operations of the physical system are part of the CPS system's software application layer. Attacks on this layer have the capability to reduce the system's functionality or force it to act maliciously. Following are some common sorts of attacks on this layer:

- Malware attacks: Offenders implant software utilizing malware so they can take over the system or steal private data.
- Exploiting vulnerabilities: Attackers locate and take pleasure in flaws in software, granting them access to the system or a chance to change how the software performs.
- Social engineering attacks: Attackers trick users into providing sensitive information or performing malicious actions, allowing them to compromise the system (Yaacoub et al. 2020).

In closing, the taxonomy of physical cyber assaults on each tier of the CPS system demonstrates different sorts of attacks that can jeopardize these systems' security. To create efficient precautions to defend CPSs, it is imperative to fully understand these attacks.

11.5 ML-BASED ANOMALY DETECTION FOR CPS SECURITY

A possible approach for alleviating the security problems related to cyber-physical systems (CPS) is the application of machine learning (ML). One of the primary objectives of ML-based safeguards for CPS is anomaly detection. Anomalies in the CPS system are anomalies from typical behaviors or projected patterns. These anomalies might be a sign of cyber-physical threats or deficiencies which is depicted in Figure 11.2 (Severino et al. 2021).

For CPS security, based on machine learning anomaly detection uses algorithms that find patterns from big datasets that depict typical system behaviors. Then, anything departing from the norm that could indicate an anomaly or a security breach is found via these patterns (Baras 2019).

Several methods using machine learning can be employed for CPS security anomaly detection. Semi-supervised methods based on learning are one such methodology. Those techniques train a machine learning (ML) framework using a restricted amount of data that is labeled, which is then applied to data without labels to find irregularities.

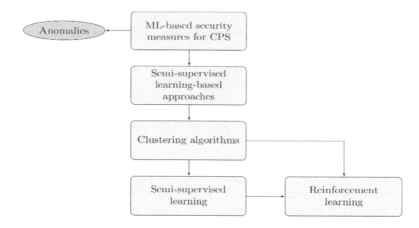

FIGURE 11.2 ML-based anomaly detection for CPS security.

In CPS security, algorithms for clustering are also applied for anomaly detection. These algorithms organize data points based on how similar they are and spot anomalies, or data points that cannot be grouped into any clusters or achieve novel clusters.

An additional approach for CPS security anomaly detection is semi-supervised learning. In this method, unlabeled and colored data are combined to construct an ML model that can detect anomalies in the CPS system (Nazarenko and Safdar 2019).

Anomaly detection in CPS security employs reinforcement learning. Using such an approach, an agent is trained to communicate with the CPS system and learn how to spot anomalies based on the rewards it earns for effective anomaly identification.

In conclusion, ML-based anomaly detection is a potential method for overcoming cyber-physical systems' security issues. ML-based security solutions could help in preventing cyber-physical threats and vulnerabilities by recognizing irregularities in the CPS system and protecting the security and privacy of CPS subscribers (Palumbo et al. 2023).

11.5.1 Semi-Supervised Learning-Based Approaches

By employing both labeled and unlabeled data to train a model for anomaly detection in cyber-physical systems (CPS), semi-supervised technology-based approaches are a classic instance of artificial intelligence (AI). The primary concept is to instruct the model to distinguish between typical and unusual conduct in the CPS using a little bit of market data and an even greater quantity of raw data. The semi-supervised learning-based approach involves the following steps in Figure 11.3:

- Manually label a small subset of the data: Using specialist knowledge or professional judgment, just a little of the data is manually labeled as reflecting typical or abnormal behavior.

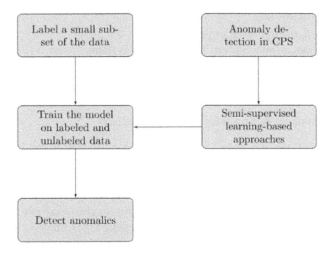

FIGURE 11.3   Semi-supervised learning-based approaches.

- Train the model on named and unlabeled data: A semi-supervised learning technique is used to train the model on both named and unlabeled data. Apart from using the unlabeled data to understand the underlying patterns and structure of the data, this technique makes use of the labeled data to direct the model toward the proper classification of both typical and abnormal activities.
- Identify abnormalities: The model can be employed to determine anomalies in the CPS once it is successfully trained. As the model is applied to fresh data, behavior is regarded as normal if the results of the model are below an established limit. As the output exceeds the threshold, the behavior is marked as strange, necessitating further investigation.

11.5.1.1   Popular Procedures or Methodologies
- Self-training: A fast and efficient methodology that involves incorporating unlabeled data into the labeled dataset for training while employing the model to predict labels for the unlabeled information.
- Co-training: The process in which two or more models receive training on various sets of features or angles of the data, and the data that is unlabeled is used to incrementally enhance the models.
- Transductive SVM: A technique for classification of unlabeled data that involves solving a support vector machine, also called an SVM, issue with both labeled and unlabeled data and then putting the resultant decision margin. Label Propagation: A method that involves propagating the labels of the labeled data to the unlabeled data based on the similarity between their feature vectors.

11.5.1.2 Applications

- Anomaly detection in smart grid systems
- Intrusion detection in industrial mechanism systems
- Fault detection in transportation systems
- Cyber-physical security in insolent home systems

11.5.2 CLUSTERING ALGORITHMS FOR CPS SECURITY

Unsupervised learning has been carried out using clustering algorithms, a sort of machine learning strategy. To find patterns and structures in the data, these algorithms group data points based on how similar they are. Clustering techniques can be used by cyber-physical systems and also for security and anomaly detection.

For CPS security, a variety various methodologies for clustering can be used. Here are thorough descriptions of a few important clustering algorithms:

- **K-Means Huddling**: One of the most used methods to cluster in machine learning is K-Means Clustering. It partitions the data into k clusters, where k is an optional parameter. The technique assigns each data point to the nearby centroid by selecting by chance k centroids, one for each of the clusters. The mean of all the data points in the cluster is then captured, and the centroids are updated. Up till convergence has been reached, this process is repeated (Severino et al. 2021).

    K-Means Clustering is commonly used in CPS security for grouping data points according to how similar they are and to find anomalies, or data points that do not fit into any given cluster or create fresh groups.
- **Hierarchical Clustering**: A clustering deal with titled hierarchical clustering develops a group with a structure imitating a tree. The technique first views each data point as a separate cluster and then iteratively joins the clusters that are most similar until all of the data points are handled as a single cluster of data.

    Hierarchical Clustering can be used in CPS security for finding anomalies as data points that do not belong to any regions or create new groups and to sort data points depending on how similar they are. The clusters' hierarchical organization can also provide context on the CPS system's essential structure (Dibaji et al. 2019).
- **Density-Based Spatial Clustering of Solicitations with Noise (DBSCAN)**: Data points are grouped via the density-based clustering algorithm DBSCAN. The algorithm expands the clusters by adding further adjacent data points that satisfy the density requirements after finding basic points, which are data points with a minimum number of siblings within a given radius.

    DBSCAN can be used in CPS security for identifying aberrations as data points that do not fit into any clusters or build new groups and to sort data points depending on their density. This technique is very effective at finding abnormalities in data that include erratic forms and transforming densities.

- **Expectation-Maximization (EM) Clustering**: A probabilistic clustering algorithm titled EM clustering makes a case that the data points were produced using a variety of probability distributions. The technique assigns each data point to the probability distribution that most closely matches the data by first estimating the variables that are part of the distributions.

  To find anomalies or points in the data that do not fit into any normal distribution or have low probabilities, EM clustering can be used in CPS security to group data points by their probability distribution (Diaz-Rozo et al. 2017).

In conclusion, the algorithms for clustering are a helpful tool for CPS security since they may be used to spot anomalies and reveal information about the system's underlying structure. Among the most prevalent clustering methods are K-Means Clustering, Pyramid Clustering, DBSCAN, and EM clustering.

11.5.3 Reinforcement Learning for CPS Security

Cyber-physical system (CPS) security has used reinforcement learning (RL), a machine learning technique. Real-world learning (RL) is a sort of learning in which an agent learns how to interact in a given environment by acting and getting rewarded or punished. RL can be used in the context of CPS control to create rules to govern the system and spot behavior that is unusual. An agent interacts with surroundings to learn how to optimally utilize a cumulative reward signal in reinforcement learning, a type of machine learning. RL can be used for CPS security to create guidelines that regulate the system and discover unusual behavior.

11.5.3.1 Performances for CPS Security

Following are some reinforcement training techniques for CPS security:

- **Markov methods for decision-making**: In CPS security, reinforcement learning uses Markov Decision Products (MDPs) to replicate the system. An MDP is a mathematical framework used to simulate how an agent interacts with its surroundings and rewards. A selection of states, actions, and transitional probabilities. To maximize the cumulative reward over time, the agent employs the MDP to identify which actions to execute in every situation as in Figure 11.4 (Palumbo et al. 2023).
- **Q-learning**: A procedure for reinforcement teaching that teaches an optimal action-value function. This function assesses what is expected cumulative reward when executing an action in a particular scenario. Based on the rewards acquired and the Q-values of the future state, the algorithm changes the Q-values.
- **Deep Reinforcement Learning**: To learn representations for the state and action spaces, deep reinforcement learning (DRL) blends reinforcement learning. In smart grid networks and industrial control systems, DRL algorithms, notably deep Q-networks (DQNs) and deep deterministic policy

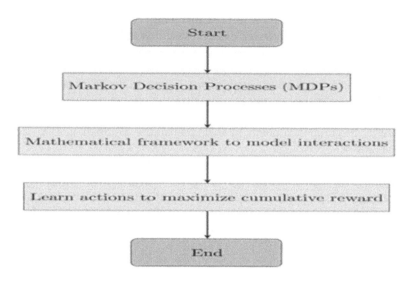

FIGURE 11.4 Markov decision processes.

gradient (DDPG), have been applied in recognizing cyber-physical warnings (Filho et al. 2021).
- **Adversarial Reinforcement Learning (ARL)**: A methodology that teaches agents to defend against attacks by replicating the behavior of the attacker. The agent gains a chance to take steps to reduce the estimated loss brought on by the attacker's actions. In smart grid networks and industrial control systems, ARL has been utilized to recognize and combat cyber-physical threats.
- **Game theory**: A mathematical model that simulates how various individuals act in a strategic context. The partnerships between cyber attackers and defenders in CPS security can be studied using game theory. The agents learn to choose actions that will increase their rewards while minimizing those of their competitors as depicted in Figure 11.5 (Baras 2019).

11.6   ENSURING SAFETY AND PRIVACY IN CPS

It is crucial for cyber-physical systems (CPSs) for them to have strong security measures in effect. Our daily lives rely upon the control of these systems over vital infrastructure, such as public transportation, power, and water distribution lines. A CPS security breach may have serious negative effects on the economy, the environment, and society (Olowononi et al. 2020).

For instance, an online criminal could gain control of a power grid, leading to substantial disturbances and blackouts. Criminals in the transportation field could have an impact on intersections, which causes catastrophes and congestion. In the field of healthcare, a hacker could compromise healthcare devices, compromising the safety of patients (Mohindru et al., 2019).

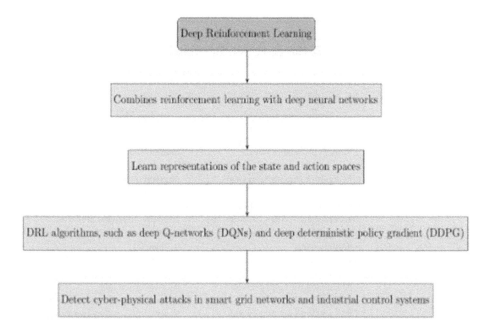

FIGURE 11.5   Deep reinforcement learning.

The interconnected nature of the systems further exacerbates potential risks related to cyber-physical threats. Numerous systems could be impacted by a hacking attack in one system, possibly resulting in a chain of failures. Therefore, to stop cyber-physical attacks and lessen the damage they cause, it is critical to design suitable safety measures for CPSs.

The implementation of CPS security measures is an intricate problem that needs an array of approaches. Security measures require taking seriously not only the technical aspects of the system along with the organizational and human components. To guarantee for illustration, security policies and processes must be established and carried out (Mohindru and Singh 2018).

Cyber-physical security breaches have ramifications that go far beyond technology. Our daily lives are dependent on the management of CPSs over crucial facilities like electrical lines, water supply mechanisms, and transportation routes. These systems' security could be deteriorating, contributing to severe disruptions and possibly catastrophic catastrophes. A hacker who acquires access to a power grid, for example, might shut down whole cities, causing mayhem and maybe compromising people's lives (Mohindru et al. 2020).

Therefore, it is essential to put together efficient security measures to shield CPSs from online threats. Identifying and addressing threats as they materialize needs not only the creation of robust safety measures but also continual surveillance and assessment.

11.7   COMPARATIVE ANALYSIS

Table 11.1 is the comparison of traditional methods vs. machine learning for early diagnosis in CPS.

TABLE 11.1
Comparison of Traditional Methods versus Machine Learning

Traditional Methods versus Machine Learning for Early Diagnosis in CPS	Traditional Methods	Machine Learning
Data Collection	Data is collected manually or through predefined rules.	Data is automatically collected in real time from the CPS network.
Data Processing	Data is processed using statistical methods or rule-based systems.	ML methods like neural networks, decision trees, and support vector machines are used to process data.
Accuracy	Traditional methods have limited accuracy due to the lack of ability to handle complex patterns and noise in data.	ML-based methods have higher accuracy due to the ability to handle complex patterns and noise in data.
Scalability	Traditional methods have limited scalability and can be time-consuming for large datasets.	ML-based methods have high scalability and can process large datasets efficiently.
Training Time	Traditional methods require less training time as they use predefined rules or statistical models.	ML-based methods require more training time as they learn patterns and relationships from data.
Detection Time	Traditional methods have a longer detection time as they require manual intervention and analysis.	ML-based methods have a shorter detection time as they can analyze data in real time and detect anomalies automatically.
Maintenance	Traditional methods require manual updates and maintenance to adjust rules or models.	ML-based methods require updates to the ML model or training data but can be automated to a large extent.
Adaptability	Traditional methods have limited adaptability and may not be suitable for detecting new types of threats.	ML-based methods can adapt to new types of threats by learning from new data and updating the ML model.
Human Involvement	Traditional methods require more human involvement for data processing and analysis.	ML-based methods require less human involvement for data processing and analysis.
Interpretability	Traditional methods are more interpretable as the rules and models are transparent.	ML-based methods can be less interpretable as the ML model may not be transparent, and it may be difficult to explain how a decision was made.
False Positives	Traditional methods may generate more false positives due to the limitations of rule-based or statistical models.	ML-based methods can be less interpretable as the ML model may not be transparent, and it may be difficult to explain how a decision was made.
False Negatives	Traditional methods may generate more false negatives due to the limitations of rule-based or statistical models.	ML-based methods may generate fewer false negatives due to the ability to handle complex patterns and noise in data.

(Continued)

TABLE 11.1 (Continued)

Traditional Methods versus Machine Learning for Early Diagnosis in CPS	Traditional Methods	Machine Learning
Type of Anomalies Detected	Traditional methods are limited in detecting anomalies that are not predefined in the rules or models.	ML-based methods can detect a wide range of anomalies, including those that are not predefined in the ML model.
Complexity of Anomalies Detected	Traditional methods may not be able to detect complex anomalies due to the limitations of rule-based or statistical models.	ML-based methods can detect complex anomalies that may not be detected by traditional methods.
Performance	Traditional methods may have lower performance in terms of truthfulness and detection time compared to ML-based methods.	ML-based methods have higher performance in terms of precision and detection time compared to traditional methods.
Integration with CPS	Traditional techniques may require manual integration with the CPS network.	ML-based procedures can be integrated with the CPS network and perform real-time analysis.
Cost	Traditional methods may have lower costs compared to ML-based methods.	ML-based methods may have a higher cost compared to traditional methods.

11.8 FUTURE DIRECTIONS FOR MACHINE LEARNING–BASED EARLY DIAGNOSIS OF UNSTABLE CPS

The field of machine learning–based early diagnosis of unstable cyber-physical systems (CPS) is still in its early stages, with many challenges and opportunities ahead. It will go about some of the ability future options in the following sections to increase the level of accuracy and reliability based on machine learning diagnoses of insecure CPS.

- **Integration of Multiple ML Approaches**: Future research might concentrate on developing hybrid algorithms that bring together several Machine Learning techniques to assist in the quick identification of Unstable CPS. This is going to reduce the potential of false positives and false negatives while also enhancing the accuracy of diagnosis. The degree of precision and quantity of data that are readily available for validation and development is heavily dependent on ML algorithms.
- **Increased Collection and Processing**: To ensure that outstanding data is readily accessible to neural networks, further studies can concentrate on establishing data collecting and processing approaches for CPS.
- **Advanced Sensor Information**: Sensors play a significant part in the precision of ML-based assessment of unstable CPS. The predictive power of ML algorithms will improve as an outcome of developments in sensor technology, which might result in better and more precise collecting of data.

- **Explainable AI**: This fledgling field tries to establish a program that can convey mathematical reasoning to people. To promote accountability and openness, further studies may concentrate on creating clarified artificial intelligence algorithms for ML-based identification of instability CPS.
- **Edge Computing**: This kind of computing involves handling and analyzing data closer to the data's source, at the network's edge. This may result in a more rapid and successful analysis of CPS data, boosting the accuracy and confidence of ML-based diagnosis.
- **Real-Time Diagnosis**: Preventing disasters while minimizing damage necessitates immediate diagnosis of fragile CPS. Future research could focus on creating artificial intelligence algorithms that can evaluate unstable CPS in real time.
- **Cybersquatting**: As a top concern for CPS, further studies could focus on developing machine learning (ML) algorithms that can distinguish and repel counterattacks on untrustworthy CPS.
- **Human Interaction**: It is extremely important to make sure that human operators are capable of communicating with the system because unstable CPS can have significant effects. The development of ML algorithms that enable individuals to communicate with dynamic CPS can be a field of future inquiry.
- **Scalability**: It is of the utmost significance that one be sure that ML algorithms can scale up to handle massive amounts of data and complex systems as the size and complexity of CPS increase.
- **Interoperability**: CPS frequently entails the fusion of many systems and technologies. To ensure interoperability, future research could focus on creating artificial intelligence (AI) algorithms that can act across various systems and platforms.

11.9 CONCLUSION

In conclusion, real-time coordination between physical and cyber automation has been made practicable by cyber-physical systems, or CPS. Safety and privacy are currently CPSs' primary priorities as an outcome of the higher challenges and liabilities that this incorporation has placed forth. The usefulness of these techniques depends strongly on the reference dataset given during training. Anomaly detection employing ML-based methodologies is essential for conserving CPS stability.

To address those issues and vulnerabilities, this chapter provided a three-layer CPS system involving the physical system, network, and software applications. Also, each layer's taxonomy of cyber-physical dangers was explored. As seen from the perspectives of the hardware system, networks, and computing subsystem, it also assessed past works on conventional machine learning (ML) techniques to spot cyber-physical security breaches.

The research paper also underlined just how important it is to carefully evaluate cybersecurity concerns to CPSs for the purpose of ensuring the security of these systems. To ensure the constant security of CPSs, which are becoming increasingly advanced, it is essential to implement appropriate security measures. Future studies and advancements in CPS security may capitalize on the findings and recommendations that are drawn from this piece of work.

In a nutshell, CPSs are complex mechanisms that require to be carefully thought out for optimal safety and confidentiality. The amalgamation of both the digital and physical realms in CPSs produces new issues and deficiencies that need to be handled. To ensure the continual security of CPSs, it is essential to implement proper safety precautions. As a result, CPS security research and development must be given top priority. The insights and suggestions made in this chapter can help move this method quickly.

REFERENCES

Ahmed, Rania Salih, Elmustafa Sayed Ali Ahmed, and Rashid A. Saeed. "Machine learning in cyber-physical systems in industry 4.0." In *Artificial Intelligence Paradigms for Smart Cyber-Physical Systems*, pp. 20–41. IGI global, 2021.

Ashibani, Yosef, and Qusay H. Mahmoud. "Cyber physical systems security: Analysis, challenges and solutions." *Computers & Security* 68 (2017): 81–97.

Baras, J. "Formal methods and tool suites for CSP security, safety and verification." *Engineering Secure and Dependable Software Systems* (2019): 1–7. 10.3233/978-1-61499-977-5-1

Bokovnya, Alexandra Yuryevna, and Ildar Rustamovich Begishev. "Taxonomy of attacks on cyber-physical systems: Technological and legal aspects." *Resmilitaris* 12, no. 2 (2022): 2200–2270.

Diaz-Rozo, Javier, Concha Bielza, and Pedro Larrañaga. "Machine learning-based CPS for clustering high throughput machining cycle conditions." *Procedia Manufacturing* 10 (2017): 997–1008.

Dibaji, Seyed Mehran, Mohammad Pirani, David Bezalel Flamholz, Anuradha M. Annaswamy, Karl Henrik Johansson, and Aranya Chakrabortty. "A systems and control perspective of CPS security." *Annual Reviews in Control* 47 (2019): 394–411.

Filho, Ênio Vasconcelos, Ricardo Severino, Anis Koubaa, and Eduardo Tovar. "A wireless safety and security layer architecture for reliable Co-CPS." In *DCE21 13 Symposium on Electrical and Computer Engineering: Book of Abstracts*, p. 27. 2021.

Jadidi, Zahra, Shantanu Pal, Nithesh Nayak, Arawinkumaar Selvakkumar, Chih-Chia Chang, Maedeh Beheshti, and Alireza Jolfaei. "Security of machine learning-based anomaly detection in cyber physical systems." In *2022 International Conference on Computer Communications and Networks (ICCCN)*, pp. 1–7. IEEE, 2022.

Junejo, Khurum Nazir, and Jonathan Goh. "Behaviour-based attack detection and classification in cyber physical systems using machine learning." In *Proceedings of the 2nd ACM International Workshop on Cyber-Physical System Security*, pp. 34–43, 2016.

Kayan, Hakan, Matthew Nunes, Omer Rana, Pete Burnap, and Charith Perera. "Cybersecurity of industrial cyber-physical systems: a review." *ACM Computing Surveys (CSUR)* 54, no. 11s (2022): 1–35.

Khojasteh, Mohammad Javad, Anatoly Khina, Massimo Franceschetti, and Tara Javidi. "Learning-based attacks in cyber-physical systems." *IEEE Transactions on Control of Network Systems* 8, no. 1 (2020): 437–449.

Kim, Sangjun, and Kyung-Joon Park. "A survey on machine-learning based security design for cyber-physical systems." *Applied Sciences* 11, no. 12 (2021): 5458.

Mohindru, Vandana, Ravindara Bhatt, and Yashwant Singh. "Reauthentication scheme for mobile wireless sensor networks." *Sustainable Computing: Informatics and Systems* 23 (2019): 158–166.

Mohindru, Vandana, and Yashwant Singh. "Node authentication algorithm for securing static wireless sensor networks from node clone attack." *International Journal of Information and Computer Security* 10, no. 2–3 (2018): 129–148.

Mohindru, Vandana, Yashwant Singh, and Ravindara Bhatt. "Securing wireless sensor networks from node clone attack: a lightweight message authentication algorithm." *International Journal of Information and Computer Security* 12, no. 2–3 (2020): 217–233.

Mozaffari, Farnaz Seyyed, Hadis Karimipour, and Reza M. Parizi. "Learning based anomaly detection in critical cyber-physical systems." *Security of Cyber-Physical Systems: Vulnerability and Impact* (2020): 107–130.

Nazarenko, Artem A., and Ghazanfar Ali Safdar. "Survey on security and privacy issues in cyber physical systems." *AIMS Electronics and Electrical Engineering* 3, no. 2 (2019): 111–143.

Olowononi, Felix O., Danda B. Rawat, and Chunmei Liu. "Resilient machine learning for networked cyber physical systems: A survey for machine learning security to securing machine learning for CPS." *IEEE Communications Surveys & Tutorials* 23, no. 1 (2020): 524–552.

Palumbo, Francesca, Raquel Lazcano, and Daniel Madroñal. "Towards a living dimension: the future of cyber-physical systems." *HiPEAC Vision 2023* (2023): 44–53.

Pan, Yao, Jules White, Douglas Schmidt, Ahmad Elhabashy, Logan Sturm, Jaime Camelio, and Christopher Williams. "Taxonomies for reasoning about cyber-physical attacks in IoT-based manufacturing systems." *International Journal of Interactive Multimedia and Artificial Intelligence (IJIMAI)* 4, no. 3 (2017): 45–54, http://doi.org/10.9781/ijimai.2017.437

Raza, Asad, Shahzad Memon, Muhammad Ali Nizamani, and Mahmood Hussain Shah. "Machine learning-based security solutions for critical cyber-physical systems." In *2022 10th International Symposium on Digital Forensics and Security (ISDFS)*, pp. 1–6. IEEE, 2022.

Mohammadi, Rouzbahani, Hossein, Hadis Karimipour, Abolfazl Rahimnejad, Ali Dehghantanha, and Gautam Srivastava. "Anomaly detection in cyber-physical systems using machine learning." *Handbook of Big Data Privacy*, pp. 219–235, Springer, Cham, 2020.

Severino, Ricardo, Anis Koubâa, and Eduardo Tovar. "A wireless safety and security layer architecture for reliable Co-CPS." In *4th Doctoral Congress in Engineering*. 2021.

Tyagi, Amit Kumar, and N. Sreenath. "Cyber physical systems: Analyses, challenges and possible solutions." *Internet of Things and Cyber-Physical Systems* 1 (2021): 22–33.

Yaacoub, Jean-Paul A., Ola Salman, Hassan N. Noura, Nesrine Kaaniche, Ali Chehab, and Mohamad Malli. "Cyber-physical systems security: Limitations, issues and future trends." *Microprocessors and microsystems* 77 (2020): 103201.

Yu, Zhenwei. "The poverty alleviation effect of smart financial services based on FPGA and wireless sensors." *Microprocessors and Microsystems* 80 (2021): 103518.

Zhang, Jun, Lei Pan, Qing-Long Han, Chao Chen, Sheng Wen, and Yang Xiang. "Deep learning based attack detection for cyber-physical system cybersecurity: A survey." *IEEE/CAA Journal of Automatica Sinica* 9, no. 3 (2021): 377–391.

Section V

Application Domains in Cyber-Physical Systems

Challenges, Trends, and Future Scope

12 Challenges Associated with Cybersecurity for Smart Grids Based on IoT

Suprava Ranjan Laha, Binod Kumar Pattanayak, and Saumendra Pattnaik

Siksha 'O' Anusandhan, Deemed to be University, Bhubaneswar, Odisha, India

Mohammad Reza Hosenkhan

Universite Des Mascareignes, Mauritius

12.1 INTRODUCTION

In recent years, the IoT has enabled virtual connectivity of everything and anything to the internet. This disrupted digital technology by connecting a wide range of items to the internet, including light bulbs, fridges, aerial vehicles, detectors, automated TVs, DST boxes, surveillance monitors, wearables, automotive systems, and medical devices. As a result, multiple industries, including healthcare, manufacturing, utilities, transportation, and homes, are now smarter than before. The development of Machine-to-Machine (M2M) communication over the past decade has created a new communication paradigm that enables machines to interact independently without human involvement, thereby enabling pervasive connectivity. M2M connectivity has endured substantial advancements and is now regarded as the primary technology driving the actualization of the IoT (Schiele and Torn, 2020; Amodu et al. 2018).

IoT devices can communicate without human or computer interaction. It is anticipated that the effortless interaction of these integrated gadgets will bring in an era of automation in virtually every industry. IoT has become a pivotal technology in various fields, including intelligent transportation, automated healthcare, intelligent homes, smart environments, smart cities, and the smart grid. With IoT, internet-connected devices like webcams, refrigerators, televisions, thermostats, routers, rice cookers, and automobiles can be easily monitored and managed through the internet (Laha et al., 2022). The emergence of IoT has paved the way for it to become a crucial component in the smart grid infrastructure, where every device is viewed as an item with a distinct IP address that enables it to be controlled remotely, linking numerous devices to create a self-sufficient, intelligent ecosystem (Ghiasi et al. 2023).

DOI: 10.1201/9781003406105-17

Currently, there are an estimated 8.4 billion IoT devices being utilized worldwide, surpassing the number of humans on the planet. Cisco has predicted that this number will rise significantly, projecting over 50 billion IoT devices to be in operation by 2025 (Mazhar et al. 2023a). Despite being a relatively new technology, IoT has expanded rapidly and shows no signs of slowing down. To ensure the widespread adoption, deployment, and maturity of IoT networks, there are still obstacles to be addressed.

As the technology continues to grow exponentially, solving these obstacles becomes increasingly important.

As shown in Figure 12.1, Cisco forecasts that over 50 billion devices will represent less than 3% of everything that might be connected to the IoT. This demonstrates that IoT has the potential to become a trillion-dollar industry that impacts everything. IoT-based smart grids are sophisticated architectures with thousands of IoT clusters and devices scattered throughout power plants and structures. They constitute the largest attack surface, and if even one node is compromised, the entire network is at risk (Li et al. 2021). Increasing mobile and web usage as well as social media are key contributors to the precipitous rise of IoT adoption (Reka et al. 2018). The smart grid system is depicted in Figure 12.1. Despite this, as the number of IoT-connected gadgets continues to rapidly increase, new obstacles continue to emerge. Among these is the possibility that these internet-facing systems could be compromised by hackers. In contrast with traditional electrical grids, where the vast majority of attacks and instances of failure emerged from actual access to vital infrastructure amenities, the

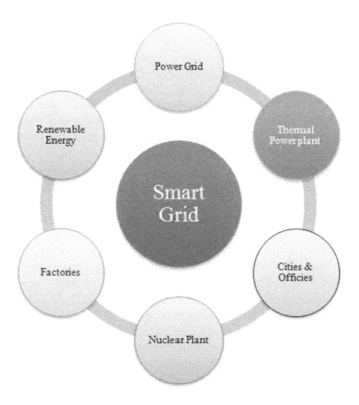

FIGURE 12.1   The smart grid model.

growing number of connected smart grid devices means that these risks are now everywhere-accessible cyber-space-based facilities (Qays et al. 2023). As IoT technology (Pattnaik and Banerjee, 2022; Laha et al., 2021) permeates further into the architecture of a smart grid, the latter becomes increasingly vulnerable to cyberattacks (Tang et al. 2019). A hacked device exposes the entire infrastructure to cyberattacks. The system is vulnerable even if the infrastructure is secure but the communications network is not. Due to the potential domino effect of closing down the energy grid, it is a primary target for cyberattacks and must be protected at all costs (Tang et al., 2023).

Smart Grids based on IoT technology have received recent focus due to their potential to increase energy efficiency, reduce costs, and facilitate the integration of green power (Bitirgen and Filik, 2023). However, the integration of IoT in Smart Grids also introduces new cybersecurity risks (Nafees et al. 2023). As Smart Grids become more connected and reliant on technology, they become more susceptible to cyber threats, which can cause significant disruption to the grid's operation and potentially lead to safety concerns (Qays et al. 2023). This research chapter aims to analyze the challenges associated with cybersecurity for Smart Grids based on IoT. Additionally, the research proposes some of the security measures that can be implemented to mitigate these risks.

12.1.1 CONTRIBUTION

A thorough examination of cybersecurity for the smart grid system was conducted, including an exploration of the various applications of IoT technology in this context and the resulting benefits. Additionally, multiple cybersecurity obstacles were identified and corresponding solutions were presented. The publication is significant in the field of cybersecurity as it focuses on the specific challenges that arise when incorporating IoT technology into smart grids. The proposed tactics have the potential to aid energy industry stakeholders in creating secure and dependable smart grid systems that can withstand cyberattacks.

This document is structured as follows: The second section provides a concise explanation of the IoT's role in the smart grid system. Section III provides a summary of the existing research on the subject. The fourth section examines the advantages of implementing an IoT-based smart infrastructure. The focus of Section V is the discussion of cybersecurity concerns. In the context of the Internet of Things, Section VI explores the most significant challenges confronting the smart grid. The seventh section examines the potential future of IoT-based smart infrastructure. In the eighth and final section, we conclude our work.

12.2 UTILIZATION OF IOT IN SMART GRID

The intelligent grid uses IoT to deploy smart devices along the energy path, from the generation plant to the end-user, to improve power systems by continuously controlling and monitoring power grid components. IoT incorporates sensors, communication networks, and data analytics to increase power grid efficiency, reliability, and sustainability (Kirmani et al. 2022). The IoT can monitor utilities and analyze data from power plants, transformers, and power lines in real time. This data can be utilized to optimize grid performance, detect faults, and manage energy demand and supply. Using IoT devices such as intelligent meters, consumers are able to monitor and control their energy consumption in real time. IoT in the smart grid makes solar and wind power integration easier and energy storage system management more efficient. IoT can help utilities to balance the energy supply and demand, reduce energy wastage, and improve the grid's resilience to disruptions such as extreme weather events or cyberattacks.

Overall, the IoT could change the energy business by making it more efficient, reliable, and environmentally friendly. However, as discussed earlier, cybersecurity is a critical challenge that must be addressed to ensure the safety and security of the grid devices connected to the internet (Reka and Dragicevic 2018).

12.3 RELATED WORK

The smart grid integrates a power grid with a communication network, making it vulnerable to security threats in both physical and cyber spaces. Smart grid systems may face a range of attacks, including DoS, DDoS, FDIA, and GPS (Global Positioning System) spoofing (Wu et al. 2020). Table 12.1 provides a summary of existing literature on cyberattacks for smart grids, which focuses mostly on FDI attacks, DoS assaults, and how to find them in the smart grid system using machine learning and deep learning.

12.4 SMART GRID IOT BENEFITS

In recent times, the deployment of smart grid technology has increased as utilities have sought to improve operating efficiency thereby cutting costs. Using IoT devices and sensors to collect data and provide real-time visibility into the grid is a significant enabler of these new systems. Nevertheless, as more IoT devices are integrated into the grid, attacks that threaten grid stability and trigger massive blackouts, become increasingly likely. In this article, we cover some of the advantages of deploying an IoT-based smart grid, as well as some of the obstacles involved in guaranteeing its cybersecurity.

A smart grid based on IoT can provide utilities with numerous benefits as detailed below.

1. With real-time data gathering and analysis, utilities can more immediately identify problems and corrective action can be taken to avert power outages and other problems. This can result in substantial cost savings by decreasing downtime and maintenance expenses.
2. By monitoring the health and performance of specific assets (such as power transformers), utilities can assist in making more informed decisions regarding whether to replace or repair them.
3. Consumers anticipate dependable electricity service and prompt replies in the event of difficulties (Liu et al. 2020). A smart grid based on IoT can assist in achieving these requirements by delivering near-real-time information on outages and expected restoration times. This enables utility companies to proactively inform customers of any impending outages.

TABLE 12.1

Summary of the Few Works of Cybersecurity of the Smart Grids

Ref.& Year	Techniques Used	Type of Attacks	Findings
Wang et al. (2020)	CNN	FDI (Power buses)	The suggested method uses a convolutional neural network and a typical bad data detector to identify the real-time locations of FDIA by detecting power flow measurement irregularity and cooccurrence dependency, which may be caused by attacks.
Li den et al. (2021)	Adaptive sliding mode	Dynamic load altering	An adaptive sliding mode controller is introduced to enable the dependable functioning of the power system in the face of unknown attacks, achieved through the utilization of an adaptive mechanism.
Nath et al. (2019)	IDS	Worst-case detection delays	The RaoCUSUM detector is utilized to estimate and track the nonstationary and time-varying states of the power grid.
Dou et al. (2020)	Variational mode decomposition	Power buses & Sensors	A method for detecting FDIA with temporal correlation is introduced and proven to be effective.
Yang et al. (2020)	LSTM	Power Shedding	Attacks are detected by analyzing feature vectors that learn temporal correlations.
Yinya et al. (2020)	LSTM	Management of Load	Feature vectors that learn temporal correlations in a time series are used to detect attacks.
Gang et al. (2020)	Optimal Partial state feedback	Switching Attack	Convex relaxation and Pontryagin's maximal principle change a selection of control signals and attack areas to degrade system performance at the lowest cost.
Yuanchang et al. (2019)	GAN-based data model	FDI	A new method for training GANs that is characterized by its smoothness has been created, and an adaptive online window has been investigated to ensure the real-time preservation of state estimation accuracy.
Oozeer and Haykin (2019)	Cognitive risk control	Power bus	CRC with task-switch control is utilized to detect and mitigate FDI attacks by leveraging the entropic state.
Uludag et al. (2021)	Attack mitigation via detection	DoS	The suggested approach for mitigating DDoS attacks is capable of detecting them promptly and can be easily expanded as needed.
Jahromi et al. (2019)	Directional unblocking scheme	DDoS	The focus of the study is solely on permissive overreaching transfer trip protection, while power system protection relays only partially address the issue of DDoS attacks.
Risbud et al. (2020)	Estimation of state weighted by least squares	Spoofing attack	It estimates nodal voltages, generator rotor angles, rotor speed, and time-varying assaults.
Sabouri et al. (2021)	Network of multilayer perceptron	Spoofing attack	Using a neural network, this method finds GPS spoofing attempts and finds out where they are happening. A neural network can only learn one thing.
Siamak et al. (2020)	Estimation of dynamic fusion using Kalman filters	Spoofing attack	The suggested method combines data from SCADAs and PMUs with a state-space model to deal with systems that change over time. The proposed method can spot repeated attempts to fake GPS signals.

12.5 CYBERSECURITY ISSUES

Demand for energy is ever-increasing, as is the need to discover more efficient and environment-friendly means to generate it. Smart grids have arisen as a response to this issue, utilizing new technology to provide a more reliable and sustainable electrical infrastructure. Nevertheless, these same technologies, particularly the Internet of Things (IoT), pose new cybersecurity threats that must be handled. Several devices are network-connected and communicate with each other to optimize energy production and distribution in a smart grid. This encompasses everything from power generation and transmission equipment to water heaters and air conditioners. Smart grids frequently include IoT devices because they can provide real-time data on electricity consumption and assist in spotting issues before they create outages.

Yet, the networked structure of smart grids also imposes new hacking vulnerabilities. Once one device is hacked, attackers can gain access to the remainder of the system (Yılmaz and Uludag 2021). This might enable them to influence energy output or completely disrupt service. In addition, attackers could utilize smart grid systems to access other sensitive networks or data. If a home's thermostat is connected to the smart grid, for instance, an attacker might theoretically exploit it to acquire information about the residents or even spy on them (Li et al. 2019).

There is a variety of initiatives that utility companies and other organizations can take to lessen the danger of smart grid hacking. They include segmenting networks to isolate essential systems from noncritical systems. Despite the rising number of assaults, 54% of US documented attacks target energy infrastructure (Figure 12.2) (Lehto, 2022). This shows the difficulty of securing IoT-based smart grid networks.

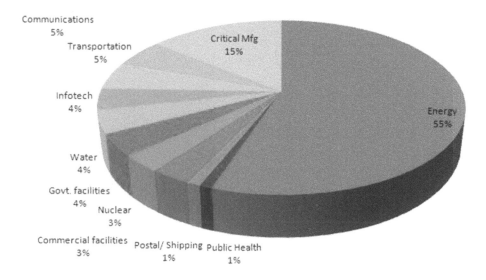

FIGURE 12.2 Cyberattacks on infrastructure.

12.5.1　Analysis of Recent Assaults

As the globe becomes increasingly digitized and networked, the demand for dependable and secure energy infrastructure is greater than ever before. To fulfill this demand, IoT-based smart grids are being created, but they confront specific cybersecurity challenges.

A number of high-profile attacks on critical infrastructure in recent years have brought to light the vulnerabilities of smart grid technologies. In December 2015, a cyberattack on the power infrastructure of Ukraine left 225,000 people without power for several hours. A similar incident in 2016 triggered an approximately one-hour outage in Kyiv. In both instances, the attackers gained access to the control systems of the power companies using malicious software and disrupted the flow of electricity (Mohindru et al. 2020a). These incidents highlight the possible repercussions of cyberattacks on smart grids and the necessity for enhanced security measures. Providing proper cybersecurity for smart grids based on the IoT involves a number of obstacles. The sheer size and complexity of these systems pose a difficulty. Smart grids can consist of tens of thousands of units and span across vast regions. This generates numerous possible entry points for attackers and makes it harder to identify and respond quickly to attacks (Mohindru et al., 2019). Several smart grid components are legacy systems that were not developed with security in mind, presenting an additional hurdle. This category contains equipment such as meters and sensors that may lack suitable security safeguards.

12.5.2　Characterization of Assaults

As global connectivity develops, the demand for adequate cybersecurity also rises. This is particularly true with the IoT. Intelligent grids are becoming more prevalent, and their functionality depends on IoT devices. Nevertheless, these gadgets frequently lack adequate protections leaving them vulnerable to assault. There are numerous forms of attacks that can be launched against intelligent grid systems. Among the most prevalent are:

1. Denial-of-service (DoS) assaults: These attacks try to flood a system with requests, preventing authorized users from gaining access. DoS assaults can be extremely challenging to recover from.
2. Infections with malware: Malware can infect IoT devices and grant attackers with control over them. Once compromised, these devices can be utilized by the attacker to conduct additional attacks or disrupt service (Mohindru et al. 2020b).
3. Man-in-the-middle (MitM) attacks: In a MitM attack, an attacker intercepts communications between two parties and inserts itself to eavesdrop or change messages. This type of assault may be employed to steal sensitive data or interrupt service.
4. Buffer overflow attacks: Buffer overflow attacks exploit poorly designed code to cause a system to crash or provide attackers with access to sensitive data. If successful, these types of attacks are frequently difficult to detect and can have severe repercussions.

12.5.3 MITIGATION OF ATTACKS

There are various measures that can be employed to avert or lessen the impact of security breaches. Among the most frequently used ones are the following:

- Robust passwords: The use of strong, intricate passwords can hinder attackers from easily guessing or cracking them.
- Two-factor authentication: Two-factor authentication (2FA) can make user accounts tougher to hack.
- Regular software updates: Consistently updating software, which includes operating systems and applications, can help patch vulnerabilities and prevent attackers from exploiting them.
- Firewall protection: Firewalls can impede unauthorized access to a network by blocking certain types of traffic.
- Encryption: The application of encryption can shield sensitive data, even if it gets into the hands of an attacker.
- Access control: Limiting user access to the resources and data necessary for their job can prevent unauthorized access and reduce the impact of an attack.
- Backup and recovery: Regularly backing up data and devising a disaster recovery plan can help lessen the impact of attacks such as ransomware.
- Security awareness training: Educating users about common attack methods, such as phishing, can help forestall successful attacks by increasing user vigilance and decreasing the likelihood of falling for scams.

12.6   OTHER SIGNIFICANT OBSTACLES TO THE EXPANSION OF IOT NETWORKS

The expansion of IoT networks has brought about various cybersecurity challenges that can hinder the functioning of these networks. These challenges include:

1. Absence of standardization: The lack of a standard security framework for IoT devices can create weak spots in the network, which can be exploited by hackers.
2. Limited device security: Many IoT devices are created with minimal security features, making them vulnerable targets for cybercriminals who can use them to initiate attacks on other devices in the network.
3. Inadequate encryption: Several IoT devices transmit data without encryption, which makes it easy for hackers to intercept and steal sensitive information.
4. Distributed denial-of-service (DDoS) attacks: IoT devices can be hijacked and used as part of a botnet to launch DDoS attacks, leading to network disruptions and downtime.
5. Concerns about data privacy and security: The vast amount of data generated by IoT devices can be exposed to interception and theft, raising issues about data privacy and security.

6. Complex network architecture: The intricate and diverse nature of IoT networks can make it challenging to implement effective security measures across all devices and systems.
7. Shortage of security expertise: The scarcity of cybersecurity professionals with knowledge in IoT security can limit the ability of organizations to adequately secure their IoT networks.

It is crucial to address these cybersecurity challenges to ensure the development and success of IoT networks. This can entail implementing standardized security frameworks, enhancing device security and encryption, improving data privacy and security, and expanding the availability of cybersecurity professionals with expertise in IoT security.

12.7   FUTURE ASPECTS

In recent years, digital systems have replaced tens of thousands of analog controls in power networks, resulting in increased control and efficiency in energy generation and transmission. Information and operational technology have enabled these benefits, but they have also made these firms more vulnerable to cyberattacks. In this age of pervasive connectivity, securing critical infrastructure from sophisticated cyber assaults is one of the hardest undertakings. Due to the constant emergence of new attack techniques and threats and the constant evolution of existing ones, the cybersecurity landscape has become highly dynamic and unpredictable. Cyberattacks on vital infrastructure could have catastrophic effects. Every day, nuclear facilities, power grids, dams, and other vital infrastructure become more susceptible to cyberattacks. Even though their infrastructure is aging and underfunded, these organizations must defend themselves from advanced cyber threats as their risk multiplies exponentially. Recent research has predicted that the number of cyberattacks will increase significantly as the number of Internet of Things devices continues to grow. Cyberattacks are expected to raise data intrusion costs to $2.5 trillion, roughly four times the 2018 projection. The pervasive use of mobile phones has also increased exposure to the internet, and the absence of security software on mobile devices, combined with the proliferation of inexpensive internet connections in homes without secure systems, makes more IoT systems susceptible to cyberattacks. Due to the increased connectivity of IoT devices, it is anticipated that the average cost of a single cybersecurity incident will rise. In the near future, there is a significant risk of a nightmare scenarios involving debilitating cyberattacks against critical infrastructure occurring if these issues are not addressed.

12.8   CONCLUSION

The Internet of Things (IoT) is a crucial technology utilized by the smart grid to facilitate a globally connected network of communication- and computation-enabled objects. Nevertheless, the deployment of IoT in the smart grid has increased cybersecurity hazards due to the vast number of network-connected devices. This presents a significant challenge for assuring the security of internet-connected grid devices. This chapter provides an in-depth analysis of the principal security issues and challenges encountered by IoT-based smart grids, as well as potential solutions. Despite these obstacles, the Internet of Things can be used to enhance existing power grids by providing real-time control and monitoring of power grid components. Consequently, it is essential to prioritize security concerns throughout the various phases of designing, implementing, and integrating IoT devices into the smart grid.

REFERENCES

Amodu, Oluwatosin Ahmed, and Mohamed Othman. "Machine-to-machine communication: An overview of opportunities." *Computer Networks* 145 (2018): 255–276.

Bitirgen, Kübra, and Ümmühan Başaran Filik. "A hybrid deep learning model for discrimination of physical disturbance and cyber-attack detection in smart grid." *International Journal of Critical Infrastructure Protection* 40 (2023): 100582.

Dou, Chunxia, Di Wu, Dong Yue, Bao Jin, and Shiyun Xu. "A hybrid method for false data injection attack detection in smart grid based on variational mode decomposition and OS-ELM." *CSEE Journal of Power and Energy Systems* 8, no. 6 (2020): 1697–1707.

Ghiasi, Mohammad, Zhanle Wang, Mehran Mehrandezh, Shayan Jalilian, and Noradin Ghadimi. "Evolution of smart grids towards the Internet of energy: Concept and essential components for deep decarbonisation." *IET Smart Grid* 6, no. 1 (2023): 86–102.

Jahromi, Amir Abiri, Anthony Kemmeugne, Deepa Kundur, and Aboutaleb Haddadi. "Cyber-physical attacks targeting communication-assisted protection schemes." *IEEE Transactions on Power Systems* 35, no. 1 (2019): 440–450.

Kirmani, Sheeraz, Abdul Mazid, Irfan Ahmad Khan, and Manaullah Abid. "A survey on IoT-enabled smart grids: Technologies, architectures, applications, and challenges." *Sustainability* 15, no. 1 (2022): 717.

Laha, Suprava Ranjan, Sushil Kumar Mahapatra, Saumendra Pattnaik, Binod Kumar Pattanayak, and Bibudhendu Pati. "U-INS: an android-based navigation system." In *Cognitive Informatics and Soft Computing: Proceeding of CISC 2020*, pp. 125–132. Springer Singapore, (2021).

Laha, Suprava Ranjan, Binod Kumar Pattanayak, and Saumendra Pattnaik. "Advancement of Environmental Monitoring System Using IoT and Sensor: A Comprehensive Analysis." *AIMS Environmental Science* 9, no. 6 (2022): 771–800.

Lehto, Martti. "Cyber-attacks against critical infrastructure." In Martti Lehto and Pekka Neittaanmäki (Eds.), *Cyber Security: Critical Infrastructure Protection*, pp. 3–42. Cham: Springer International Publishing, (2022).

Li, Jian, De-Fu Yang, Yan-Chao Gao, and Xin Huang. "An adaptive sliding-mode resilient control strategy in smart grid under mixed attacks." *IET Control Theory & Applications* 15, no. 15 (2021): 1971–1986.

Li, Yuancheng, Yuanyuan Wang, and Shiyan Hu. "Online generative adversary network based measurement recovery in false data injection attacks: A cyber-physical approach." *IEEE Transactions on Industrial Informatics* 16, no. 3 (2019): 2031–2043.

Liu, Tianbin, Yinya Zhang, Hang Zhao, Xiaohong Liu, Tianlu Gao, Hongxia Yuan, and Jun Zhang. "Social implications of cyber-physical systems in electrical load forecasting." In *IEEE 16th International Conference on Automation Science and Engineering (CASE)*, pp. 582–587. IEEE, (2020).

Mazhar, Tehseen, Hafiz Muhammad Irfan, Inayatul Haq, Inam Ullah, Madiha Ashraf, Tamara Al Shloul, Yazeed Yasin Ghadi, Imran, and Dalia H. Elkamchouchi. "Analysis of challenges and solutions of IoT in smart grids using AI and machine learning techniques: A review." *Electronics* 12, no. 1 (2023b): 242.

Mazhar, Tehseen, Hafiz Muhammad Irfan, Sunawar Khan, Inayatul Haq, Inam Ullah, Muhammad Iqbal, and Habib Hamam. "Analysis of Cyber Security Attacks and Its Solutions for the Smart Grid Using Machine Learning and Blockchain Methods." *Future Internet* 15, no. 2 (2023a): 83.

Mohindru, Vandana, Ravindara Bhatt, and Yashwant Singh. "Reauthentication scheme for mobile wireless sensor networks." *Sustainable Computing: Informatics and Systems* 23 (2019): 158–166.

Mohindru, Vandana, Yashwant Singh, and Ravindara Bhatt. "Hybrid cryptography algorithm for securing wireless sensor networks from Node Clone Attack." *Recent Advances in Electrical & Electronic Engineering (Formerly Recent Patents on Electrical & Electronic Engineering)* 13, no. 2 (2020a): 251–259.

Mohindru, Vandana, Yashwant Singh, and Ravindara Bhatt. "Securing wireless sensor networks from node clone attack: a lightweight message authentication algorithm." *International Journal of Information and Computer Security* 12, no. 2–3 (2020b): 217–233.

Nafees, Muhammad Nouman, Neetesh Saxena, Alvaro Cardenas, Santiago Grijalva, and Pete Burnap. "Smart grid cyber-physical situational awareness of complex operational technology attacks: A review." *ACM Computing Surveys* 55, no. 10 (2023): 1–36.

Nath, Samrat, Israel Akingeneye, Jingxian Wu, and Zhu Han. "Quickest detection of false data injection attacks in smart grid with dynamic models." *IEEE Journal of Emerging and Selected Topics in Power Electronics* 10, no. 1 (2019): 1292–1302.

Qays, Md Ohirul, Iftekhar Ahmad, Ahmed Abu-Siada, Md Liton Hossain, and Farhana Yasmin. "Key communication technologies, applications, protocols and future guides for IoT-assisted smart grid systems: A review." *Energy Reports* 9 (2023): 2440–2452.

Oozeer, Mohammad Irshaad, and Simon Haykin. "Cognitive risk control for mitigating cyber-attack in smart grid." *IEEE Access* 7 (2019): 125806–125826.

Pattnaik, Saumendra, Sayan Banerjee, Suprava Ranjan Laha, Binod Kumar Pattanayak, and Gouri Prasad Sahu. "A Novel Intelligent Street Light Control System Using IoT." In *Intelligent and Cloud Computing: Proceedings of ICICC 2021*, pp. 145–156. Springer Nature Singapore, (2022).

Reka, S. Sofana, and Tomislav Dragicevic. "Future effectual role of energy delivery: A comprehensive review of Internet of Things and smart grid." *Renewable and Sustainable Energy Reviews* 91 (2018): 90–108.

Risbud, Paresh, Nikolaos Gatsis, and Ahmad Taha. "Multi-period power system state estimation with PMUs under GPS spoofing attacks." *Journal of Modern Power Systems and Clean Energy* 8, no. 4 (2020): 597–606.

Sabouri, Mohammad, Sara Siamak, Maryam Dehghani, Mohsen Mohammadi, and Mohammad Hassan Asemani. "Intelligent GPS spoofing attack detection in power grid." In *11th Smart Grid Conference (SGC)*, pp. 1–6. IEEE, (2021).

Schiele, Holger, and Robbert-Jan Torn. "Cyber-physical systems with autonomous machine-to-machine communication: Industry 4.0 and its particular potential for purchasing and supply management." *International Journal of Procurement Management* 13, no. 4 (2020): 507–530.

Siamak, Sara, Maryam Dehghani, and Mohsen Mohammadi. "Dynamic GPS spoofing attack detection, localization, and measurement correction exploiting PMU and SCADA." *IEEE Systems Journal* 15, no. 2 (2020): 2531–2540.

Tang, Daogui, Yi-Ping Fang, and Enrico Zio. "Vulnerability analysis of demand-response with renewable energy integration in smart grids to cyber attacks and online detection methods." *Reliability Engineering & System Safety* 235 (2023): 109212.

Tang, Shu, Dennis R. Shelden, Charles M. Eastman, Pardis Pishdad-Bozorgi, and Xinghua Gao. "A review of building information modeling (BIM) and the internet of things (IoT) devices integration: Present status and future trends." *Automation in Construction* 101 (2019): 127–139.

Wang, Shuoyao, Suzhi Bi, and Ying-Jun Angela Zhang. "Locational detection of the false data injection attack in a smart grid: A multilabel classification approach." *IEEE Internet of Things Journal* 7, no. 9 (2020): 8218–8227.

Wu, Guangyu, Gang Wang, Jian Sun, and Jie Chen. "Optimal partial feedback attacks in cyber-physical power systems." *IEEE Transactions on Automatic Control* 65, no. 9 (2020): 3919–3926.

Yang, Liqun, Xiaoming Zhang, Zhi Li, Zhoujun Li, and Yueying He. "Detecting bi-level false data injection attack based on time series analysis method in smart grid." *Computers & Security* 96 (2020): 101899.

Yılmaz, Yasin, and Suleyman Uludag. "Timely detection and mitigation of IoT-based cyberattacks in the smart grid." *Journal of the Franklin Institute* 358, no. 1 (2021): 172–192.

13 Cybersecurity Challenges in IoT-Based Healthcare Systems
A Survey

Suprava Ranjan Laha and
Debasish Swapnesh Kumar Nayak

Siksha 'O' Anusandhan (Deemed to be) University, Odisha, India

13.1 INTRODUCTION

IoT will bring about a major technological revolution because it provides humans with a number of benefits. By 2025, it's anticipated that there will be more than 75 billion objects, including mobile devices, sensors, and actuators, connected to the internet. IoT will play a significant function across all industries since it offers a chance to advance precision and productivity (Ferrag et al. 2017).

The capacity to track patients' illnesses outside of medical and hospital facilities using technological devices and sensors connected to the patient's body is one of the most important advancements in healthcare today, second only to changes in diet and lifestyle. Another significant development concerns rural areas, which frequently experience a shortage of medical knowledge. However, by utilizing connected device healthcare systems, people in remote locations may receive the correct benefit from doctors by providing them with all records and sensor readings, allowing them to treat patients conveniently based on their records. Additionally, IoT-enabled healthcare goes from immobile to mobile, allowing for the monitoring of elderly patients while they are in motion (Joshitta et al. 2017). The availability of resources, security, and networking is a top concern for developers when it comes to the Internet of Things (IoT). Adding potential key limitations to it causes a number of issues (Patel and Shah 2022).

With new technologies, security continues to be a concern, and this situation is no different. It is an issue of life and death if the security of IoT devices and medical data is compromised. Internet-connected medical equipment such as a pacemaker, support for life, or supply of oxygen system might leave a patient defenseless and open to a variety of threats. IoT devices that are linked in healthcare can pose dangers to the devices and patients' security and privacy (Elhoseny et al. 2021).

DOI: 10.1201/9781003406105-18

13.1.1 DIFFERENT TYPES OF SECURITY

IT security is the safeguarding of IT (information technology) assets and digital data from attacks (Hong 2019). There may be external, internal, accidental, or malevolent threats. Following are the various forms of security:

1) Physical security protects hardware, software, staff, network, and data from physical acts, invasions, and internal occurrences that could destroy an organization (Hong 2019).
2) Information security encompasses a vast array of tactics for detecting, preventing, and responding to threats (Jayalakshmi and Gomathi 2020) Information security programs are focused on three primary objectives: Confidentiality, integrity, and availability (Gopalan, Raza, and Almobaideen 2021). Cybersecurity is centered on information security. Figure 13.1 shows various information security types that are present in a cyber-related model design.

FIGURE 13.1   Types of information security.

13.1.2 CONTRIBUTION

- A survey of relevant publications from 2017 to 2022.
- Summary of IoT security challenges, frameworks, and supporting methods/ techniques for these mechanisms.
- Inspection and observation of these tables to illustrate how to address IoT security concerns in various healthcare contexts.

13.2 LITERATURE SURVEY

Despite the fact that IoT-enabled healthcare system innovations are still in their infancy, prospective industrial applications are surfacing and growing quickly. IoT-related industrial cases and research initiatives with a focus on healthcare have both been created and put into use. By facilitating collaboration across a wide range of industries, IoT-based mechanisms will expedite healthcare treatment procedures and improve patient care outcomes. Particularly, ambient assisted living attempts to make it easier for those with disabilities and major medical conditions to go about their daily lives. The usage of IoT in this industry can deliver a number of groundbreaking services, including efficient management of sensor data as well as the collection of critical health data using a sensor network, and relocation to a cloud (remote) for medical convenience and storage and analysis (Awotunde et al. 2021; Darwish et al. 2019).

The aging population, increasing number for chronic illnesses, scarcity of healthcare professionals, and unpredictable rising costs of healthcare are just a few of the significant problems that contemporary healthcare systems are facing. Entities from the private and public sectors should collaborate to address these issues and discover more creative and approachable solutions that can be used outside of hospitals. Current technological advancements have significantly altered how people understand conventional ways of carrying out daily tasks. The Internet of Things has been a growing trend in various sectors of everyday life, including the healthcare industry. However, this quick IoT revolution has also led to several ambiguities and worries about how data held in various linked gadgets would be protected.

Secure and safe patients must be reassured by IoT healthcare applications regarding the security and confidentiality risks posed to their lives, as well as other impacts, such as privacy violations and financial threats. Healthcare providers and applications support remote patient management processes and alerting mechanisms. Since knowledge produced through these methods is considered to be susceptible, data are these applications' most important commodity (Vermesan and Friess 2014; Malan et al. 2004; Kumar and Lee 2011).

However, the sheer volume of sensitive datasets that have been gathered by gadgets that are connected and the enormous amount of these records has led to new issues with information confidentiality and safety. With the IoT's quick expansion, cyberattacks have also altered, opening up a new front for intrusion and risk to the entire medical sector. Numerous studies have investigated IoT's numerous security and privacy issues, as well as device flaws pertinent to connected device healthcare management devices in cloud and fog computing environments. Kumar and Lee (2011) and Abdulraheem et al. (2020) examined the IoMT security and privacy taxonomy in depth.

Since IoT devices lack enough memory, processing, and information transmission capabilities, they require a powerful, immediately accessible high-performance computing system as well as a greater storage system for real-time processing and record warehousing. Numerous IoT organizations have recently extended their various application servers into the cloud and deposited the health records they have gathered. Cloud-based apps will properly transfer medical activity data. Through its resistance and ability to access shared resources and infrastructure globally, cloud facilities provide a positive explanation for the efficient management of ubiquitous medical records.

Users' security concerns with IoT applications are complicated by the variety of IoT components. In light of this, identifying and resolving these security issues is of utmost importance for the development of these IoT applications. The minimal security requirements for the applications can be summed up as confidentiality, integrity, and availability (CIA) (Awotunde et al. 2021).

Technologies for connection and security risks multiple issues can occur in IoT-based healthcare networks. These technologies are vulnerable to DoS/DDoS attacks, including as overflow, black hole, and domestic attacks. These systems are also vulnerable to linkage interference, baritone loss, identity fraud, monitoring, usability, power utilization, and switching on and off of the exploration mode while exploiting the core exchange function. Intruder 27 to trace abnormal activations, identity-based confirmation, anti-jamming, and packet filtering should be used in this community to prevent unauthorized users from gaining access. The encryption of all wireless traffic frequently provides the assurance that the data sent over wireless networks is private.

Big data analytics and IoT have been widely adopted by numerous organizations. However, the development of these machines is still in its early stages. It still hasn't addressed a number of pressing workplace issues. Big data analysis is a contentious issue for many applications due to the nature of the data and the scalability of the processes that undergird these methodologies. As a result, this section presents several challenges for big data analytics centered on IoT. Data security issues arise when an anonymous user creates data on a network and then uses big data analytics tools to infer or reconstruct personal information. With the introduction of big data analytics technologies used in IoT, the confidentiality issue must become a primary concern in the data mining industry. Because these networks lack clear service-level agreements (SLAs) regarding customer abuse or misuse of personal information, the majority of consumers are reluctant to rely on them. Sensitive information about users must be kept private and protected against unauthorized access. It is important to address ethical issues such as what to use, how to use, and why to use big data generated by IoT, despite the fact that there are several approaches to data protection, including temporary identification, hiding, and encryption. The range of system types used and the complexity of the data produced, such as new computers, data formats, and communication protocols, are additional security risks associated with IoT data. These systems, which might have a variety of extents and forms outside the system, are designed to interact with supportive utilization. Therefore, each unit should be supplied by an IoT system with a nonrepudiable identifying technique in order to authenticate these devices. Organizations will also maintain a meta-archive of these associated tools for analysis purposes. IoT's composite design is novel in terms of security, which increases security vulnerabilities. Thus, any intrusion compromises network security and disconnects associated devices (Adeniyi, Ogundokun, and Awotunde 2021; Thomas 2020; Mutlag et al. 2019).

When it comes to collecting and storing enormous amounts of data in the context of IoT-based Big data analytics, security and privacy are major issues. Similar to other systems, these ones heavily rely on third-party infrastructure and facilities carrying out crucial functions and holding private data. As a result, obtaining all relevant data in its whole is difficult due to the enormous expansion in data volume. Big data scenarios based on IoT do not now have any established security measures that offer complete protection. Current algorithms are not implemented effectively because they are not designed for sophisticated data interpretation. Legacy data protection methods are designed for static datasets, but data requirements change. Thus, aggressively accumulating data safety resolutions is difficult (Burhan et al. 2018).

13.3 HEALTHCARE SYSTEM AUTHENTICATION USING ANONYMOUS CREDENTIALS

User IDs and passwords are no longer enough for offline and online identification due to the rising demand. Password, certificate, multifactor, facial, and biometric authentication are described (Tsai et al. 2015; Alassaf et al. 2019). Examples of authenticating attacks using anonymity are as follows:

- Sensor node capturing attack: It is a crucial assault that allows an adversary to do several activities on the network and simply breach the entire system.
  - Desynchronization offensive: Infiltration that changes RFID tag and reader values. If the intrusion succeeds, subsequent transactions involving the identifier will not be verified.
  - Offline attempt to guess a password: In this case, the password hash will be retrieved offline and the clear-text password will be compared to the hash value. A machine generates the password hash function and swiftly compares it to the selected password's hash until a match is found.
  - Attacks of stolen verifier: This allows an intruder to impersonate a user using a stolen password verifier. Clearly, if weak credentials are employed, the stolen verifier attack is susceptible to a dictionary attack.
  - Privileged insider assault: Authorized users attack networks or computers without permission.

Scyther was utilized to simulate the proposed authentication mechanism by Tsai et al. (2015) based on symmetric keys. Unique passwords (OTPs) were produced using an encrypted symmetric key (counter technique) and the crypto-hash function to secure communication between IoT-embedded devices and cloud servers (Marjani et al. 2017). They utilized the BAN technique and Scyther to validate the security of the deployed protocol. In Iyengar et al. (2010), the users are permitted to freely select and modify their passwords, and no password verifier table is maintained. Using a dynamic ID, the system is secured against theft of ID. Using user passwords, fingerprints, and smart cards, Fortino et al. (2009) created a cloud-centric three-factor authentication strategy for autonomous vehicles. The authors of Aloi et al. (2016) described a three-factor UCSSO technique that provides rapid authentication and privacy safeguarding for TMIS. Their solution enables users and servers to generate anonymous, secure, and swift shared session keys. They utilized the BAN technique, the ROR model, and a tool named AVISPA to demonstrate the security of the proposed system. The approach presented by Fortino et al. (2015) provides mobile customers who roam with secure services. The proposed ES-HAS approach is impervious to security assaults. The joint session identifier is produced using ECC and distributed within two entities to authenticate each other during communication. In Jiang et al.'s (2020) system, users and servers are able to generate shared session keys rapidly, securely, and anonymously. They demonstrated that the suggested method is protected by the BAN technique, the ROR model, and the tool AVISPA. A protocol is used to communicate between the user, IoT gadgets, and the gateway node. A session key is generated following successful authentication and transferred across the user and the IoT device. One of the most difficult components of the protocol design is identity desynchronization (ID-S). In Qiu et al. (2020), the causes and drawbacks of ID-S are examined. The authors revealed that the old authentication mechanism for the Internet of Vehicles (IoV) employing symmetric keys was vulnerable to ID-S. The authors proposed a blockchain-based access control approach for embedded IoT devices in drones and for the Ground Station Server (GSS).

13.4 SECURITY ATTACKS

There are various forms of security attacks that aim to undermine the security of a system or network. These attacks can be carried out through deliberate actions.

- **Malware attacks**: It is forms of malicious software designed to damage or disrupt computer systems. An email, attachments, downloads, and infected websites can all be used to transmit malware. Malware includes viruses, worms, Trojan horses, and ransomware (Rudd et al. 2016; Qamar, Karim, and Chang 2019; Hsu et al. 2020).
- **Phishing attacks**: These attacks utilize fraudulent emails, text messages, or websites to deceive users into divulging sensitive information such as usernames, passwords, and credit card information. Phishing attacks can be extremely effective because they frequently appear to originate from a reliable source (Hong 2012; Gupta et al. 2017; Alkhalil et al. 2021).
- **Denial-of-service attacks (DoS)**: By saturating a network or website with traffic, a DoS attack aims to render it inaccessible. DoS assaults can be carried out using botnets, which are networks of compromised devices that a single perpetrator can control (Pelechrinis, Iliofotou, and Krishnamurthy 2010).
- **MITM (Man-in-the-middle attacks)**: In a man-in-the-middle (MITM) attack, an adversary interprets the communication between two parties and eavesdrops on the conversation or modifies the data being exchanged. Because they can be used to steal sensitive information such as login credentials, these attacks are particularly dangerous (Ornaghi and Valleri 2003).

- **Password attacks**: Password assaults include attempts to decipher a user's password to gain access to a system or network. Common password attack types include brute force, dictionary, and fraud (Tasevski 2011; Raza et al. 2012).
- **SQL injection attacks**: These attacks are a form of web-based attack that makes use of vulnerabilities in web-based applications to reach access to sensitive data stored in databases. By injecting malicious SQL code into a web form, an attacker can gain access to sensitive information such as usernames, passwords, and credit card information (Halfond, Viegas, and Orso 2006).

13.5   SECURITY FEATURES

Systems, networks, devices, and data are protected against unauthorized access, theft, disruption, and injury by security features. These features may be physical, technical, or administrative in nature and may include:

- The process of limiting a user's access to resources based on his or her identity, role, or privileges for access control, permissions, firewalls, and other security mechanisms may be used (Mohindru et al. 2020a).
- Authentication is the procedure used to verify the identity of a user or device aiming to access a system or network. Authentication can be achieved through the use of passwords, biometrics, smart cards, and other methods.
- Encryption is the process of encapsulating plaintext data in order to prevent unauthorized access. Encryption is applicable to both data in transit and data in storage.
- Intrusion detection and prevention refer to the monitoring of a system or network for suspicious activity and the implementation of measures to prevent or stop intrusions. Utilizing intrusion detection and prevention systems (IDPS) to identify and block malicious traffic (Mohindru et al. 2019).
- ID and prevention refer to the preservation of physical assets, such as servers, data centers, and other equipment. As physical security measures, access control systems, surveillance cameras, and alarms may be utilized.
- Physical security refers to the processes and procedures established to recover from a disaster or business interruption. Planning for disaster recovery and business continuity includes procedures for backup and recovery, redundant systems, and other measures to ensure the continuation of essential operations.
- Disaster recovery refers to programs designed to educate employees about security hazards and how to avoid them. Security awareness training can prevent social engineering attacks, phishing attempts, and other types of attacks that exploit human vulnerabilities. Physical and digital systems may implement security awareness training programs to assist employees in identifying potential security risks and implementing preventative measures.
- Session key agreement is the process by which two or more parties agree on a confidential key to be used during a specific communication session

(Mohindru et al. 2020b). The session key is typically used to encrypt and decrypt communications exchanged between participants during a session.

- There are numerous session-key agreement mechanisms, including:
  - RSA key exchange: Using the RSA algorithm, this method exchanges public keys and generates a shared secret key. It is widely employed in internet protocols like SSL, TLS, and SSH.
  - Diffie Hellman key exchange: Using this standard method, two parties may agree on a secret key over an insecure medium (channel). Using public-key cryptography and a shared secret, it generates a secret key that only the two parties know.
  - Elliptic curve cryptography (ECC): This method uses elliptic curves to generate public and private keys for secure key exchange. It is a popular choice for secure communication systems due to its effectiveness and safety.
  - Password-based key agreement: Using a shared password, this method allows parties to agree on a secret key. Because passwords are easily surmised or intercepted, this method is less secure than others.
- Anonymity refers to the condition of being anonymous or unidentified. It is commonly used in the context of online activities in which users may desire to protect their identity and personal information. There are numerous methods to achieve anonymity, such as using pseudonyms, virtual private networks (VPNs), and anonymous browsers.

13.5.1 COMPARISON OF DIFFERENT SECURITY FEATURES

There are various security features that can be implemented to enhance the security of a system or network. Here is a comparison of some common security features shown in Table 13.1.

TABLE 13.1
Comparison of Different Security Features

Authors & Year	Authentication	Anonymity	Nontraceability	Session Key Agreement	Forward and Backward Secrecy
Abdussami, Amin, and (Vollala 2023)	✓	✓	✓	✓	–
Wu et al. (2018)	✓	✓	✓	✓	–
Vangala et al. (2023)	✓	✓	✓	✓	✓
Fan et al. (2018)	✓	–	–	✓	✓
Aghili et al. (2019)	✓	–	–	✓	✓
Li and Liu (2021)	✓	✓	✓	✓	✓

13.6   CRITICAL FINDINGS AND RECOMMENDATION

Cybersecurity is an essential aspect of the IoT in healthcare that must be carefully considered. The following are essential findings concerning the topic:

- Due to the dearth of standardization among healthcare IoT devices, it is difficult for organizations to implement effective cybersecurity measures.
- Cyberattacks can easily target healthcare IoT devices that are frequently connected to the internet, potentially granting hackers access to sensitive patient data or control over the devices.
- Medical devices may not receive timely security patches, leaving them vulnerable to cyberattacks.
- Human error, such as the use of insecure passwords or falling for phishing emails, is a significant factor in cyberattacks against healthcare systems.
- Health services firms must place a high priority on cybersecurity to protect their systems and devices.
- Healthcare organizations, technology providers, and cybersecurity experts must collaborate to resolve the complex cybersecurity issues posed by healthcare IoT.
- Loss of patient information, disruption of medical devices, and the risk of patient injury are all possible outcomes of cyberattacks on healthcare IoT.
- Privacy for the IoT in healthcare has now become a serious concern, necessitating concerted efforts to mitigate risks, safeguard patient data, and guarantee patient safety.

Following are the recommendations on cybersecurity in healthcare IoT:

1. Implement robust password policies and multifactor authentication to reduce human error and unauthorized access.
2. Ensure that all healthcare IoT devices are updated and patched on a regular basis with the most recent security measures and adjustments.
3. Utilize network segmentation to isolate sensitive patient information and medical devices from the remainder of the network.
4. Conduct routine security audits and risk assessments to identify and eliminate vulnerabilities.
5. Provide all employees with regular cybersecurity training and awareness programs to assist them in recognizing and preventing cyber threats.
6. Utilize encryption technologies to secure patient data and guarantee secure data transmission.
7. Collaborate with technology providers and cybersecurity specialists to ensure that healthcare IoT devices adhere to best practices and meet industry standards.
8. Establish and periodically test an incident response plan to assure readiness in the event of a cyberattack.
9. Monitor and defend the healthcare IoT network with tools like firewalls, intrusion detection systems, and antivirus software.
10. Implement a secure backup system to restore systems and data quickly in the event of a cyberattack or system failure.

By following these recommendations, healthcare organizations can enhance their cybersecurity stance and better safeguard patient data and safety amid the rapidly changing healthcare IoT landscape.

13.7 CONCLUSION

The primary obstacle for IoT devices is the security of IoT infrastructure, particularly in critical applications such as healthcare environments where sensitive data is exchanged and must be protected from unauthorized access. This chapter examined the dearth of research on authentication for healthcare in the Internet of Things, specifically anonymous authentication. To address this gap, we conducted a review of notable papers that discussed security challenges in IoT, as well as anonymous authentication in healthcare environments. Taking into account the computational, storage, and speed limitations of IoT devices, the reviewed papers proposed a variety of methods to surmount IoT security challenges. However, some of these methods have drawbacks, such as being susceptible to different types of security attacks due to weak cryptography. Additionally, some approaches were not capable of concealing the user's identity, which is crucial in healthcare environments. Future studies must also consider denial of service, modification, and nontraceability security techniques. It is worth noting that most of the papers reviewed in this study support mobility, which prompts us to consider solutions that hide the location of mobile patients for the purpose of achieving location privacy in addition to the authentication protocol. Based on our analysis of the tables in this survey, we provide recommendations to researchers as guidelines for future research in this area.

REFERENCES

Abdulraheem, Muyideen, Joseph Bamidele Awotunde, Rasheed Gbenga Jimoh, and Idowu Dauda Oladipo. 2020. "An efficient lightweight cryptographic algorithm for IoT security." *International Conference on Information and Communication Technology and Applications.*

Abdussami, Mohammad, Ruhul Amin, and Satyanarayana Vollala. 2023. "Provably secured lightweight authenticated key agreement protocol for modern health industry." *Ad Hoc Networks* 141:103094.

Adeniyi, Emmanuel Abidemi, Roseline Oluwaseun Ogundokun, and Joseph Bamidele Awotunde. 2021. "IoMT-based wearable body sensors network healthcare monitoring system." *IoT in Healthcare and Ambient Assisted Living*, 103–121.

Aghili, Seyed Farhad, Hamid Mala, Pallavi Kaliyar, and Mauro Conti. 2019. "SecLAP: Secure and lightweight RFID authentication protocol for medical IoT." *Future Generation Computer Systems* 101:621–634.

Alassaf, Norah, Adnan Gutub, Shabir A Parah, and Manal Al Ghamdi. 2019. "Enhancing speed of SIMON: A light-weight-cryptographic algorithm for IoT applications." *Multimedia Tools and Applications* 78:32633–32657.

Alkhalil, Zainab, Chaminda Hewage, Liqaa Nawaf, and Imtiaz Khan. 2021. "Phishing attacks: A recent comprehensive study and a new anatomy." *Frontiers in Computer Science* 3:563060.

Aloi, Gianluca, Giuseppe Caliciuri, Giancarlo Fortino, Raffaele Gravina, Pasquale Pace, Wilma Russo, and Claudio Savaglio. 2016. "A mobile multi-technology gateway to enable IoT interoperability." *2016 IEEE First International Conference on Internet-of-Things Design and Implementation (IoTDI).*

Awotunde, Joseph Bamidele, Rasheed Gbenga Jimoh, Sakinat Oluwabukonla Folorunso, Emmanuel Abidemi Adeniyi, Kazeem Moses Abiodun, and Oluwatobi Oluwaseyi Banjo. 2021. "Privacy and security concerns in IoT-based healthcare systems." In Patrick Siarry, M.A. Jabbar, Rajanikanth Aluvalu, Ajith Abraham, Ana Madureira (Eds.), *The Fusion of Internet of Things, Artificial Intelligence, and Cloud Computing in Health Care*, 105–134. Springer.

Burhan, Muhammad, Rana Asif Rehman, Bilal Khan, and Byung-Seo Kim. 2018. "IoT elements, layered architectures and security issues: A comprehensive survey." *Sensors* 18 (9):2796.

Darwish, Ashraf, Aboul Ella Hassanien, Mohamed Elhoseny, Arun Kumar Sangaiah, and Khan Muhammad. 2019. "The impact of the hybrid platform of internet of things and cloud computing on healthcare systems: Opportunities, challenges, and open problems." *Journal of Ambient Intelligence and Humanized Computing* 10:4151–4166.

Elhoseny, Mohamed, Navod Neranjan Thilakarathne, Mohammed I Alghamdi, Rakesh Kumar Mahendran, Akber Abid Gardezi, Hesiri Weerasinghe, and Anuradhi Welhenge. 2021. "Security and privacy issues in medical internet of things: Overview, countermeasures, challenges and future directions." *Sustainability* 13 (21):11645.

Fan, Kai, Wei Jiang, Hui Li, and Yintang Yang. 2018. "Lightweight RFID protocol for medical privacy protection in IoT." *IEEE Transactions on Industrial Informatics* 14 (4):1656–1665.

Ferrag, Mohamed Amine, Leandros A Maglaras, Helge Janicke, Jianmin Jiang, and Lei Shu. 2017. "Authentication protocols for internet of things: a comprehensive survey." *Security and Communication Networks* 2017, 1–41.

Fortino, Giancarlo, Stefano Galzarano, Raffaele Gravina, and Wenfeng Li. 2015. "A framework for collaborative computing and multi-sensor data fusion in body sensor networks." *Information Fusion* 22:50–70.

Fortino, Giancarlo, Antonio Guerrieri, Fabio L Bellifemine, and Roberta Giannantonio. 2009. "SPINE2: developing BSN applications on heterogeneous sensor nodes." *2009 IEEE International Symposium on Industrial Embedded Systems*.

Gopalan, Subiksha Srinivasa, Ali Raza, and Wesam Almobaideen. 2021. "IoT security in healthcare using AI: A survey." *2020 International Conference on Communications, Signal Processing, and their Applications (ICCSPA)*.

Gupta, Brij B, Aakanksha Tewari, Ankit Kumar Jain, and Dharma P Agrawal. 2017. "Fighting against phishing attacks: state of the art and future challenges." *Neural Computing and Applications* 28:3629–3654.

Halfond, William G, Jeremy Viegas, and Alessandro Orso. 2006. "A classification of SQL-injection attacks and countermeasures." *Proceedings of the IEEE International Symposium on Secure Software Engineering*.

Hong, Jason. 2012. "The state of phishing attacks." *Communications of the ACM* 55 (1): 74–81.

Hong, Sunghyuck. 2019. "Authentication techniques in the internet of things environment: A survey." *International Journal of Network Security* 21 (3):462–470.

Hsu, Chien-Lung, Tuan-Vinh Le, Mei-Chen Hsieh, Kuo-Yu Tsai, Chung-Fu Lu, and Tzu-Wei Lin. 2020. "Three-factor UCSSO scheme with fast authentication and privacy protection for telecare medicine information systems." *IEEE Access* 8:196553–196566.

Iyengar, Sameer, Filippo Tempia Bonda, Raffaele Gravina, Antonio Guerrieri, Giancarlo Fortino, and Alberto Sangiovanni-Vincentelli. 2010. "A framework for creating healthcare monitoring applications using wireless body sensor networks." *3rd International ICST Conference on Body Area Networks*.

Jayalakshmi, M., and V. Gomathi. 2020. "Pervasive health monitoring through video-based activity information integrated with sensor-cloud oriented context-aware decision support system." *Multimedia Tools and Applications* 79:3699–3712.

Jiang, Qi, Ning Zhang, Jianbing Ni, Jianfeng Ma, Xindi Ma, and Kim-Kwang Raymond Choo. 2020. "Unified biometric privacy preserving three-factor authentication and key agreement for cloud-assisted autonomous vehicles." *IEEE Transactions on Vehicular Technology* 69 (9):9390–9401.

Joshitta, R., Shantha Mary, and L. Arockiam. 2017. "Device authentication mechanism for IoT enabled healthcare system." *2017 International Conference on Algorithms, Methodology, Models and Applications in Emerging Technologies (ICAMMAET).*

Kumar, Pardeep, and Hoon-Jae Lee. 2011. "Security issues in healthcare applications using wireless medical sensor networks: A survey." *sensors* 12 (1):55–91.

Li, Yuchong, and Qinghui Liu. 2021. "A comprehensive review study of cyber-attacks and cyber security: Emerging trends and recent developments." *Energy Reports* 7:8176–8186.

Malan, David J, Thaddeus Fulford-Jones, Matt Welsh, and Steve Moulton. 2004. "Codeblue: An ad hoc sensor network infrastructure for emergency medical care." *International Workshop on Wearable and Implantable Body Sensor Networks.*

Marjani, Mohsen, Fariza Nasaruddin, Abdullah Gani, Ahmad Karim, Ibrahim Abaker Targio Hashem, Aisha Siddiqa, and Ibrar Yaqoob. 2017. "Big IoT Data Analytics: Architecture, Opportunities, and Open Research Challenges." *IEEE Access* 5:5247–5261.

Mohindru, Vandana, Ravindara Bhatt, and Yashwant Singh. "Reauthentication scheme for mobile wireless sensor networks." *Sustainable Computing: Informatics and Systems* 23 (2019): 158–166.

Mohindru, Vandana, Yashwant Singh, and Ravindara Bhatt. "Hybrid cryptography algorithm for securing wireless sensor networks from node clone attack." *Recent Advances in Electrical & Electronic Engineering (Formerly Recent Patents on Electrical & Electronic Engineering)* 13, no. 2 (2020a): 251–259.

Mohindru, Vandana, Yashwant Singh, and Ravindara Bhatt. "Securing wireless sensor networks from node clone attack: a lightweight message authentication algorithm." *International Journal of Information and Computer Security* 12, no. 2–3 (2020b): 217–233.

Mutlag, Ammar Awad, Mohd Khanapi Abd Ghani, Net al Arunkumar, Mazin Abed Mohammed, and Othman Mohd. 2019. "Enabling technologies for fog computing in healthcare IoT systems." *Future Generation Computer Systems* 90:62–78.

Ornaghi, Alberto, and Marco Valleri. 2003. "Man in the middle attacks." *Blackhat Conference Europe.*

Patel, Bimal, and Parth Shah. 2022. "Operating system support, protocol stack with key concerns and testbed facilities for IoT: A case study perspective." *Journal of King Saud University-Computer and Information Sciences* 34 (8):5420–5434.

Pelechrinis, Konstantinos, Marios Iliofotou, and Srikanth V Krishnamurthy. 2010. "Denial of service attacks in wireless networks: The case of jammers." *IEEE Communications surveys & tutorials* 13 (2):245–257.

Qamar, Attia, Ahmad Karim, and Victor Chang. 2019. "Mobile malware attacks: Review, taxonomy & future directions." *Future Generation Computer Systems* 97:887–909.

Qiu, Shuming, Ding Wang, Guoai Xu, and Saru Kumari. 2020. "Practical and provably secure three-factor authentication protocol based on extended chaotic-maps for mobile lightweight devices." *IEEE Transactions on Dependable and Secure Computing* 19 (2):1338–1351.

Raza, Mudassar, Muhammad Iqbal, Muhammad Sharif, and Waqas Haider. 2012. "A survey of password attacks and comparative analysis on methods for secure authentication." *World Applied Sciences Journal* 19 (4):439–444.

Rudd, Ethan M, Andras Rozsa, Manuel Günther, and Terrance E Boult. 2016. "A survey of stealth malware attacks, mitigation measures, and steps toward autonomous open world solutions." *IEEE Communications Surveys & Tutorials* 19 (2):1145–1172.

Tasevski, Predrag. 2011. "Password attacks and generation strategies." *Tartu University: Faculty of Mathematics and Computer Sciences.* https://scholar.google.com/citations?view_op=view_citation&hl=en&user=5EEZXMoAAAAJ&citation_for_view=5EEZXMoAAAAJ:u5HHmVD_uO8C

Thomas, Ciza. 2020. "Introductory chapter: Computer security threats." In *Computer security threats.* IntechOpen.

Tsai, Chun-Wei, Chin-Feng Lai, Han-Chieh Chao, and Athanasios V Vasilakos. 2015. "Big data analytics: A survey." *Journal of Big data* 2 (1):1–32.

Vangala, Anusha, Ashok Kumar Das, Vinay Chamola, Valery Korotaev, and Joel JPC Rodrigues. 2023. "Security in IoT-enabled smart agriculture: Architecture, security solutions and challenges." *Cluster Computing* 26 (2):879–902.

Vermesan, Ovidiu, and Peter Friess. 2014. *Internet of things applications-from research and innovation to market deployment.* Taylor & Francis.

Wu, Fan, Xiong Li, Arun Kumar Sangaiah, Lili Xu, Saru Kumari, Liuxi Wu, and Jian Shen. 2018. "A lightweight and robust two-factor authentication scheme for personalized healthcare systems using wireless medical sensor networks." *Future Generation Computer Systems* 82:727–737.

14 Rapid Advancement and Trends of Big Data Analytics and Cyber-Physical System Embedded in Healthcare and Industry 4.0

Chintan Singh, Himanshu Khajuria, and Biswa Prakash Nayak

Amity University, Uttar Pradesh, India

14.1 INTRODUCTION

With the increasing prevalence of the internet and advancements in technology, numerous rooted structures have ensued that can manage physical objects, including machinery, equipment, and structures. This integration of information communication technologies with physical elements has led to the development of smart or intelligent systems, boosting effectiveness, productivity, safety, and speed while allowing for new functions. This has caused the usage of cyber-physical systems (CPS) to significantly rise, which merges cyber systems with physical objects. As noted by Yaacoub et al. (2020), aspects of daily life impacted by CPS include transportation networks, medical equipment, home appliances, oil and gas transportation, and electrical power grids (Yaacoub et al. 2020).

Ever since H. Gill, the person working for the National Science Foundation, first coined the term CPS in 2006, research in this field has been closely associated with emerging IT trends such as Industry 4.0, and the Internet of Things (IoT). As stated by Woschank (2020), Industry 4.0, which implies the fourth revolution of industrialization, is a German strategic effort that opens the way for an IoT, data, and service-oriented approach as well as a change from centralized to decentralized manufacturing (Woschank, Rauch, and Zsifkovits 2020). According to Almadani (2020), big data is massive, dynamic, and complicated information that is characterized by volume, velocity, and diversity (Almadani et al. 2020). According to Mohamed (2019), with immediate modifications to user needs, cloud computing (CLC) provides computer resources including software, infrastructure, and services through a network

DOI: 10.1201/9781003406105-19

(Mohamed, Al-Jaroodi, and Lazarova-Molnar 2019). Last but not least, IoT is described by Pivoto et al. as the interconnection of numerous objects, implementing the gadgets made up of sensors (Pivoto et al. 2021).

The major concept behind Industry 4.0 was the creation of intelligent networks that can autonomously control each other throughout the value chain by linking machines, workpieces, and systems (Zhou et al. 2021). To accomplish such a goal, CPS and other developing IT leanings, including (1) CPS as autonomous factories or production entities, (2) IoT as an infrastructure for CPS communications, (3) cloud-based interpretation for distributed offerings, and (4) big data solutions for rapid manufacturing enormous, intricate, variable, and precise information during production (Lv et al. 2021), have been explored. Ahmad and Pothuganti (2020) transmit a clarification of how IoT, big data, CLC, and Industry 4.0 attributes intersect with CPS parameters (Ahmad and Pothuganti 2020). Zheng et al. (2021) suggest that Industry 4.0 has been constructed on CPS and IoT, which are implemented on a cloud platform using the internet as a service, as illustrated in Figure 14.1 (Ding et al. 2021).

Linking the concepts of CPS with Industry 4.0, IoT, big data, and CLC can lead to more diverse and flexible research ideas, as these sections are directly interconnected but imply different perceptions and expertise. However, there aren't many publications that completely explain the CPS research trends relevant to these recent IT advancements (Tao et al. 2019). As an outcome, this chapter's objective is to examine

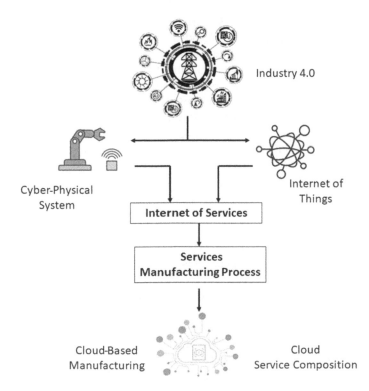

FIGURE 14.1   Relation of CPS to Industry 4.0 and IoT.

CPS research topics connected to current IT trends as well as how CPS technologies have been used in different industries. It is intended to convey these vast trends and information to aid researchers in concentrating on interdisciplinary research into CPS and upcoming IT trends and to offer insights that can assist in overcoming difficulties associated with industrial integration. A more active and innovative research environment will result from this.

In this chapter, we focus on the rapid advancement of big data analytics and CPS that has had a significant influence on healthcare manufacturing and Industry 4.0. The incorporation of these advancements has led to improved patient care, reduced costs, and increased efficiency in healthcare systems. In Industry 4.0, big data analytics (BDA) and CPS have transformed traditional manufacturing processes into smart factories that use immediate data to enhance production. Adoption of these technologies is, however, complicated by a variety of obstacles, such as concerns about data security and privacy. Despite these challenges, BDA and cyber-physical systems are still crucial areas for research and investment in the future because of the major advantages they might have for Industry 4.0 and healthcare. Furthermore, this chapter also focuses on the application, challenges, and future direction of CPS for other aspects of the advancement.

14.2   CURRENT TRENDS ON BIG DATA AND CPS

The incorporation of BDA and CPS is transforming various industries, including healthcare and manufacturing. The rapid advancement of these technologies has led to improved patient care, reduced costs, and increased efficiency in healthcare systems, as well as transformed traditional manufacturing processes into smart factories (Bayne 2018). The healthcare industry has seen significant improvements through the integration of BDA and CPS. The use of BDA has transformed the way healthcare providers operate (Irons-Forth 2014; Iskandarani 2014). It has allowed for better patient care and has helped in the development of personalized treatment plans. The use of CPS has also improved healthcare delivery by enabling remote monitoring and diagnosis.

The manufacturing industry has also seen significant improvements through the incorporation of BDA and CPS. Industry 4.0 in terms of use characterizes the present enterprise trend, which involves the integration of various technologies, including BDA and CPS (Sugawara and Nikaido 2014). The use of these technologies has transformed traditional manufacturing processes into smart factories, where everything is interconnected and intelligent. This has led to significant improvements in efficiency, productivity, and cost reduction. Despite the potential benefits, there are challenges that must be addressed when it comes to the incorporation of BDA and CPS (Mishra et al. 2022). Data security and privacy concerns ranked among the most significant challenges. There is a jeopardy of data breaches as more data is gathered and analyzed, which may cause serious financial and social damage (Zhang et al. 2021). There is also a threat of cyberattacks which can further disrupt the operations of healthcare providers and manufacturers (Napoleone, Macchi, and Pozzetti 2020).

To address these challenges, there is a need for collaboration between industry stakeholders, policymakers, and researchers. The development of standards and regulations can help ensure that data authenticity and security concerns are addressed. Utilization of encryption and other security protocols can also help protect data from cyberattacks. Despite these challenges, BDA and CPS remain a crucial part of research and investment for the future. The potential benefits of these technologies are too significant to ignore. Employing BDA and CPS in healthcare may optimize patient outcomes and safeguard expenses (Keshk et al. 2022; Niu and Wang 2022). Incorporation of these technologies can increase profitability and effectiveness in the industrial sector, leading to cost reductions and increased profitability (Li et al. 2021; Cao et al. 2021).

14.3 RAPID ADVANCEMENT OF BDA (HEALTHCARE AND INDUSTRY 4.0 PERSPECTIVE)

14.3.1 ADVANCEMENT IN HEALTHCARE SECTOR

BDA and CPS are rapidly transforming the healthcare and manufacturing industries. In healthcare, big data is being used to improve patient outcomes, reduce costs, and enhance clinical decision-making. The tendency to compile and examine vast amounts of patient data from electronic health records, wearables, and other sources has enabled healthcare providers to develop personalized treatment plans and deliver precision medicine (Cassoli et al. 2022). Additionally, BDA has the potential to revolutionize clinical trials by identifying patient subgroups and predicting treatment efficacy, ultimately leading to more effective and efficient drug development.

The American healthcare system is said to have more data than 150 exabytes in 2011. Given its present rate of growth, it is anticipated that we will soon transcend the zettabyte (1021 gigabytes) and yottabyte (1024 gigabytes) scales (Clinics and 2018). Kaiser Permanente, a California-based healthcare organization with more than nine million members, is estimated to be holding between 26.5 and 44 petabytes of potentially accessible EHR data, including pictures and annotations. Big data is a concept commonly employed by the healthcare sector to describe large and complex electronic health data sets that are challenging or impossible to handle using standard software and hardware as well as conventional data management techniques and processes (Shafqat et al. 2020; Asri et al. 2015). The overwhelming amount and diversity of data types, as well as the speed at which it must be managed, present significant challenges. However, BDA has the latent power to extract insights from this vast amount and array of data, enabling better-informed decisions, improving care, saving survivors, and lowering expenditure. BDA applications in healthcare are described as a growing research category (Shafqat et al. 2020).

Healthcare organizations, from solitary clinicians to tremendous hospital systems with oversight health organizations, may considerably benefit from digitizing, combining, and effectively exploiting big data., as reported in previous studies (Raghupathi and Raghupathi 2014; Sugawara and Nikaido 2014). Some of the potential advantages of this approach include detecting diseases in their early stages, managing the health of specific individuals and populations, and faster and more efficient detection of healthcare fraud. BDA can answer a broad range of queries, such as predicting convinced outcomes or large amounts of past statistics that have been used to make discoveries about the length of hospital stays, the likelihood that patients will choose elective surgery, the identification of patients who would not benefit from surgery, the detection of problems, and the identification of patients who are at risk for medical issues, hospital-acquired infections such as sepsis, MRSA, or *C. difficile*, predicting disease progression, and identifying patients at risk of advancing illness states. According to Mansourvar and Grover, BDA can potentially save more than $300 billion annually in U.S. healthcare, with deuce-thirds of the savings resulting in a reduction of approximately 8% in healthcare expenses (Mansourvar et al. 2020; Grover et al. 2018). Healthcare services and development and research, with $165 billion and $108 billion in opportunity reductions in waste, accordingly, are two of the sectors with the highest potential for savings. In the following three categories, according to Haafza, big data might assist with eliminating waste and inefficiency (Haafza et al. 2022):

Medical operations: In order to develop more cheap strategies for patient diagnosis and treatment, a comparative effectiveness research is being conducted.

Research and development:
- Using extrapolative shaping to streamline the R&D process and develop targeted drugs and devices.
- Accelerating the development of innovative medicines by improving patient recruitment and clinical trial design through the application of statistical techniques and algorithms.

Analyzing patient data and clinical trials to look for additional applications and adverse reactions before a medicine is released.

Society Healthiness:
- Tracking disease outbreaks and transmission and analyzing illness trends to enhance public health surveillance and quicken response.
- Creating vaccinations that are more precisely targeted.
- Converting enormous amounts of data into information that may be put to good use, especially for the benefit of populations, in order to identify needs, provide services, and foresee and prevent calamities.
- Other potential areas where BDA can put up to healthcare include the following:

Evidence-driven medical practice: Using different forms of sources of data to combine, examine, and analyze in order to forecast illness or relapse risk in patients, match therapies with outcomes, and deliver improved treatment.

Genetic statistical analysis: Increasing the effectiveness and economy of gene sequencing, as well as the use of genomic data in patient records and clinical decisions.

Preadjudication fraud analysis: Rapidly analyzing to minimize deception through claim requests, waste, and abuse.

Patient profiling statistics: Determining those who might profit from preventative measures or changes in behavior, such as those who are at risk of developing a certain disease, using patient profiling statistics.

14.3.2 ADVANCEMENT TOWARD INDUSTRY 4.0

BDA has become a critical tool for businesses in Industry 4.0. As the world becomes more connected through the IoT, the amount of information generated increases exponentially. This data can be analyzed to reveal insights that can improve business operations, increase efficiency, and ultimately boost profits.

One of the elementary advantages of BDA in Industry 4.0 is its ability to anticipate maintenance. Predictive maintenance allows businesses to anticipate when a gear is probably going to crash, allowing for repairs or replacement before a catastrophic failure occurs. This not only reduces downtime and repair costs but also improves safety. By examining data from other sources such as sensors, companies may forecast when a product is going to break and accordingly take precautions to accompt it (Karimi et al. 2021; Waheed et al. 2021). Another important application of BDA in Industry 4.0 is quality control. By analyzing data from production processes, organizations may recognize patterns and trends that can point to a manufacturing process issue. This can help prevent defects and improve overall product quality. Additionally, BDA can assist in recognizing the source of quality issues, thus allowing for targeted fixes and improvements.

BDA can also be used for supply chain optimization. Organizations may spot supply chain inefficiencies and bottlenecks by analyzing information gathered by suppliers, logistics providers, and other sources. This can help improve delivery times, reduce costs, and improve overall supply chain performance. In accumulation, BDA can help reduce healthcare costs by improving operational efficiency and reducing waste. Data from healthcare systems and insurance firms may be analyzed by healthcare providers to identify areas where expenses could be lowered without jeopardizing patient care (Z Lv et al. 2021).

However, the advancement of BDA in Industry 4.0 also brings challenges. Data security and privacy issues should be addressed for resulting in prevention of exposure to sensitive information. Collaboration and regulation are needed to ensure the ethical and responsible use of these technologies. A conceptual framework is illustrated in Figure 14.2 for BDA which represents its application and other uses.

In the manufacturing industry, Industry 4.0 is directing the adoption of CPS, which enables real-time data gathering and analysis to optimize production processes. The integration of BDA with CPS can help manufacturers provide better product value, moderate costs, and strengthen effectiveness. For example, predictive maintenance, aided by BDA, may reduce unplanned downtimes by identifying potential equipment problems early on. However, there are also significant issues with BDA and CPS implementation. A significant pressing problem is the security and privacy of personal information. As healthcare and manufacturing organizations collect and store more data, they must ensure that sensitive information is kept secure and confidential. Additionally, there is a need for collaboration and regulation to ensure that these technologies are used ethically and responsibly.

In conclusion, BDA has become a critical tool for businesses in Industry 4.0. It allows businesses to predict equipment failures, improve quality control, optimize supply chains, and transform patient care in the healthcare industry. An illustration of BDA architecture is shown in Figure 14.2. However, data privacy and security concerns must be addressed, and collaboration and regulation are needed to ensure the

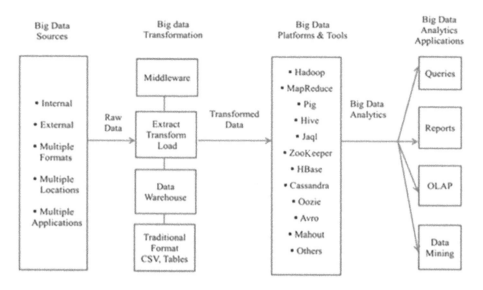

FIGURE 14.2   Applied framework for BDA and its applications.

ethical and responsible use of these technologies. Despite these challenges, BDA remains a crucial area of research and investment for the future.

14.4   CYBER-PHYSICAL SYSTEM (CPS) EMBEDDED IN ORGANIZATIONS

14.4.1   CPS RESEARCH AND INTEGRATION APPLICATION IN HEALTHCARE AND INDUSTRY 4.0

A CPS architecture provides a modular and organized structure that facilitates the integration of technology into existing or new systems with minimal effort (Yilma, Panetto, and Naudet 2019). Unified architectures have been suggested as a means of defining the CPS's structure and approach. As shown in Figure 14.3, Kotronis (2019) proposes a five-level CPS structure known as the 5C architecture, which offers a comprehensive guide for developing and using CPS in industrial applications (Kotronis et al. 2019). The initial stage entails gathering precise and trustworthy data from machines and their components at the smart interconnection level. This data might be collected via controllers or commercial manufacturing systems, measured by sensors, or obtained from assessments made by detectors. The second stage is to convert the data into information and get useful information from it. Using the architecture described by Kotronis (2019), Bagula et al. (2018) established the 5C paradigm for CPS implementation by combining autonomous and cooperative parts and subsystems dependent on the context across all the production stages and production lines. Information circulated throughout various components of Industry 4.0 is depicted in Figure 14.4 (Bagula et al. 2018; Kotronis et al. 2019).

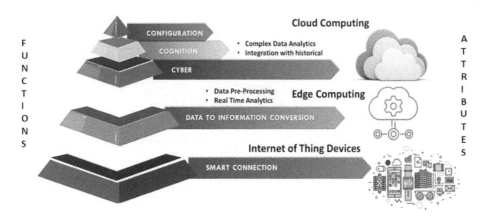

FIGURE 14.3   5C architecture for IoTH-based cyber-physical system (CYPS) paradigm.

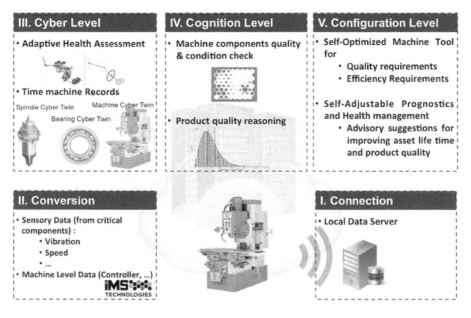

FIGURE 14.4   Illustration shows the production line utilizing the 5C CPS architecture, data, and information seamlessly circulated throughout the CPS-enabled factory's machine tools.

14.4.2   CPS MODELS: IMPLEMENTATION AND MATURITY

Sampath and Scheuermann (2017) addressed management issues arising from the complexity of CPS by designing innovations and designs geared toward databases that combine networking, AI, and real-time control challenges into a single computer paradigm (Khargonekar and Sampath 2020; Scheuermann et al. 2017). The stages of CPS maturity were described as follows: Establishing the fundamentals, fostering transparency, raising awareness, enhancing decision-making, and

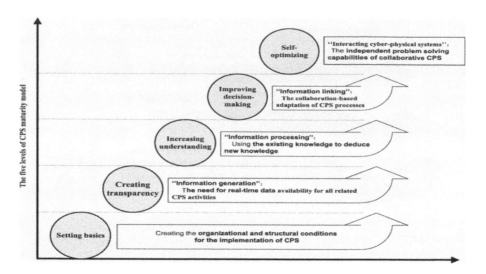

FIGURE 14.5 Five-layer maturity model for CPS.

self-optimizing. The base level establishes the organizational and structural framework for CPS implementation, while each of the higher levels shows the maturity of realizations regarding knowledge and information processing, as well as features of working together and collaborating. The integration of expanded CPS domains, such as industrial cyber-physical systems (ICPSs) and CPSs, has been covered in a number of studies. According to Taimoor and Rehman (2022), ICPS can be explained best by their ability to obtain physical data and analyze it intelligently for a particular industrial automation-related goal (Taimoor and Rehman 2022; Taimoor and Rehman 2022). IoT, service-based interactions, cloud capabilities, and big data are merely a few of the significant upcoming technological developments that the authors predicted will be combined to form ICPS. They additionally glanced to see how automation technologies may be integrated into ICPS modules and subsystems. A five-layer maturity model is illustrated in Figure 14.5. Poursoltan et al. (2023) rendered a framework for the establishment of a database and provided suggestions for implementing the Digital Twin as a crucial requirement of a CPS in small and medium-sized enterprises (SMEs) for establishing a CPS, which is an essential facet of Industry 4.0 (Poursoltan et al. 2023; R. S. Nandhini and Ramanathan 2022).

14.5 CPS: MANAGEMENT AND CONTROL

In order to develop designs for products that incorporate essential manufacturing characteristics, an evolutionary feature-based management approach for distributed manufacturing resources in CPS was proposed by Latif et al. (2022). The authors also provided a structure for information that supports this approach (Latif et al. 2022). Conversely, Cao et al. (2021) evaluated a highly computerized manufacturing system using digital representations including important product-specific information (Cao et al. 2021). Alsufayani et al. (2021) developed a framework for

CPS experimentation based on CLC and software-defined networks classified into three sublevels: The physical layer, the cloud layer, and the application layer. This design was established to evaluate the privacy of CPS systems (Alsufyani et al. 2021). Azamfar et al. adopted a structure-driven dynamic control (SDC) procedure based on optimum program control (OPC) theory and mathematical programming (MP) to deal with the dynamic scheduling of service provision in the CPS. This service-focused tactic, which also takes advantage of recent advancements in decentralized information services like CLC, specifically includes the CPS material and information processes (Ahmad and Pothuganti 2020; Lee, Azamfar, and Singh 2019).

14.6   CPS FOR CLC

According to Xu et al. (2020), leveraging CLC infrastructure may enhance the reliability, interoperability, and sustainability of CPS by providing versatile and agile processing power and storage space (Xu et al. 2020). The CPS cyber layer needs to incorporate cloud technologies, according to Cao et al. (2021), complying with academics' recommendations, to ensure the scalability of storage, computation, and cross-domain interaction capabilities. The conceptualization of a cloud-integrated CPS has been the subject of several research studies (Cao et al. 2021). Xu et al. (2020) render a model-based framework paradigm of cloud-based CPS that is adaptable, changeable, and reproducible for a variety of applications by utilizing CLC to allow scalable computing power and data storage. Similar to this, R. Nandhini and Ramanathan (2022) convey a reference model for a digital twin framework that evaluates a system's current state and recommends control measures for the physical environment. To tackle the drawbacks of the current cloud-based CPS design, Wang et al. (2022) suggest decentralizing the CPS architecture into three layers: The sensor-based and activation layer, the communications, and the processing and application layer. In their final contribution, Chen et al. (2020) establish an architecture for the cyber-physical indication relationship that combines signage, consumer, website, and CLC to support recognition and detection of face applications and improve audience engagement with digital signage so that users can quickly get information or feedback, Figure 14.6 depicts the framework of CPS with respect to Industry 4.0.

14.6.1   COMMUNICATION AND NETWORK OF CPS

Wireless sensor networks (WSNs) should be used by CPS to collect physical data on the internet and the tangible world is integrated, claim R. Nandhini and Ramanathan (2022). An illustration of all the components of networking and communication in CPS is shown in Figure 14.7. For real-time environmental monitoring, the authors discuss the WSN, multiagent, and CLC capabilities used in the CPS paradigm. According to Xu et al. (2020), in automobile networks, cloud-assisted dynamic spectrum access may offer an ideal communication path that satisfies data rate requirements. In a cyber-physical industrial production cloud, Xu et al. (2020) devised an MT Connect RESTful protocol for monitoring networked open-sourced RepRap-based 3D printers. MT Connect is an internet communication protocol for

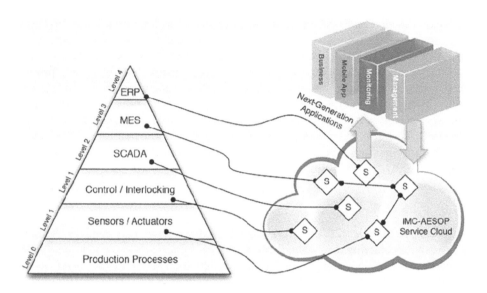

FIGURE 14.6   Cloud-based CPS framework for Industry 4.0.

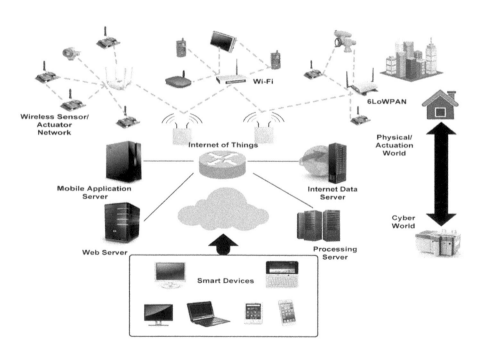

FIGURE 14.7   Elements of network and communications in CPS.

factories. Network-on-Chip (NoC) technology is used by Xu et al. (2020) to propose an energy-aware virtual machine deployment approach for cloud-supported systems that ensures lower signal problems, better execution, and low power feeding in order to reduce power consumption management costs. According to Lee, Azamfar, and Singh (2019), an integrated CPS increases the accessibility and remote controllability of industrial equipment while reducing network traffic.

14.7 APPLICATION TOWARD INDUSTRY 4.0 AND HEALTHCARE

Although the CPS model was still in use in 2006, the organization's efforts are still in their infancy. Nevertheless, CPS has an immense ability to revolutionize our day-to-day lifestyle and various industries. According to Semwal and Handa (2022), there are already multiple practical applications of CPS that include autonomous vehicles, surgical robots, smart frameworks, intelligent energy grids, smart manufacturing, and implantable medical technology. CPS has been used in four significant areas, including production, transport, energy management, and healthcare, according to the papers that were chosen. A few CPS applications also exist in the sectors of smart cities, the environment, and advertising.

14.7.1 MANUFACTURING AND TRANSPORTATION

According to Pathak et al. (2019), the adoption of CPS in industrial settings has enhanced the productivity of the whole manufacturing process by sharing immediate data on manufacturing equipment, distribution networks, business systems, and customer activities that add value. Using smart factory hardware Gupta et al. (2020) designed a CPS to create a flexible factory that permits product order modifications during assembly. Three CPS application scenarios for smart manufacturing – cyber-physical logistics system, safe human–robot interaction, and video surveillance use as a service – are suggested by Ahmad and Pothuganti (2020). Napoleone, Macchi, and Pozzetti (2020) also use CPS in anticipatory production systems in order to boost productivity by including robustness and interoperability.

The abilities and capabilities of systems with embedded components are also able to improve through CPS. CPS, as defined by Fang et al. (2020), are embedded systems, for which he devised a commercial caffeine maker that offers a variety of services, including remote diagnostics and firmware upgrades. Using the five-level CPS architecture, Neal et al. (2021) constructed self-aware band-saw machines. Finally, using a UML methodology, Neal et al. (2021) and Akanmu, Anumba, and Ogunseiju (2021) developed a completely automated and inexpensive cyber-physical component-based liquor plant system.

14.7.2 SMART GRIDS

ICT-based smart grid architecture makes it feasible to deliver a dependable energy supply to end consumers. Smart grids are regarded as part of modern CPS, according to Nafees et al. (2023), where smart devices are situated in the realm of reality and organized algorithms are carried out in the cloud network. Jha et al. (2021) suggest a cyber-physical cloud-based system to provide safe smart grids and IoT integration. On the contrary, Pathak et al. (2019) employed distributed smart solar-powered microgrids that will enable CPS and CLC to improve the duration of electric car charging. To reduce the number of tracking movements and enable significant code reclaim of algorithms, they construct the smart subsystems framework (SSF) for a two-axis solar tracker system.

14.7.3 HEALTHCARE

According to Khujamatov et al. (2021), CPS is growing as a potential option for healthcare applications, particularly in-hospital and personal patient care, as wireless sensing networks (WSN), medical devices, and CLC continue to advance. The utilization of CPS to remotely monitor the physical status of elderly or handicapped patients is suggested by Neal et al. (2021). Fang et al. (2020) propose a CPS-based healthcare system to solve the shortcomings of conventional medical systems in order to propose a wearable and wireless system that allows local actions and distant data collecting for elderly people monitoring, patients with mild cognitive impairment, and early Alzheimer's disease treatment. Pathak et al. (2019) integrate CPS with Wireless Body Area Networks (WBAN).

14.8 CHALLENGES AND OPPORTUNITIES AND FUTURE RESEARCH

For performing control experiments on embedded computer systems, a multidisciplinary system called CPS incorporates methods for correspondence, computing, and control (Mohindru et al. 2021). Industry 4.0 depends on CPS's expansion, which will be sped up through collaborations that include IoT, big data, and CLC. Although there have been considerable studies in CPS on Industry 4.0 and big data, collaboration, network, and security-related concerns have received little attention (Mohindru et al. 2020a). Technologies for communication, networks, and security are essential for securing connections between smart factories in the CPS environment (Mohindru et al. 2020b). Additionally, by incorporating cutting-edge IT trends like IoT, big data, and CLC, CPS may be utilized in various industries like agricultural and supply chain management. Investigators can develop a more comprehensive perspective and reveal novel solutions to these technological difficulties by using an interdisciplinary approach that is not achievable with dispersed strategies.

14.9 CONCLUSION

In conclusion, the rise of BDA, CPS, Industry 4.0, and other technologies is rapidly changing the way individuals live, work, and interact with technology. Organizations across areas are using BDA to get useful insights and motivate educated decision-making as a result of the data's fast expansion. Healthcare practitioners are now equipped to better patient outcomes, cut costs, and improve overall care quality because of the integration of CPS. Manufacturing procedures are being revolutionized by Industry 4.0, they becoming more effective and efficient. It is apparent that as these trends advance, the potential of big data analytics and CPS will continue to transform the way we work, live, and confront problems. Organizations have to adapt to these developments and take advantage of them if they are to continue to be competitive and inventive in a quick-paced and always-evolving world of technology.

REFERENCES

Ahmad, Irfan, and Karunakar Pothuganti. 2020. "Smart Field Monitoring Using ToxTrac: A Cyber-Physical System Approach in Agriculture." *Proceedings - International Conference on Smart Electronics and Communication, ICOSEC 2020*, 723–27. https://doi.org/10.1109/ICOSEC49089.2020.9215282

Akanmu, Abiola A, Chimay J Anumba, and Omobolanle O Ogunseiju. 2021. "Towards next Generation Cyber-Physical Systems and Digital Twins for Construction." *Journal of Information Technology in Construction* 26: 505–25. https://doi.org/10.36680/j.itcon.2021.027

Almadani, Yousef, David Plets, Sander Bastiaens, Wout Joseph, Muhammad Ijaz, Zabih Ghassemlooy, and Sujan Rajbhandari. 2020. "Visible Light Communications for Industrial Applications—Challenges and Potentials." *Electronics (Switzerland)*. https://doi.org/10.3390/electronics9122157

Alsufyani, Abdulmajeed, Youseef Alotaibi, Alaa Omran Almagrabi, Saleh Ahmed Alghamdi, and Nawal Alsufyani. 2021. "Optimized Intelligent Data Management Framework for a Cyber-Physical System for Computational Applications." *Complex and Intelligent Systems* 1: 3. https://doi.org/10.1007/s40747-021-00511-w

Asri, Hiba, Hajar Mousannif, Hassan Al Moatassime, and Thomas Noel. 2015. "Big Data in Healthcare: Challenges and Opportunities." In *Proceedings of 2015 International Conference on Cloud Computing Technologies and Applications, CloudTech 2015*. https://doi.org/10.1109/CloudTech.2015.7337020

Bagula, A., M. Mandava, and H. Bagula. 2018. "A Framework for Healthcare Support in the Rural and Low Income Areas of the Developing World." *Journal of Network and Computer Applications* 120: 17–29. https://doi.org/10.1016/j.jnca.2018.06.010

Bayne, Lynn E. 2018. "Big Data in Neonatal Health Care: Big Reach, Big Reward?" *Critical Care Nursing Clinics of North America*. https://doi.org/10.1016/j.cnc.2018.07.005

Cao, Kun, Shiyan Hu, Yang Shi, Armando Walter Colombo, Stamatis Karnouskos, and Xin Li. 2021. "A Survey on Edge and Edge-Cloud Computing Assisted Cyber-Physical Systems." *IEEE Transactions on Industrial Informatics* 17 (11): 7806–19. https://doi.org/10.1109/TII.2021.3073066

Cassoli, Beatriz Bretones, Nicolas Jourdan, Phu H. Nguyen, Sagar Sen, Enrique Garcia-Ceja, and Joachim Metternich. 2022. "Frameworks for Data-Driven Quality Management in Cyber-Physical Systems for Manufacturing: A Systematic Review." In *Procedia CIRP*, 112:567–72. https://doi.org/10.1016/j.procir.2022.09.062

Chen, Gaige, Pei Wang, Bo Feng, Yihui Li, and Dekun Liu. 2020. "The Framework Design of Smart Factory in Discrete Manufacturing Industry Based on Cyber-Physical System." *International Journal of Computer Integrated Manufacturing* 33 (1): 79–101. https://doi.org/10.1080/0951192X.2019.1699254

Ding, Derui, Qing Long Han, Xiaohua Ge, and Jun Wang. 2021. "Secure State Estimation and Control of Cyber-Physical Systems: A Survey." *IEEE Transactions on Systems, Man, and Cybernetics: Systems*. https://doi.org/10.1109/TSMC.2020.3041121

Fang, Pengcheng, Jianjun Yang, Lianyu Zheng, Ray Y. Zhong, and Yuchen Jiang. 2020. "Data Analytics-Enable Production Visibility for Cyber-Physical Production Systems." *Journal of Manufacturing Systems* 57: 242–53. https://doi.org/10.1016/j.jmsy.2020.09.002

Grover, Varun, Roger H.L. Chiang, Ting Peng Liang, and Dongsong Zhang. 2018. "Creating Strategic Business Value from Big Data Analytics: A Research Framework." *Journal of Management Information Systems* 35 (2): 388–423. https://doi.org/10.1080/07421222.2018.1451951

Gupta, Rajesh, Sudeep Tanwar, Fadi Al-Turjman, Prit Italiya, Ali Nauman, and Sung Won Kim. 2020. "Smart Contract Privacy Protection Using AI in Cyber-Physical Systems: Tools, Techniques and Challenges." *IEEE Access* 8: 24746–72. https://doi.org/10.1109/ACCESS.2020.2970576

Haafza, Shahra Asif, Muhammad Subhan Dar, Muhammad Imran Tariq, Muhammad Arfan Jaffar, and Shariq Aziz Butt. 2022. "Impact of Big Data in Healthcare and Management Analysis." *Security and Privacy Trends in Cloud Computing and Big Data*, April, 165–89. https://doi.org/10.1201/9781003107286

Irons-Forth, Roseline Pamella. 2014. "An Exploratory Study of Factors Affecting Adoption of Technology by Small Physician Practices." *Dissertation Abstracts International Section A: Humanities and Social Sciences* 75: No-Specified. https://search.proquest.com/openview/df548027f0c9d571f646407bad07e7aa/1?pq-origsite=gscholar&cbl=18750

Iskandarani, Khalid M. 2014. "Review of Transforming Health Care: The Financial Impact of Technology, Electronic Tools, and Data Mining." *Sociology of Health & Illness*. https://books.google.com/books?hl=en&lr=&id=Lx4i2brzh4IC&oi=fnd&pg=PT4&dq=Healthcare+organizations,+ranging+from+single-physician+practices+to+large+hospital+networks+and+accountable+care+organizations,+can+reap+significant+benefits+by+digitizing,+combini

Jha, A. V., B. Appasani, A. N. Ghazali, P. Pattanayak, D. S. Gurjar, E. Kabalci, and D. K. Mohanta. 2021. "Smart Grid Cyber-Physical Systems: Communication Technologies, Standards and Challenges." *Wireless Networks* 27 (4): 2595–2613. https://doi.org/10.1007/S11276-021-02579-1

Karimi, Yaghoob, Mostafa Haghi Kashani, Mohammad Akbari, and Ebrahim Mahdipour. 2021. "Leveraging Big Data in Smart Cities: A Systematic Review." *Concurrency and Computation: Practice and Experience* 33 (21). https://doi.org/10.1002/CPE.6379

Keshk, Marwa, Nour Moustafa, Elena Sitnikova, and Benjamin Turnbull. 2022. "Privacy-Preserving Big Data Analytics for Cyber-Physical Systems." *Wireless Networks* 28 (3): 1241–49. https://doi.org/10.1007/S11276-018-01912-5

Khargonekar, Pramod P., and Meera Sampath. 2020. "A Framework for Ethics in Cyber-Physical-Human Systems." In *IFAC-PapersOnLine* 53: 17008–15. https://doi.org/10.1016/j.ifacol.2020.12.1251

Khujamatov, Halim, Ernazar Reypnazarov, Doston Khasanov, and Nurshod Akhmedov. 2021. "IoT, IIoT, and Cyber-Physical Systems Integration." *Advances in Science, Technology and Innovation*, 31–50. https://doi.org/10.1007/978-3-030-66222-6_3

Kotronis, Christos, Ioannis Routis, Anargyros Tsadimas, Mara Nikolaidou, and Dimosthenis Anagnostopoulos. 2019. "A Model-Based Approach for the Design of Cyber-Physical Human Systems Emphasizing Human Concerns." In *Proceedings - 2019 IEEE International Congress on Internet of Things, ICIOT 2019 - Part of the 2019 IEEE World Congress on Services*, 100–107. https://doi.org/10.1109/ICIOT.2019.00028

Latif, Sohaib A, Fang B. Xian Wen, Celestine Iwendi, Li Li F. Wang, Syed Muhammad Mohsin, Zhaoyang Han, and Shahab S Band. 2022. "AI-Empowered, Blockchain and SDN Integrated Security Architecture for IoT Network of Cyber Physical Systems." *Computer Communications* 181: 274–83. https://doi.org/10.1016/j.comcom.2021.09.029

Lee, Jay, Moslem Azamfar, and Jaskaran Singh. 2019. "A Blockchain Enabled Cyber-Physical System Architecture for Industry 4.0 Manufacturing Systems." *Manufacturing Letters* 20: 34–39. https://doi.org/10.1016/j.mfglet.2019.05.003

Li, Beibei, Yuhao Wu, Jiarui Song, Rongxing Lu, Tao Li, and Liang Zhao. 2021. "DeepFed: Federated Deep Learning for Intrusion Detection in Industrial Cyber-Physical Systems." *IEEE Transactions on Industrial Informatics* 17 (8): 5615–24. https://doi.org/10.1109/TII.2020.3023430

Lv, Zhihan, Dongliang Chen, Ranran Lou, and Ammar Alazab. 2021. "Artificial Intelligence for Securing Industrial-Based Cyber–Physical Systems." *Future Generation Computer Systems* 117: 291–98. https://doi.org/10.1016/j.future.2020.12.001

Mansourvar, M., U. K. Wiil, C. Nøhr -, iCETiC 2020, undefined London, undefined UK, August 19, and undefined 2020. 2020. "Big Data Analytics in Healthcare: A Review of Opportunities and Challenges." *Springer* 2020: 126–41. https://doi.org/10.1007/978-3-030-60036-5_9

Mishra, Ayaskanta, Amitkumar V. Jha, Bhargav Appasani, Arun Kumar Ray, Deepak Kumar Gupta, and Abu Nasar Ghazali. 2022. "Emerging Technologies and Design Aspects of next Generation Cyber Physical System with a Smart City Application Perspective." *International Journal of Systems Assurance Engineering and Management.* https://doi.org/10.1007/s13198-021-01523-y

Mohamed, Nader, Jameela Al-Jaroodi, and Sanja Lazarova-Molnar. 2019. "Leveraging the Capabilities of Industry 4.0 for Improving Energy Efficiency in Smart Factories." *IEEE Access* 7: 18008–20. https://doi.org/10.1109/ACCESS.2019.2897045

Mohindru, Vandana, Yashwant Singh, and Ravindara Bhatt. 2020a. "Hybrid cryptography algorithm for securing wireless sensor networks from Node Clone Attack." *Recent Advances in Electrical & Electronic Engineering (Formerly Recent Patents on Electrical & Electronic Engineering)* 13 (2): 251–259.

Mohindru, Vandana, Yashwant Singh, and Ravindara Bhatt. 2020b. "Securing wireless sensor networks from node clone attack: a lightweight message authentication algorithm." *International Journal of Information and Computer Security* 12, no. 2–3: 217–233.

Mohindru, Vandana, Sunidhi Vashishth, and Deepak Bathija. 2021 "Internet of Things (IoT) for Healthcare Systems: A Comprehensive Survey." *Recent Innovations in Computing: Proceedings of ICRIC* 1 (2022): 213–229.

Nafees, Muhammad Nouman, Neetesh Saxena, Alvaro Cardenas, Santiago Grijalva, and Pete Burnap. 2023. "Smart Grid Cyber-Physical Situational Awareness of Complex Operational Technology Attacks: A Review." *ACM Computing Surveys* 55 (10): 1–36. https://doi.org/10.1145/3565570

Nandhini, RS, and L. Ramanathan. 2022. "Integration of Big Data Analytics Into Cyber-Physical Systems." In *Cyber-Physical Systems*, 19–41. https://doi.org/10.1002/9781119836636.ch2

Napoleone, Alessia, Marco Macchi, and Alessandro Pozzetti. 2020. "A Review on the Characteristics of Cyber-Physical Systems for the Future Smart Factories." *Journal of Manufacturing Systems.* https://doi.org/10.1016/j.jmsy.2020.01.007

Neal, Aaron D., Richard G. Sharpe, Katherine van Lopik, James Tribe, Paul Goodall, Heinz Lugo, Diana Segura-Velandia, et al. 2021. "The Potential of Industry 4.0 Cyber Physical System to Improve Quality Assurance: An Automotive Case Study for Wash Monitoring of Returnable Transit Items." *CIRP Journal of Manufacturing Science and Technology* 32: 461–75. https://doi.org/10.1016/j.cirpj.2020.07.002

Niu, C., and L. Wang. 2022. "Big Data-Driven Scheduling Optimization Algorithm for Cyber–Physical Systems Based on a Cloud Platform." *Elsevier* 181: 173–81. https://doi.org/10.1016/j.comcom.2021.10.020

Pathak, Pankaj, Parashu Ram Pal, Manish Shrivastava, and Priyanka Ora. 2019. "Fifth Revolution: Applied AI & Human Intelligence with Cyber Physical Systems." *International Journal of Engineering and Advanced Technology* 8 (3): 23–27. https://www.researchgate.net/profile/Parashu-Pal/publication/331966435_Fifth_revolution_Applied_AI_human_intelligence_with_cyber_physical_systems/links/5ca5efa2299bf118c4b0a484/Fifth-revolution-Applied-AI-human-intelligence-with-cyber-physical-systems.pdf

Pivoto, Diego G.S., Luiz F.F. de Almeida, Rodrigo da Rosa Righi, Joel J.P.C. Rodrigues, Alexandre Baratella Lugli, and Antonio M. Alberti. 2021. "Cyber-Physical Systems Architectures for Industrial Internet of Things Applications in Industry 4.0: A Literature Review." *Journal of Manufacturing Systems* 58: 176–92. https://doi.org/10.1016/j.jmsy.2020.11.017

Poursoltan, Milad, Mamadou Kaba Traore, Nathalie Pinède, and Bruno Vallespir. 2023. "A Digital Twin Model-Driven Architecture for Cyber-Physical and Human Systems." In *Proceedings of the I-ESA Conferences*, 10: 135–44. Springer Science and Business Media Deutschland GmbH. https://doi.org/10.1007/978-3-030-90387-9_12

Raghupathi, Wullianallur, and Viju Raghupathi. 2014. "Big Data Analytics in Healthcare: Promise and Potential." *Health Information Science and Systems* 2 (1). https://doi.org/10.1186/2047-2501-2-3

Scheuermann, Constantin, Bernd Bruegge, Jens Folmer, and Stephan Verclas. 2017. "Incident Localization and Assistance System: A Case Study of a Cyber-Physical Human System." In *2015 IEEE/CIC International Conference on Communications in China - Workshops, CIC/ICCC 2015*, 57–61. https://doi.org/10.1109/ICCChinaW.2015.7961580

Semwal, Prabhat, and Akansha Handa. 2022. "Cyber-Attack Detection in Cyber-Physical Systems Using Supervised Machine Learning." In *Handbook of Big Data Analytics and Forensics*, 131–40. Springer International Publishing. https://doi.org/10.1007/978-3-030-74753-4_9

Shafqat, Sarah, Saira Kishwer, Raihan Ur Rasool, Junaid Qadir, Tehmina Amjad, and Hafiz Farooq Ahmad. 2020. "Big Data Analytics Enhanced Healthcare Systems: A Review." *Journal of Supercomputing* 76 (3): 1754–99. https://doi.org/10.1007/s11227-017-2222-4

Sugawara, Etsuko, and Hiroshi Nikaido. 2014. "Properties of AdeABC and AdeIJK Efflux Systems of Acinetobacter Baumannii Compared with Those of the AcrAB-TolC System of Escherichia Coli." *Antimicrobial Agents and Chemotherapy* 58 (12): 7250–57. https://doi.org/10.1128/AAC.03728-14

Taimoor, Najma, and Semeen Rehman. 2022. "Reliable and Resilient AI and IoT-Based Personalised Healthcare Services: A Survey." *IEEE Access* 10: 535–63. https://doi.org/10.1109/ACCESS.2021.3137364

Tao, Fei, Qinglin Qi, Lihui Wang, and A. Y.C. Nee. 2019. "Digital Twins and Cyber–Physical Systems toward Smart Manufacturing and Industry 4.0: Correlation and Comparison." *Engineering* 5 (4): 653–61. https://doi.org/10.1016/j.eng.2019.01.014

Waheed, Nazar, Xiangjian He, Muhammad Ikram, Muhammad Usman, Saad Sajid Hashmi, and Muhammad Usman. 2021. "Security and Privacy in IoT Using Machine Learning and Blockchain: Threats and Countermeasures." *ACM Computing Surveys* 53 (6). https://doi.org/10.1145/3417987

Wang, B., P. Zheng, Y. Yin, A. Shih, and L. Wang 2022. "Toward Human-Centric Smart Manufacturing: A Human-Cyber-Physical Systems (HCPS) Perspective." *Elsevier*. Accessed May 7, 2023. https://www.sciencedirect.com/science/article/pii/S0278612522000759

Woschank, Manuel, Erwin Rauch, and Helmut Zsifkovits. 2020. "A Review of Further Directions for Artificial Intelligence, Machine Learning, and Deep Learning in Smart Logistics." *Sustainability (Switzerland)* 12 (9). https://doi.org/10.3390/su12093760

Xu, Zhanyang, Yanqi Zhang, Haoyuan Li, Weijing Yang, and Quan Qi. 2020. "Dynamic Resource Provisioning for Cyber-Physical Systems in Cloud-Fog-Edge Computing." *Journal of Cloud Computing* 9 (1). https://doi.org/10.1186/s13677-020-00181-y

Yaacoub, J. P. A., O. Salman, … H. N. Noura. 2020. "Cyber-Physical Systems Security: Limitations, Issues and Future Trends." *Elsevier*. Accessed May 6, 2023. https://www.sciencedirect.com/science/article/pii/S0141933120303689

Yilma, Bereket Abera, Hervé Panetto, and Yannick Naudet. 2019. "A Meta-Model of Cyber-Physical-Social System: The CPSS Paradigm to Support Human-Machine Collaboration in Industry 4.0." In *IFIP Advances in Information and Communication Technology*, 568:11–20. Springer New York LLC. https://doi.org/10.1007/978-3-030-28464-0_2

Zhang, Dan, Qing Guo Wang, Gang Feng, Yang Shi, and Athanasios V. Vasilakos. 2021. "A Survey on Attack Detection, Estimation and Control of Industrial Cyber–Physical Systems." *ISA Transactions* 116: 1–16. https://doi.org/10.1016/j.isatra.2021.01.036

Zhou, Xiaokang, Wei Liang, Shohei Shimizu, Jianhua Ma, and Qun Jin. 2021. "Siamese Neural Network Based Few-Shot Learning for Anomaly Detection in Industrial Cyber-Physical Systems." *IEEE Transactions on Industrial Informatics* 17 (8): 5790–98. https://doi.org/10.1109/TII.2020.3047675

15 Blockchain-Based Cyber-Physical System
Opportunities and Challenges

Veerpal Kaur and Devershi Pallavi Bhatt

Manipal University, Jaipur, India

Sumegh Tharewal

Symbiosis Institute of Computer Studies and Research (SICSR), Symbiosis International (Deemed) University (SIU), Pune, India

Pradeep Kumar Tiwari

Dr. Vishwanath Karad MIT World Peace University, Pune, India

15.1 INTRODUCTION

Cyber-physical systems are highlighted by recent developments in the industry of the future; Industry 4.0's cyber-physical systems (CPS) are a new category of systems with combined physical and computational abilities that can interact with people using a wide range of novel modalities (Mo, Wagle, and Zuba 2014). CPS's objective is to function as a channel for communication between the cyber and physical worlds. The natures of these two words, however, differ so greatly from one another that any interaction poses risks to safety and security. For instance, CPS frequently monitors the part's dimensions in real time and sends them online for computation and analysis to determine the machining operations. These results are then returned to real-world numerical control systems (Alam and El Saddik 2017). Cyber-physical systems are becoming increasingly important in vital infrastructure around the world that includes smart grid systems, water, energy, gas, healthcare, and transportation. These systems contain Internet of Things (IoT) devices, which produce enormous amounts of data and transfer that data to a centralized server. Unfortunately, these devices have limited resources for data processing, storage, and safety precautions that present serious difficulties to ensure the security and effectiveness of CPS. CPS has become a major target as attackers carry out more targeted attacks to have the greatest impact. The recent Colonial Pipeline malware attack is a current illustration of the extensive

DOI: 10.1201/9781003406105-20

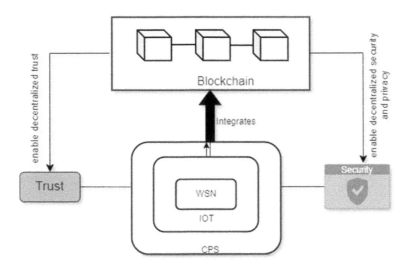

FIGURE 15.1 Broad perspective utilizing blockchain.

effects of a CPS attack. This increases the value of efficient CPS security solutions on a global scale (Khalil et al. 2022). Effective CPS security solutions become even more crucial globally as a result. Blockchain has become a key element in rebuilding CPS systems for better efficiency and safety as examples of these networked devices keep going increase. By 2023, there will be 29.3 billion networked devices.

The most well-known decentralized system in use today is blockchain, which has attracted a lot of attention recently because of its decentralized architecture, and the elimination of centralized regulatory power. A peer-to-peer (P2P) network called the blockchain stores every timestamp transaction created by users and smart devices of the CPS (Bhawana and Kumar 2021). To prevent disputes, each transaction is recorded in an immutable ledger that is kept up to date by network users who are a part of the CPS ecosystem. Many CPS-related problems, including scalability, data integrity, security, reliability, and transparency, are resolved by the blockchain's decentralized architecture, which also lowers the installation and maintenance costs of the centralized system. A broad perspective utilizing blockchain to reconstruct CPS to handle many issues, including WSN and IoT, is shown in Figure 15.1.

15.2 BLOCKCHAIN

Blockchain technology is a distributed, immutable database to which new transactions with time stamps can be added and which can then be organized into blocks by hashing them. The blockchain protocol that supports it specifies how many copies of these blocks can be created and kept in a distributed form. Choosing how a network of users, known as miners, may reach a consensus on the blockchain's present state is a crucial component of this protocol (Rathore, Mohamed, and Guizani 2020). In blockchain blocks contain specific information related to transactions. Hash values are used to store the data to conserve storage space. A block consists of two sections: The first is the block header containing metadata, and the second is the block body

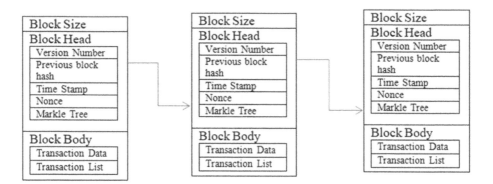

FIGURE 15.2   Sections of blocks.

which contains the value of the block as shown in Figure 15.2. The block header contains the nonce, timestamp, preceding block hash, and hash value, and the Markle tree root summarizes all the data of transactions (Gu et al. 2020). The block body contains transaction data and a list.

15.3   LITERATURE REVIEW

There have been various publications on blockchain-enabled CPS that each focus on a different aspect of this research methodology. These studies frequently concentrate on CPS security. Keshk et al. (2021) provide an overview of the current privacy-preserving methods being utilized to save CPS systems and data from online attacks. They categorize and describe privacy-protection strategies, such as blockchain. Bodkhe et al. (2020) explored the latest developments in consensus techniques, highlighting both their advantages and disadvantages in decentralized CPS applications. They also outline the gaps in the surveys that have already been conducted and offer taxonomy of decentralized consensus mechanisms as a potential solution for various CPS applications.

Dedeoglu et al. (2020) addressed the fact that computationally expensive consensus procedures, limited scalability and throughput, and high latency significantly hinder the broad use in the CPS application of blockchain. Gupta et al. (2020) focused on the cybersecurity flaws of blockchain-enabled CPS applications with smart contracts, where it is simple to change software code exploitable by malicious users. They discovered that even advanced smart contract designs could not completely address security concerns, so they researched artificial intelligence (AI) methods for protecting smart contract privacy.

In Khalil et al. (2022) the authors suggested a CPS based on blockchain from a security and practical standpoint. Additionally, a graphic representation is suggested to illustrate the research work and provides an organized summary of the previous study. In Zhao et al. (2021) the authors gave a thorough analysis of CPS with blockchain support. Through subjective logic, the benefit of adopting blockchain for CPS is demonstrated. In addition, nine blockchain-based operations are taken into account in CPS applications. These operations are categorized into groups according to their throughput and sensitivity, which are connected to the blockchain.

15.4 BLOCKCHAIN'S ROLE IN CPS

The blockchain-based approach, which preserves the information with reliable third parties in a decentralized manner, has been implemented to address the CPS concerns. This section offers a thorough analysis of blockchain use potential advances in the CPS sector using IoT. Trust, security, and privacy are the three divisions of this.

15.4.1 BLOCKCHAIN FOR CPS PRIVACY PROTECTION

For CPS applications, privacy is important. Blockchain technology was used in the development of CPS apps to handle security, privacy, and trust. Smart contracts are required for the verification and authentication of every element of the CPS system. Consequently, the information from the device is safely recorded in the blockchain (Das et al. 2023). Each participating node in a blockchain is identified by the use of a Public Key (PK), which can be modified to create new transactions and thus boost user anonymity. However, research into the Blockchain for Bitcoin reveals that attackers can try to make a user less anonymous by connecting several blockchain transactions with a real-world identity, threatening the user's privacy (Dorri et al. 2019a). In a CPS environment, every contact in a blockchain is permanently recorded between the participating nodes that the node can access. Due to the attackers' ability to view the entire history of user interactions since joining the blockchain, this could raise significant concerns about privacy for CPS users (Dorri, Roulin, et al. 2019b).

Blockchain-based privacy-preserving techniques take advantage of the idea of peer-to-peer cryptography link, or blockchain, to keep network nodes safe or transmission of data (Gaoqi et al. 2018). Peers emerge from different distributed networks, and each peer performs the role of a network node and can help with the computation of the solution to a puzzling problem based on hashes that verify the integrity of the transactions. The current blockchains are packed into every block of transaction records. The block contents that have been recorded are regarded as a ledger. Every peer maintains a copy of the same ledger because the full blocks are updated synchronously across the entire network (Shen et al. 2019). Proof of work (PoW) and proof of stake (PoS), two well-known miner techniques, have been utilized in Ethereum and Bitcoin, respectively, to generate new blocks and verify the authenticity of existing ones (Huang et al. 2019).

15.4.2 BLOCKCHAIN FOR SECURITY IN CPS

Blockchain offers a reliable and secure environment. Before being recorded by the network's nodes, transactions (records) initiated by end users must be verified. A transaction is always encrypted for security purposes and, after being verified, is linked to the previous node through blockchain technology. Instead of having a central server to store data, the Internet of Things network distributes information throughout the system, preventing hackers and intrusions from collecting sensitive data (Mathur and Prakash 2022). Blockchain technology's employment in the context of CPSs enables distributed security since the cryptographic mechanisms enable it to offer a desirable alternative to centralized security. Because a secure blockchain-based system is intended for decentralized governance, it should be more scalable than a conventional one (Veerpal, Bhatt, and Tharewal, 2023). Blockchain's strong security features would also assist prevents malicious devices from transmitting false information and destabilizing a home, industry, or transit system. Blockchain technology may thus securely unlock the operational and financial value of CPSs to enable common functions including information detection, processing, storing, and transmission (Das et al. 2023).

To prevent hackers from compromising transaction data, instead of being kept on a single server, information is spread over a network of computers. Using PKI (private/public key) is the primary method of security in blockchain. Blockchain systems employ Asymmetric Encryption is used to secure transactions between participants. To create these keys, random integers, and strings are used, thus making it impossible for someone to calculate the private key from the public key. This increases the blockchain network's security and secures against future attacks on blockchain records (Yu et al. 2018).

15.4.3 Blockchain for Trust in CPS

The use of CPS like the Internet of Things (IoT), Industrial Control Systems (ICS), Industrial IoT, and Internet of Vehicles (IoV) is growing, and, with it, cyber-attacks, thus having negative impacts on society, the environment, and human lives (Khaitan and Kumar 2014). By enforcing the rules, blockchain technology is used to create trusted systems that correct themselves without any help from an intermediary or a third person. The consensus algorithm is the method employed to achieve this. Simply put, reaching a consensus is reaching an understanding among a group of stockholders who typically do not trust one another. Because every blockchain generates a unique set of data, there are many alternative approaches for creating a consensus. Proof-of-Stake (PoS), Proof-of-Work (PoW), and other similar models are a few examples of consensus algorithms (Mohanta et al. 2019).

15.4.4 Blockchain-Enabled CPS Applications

'In recent years, fuelled by the growth of IoT and sensors-driven technologies, humans are now being replaced as the primary source of data collection by machines' (Rathore, Mohamed, and Guizani 2020). The term 'cyber-physical systems' (CPS) means integrated systems that utilize the power of cyber computation to integrate physical systems, machine worlds, and industrial facilities (Tawalbeh and Tawalbeh 2017). These days, there is a significant advancement, including blockchain-based CPS applications, which benefit various industries in numerous ways. In this section, we will discuss different uses of blockchain in cyber-physical systems, including smart cities, smart grid technology, industrial manufacturing methods, transportation applications, supply chains, IoT, banking, e-voting and medical device security, as shown in Figure 15.3.

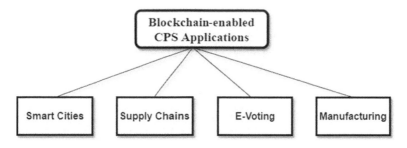

FIGURE 15.3   Applications of blockchain.

15.4.5   SMART CITIES

Smart cities are becoming a necessary demand and a solution to the issues that urban cities face in the modern world. Global population growth means that people no longer simply need just the right amount of infrastructure to support their existence, but also improved facilities that would make their lives more pleasant and comfortable. Smart cities can offer smart services shown in Figure 15.4, such as smart governance, smart living, smart parking, smart education, smart medicare, smart economy, and smart mobility, to their citizens and can do so with the aid of cutting-edge IT-based technologies including ICT, IoT, big data, blockchain, cybersecurity, artificial intelligence, image processing, machine learning, etc. (Gade 2019).

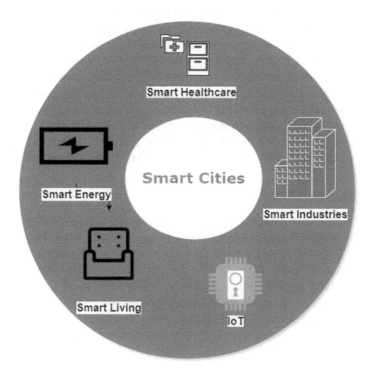

FIGURE 15.4   Smart services by smart cities.

15.4.6 Smart Healthcare

Blockchain is now being employed in applications using individual patient data for record-keeping and conducting medical and public health research. Blockchain-based decentralized solutions in the field of healthcare can be evaluated using metrics based on viability, desired capability, and compliance (Peng et al. 2017). A healthcare system is a combination of industries that offer patients products and services. Sensitive data is frequently exchanged within and outside of the healthcare industry. Healthcare can benefit from the blockchain by better managing electronic medical records (EMR) and safeguarding patient data. The cost of healthcare is currently \$2.3 trillion worldwide, and it is continuously rising by 5.6% annually (Shah et al. 2018).

Blockchain offers patients ownership and control over their data by setting smart contracts for limiting access to healthcare data. A patient can view the history of his data regarding actions like record addition and access. In addition to patients, blockchain allows a safe, common format for the swift processing of services relating to healthcare, and it is used by many organizations to connect and share healthcare data across organizational boundaries. Blockchain-based hospital integration with pharmaceutical and health insurance businesses offers a secure platform for quickly and effectively handling tasks like processing insurance claims and managing the medication distribution chain (Pandey et al. 2021).

15.4.7 Smart Industries

Applications for smart manufacturing frequently use resources and services that are distributed and are available on various platforms, including manufacturing hardware and software-based systems, including CPS, cloud, fog, and other systems. These services and resources could come from a single huge manufacturing company or several connected businesses that work to support a targeted value chain. Without a suitable and flexible execution and development environment assisting their operations and following proper protocols allowing all scattered resources and services to be combined, smart manufacturing apps cannot function effectively. Blockchain offers a secure platform for quickly completing tasks like processing insurance claims and managing the medicine delivery chain (Mohamed and Al-Jaroodi 2019).

15.4.8 Smart Energy

For today's society and economy, having access to power is essential. Over the next 15 years, the energy infrastructure will require an estimated \$48 trillion in investment (Goldthau 2014). This creates a pressing need for and a chance to transition to a clean, efficient, and low-carbon energy system. Smart grid technology serves as a crucial enabler for this change. Figure 15.5 illustrates smart grids function as an intelligent, digitalized system for transporting electricity from a source to a consumer in an efficient manner. The present energy infrastructure is combined with information, telecommunication, and power technologies to achieve this.

A new grid infrastructure known as a 'smart grid' has been suggested as a method to replace the outdated conventional grid with a more precise, effective, and smart

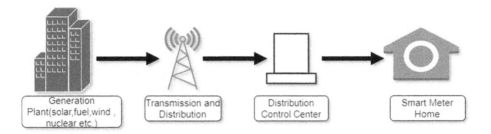

FIGURE 15.5 Smart grid's functions.

energy access and delivery system. Due to the rapid climate change rate of progression and the necessity for sustainable energy sources, several changes and modernizations have taken place (Mollah et al. 2021).

15.5 SUPPLY CHAINS

The full manufacturing and shipping process starts with the procurement, production, and distribution stages in the supply chain. Every industry's supply chain has a very complex framework and architecture. All sectors must modernize their supply chains to increase production and financial success. Among stakeholders, there is trust, transparency, and efficiency at every stage of the supply chain. There are some difficulties and challenges that occur when maintaining a good supply chain. Supply chain operations could benefit from greater flexibility and agility because of blockchain (Cole, Stevenson, and Aitken 2019). Due to blockchain technology, everyone who is a part of the ecosystem can take part in, share, and validate all information and data. Blockchain can be utilized as an append-only transactional data store or as a centralized broker run by a single trusted authority (Viriyasitavat, Anuphaptrirong, and Hoonsopon 2019).

15.6 E-VOTING

Every citizen has the right to vote. Elections are an extremely expensive instrument for exercising this freedom. The residents of the constituency where the elections will take place typically receive a day off work so they can cast their votes. But many people continue to not cast votes (Johari et al. 2022). People don't want to wait around for a long period in the queue. Additionally, those in charge of the election must follow a new voting process that is transparent and takes more time. The blockchain-based election system makes it simpler for voters to cast ballots as well as for the committee to keep track of the results. The blockchain method will enable voters to cast their ballots from anywhere. A sizable number of Indians leave the nation each year, rendering them frequently unable to exercise their right to vote (Li et al. 2019). They would be able to cast their votes via the blockchain system even if they do not have a physical presence in India at the time of the election (Leema, Zameer Gulzar, and Padmavathy, n.d.).

15.7 MANUFACTURING

The CPS system for intelligent manufacturing has a large number of nodes and frequent interactions. The blockchain system's single-chain storage architecture, which is currently in widespread usage, cannot meet the demands of high concurrency and huge amounts of data for various equipment productions in the CPS system for intelligent manufacturing from the standpoint of function and performance (Shobanadevi et al. 2022). It primarily shows up in the next two areas. First off, the immutable data entry feature of blockchain will create the CPS system's intelligent manufacturing nodes exceedingly bulky and large, using a lot of the equipment's storage capacity. Second, the node-to-node communication speed cannot fulfill the criteria for increased concurrency and rapid reaction to the manufacturing industry's speed due to the slow execution speed and significant uniformity of node types (Bhawana and Kumar 2021). The interaction between nodes in a CPS manufacturing system that is intelligent must adhere to real-time specifications to satisfy the needs of flexible production processes (Mohindru et al. 2019). As a result, efficient processing and data storage become crucial components in maximizing system performance.

15.8 BLOCKCHAIN CHALLENGES FOR CPS

Directly implementing blockchain in the CPS domain or applications comes with many challenges shown in Figure 15.6. The CPS's integrated smart sensor devices are in charge of producing a significant amount of data. The mining nodes, who control all of the blockchain's details, may incur a large storage cost as a result of storing this continuously expanding CPS information on the blockchain (Mohindru et al. 2020). Additionally, the blockchain mining process uses a lot of processing power and specialized hardware to validate newly formed blocks, which uses a lot of energy. Thus, scalability problems are presented by this dedicated hardware. The growing number of CPS smart devices in P2P or distributed networks has an indirect impact on the consensus process, which increases the time it takes for a transaction to be confirmed. Additionally, privacy concerns arise in blockchain-based CPS systems since an attacker can utilize transaction information to determine a user's or participant's true identity for illegal reasons. On the other hand, forking, or fraudulent block generation is a serious issue in the blockchain.

The challenges mentioned above can be solved by combining the blockchain with the latest technologies like ML and AI. These technologies assist CPS in

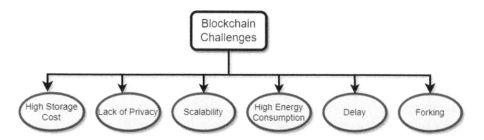

FIGURE 15.6 Challenges in blockchain.

safeguarding against multiple attacks by identifying the various types of attacks (Mohindru & Singh 2018). When developing a way for the CPS to provide anonymity to an interoperable network, zero-knowledge proofs, rings, and group signatures can be used in dealing with privacy issues.

15.9 CONCLUSION

Cyber-physical systems (CPS) allow the exchange of data within a distributed system of systems and objects by integrating physical elements with computing power and storage capacity. Blockchain is a relatively new concept, using the distributed computing paradigm, and provides promising answers for today's CPS applications. Blockchain technology holds great promise for overcoming CPS issues including security, confidentiality, resource limitations, centralization and scalability, a lack of audibility and control, and complex interactions. An example of how industrial applications can create methods of operation, procedure, and adaptability is the blockchain in CPS's IoT, which provides secure and stored data for applications related to production, transportation, healthcare, and energy. This chapter explains how IoT devices, autonomous vehicles, and smart grid applications have profited by transferring the responsibility for the validation of information for network peers, hence removing the risks connected to a centralized architecture.

REFERENCES

Alam, Kazi Masudul, and Abdulmotaleb El Saddik. 2017. "C2PS: A Digital Twin Architecture Reference Model for the Cloud-Based Cyber-Physical Systems." *IEEE Access: Practical Innovations, Open Solutions* 5: 2050–62. https://doi.org/10.1109/access.2017.2657006

Bhawana, and Sushil Kumar. 2021. "A Review on Cyber-Physical Systems Based on Blockchain: Possibilities and Challenges." In *2021 IEEE 6th International Conference on Computing, Communication and Automation (ICCCA)*. IEEE.

Bodkhe, Umesh, Dhyey Mehta, Sudeep Tanwar, Pronaya Bhattacharya, Pradeep Kumar Singh, and Wei-Chiang Hong. 2020. "A Survey on Decentralized Consensus Mechanisms for Cyber-Physical Systems." *IEEE Access* 8: 54371–401.

Cole, Rosanna, Mark Stevenson, and James Aitken. 2019. "Blockchain Technology: Implications for Operations and Supply Chain Management." *Supply Chain Management: An International Journal* 24 (4): 469–83. https://doi.org/10.1108/scm-09-2018-0309

Das, Debashis, Sourav Banerjee, Pushpita Chatterjee, and Uttam Ghosh. 2023. "Security, Trust, and Privacy Management Framework in Cyber-Physical Systems Using Blockchain." In *2023 IEEE 20th Consumer Communications & Networking Conference (CCNC)*. IEEE.

Dedeoglu, Volkan, Ali Dorri, Raja Jurdak, Regio A. Michelin, C. Roben, Salil S. Lunardi, and Avelino F. Kanhere. 2020 "A Journey in Applying Blockchain for Cyber-Physical Systems." In *2020 International Conference on COMmunication Systems & NETworkS (COMSNETS)*. IEEE.

Dorri, Ali, Salil S. Kanhere, Raja Jurdak, and Praveen Gauravaram. 2019a. "LSB: A Lightweight Scalable Blockchain for IoT Security and Anonymity." *Journal of Parallel and Distributed Computing* 134: 180–97. https://doi.org/10.1016/j.jpdc.2019.08.005

Dorri, Ali, Clemence Roulin, Raja Jurdak, and Salil S. Kanhere. 2019b. "On the Activity Privacy of Blockchain for IoT." In *2019 IEEE 44th Conference on Local Computer Networks (LCN)*. IEEE.

Gade, Dipak. 2019. "Introduction to Smart Cities and Selected Literature Review." *International Journal of Advance and Innovative Research* 6 (2): 7–15.

Gaoqi, Steven R., Fengji Weller, Junhua Luo, and Zhao Yang Zhao. 2018. "Distributed Blockchain-Based Data Protection Framework for Modern Power Systems against Cyber-Attacks." *IEEE Transactions on Smart Grid* 10 (3): 3162–73.

Goldthau, Andreas. 2014. "Rethinking the Governance of Energy Infrastructure: Scale, Decentralization and Polycentrism." *Energy Research & Social Science* 1: 134–40. https://doi.org/10.1016/j.erss.2014.02.009

Gu, Ai, Zhenyu Yin, Chuanyu Cui, and Yue Li. 2020. "Integrated Functional Safety and Security Diagnosis Mechanism of CPS Based on Blockchain." *IEEE Access: Practical Innovations, Open Solutions* 8: 15241–55. https://doi.org/10.1109/access.2020.2967453

Gupta, Rajesh, Sudeep Tanwar, Fadi Al-Turjman, Prit Italiya, Ali Nauman, and Sung Won Kim. 2020. "Smart Contract Privacy Protection Using AI in Cyber-Physical Systems: Tools, Techniques, and Challenges." *IEEE Access* 8: 24746–72.

Huang, Junqin, Linghe Kong, Guihai Chen, Min-You Wu, Xue Liu, and Peng Zeng. 2019. "Towards Secure Industrial IoT: Blockchain System with Credit-Based Consensus Mechanism." *IEEE Transactions on Industrial Informatics* 15 (6): 3680–89. https://doi.org/10.1109/tii.2019.2903342

Johari, Rahul, Arvinder Kaur, Mohammad Hashim, Prateek Kumar Rai, and Kanika Gupta. 2022. "SEVA: Secure E-Voting Application in Cyber-Physical System." *Cyber-Physical Systems* 8 (1): 1–31.

Keshk, Marwa, Benjamin Turnbull, Elena Sitnikova, Dinusha Vatsalan, and Nour Moustafa. 2021. "Privacy-Preserving Schemes for Safeguarding Heterogeneous Data Sources in Cyber-Physical Systems." *IEEE Access: Practical Innovations, Open Solutions* 9: 55077–97. https://doi.org/10.1109/access.2021.3069737

Khaitan, Siddhartha, and James D. Kumar. 2014. "Design Techniques and Applications of Cyber-Physical Systems: A Survey." *IEEE Systems Journal* 9 (2): 350–65.

Khalil, Alvi Ataur, Javier Franco, Imtiaz Parvez, Selcuk Uluagac, Hossain Shahriar, and Mohammad Ashiqur Rahman. 2022. "A Literature Review on Blockchain-Enabled Security and Operation of Cyber-Physical Systems." In *2022 IEEE 46th Annual Computers, Software, and Applications Conference (COMPSAC)*. IEEE.

Leema, Anny, A. Zameer Gulzar, and P. Padmavathy. n.d. "Trusted and Secured E-Voting Election System Based on Blockchain Technology." In *Proceeding of the International Conference on Computer Networks, Big Data and IoT (ICCBI-2019)*. Springer International Publishing.

Li, Suisheng, Hong Xiao, Hao Wang, Tao Wang, Jingwei Qiao, and Shaofeng Liu. 2019. "Blockchain Dividing Based on Node Community Clustering in Intelligent Manufacturing CPS." In *2019 IEEE International Conference on Blockchain (Blockchain)*. IEEE.

Mathur, Ashish, and Shiva Prakash. 2022. "Review of Security Enhancement in IoT Using Blockchain." In *2022 IEEE World Conference on Applied Intelligence and Computing (AIC)*. IEEE.

Mo, Haining, Neeti Sharad Wagle, and Michael Zuba. 2014. "Cyber-Physical Systems." *XRDS Crossroads The ACM Magazine for Students* 20 (3): 8–9. https://doi.org/10.1145/2590778

Mohamed, Nader, and Jameela Al-Jaroodi. 2019. "Applying Blockchain in Industry 4.0 Applications." In *2019 IEEE 9th Annual Computing and Communication Workshop and Conference (CCWC)*. IEEE.

Mohanta, Bhabendu K., Soumyashree S. Panda, Utkalika Satapathy, Debasish Jena, and Debasis Gountia. 2019. "Trustworthy Management in Decentralized IoT Application Using Blockchain." In *2019 10th International Conference on Computing, Communication and Networking Technologies (ICCCNT)*. IEEE.

Mohindru, Vandana, Ravindara Bhatt, and Yashwant Singh. "Reauthentication scheme for mobile wireless sensor networks." *Sustainable Computing: Informatics and Systems* 23 (2019): 158–66.

Mohindru, Vandana, and Yashwant Singh. "Node Authentication Algorithm for Securing Static Wireless Sensor Networks from Node Clone Attack." *International Journal of information and computer security* 10, no. 2–3 (2018): 129–48.

Mohindru, Vandana, Yashwant Singh, and Ravindara Bhatt. "Securing wireless sensor networks from node clone attack: a lightweight message authentication algorithm." *International Journal of Information and Computer Security* 12, no. 2–3 (2020): 217–33.

Mollah, Muhammad Baqer, Jun Zhao, Dusit Niyato, Kwok-Yan Lam, Xin Zhang, Amer M. Y. M. Ghias, Leong Hai Koh, and Lei Yang. 2021. "Blockchain for Future Smart Grid: A Comprehensive Survey." *IEEE Internet of Things Journal* 8 (1): 18–43. https://doi.org/10.1109/jiot.2020.2993601

Pandey, Mayank, Rachit Agarwal, Sandeep K. Shukla, and Nishchal K. Verma. 2021. "Security of Healthcare Data Using Blockchains: A Survey." ArXiv [Cs.CR]. http://arxiv.org/abs/2103.12326

Peng, Michael A., Jules Walker, Douglas C. White, and Gunther Schmidt. 2017. "Metrics for Assessing Blockchain-Based Healthcare Decentralized Apps." In *2017 IEEE 19th International Conference on E-Commerce Networking, Applications and Services (Healthcom)*, 1–4. IEEE.

Rathore, Heena, Amr Mohamed, and Mohsen Guizani. 2020. "A Survey of Blockchain-Enabled Cyber-Physical Systems." *Sensors* 20 (1): 1–28.

Shah, Bhavya, Niket Shah, Shruti Shakhla, and Vinaya Sawant. 2018. "Remodeling the Healthcare Industry by Employing Blockchain Technology." In *2018 International Conference on Circuits and Systems in Digital Enterprise Technology (ICCSDET)*. IEEE.

Shen, Meng, Xiangyun Tang, Liehuang Zhu, Xiaojiang Du, and Mohsen Guizani. 2019. "Privacy-Preserving Support Vector Machine Training over Blockchain-Based Encrypted IoT Data in Smart Cities." *IEEE Internet of Things Journal* 6 (5): 7702–12. https://doi.org/10.1109/jiot.2019.2901840

Shobanadevi, A., Sumegh Tharewal, Mukesh Soni, D. Dinesh Kumar, Ihtiram Raza Khan, and Pankaj Kumar. 2022. "Novel Identity Management System Using Smart Blockchain Technology." *International Journal of System Assurance Engineering and Management* 13 (S1): 496–505. https://doi.org/10.1007/s13198-021-01494-0

Tawalbeh, Lo'ai A., and Hala Tawalbeh. 2017. "Lightweight Crypto and Security." In Houbing Song, Glenn, A. Fink, and Sabina Jeschke (Eds.), *Security and Privacy in Cyber-Physical Systems*, 243–61. Chichester, UK: John Wiley & Sons, Ltd.

Veerpal, Devershi Pallavi, Sumegh Bhatt, and Pradeep Kumar Tharewal. 2023 "Blockchain-Based Secure Storage Model for Multimodal Biometrics Using 3D Face and Ear." In *2023 International Conference on Advancement in Computation & Computer Technologies (InCACCT)*. IEEE.

Viriyasitavat, Wattana, Tharwon Anuphaptrirong, and Danupol Hoonsopon. 2019. "When Blockchain Meets Internet of Things: Characteristics, Challenges, and Business Opportunities." *Journal of Industrial Information Integration* 15: 21–8. https://doi.org/10.1016/j.jii.2019.05.002

Yu, Yong, Yannan Li, Junfeng Tian, and Jianwei Liu. 2018. "Blockchain-Based Solutions to Security and Privacy Issues in the Internet of Things." *IEEE Wireless Communications* 25 (6): 12–18. https://doi.org/10.1109/mwc.2017.1800116

Zhao, Wenbing, Congfeng Jiang, Honghao Gao, Shunkun Yang, and Xiong Luo. 2021. "Blockchain-Enabled Cyber–Physical Systems: A Review." *IEEE Internet of Things Journal* 8 (6): 4023–34. https://doi.org/10.1109/jiot.2020.3014864

16 Cybersecurity Challenges, Trends, and Future Directions for Smart Agriculture

Aditya Sharma and Kamal Deep Garg

Chitkara University Institute of Engineering & Technology, Chitkara University, Punjab, India

16.1 INTRODUCTION

Agriculture is a sector that helps the entire world to provide food-related items and plays a very important part in the profitable growth of a country. As we know, population is increasing rapidly which can lead to a lack (Udayanga and Bellanthudawa 2023) of resources in the future. The current state of production is not even able to fulfill the full nutrition diet of the overall world population (Li et al. 2022). People in some areas are still suffering from the lack of healthy food resources which is causing malnutrition among them. According to actionagainstthehunger.org, 783 million people still go hungry because of the lack of food production in some parts of the world which are also labeled as the world's most hungriest countries according to Google – Yemen, South Sudan, Ethiopia, Nigeria, Somalia, Afghanistan, Haiti, and many more in the list. Reviewing this could raise a lot of issues for both the present and the future. In order to meet this need, we must adopt a few critical actions that should totally eradicate the world's population's scarcity of food supplies. As per the United Nations World Population Prospects (Table 16.1), the global population of different countries now vs the 2050 predicted population, for instance, Prospects 2022 has predicted that India's population will rise up to 166.8 crores by the year 2050 which might become a huge concern in fulfilling the diet-related needs of every individual of such a huge population in the coming years. Figure 16.1 shows a graph relation which shows the population now versus 2050 globally. This will impact the yearly grain production that needs to be increased by five billion tons, and meat eating population must be increased up to 250% by 2060 to meet and fulfill the dietary needs of every individual. We have to cultivate and increase more number of lands that are doing crop yielding for the population with almost a zero-failure rate for the farmers all over the world. upon reviewing the above graph, the food production and improvement in crop growing sectors must increase to meet the global needs. Global food production needs must increase in well-organized, smooth-running, and modernized ways and so smart agriculture comes into play and fulfills the requirement globally. Table 16.1 shows

DOI: 10.1201/9781003406105-21

TABLE 16.1
World Population Now versus Predicted

Country	Population (Now)	Population (2050 Predicted)
India	1,428,627,663	166.8 crores
USA	339,996,563	379.4 million
China	1,425,671,352	1.313 billion
Australia	26,439,111	32,814,113
Japan	123,294,513	10.84 million
[27]	2020	Generic NG-CPS framework

Source: 'World Population Now vs 2050', n.d.

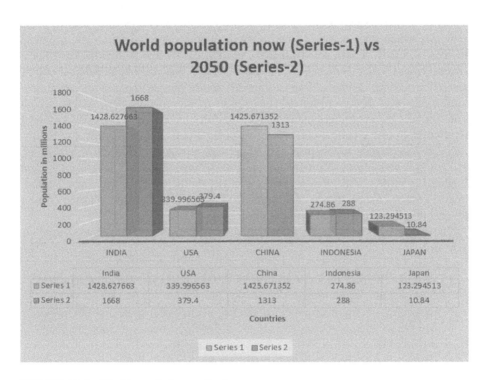

FIGURE 16.1   World population prediction.

the data on the world population now versus the predicted for 2050. This table shows the population of different countries like India, the USA, China, Australia, and Japan.

The term 'smart agriculture' means the application of newly developed devices, models, technologies, and transformations in agriculture. Agriculture 4.0 and Internet of things (IoT) helped a lot in scaling up the agriculture processes to high speed. The fourth generation of Industrial Revolution helps us to provide some information on improving cultivation productivity without increasing the land for growing crops. The internet of things helps to make automating tools for farming. New opportunities and innovations created by smart agriculture allow crop production or cultivation processes to improve by using less natural resources. Smart farming merges different tools, rules, and modern technology that help the farmers to produce high yields or crop productions. The farming sector depends on technologies like remote sensing, cloud, big data, analysis, intelligent models, and cybersecurity. Smart agriculture has some security problems which may also lead to failure. The biggest security issues that are related to smart agriculture are shielding of huge data, processing, limitation of devices, etc. To build strong and accurate models or systems, we need to properly review the generation of large data from devices, transferring of accurate data, processing data in a correct manner, and having some security features to prevent cybersecurity attacks (Drape et al. 2021). Smart agriculture is a technology that requires a lot of data generation and accurate ones; so, failures or attacks can put the security protocols at risk which may raise concerns like privacy, trust, and proper functioning. Smart agriculture contains elements from the Internet of Things (IoT) and wireless networks which may also lead to security problems, especially the data, trustable devices, accuracy of data, and availability of data. Smart agriculture devices consist of sensors and actuators and communication devices that work in all weather conditions. For instance, animals, farm equipment, and/or people could harm smart agriculture deployed devices in fields. They might unintentionally destroy this, which would hinder the smart agriculture gadgets' ability to operate properly. To prevent external harm to the equipment, protective installations and protocols must be created. New advancements in smart agriculture can also lead to agro-terrorism which will lead to cyberattacks through computers to damage crops and generate a critical downfall in profits. This chapter mainly focuses on the cybersecurity threats, challenges, security issues, trends, and future work of smart agriculture and the current advancements and intelligent systems.

The most significant contributions made by this chapter are summarized as follows:

- Describe the idea of smart farming in detail and explain its importance to contemporary agriculture.
- Examine how smart farming can use precision agriculture, and talk about ways in which sensors for the Internet of Things, drones, and satellite imaging may help.
- Discuss the difficulties with internet connection that rural regions experience and how this affects the widespread implementation of smart agricultural devices.
- Determine the difficulties and impediments to the broad application of smart farming.

16.1.1 ORGANIZATION OF THE CHAPTER

The remainder of this chapter is organized as follows. Section 16.2 summarizes the contribution made by experts in smart agriculture culture and lists a table that also includes the limitations of a particular paper. Section 16.3 consists of an overview of smart agriculture. Section 16.4 consists of smart agriculture security challenges that contain different layers of security issues. Section 16.5 consists of trends in smart agriculture. Section 16.6 includes current advancements in smart agriculture. Section 16.7 tells about the future direction or scope in smart agriculture. Section 16.8 gives a conclusion about this chapter.

16.2 LITERATURE WORK

Literature work helps us to get information about smart agriculture and helps the researchers to start the research on who are interested in applications of smart agriculture and its subfields.

Zhao et al. (2023) (Zhao, Liu, and Huang 2023) review the recent advancements, future directions, and challenges that agricultural development faces and the definition and development goals of climate smart agriculture. The paper promotes new strategies for environmental protection, green development, and climate change. It also provides new ideas and strategies for strengthening the environment.

Elsa Jerhamre et al. (2022) explored the opportunities of implementing Artificial intelligence in the agriculture sector business. This study identifies the main technical challenges to data owning, cybersecurity threats, and lack of technical knowledge in the agriculture sector and concludes by discussing macro trends in smart agriculture depending upon obstacles.

Annepu Divya Chandana et al. and Jummelal (2022) provide a detailed review of harvesting and seeding in agriculture sector and also forecast the quantity of pesticides needed to manage the pests. In these papers, the authors monitor crops using 5G connections and IoT devices by capturing crop images and then sending them to a centralized machine learning model or algorithm that will predict diseases and suggest chemicals to farmers. The authors used the PLANT VILLAGE disease dataset that contains 20 diseases of plants and also used the CNN ML model to forecast disease and drugs.

Zaharadeen Yusuf Abdullahi et al. (2022) focus on the implementation of artificial intelligence (AI) in smart agriculture. This helps to enhance crop yield production of different varieties. This paper provides information about current AI trends for boosting crop production using AI tools by utilizing the features from recent years.

Widianto et al. (2022) provide information on artificial intelligence which helps to improve the agriculture sector and develop automation tools by utilizing current trends paper. This study aims to gather trends in the field of artificial intelligence in agriculture, with a focus on factors that improve agricultural productivity and current developments in AI.

Vivek Sharma et al. (2022) and Sharma, Tripathi, and Mittal (2022) review crop diseases and pest recognition using image processing to get the features and algorithms by having different inputs by applying artificial intelligence and machine learning and developing a framework to automate crop pests and detect diseases on crops. In-depth research has been done on a number of issues in order to provide an automated framework for illness and pest disease detection.

Yang et al. (2021) gave the smart farming approach which has a valuable collection of various types of data, control on high precision, and an automated monitor approach. This paper shows a smart farming monitoring system that collects inputs as data and monitors soil moisture, temperature, and humidity. This research contains smart sensors that do the decision-making process for spraying of weed and collection of data.

M. Gupta et al. (2020) provide a comprehensive analysis of security and privacy in the ecosystem of smart farming. The study examines the security and privacy concerns in this dynamic and distributed cyber-physical environment, as well as a multilayered architecture that is pertinent to the precision agricultural area. This paper's main objectives are to outline the multilayer architecture to accurate smart farming environment.

Rettore de Araujo Zanella et al. (2020) provide and review the security addresses challenges such as compatibility, constrained protection schemes used in prior internet or IoT. This paper reviews smart agriculture security, architecture, security threats, challenges, and future directions. Devices or tools demand a lot of data and accuracy which will be very helpful for farmers in various sectors.

Pankaj Dariya et al. (2019) and Pankaj Dariya, Vanshuka Puri, and Amandeep Kaur (2019) address the concept of Internet of Things(IoT) by doing automation in agriculture tools and devices by adding digital intelligence to physical tools. Their papers have shown experimental research on IoT since 2013. They provide information on data sharing and data controlling and doing automation. They summarized various applications of Internet of Things in different fields having various challenges in farming/agriculture related to IoT devices. Table 16.2 displays the title of the study article, the year it was published, and its restrictions.

16.3 OVERVIEW OF SMART AGRICULTURE

Smart agriculture is also known as the digital era of farming/agriculture which combines the new ideas of modernized devices and massive data collection techniques into the agriculture sector or food-related practices. Smart farming/agriculture mainly focuses on agriculture management, a hike in productivity, and emerging new practices by using least amount of resources and doubling the profits and crops of agriculture sector. One of the most beneficial aspects of smart agriculture, according to Singh (2022), is productivity. This allows the industry to realize its full potential, which includes doubling output while using less resources and increasing profitability. Smart agriculture also plays a major role in resource management which helps the practices by refining the use of water, pesticides, and fertilizers. By using automated irrigation or watering system for crops by applying the targeted input based on collected data, it will help the farmers to use less water and cut usage of chemicals and preserve the natural resources for the upcoming generations. Smart agriculture also plays a crucial role in cost saving which was the initial plan of this technique to get long term profits, improve the resource management process, and increase productivity leads to cost savings by reducing the operational cost and doubling the crop production. Smart agriculture also raises a (Kalinaki et al. 2023) concern regarding data management and privacy because in the smart agriculture process massive

TABLE 16.2
Research Paper Titles, Published Year, and Limitations

Sr. No	Research Title	Year	Limitations
1	A Review of Climate-Smart Agriculture: Recent Advancements, Challenges, and Future Directions (Zhao, Liu, and Huang 2023)	2023	The lack of farming water availability, climate variability, and change, agricultural GHG emissions, information resource integration, developing the caliber of agricultural services, and executing agricultural weather index-based insurance have been deemed to be the main development directions of CSA. These issues and challenges are still present in CSA.
2	Exploring the susceptibility of smart farming (Jerhamre, Carlberg, and van Zoest 2022)	2022	The respondents' reported economic concerns are a significant factor slowing the adoption of AI and smart agricultural technology in agriculture. Of course, the high price of investments play a significant role in this, but there are other economic factors at play as well.
3	Smart and safe agriculture in arid locations (Jummelal 2022)	2022	The PLANT VILLAGE Diseases dataset, which includes information on more than twenty different plant ailments, is what we're utilizing instead because we don't have any IOT sensors of this kind.
4	Effects of Modern AI Trends on Smart Farming to Boost Crop Yield Renewable energy View project Security system View project Effects of Modern AI Trends on Smart Farming to Boost Crop Yield (Zaharadeen Yusuf Abdullahi et al. 2022)	2022	Other approaches, such as statistical models, system recommenders, and multi-agent systems, can be used to review further research are not applied.
5	A Systematic Review of Current Trends in Artificial Intelligence for Smart Farming to Enhance Crop Yield (Widianto et al. 2022)	2022	Other approaches, such as statistical models, system recommenders, and multi-agent systems, may be used to look at additional studies but haven't. The outcomes of intelligent agricultural systems can also be explored.
6	Technological Advancements in Automated Crop Pest and Disease Detection: A Review & Ongoing Research (Sharma, Tripathi, and Mittal 2022)	2022	Researchers have not focused on identifying a syndrome in illness that affects several plant parts, such as the stem.
7	IoT-Based Framework for Smart Agriculture (Chitkara university) (Yang, Sharma, and Kumar 2021)	2021	It is possible to add diagnosing crop weeds, insects, and diseases to the work. Machine learning and image processing can be used to detect and diagnose crop problems in agricultural fields by installing photography equipment there.*

TABLE 16.2   (Continued)

Sr. No	Research Title	Year	Limitations
8	Security and Privacy in Smart Farming: Challenges and Opportunities (M. Gupta et al. 2020)	2020	The widespread usage of these based on information apps and internet-connected devices across a variety of industries has created security and privacy concerns, leaving these infrastructures vulnerable to cyberattacks.
9	Security challenges to smart agriculture: Current state, key issues, and future directions (Rettore de Araujo Zanella, da Silva, and Pessoa Albini 2020)	2020	Despite the fact that various security risks might have an impact on the agricultural sector, these solutions nonetheless include certain security measures. It's possible that this is a result of these solutions' immature state. For the majority of the time, only automated resources with little computational resources are used.
10	Understanding Current Trends on Internet of Things – An Overview (Chitkara university) (Pankaj Dariya, Vanshuka Puri, and Amandeep Kaur 2019)	2019	Future studies may be conducted to address a variety of societal problems because IoT is a thriving topic to examine with the help of cloud computing and wireless sensor networks.

data is generated; although it is beneficial, it raises some risks of ownership of data, security, and privacy from cyber-attacks. Farmers or agriculture department must keep the data safe and confidential and protected from hackers. Smart agriculture should focus on making eco-friendly and recyclable devices to minimize the damage to environment. Smart farming/agriculture has many (Vamadeva, Almuraqab, and Khatib 2023) expectations for the future of agriculture. By advancing the technology, proper data collection and analysis of data will enable farmers to optimize the overall productivity by successfully implementing smart farming machines or models and adapting to their usage. Smart agriculture plays an important role in removing the global food insecurity and can be more beneficial due to its cost-effectiveness. Smart farming can also do live monitoring and can also control the smart devices to help the farmers to increase overall crop productions of various crops with different climate conditions and lands by adopting new farming techniques which will make less impact on our environment (eco-friendly) and resource efficient and hike in productivity. The current technological era of smart farming and agriculture is, as of Talero-Sarmiento et al. (2023), developing at a faster pace and with the potential to bring about a significant revolution in the farming sector. This will benefit farmers worldwide and increase overall production. Long-term success can be ensured through extensive knowledge and the appropriate adaptation of new technology. 5G network will overall help the agriculture sector by giving them proper connectivity which will help the farmers to run the smart devices without any drawbacks and full connectivity. Smart agriculture will be a growing sector in the coming years. Smart agriculture involves smart irrigation system, smart drones, smart harvesting tools, some electronic devices, etc. Smart farming also helps farmers to make predictions about their crop prediction. Smart agriculture/farming helps farmers earn more profits due to less hiring of workers and less resource usage.

Smart agriculture has many challenges and limitations to developing new machines, farming tools, and software- and hardware-related technologies; however, at the initial stage, it will involve high cost and will be a challenging task for small crop-producing farmers to adapt to these trends. Security breach is also a big security threat in smart farming as smart agriculture completely relies on data collection and analyzes collected data. So, any hackers or cybercriminal can breach the data and can modify data according to their requirements. As smart farming depends on connectivity it can also be a huge limitation to small crop production farmers or some farmers not having proper internet facility in their areas. Another limitation is that all the crop production farmers must acquire required technical skills and training to properly use the smart devices or machines which can help them to increase their crop production. In some cases, technology can predict or make wrong decisions, so we should also not fully rely on these predictions as machines can give inaccurate predictions due to pseudo-reading of fields. Figure 16.2 depicts some smart agriculture applications.

FIGURE 16.2 Smart agriculture applications.

16.4 SMART AGRICULTURE SECURITY CHALLENGES

Smart agriculture contains mainly four layers – perception layer, network layer, edge layer, and application layer – which help the smart agriculture devices to collect, transport, store, and process massive dataFarming devices are connected to several protocols and use the data to examine the practices brings several security threats (Koduru and Koduru 2022). Smart agriculture uses machine-to-machine communication, and some security measures are also implemented by developers in communication model by TCP/IP networks. Smart farming is can be exposed to many cyberattacks if not implemented carefully and in a perfect manner. These four layers contain many security threats or challenges which can completely harm the crop production and affect the overall quality of the yield. Table 16.3 shows different layers of security challenges with security issues. These threats can also damage the smart devices or machines used by farmers. Figure 16.3 shows the various smart agriculture layers. The threats or security issues which are faced by every layer of smart agriculture are as follows:

16.4.1 PERCEPTION LAYER AND ITS SECURITY CHALLENGES

The perception layer consists of sensors, a camera, GPS, an RFID tag, and an actuator. This layer deals with physical devices that can be implemented in farms and agriculture places that produce crops. Security issues (Kethineni and Gera 2023)

TABLE 16.3
Security Issues in Different Layers ("Security Issues," n.d.)

Layer	Security Issues
Perception Layer	• System hacking
	• Sensor accidents
	• System disruption
	• Fake node
	• Sensor damaging
	• Inaccurate Readings
	• Battery draining attack
	• Optical instability
Network Layer	• Data transit threats
	• Routing security threats
	• Signal disturbance
	• Dos/DDoS
Edge Layer	• Booting
	• Anonymous unauthorized access
	• Middle-men
	• Flooding
	• Illegal control over actuators
Application layer	• Dos/DDoS
	• Phishing
	• Hostile scripts

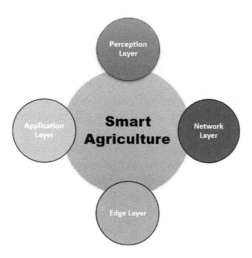

FIGURE 16.3   Smart agriculture layers.

occur due to unauthorized (Freyhof et al. 2022) human activities intentionally, cyber-criminals, viruses, malware, etc.

- **Sensors accident** – It is an unauthorized attack that involves the modification of a smart agriculture implemented device which stops it from doing its desired tasks. Sensors can be damaged by animals or humans or any intense hit will destroy the sensor working. It is a genuine issue that should be handled carefully (Padhy et al. 2023), but in some cases, there is no way to protect the sensors that are inside the devices. Farmers have to identify these and try to avoid damage to the sensors.
- **System hacking** – Drones, robots, and many farming tools are a part of autonomous systems. If unauthorized hackers hack these systems, they can control and make changes according to their needs without official authorization. This cyberattack can lead to the incompletion of required tasks and overall result in crop damage or failure.
- **Inaccurate Reading** – The main reason behind the inaccurate readings or measurements is due to severe weather, malfunction, or false reading input by hackers. Or mainly due to corruption of data due to these causes, the system is unable to give or boost the results required.
- **Sensor Degeneration** – The main reason behind the weakening of sensors is due to oxidation of source material, corrosion of applied metals, and some environmental or chemical conditions. Sensors should be repaired or replaced via management authority to collect accurate data so it is necessary to check the sensors on a yearly basis. Cybercriminals and hackers attempt to compromise the security of the smart farm machinery or device system by gaining access to data, manipulating actuators and sensors, and causing malfunctions or battery drains in the sensors.

- **Battery draining attack** – This attack restricts the machines' battery energy and drains the batteries until they are fully dead. This attack affects the functioning of the overall system and model. Due to this, sensors will also be disoriented (Narayana, Humphreys, and Shelton 2023) and readings will also not be properly taken as required. In this attack, the hackers send several requests; due to this, the system will not enter into sleep mode and its battery will drain faster due to full day working.
- **Optical instability** – This is caused by damaging cameras installed in systems, and due to this they cannot take pictures or scan the data accurately. Cameras are the main visual sensors that capture images to smooth the overall process. They store low-quality images but what if they select misleading data images and bad crop condition images? It may affect overall production and profits. It may affect overall production and profits.

16.4.2 Network Layer and Its Security Challenges

The network layer takes its data from the perception layer. This layer is the most attacked layer due to a large amount data transferring from one communication network to other. They have some threats such as the following:

- **Data transit threats** – These attacks are usually done by hackers or cybercriminals taking control of the sensitive information of network communication. Hackers and cybercriminals can breach the data and make the data corrupt or inaccurate by intervening in the connection between wireless networks containing unencrypted data, or some staff can also provide the data to hackers or cybercriminals.
- **DoS/DDoS** – Denial of services is the most dangerous attack on the smart agriculture systems which exploits the rules and regulations of the systems by preventing use the services of a particular device by making its services unavailable. These types of attacks can prevent farmers from getting or boosting high yield and getting more profits.

16.4.3 Edge Layer and Its Security Challenges

The edge layer consists of control and monitoring tasks and has a connection with all the four layers in the system. It ensures system reliability. Threats faced by it are as follows:

Anonymous unauthorized access – access to massive data and all protocols that are very important for the security of the system. But, if they get breached by hackers and cybercriminals, they will completely disrupt the data and machine from working and can lead to many failures and harmful actions. So, to be safe from this attack the persons handling the access should change the passwords after every deployment so that it would not be easy for hackers to hack it easily.

- **Middle-men** – The attackers who become men in the middle or broker of data may get the overall data and he/she can completely harm the system protocols and can cause some dangerous attacks and total device destruction.
- **Flooding** – A DDoS attack's task is to overload the systems by sending packets to breach the quality of services or even fully discontinued. Attackers send multiple requests to service to make the device exhausted, and this may lead to not proper functioning of the device. It leads the device battery to drain and overuse of smart devices.

16.4.4 APPLICATION LAYER AND ITS CHALLENGES

The application layer focuses on security threats and prevents massive data theft from hackers and cybercriminals. This layer's main function is to provide services to the end users by storing data and making decisions. But, some security issues or threats also may occur to different challenges as follows:

- **Phishing** – It is a digital technique that tries to obtain user data like ID and password by entering systems through emails and websites which gather our system information and give our user data to frauds like hackers and cybercriminals. In the case of smart agriculture, the attackers can take access to user data and change the decision-making processes as per their requirements. It is very difficult to avoid a phishing attack but secure access systems can help to avoid it sometimes. Users should be attentive while browsing the internet.
- **Hostile scripts** – Java applets, Active-X scripts, XSS, and some malicious scripts are used by attackers which can mislead persons and put some hostile information by accessing sensitive information or breaking system regulations and breaking the security of the systems. Cybercriminals can disrupt the services by showing different advertisements and demanding money.

16.5 TRENDS IN SMART AGRICULTURE

Smart agriculture practices have already been a growing trend for the past many years, and it will continue to evolve by emerging technologies (Thilakarathne et al. 2021). Some trends in smart agriculture are as follows, and Figure 16.4 depicts the Internet of Things (IoT) for smart agriculture:

- **Internet of Things (IoT)** – This helps the farmers to increase their yields and production and increase resources. It works on data. IoT devices contain sensors and actuators that analyze many parameters such as land moisture, humidity, and health of the cultivation land. This technology overall helps farmers in some tasks like irrigation and fertilization, using their overall resources, and doubling the production of the crops.

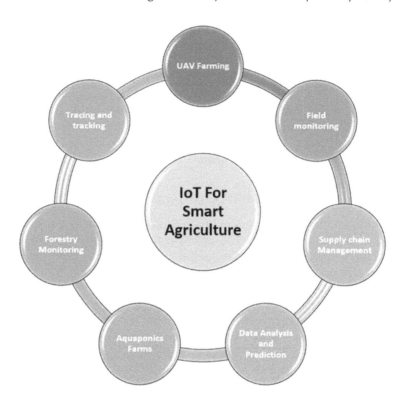

FIGURE 16.4   Internet of Things (IoT) for smart agriculture.

Internet of things devices consist of sensors and hardware and some new technologies that allow them to interact and exchange data within devices or systems connected over the internet. Connectivity technologies and gadgets like Bluetooth, Wi-Fi, and Zigbee are some of the components that make up the Internet of Things. Wearable technology is one example of an IoT gadget. IoT devices have many applications in various sectors like industries, homes, cities, and agriculture.

- **Accuracy Farming** – Accuracy agriculture techniques consist of many technologies GPS and analysis of data to create a field overview which helps farmers to irrigate the required amount of water in their fields and prevent water wastage. This technique not only increases crop yielding but also follows eco-friendliness. Accuracy farming helps the farmers to predict their crop production of their fields through AI/ML model which help them in using limited resources.

- **Data Analysis** – Smart agriculture generates a massive amount of data from fields and installed smart devices from the various crop fields. This data helps the farmers to analyze their land and grow crops according to the historical data and farmers can also plan a successful and more accurate yielding of crops. Data analysis mainly helps to filter a recorded the data and split them into suitable categories which will help the model or device to predicted an accurate output or result and help the farmers to have a high crop yield.

- **Artificial Intelligence (AI)** – AI assists farmers with disease identification, agricultural production forecasting, and crop forecasting through trained models (Baballe, 2022). AI can offer farmers a lot of advice on how to increase their total crop yield. Artificial intelligence (Talaviya et al. 2020) offers innovative models or machines which will help the agriculture sector to enhance its productivity and optimize the overall productivity in the domain of agriculture. Artificial intelligence helps to have a precision farming, automated farming equipment, crop yield prediction, management of livestock (Svetskiy 2022), optimization of livestock, management of various soil conditions or optimizing fertility, weather prediction, irrigation in fields managements (Sarkar, Banerjee, and Ghosh 2023), and agricultural machines, devices, and robots. Artificial Intelligence is one of the sectors that will ensure sustainable food security and lessen the demand for field labor. AI will play a vital role in constructing the future of smart agriculture.
- **Automation tools** – These tools help the farmers and agriculture sectors to transform the overall crop production like drone monitoring of crops, harvesting tools, and actuators. Automation tools are made of sensors and actuators which help the automation device to collect data from its environment and record real and accurate data to get best predictive output. These tools also include farming autonomous robots which are designed to perform important tasks in fields like, pruning, weeding, and picking up of fruits. These robots can work more as compared to manual labor.
- **Data-security and privacy** – It ensures that sensitive or massive agriculture data is safe and follows all safety protocols (Majore 2022). It protects agriculture data from cybercrimes and hackers.

Smart agriculture has many more trends which are developing with a very high speed which are aiming to increase the production of crops and fulfill the global need. Developers have to construct an environment so that the data will be in safe hands and cannot be breached or attacked by hackers and cybercriminals who are trying to steal the data from the smart agriculture devices and machines.

16.6   RECENT ADVANCEMENTS IN SMART AGRICULTURE

Current generation of smart agriculture has many advanced developments which have been developed in recent years globally. Many regulations and protocols (Aslam Ansari & Mohammad 2022) are considered by reviewing the challenges. Recent advancements in smart agriculture (Tavakoli et al. 2022) sector. Table 16.4 gives details about the current advancements in smart agriculture around different parts of the world with its difficulties and the advancements or steps taken to improve the smart agriculture sector.

TABLE 16.4

Current Advancements in Smart Agriculture ('Table of Advancements', n.d.)

Countries	Difficulties	Steps Taken for Smart Agriculture
Maharashtra (India)	• Greenhouse gas (GHC) emissions • Not enough required water • Climate risks	• Water technologies for managing irrigation system by digging well, rainwater harvesting, irrigation of drips, extraction of groundwater collection methods. • Management of ground nutrients methods, manure, straw residue incorporation.
Nepal (Asia)	• Low crop yield • Forecast risks • Greenhouse gas emissions	• Crop rotation, straw return to cultivate land by adapting measures. • Improving land fertility and its properties
Pakistan (Asia)	Same conditions and regulations as Nepal and Maharashtra.	• Crop rotation, straw return to cultivate land by adapting measures. • Improving land fertility and its properties.
California (United States)	• Agriculture flexibility • GHC emissions • Systematic production	• Upgradation of underground water. • Micro sprinkler irrigation systems. • Implementing rules
Netherlands (Europe)	• Agriculture impact changes • GHC emissions	• LED horticulture tech. • Feasible increased in horticulture

16.7   FUTURE DIRECTIONS/SCOPE IN SMART AGRICULTURE

The current generation of smart agriculture devices and models has shown many encouraging results of food productions in agriculture sector.(Iaksch, Fernandes, and Borsato 2020) Some research work is going on for future use for betterment of farmers and current agriculture status (Jackson, Marvin, and Chakrabarty 2022). Future directions are as follows:

• **Smart agriculture irrigation system** – Water shortage is a huge concern for farming sector, and smart agriculture irrigation systems will help the farmers to use the right amount of water without any wastage and crop damage (Wu and Bulut 2022). The developed systems will be able to adjust water schedule based on real-time data or historical data or according to weather forecast. These irrigation systems collect data, automate, and improve crop production (Akella et al. 2023). These systems can be applied on large-scale and small-scale agriculture lands and can also be installed on any soil condition with various settings.

By such water usage and decreasing the use of agro based chemicals on crops smart irrigation helps with reducing the environmental impact and using smart modes of practices.

- **Remote sensing** – This can help farmers to analyze huge agriculture area with help of advancements in remote sensing and satellite image capturing. This can detect crop condition, pest infest, and changes in crop (Aboneh 2023). It is an important technique in smart agriculture. It helps us to collect information and condition of a particular crop field by using various tools like drones and ground platforms to collect data, which is processed and then optimized for agricultural tasks. It basically tell us about estimation of crop production, analysis of soil, managing of water usage, weather viewing and management, disease and pest detection, weed detection, planning the use of land, and doing crop growth modeling.

- **Urban Agriculture** – This technique could play an important role in food production. This will support increasing crop productivity by optimizing the use of energy, resources, and many other sectors (Rahu et al. 2023). Vertical farming will also be so valuable in future. It is a practice that helps in crop production growth.

- **Drone technique** – This will help in aerial watch for crops, analysis, and spraying pesticides. This is a cost-friendly method which can cover large size fields and obtain high-resolution data. In future drones can become more advanced with advance image tech, making real-time decisions with the help of artificial intelligence models. Use of drones has various benefits such as surveillance planning and mapping of field, spraying on crops and application inputs, pollination assistance, and data collection (L. Gupta, Malhotra, and Kumar 2022). It helps to lower the production cost and increase productivity.

- **Machine Learning (ML models)** – AI and ML models enable better decision-making in agriculture by analyzing the data and prediction models. Smart agriculture will be highly dependent on artificial intelligence and machine learning models to take its own decisions and increase the crop growth by doing crop management and disease management (Mohindru et al. 2021). ML models play a vital role in smart agriculture by collecting data and pass them through advanced ML models algorithms. It learns from historical data to overall crop yield production by predicting the crop yield, detection of anomaly in field, optimization of irrigation, management of nutrients, health prediction, sorting and quality grading, behavior analysis, and price prediction after harvesting.

- **Expansion of Internet of Things (IoT)** – In future (Chattopadhyay, Patel, and Parmar 2022) more developed applications will be launched with many innovative features which will help the overall crop production with

advanced motion sensors and devices with precisions. It will help to analyze temperature, moisture in soil, and better conditions for crop growth
(Mohindru et al. 2020).

- **Data analysis** – The future of smart agriculture will highly rely on big data
  as it requires advanced modes of data collection and analysis to increase
  the crop production. Data integration and collection is a crucial task in data
  analysis. It empowers the farmers to use their resources and improve stock
  management (Mohindru & Singh 2018). It also uses machine learning and
  artificial intelligence application systems and decision support systems for
  crop classification and collects data to automate the tasks which will be
  valuable to farmers.
- **Automation and Robotics** – These will play a crucial role in growing the
  smart agriculture sector by developing the robots or technology which will
  work 24/7 on field by performing the tasks of harvest, planting, watching
  over the crops, etc.

16.8 CONCLUSION

As the time progresses, many more advancements and technologies in smart agriculture will take place and help the farmers and global population to increase food production and minimize the shortage of food resources which will help the population
to fulfill their diet needs. In conclusion, smart agriculture/farming is a life-changing,
advanced technology that helps farmers to optimize crop yield production by following advanced smart farming/agriculture practices, increase efficiency by using less
resources with the help of Internet of Things (IoT) devices, which include drones,
crops monitoring system, data-dependent decision-making through ML/AI tools or
models, and keep the resources efficiently. The primary benefits of smart farming are
extremely helpful to the agricultural industry because they enable farmers to obtain
the desired crop yield by using resources like water, fertilizers, and pesticides that
will minimize water waste and have a minimal negative impact on the environment.
Smart farming also helps to reduce the usage of chemical and water consumption and
promotes a greener and balanced agriculture approach. The adoption of smart farming has brought about a number of revolutions for the farming industry, including the
need to adapt to new investment requirements, data security concerns, privacy risks,
and the requirement to teach farmers or other users how to properly use developed
technology. Smart agriculture is a valuable thing to uplift the overall food production. Using AI/ML models helps in decision-making. It can lead to solving the overall food crisis by advancing the technology and ecosystem for the future. It will help
farmers to grow more crops and safeguard earth's resources.

REFERENCES

Abdullahi, Z.Y., Saad, A.M., Abdulsalam, S.S., Sulaiman, K., Abubakar, A.B. and Baballe,
    M.A. 2022, July. Effects of Modern AI Trends on Smart Farming to Boost Crop Yield.
    In *3rd International Conference on Applied Engineering and Natural Sciences*, https://
    www.icaens.com (pp. 627–36).

Aboneh, Tagel. 2023. "Fusion of Multiple Sensors to Implement Precision Agriculture Using IOT Infrastructure." (April): 1–13. https://doi.org/10.20944/preprints202304.0119.v1

Akella, Gopi Krishna, Santoso Wibowo, Srimannarayana Grandhi, and Sameera Mubarak. 2023. "A Systematic Review of Blockchain Technology Adoption Barriers and Enablers for Smart and Sustainable Agriculture." *Big Data and Cognitive Computing* 7 (2): 86. https://doi.org/10.3390/bdcc7020086

Aslam Ansari, B., and G. Mohammad. 2022. "Climate Smart Agriculture Interventions-Lessons Learned and Implications for Future." (April). https://www.researchgate.net/publication/359867252

Baballe, Muhammad Ahmad. 2022. "An Organized Review of Current AI Trends for Smart Farming to Boost Crop Yield and Its Advantages Some of the Authors of This Publication Are Also Working on These Related Projects: Image Processing View Project Security System View Project." *Gjrpublication*. https://doi.org/10.5281/zenodo.7026553

Chattopadhyay, Pratyay, Homak P. Patel, and Viral Parmar. 2022. "Internet of Things (IoT) in Smart Agriculture." *3rd International Conference on Electronics and Sustainable Communication Systems, ICESC 2022 - Proceedings*, August: 536–40. https://doi.org/10.1109/ICESC54411.2022.9885655

Pankaj Dariya, Vanshuka Puri, and Amandeep Kaur. 2019. "Understanding Current Trends on Internet of Things - An Overview." *Journal of Technology Management for Growing Economies* 10 (2): 66–71. https://doi.org/10.15415/jtmge.2019.102005

Drape, Tiffany, Noah Magerkorth, Anuradha Sen, Joseph Simpson, Megan Seibel, Randall Steven Murch, and Susan E. Duncan. 2021. "Assessing the Role of Cyberbiosecurity in Agriculture: A Case Study." *Frontiers in Bioengineering and Biotechnology* 9 (August). https://doi.org/10.3389/fbioe.2021.737927

Freyhof, Mark, George Grispos, Santosh Pitla, and Cody Stolle. 2022. "Towards a Cybersecurity Testbed for Agricultural Vehicles and Environments." May. http://arxiv.org/abs/2205.05866

Gupta, Lipika, Shivani Malhotra, and Amit Kumar. 2022. "Study of Applications of Internet of Things and Machine Learning for Smart Agriculture." *Proceedings of 2022 IEEE International Conference on Current Development in Engineering and Technology, CCET 2022* (December): 1–5. https://doi.org/10.1109/CCET56606.2022.10080342

Gupta, Maanak, Mahmoud Abdelsalam, Sajad Khorsandroo, and Sudip Mittal. 2020. "Security and Privacy in Smart Farming: Challenges and Opportunities." *IEEE Access* 8: 34564–84. https://doi.org/10.1109/ACCESS.2020.2975142

Iaksch, Jaqueline, Ederson Fernandes, and Milton Borsato. 2020. "Digitalization and Big Data in Smart Farming - Bibliometric and Systemic Analysis." *Advances in Transdisciplinary Engineering* 12: 115–24. https://doi.org/10.3233/ATDE200068

Jackson, Majwega, Ggaliwango Marvin, and Amitabha Chakrabarty. 2022. "Robust Ensemble Machine Learning for Precision Agriculture." *2022 International Conference on Innovations in Science, Engineering and Technology, ICISET 2022* (May): 492–97. https://doi.org/10.1109/ICISET54810.2022.9775879

Jerhamre, Elsa, Carl Johan Casten Carlberg, and Vera van Zoest. 2022. "Exploring the Susceptibility of Smart Farming: Identified Opportunities and Challenges." *Smart Agricultural Technology*. Elsevier B.V. https://doi.org/10.1016/j.atech.2021.100026

Jummelal, Karamtothu. 2022. "Smart and Safe Agriculture in Arid Locations Utilizing 5G, IOT and Machine Learning." www.ijsdr.org

Kalinaki, Kassim, Wasswa Shafik, Tar J. L. Gutu, and Owais Ahmed Malik. 2023. "Computer Vision and Machine Learning for Smart Farming and Agriculture Practices." *IGI Global*, 79–100. https://doi.org/10.4018/978-1-6684-8516-3.ch005

Kethineni, Keerthi, and Pradeepini Gera. 2023. "Iot-Based Privacy-Preserving Anomaly Detection Model for Smart Agriculture." *Systems* 11 (6): 304. https://doi.org/10.3390/systems11060304

Koduru, Tejaswi, and Naga Padmasri Koduru. 2022. "An Overview of Vulnerabilities in Smart Farming Systems." *Journal of Student Research* 11 (1): 1–14. https://doi.org/10.47611/jsrhs.v11i1.2303

Li, Jun, Enjun Xia, Lingling Wang, Kuan Yan, Li Zhu, and Jieping Huang. 2022. "Knowledge Domain and Emerging Trends of Climate-Smart Agriculture: A Bibliometric Study." *Environmental Science and Pollution Research* 29 (46): 70360–79. https://doi.org/10.1007/s11356-022-20796-9

Majore, Ginta. 2022. "Enterprise Modelling Methodology for Socio-Cyber-Physical Systems Design: Case from Cybersecurity Education and Climate-Smart Agriculture." *Society. Technology. Solutions. Proceedings of the International Scientific Conference* 2 (April): 4. https://doi.org/10.35363/via.sts.2022.74

Mohindru, Vandana, and Yashwant Singh. 2018. "Node Authentication Algorithm for Securing Static Wireless Sensor Networks from Node Clone Attack." *International Journal of Information and Computer Security* 10, no. 2–3: 129–48.

Mohindru, Vandana, Yashwant Singh, and Ravindara Bhatt. 2020. "Hybrid Cryptography Algorithm for Securing Wireless Sensor Networks from Node Clone Attack." *Recent Advances in Electrical & Electronic Engineering (Formerly Recent Patents on Electrical & Electronic Engineering)* 13 (2): 251–59.

Mohindru, Vandana, Sunidhi Vashishth, and Deepak Bathija. 2021. "Internet of Things (IoT) for Healthcare Systems: A Comprehensive Survey." *Recent Innovations in Computing: Proceedings of ICRIC*, 1 (2022): 213–29.

Narayana, Ravishankar, Brianna Humphreys, and Kyle Shelton. 2023. "I-Farming: Managing Crop Production in the Digital Era i-Farming: Managing Crop Production in the Digital Era." (January): 2.

Padhy, Sasmita, Majed Alowaidi, Sachikanta Dash, Mohamed Alshehri, Prince Priya Malla, Sidheswar Routray, and Hesham Alhumyani. 2023. "AgriSecure: A Fog Computing-Based Security Framework for Agriculture 4.0 via Blockchain." *Processes* 11 (3). https://doi.org/10.3390/pr11030757

Rahu, Mushtaque Ahmed, Sarang Karim, Rehan Shams, Ayaz Ahmed Soomro, and Abdul Fattah Chandio. 2023. "Wireless Sensor Networks-Based Smart Agriculture: Sensing Technologies, Application and Future Directions." *Sukkur IBA Journal of Emerging Technologies* 5 (2): 18–32. https://doi.org/10.30537/sjet.v5i2.1104

Rettore de Araujo Zanella, Angelita, Eduardo da Silva, and Luiz Carlos Pessoa Albini. 2020. "Security Challenges to Smart Agriculture: Current State, Key Issues, and Future Directions." *Array* 8 (December): 100048. https://doi.org/10.1016/j.array.2020.100048

Sarkar, Uditendu, Gouravmoy Banerjee, and Indrajit Ghosh. 2023. "Artificial Intelligence in Agriculture: Application Trend Analysis Using a Statistical Approach." *International Journal of Applied Science and Engineering* 20 (1): 1–8. https://doi.org/10.6703/IJASE.202303_20(1).002

"Security Issues." n.d. https://www.sciencedirect.com/science/article/pii/S2590005620300333

Sharma, Vivek, Ashish Kumar Tripathi, and Himanshu Mittal. 2022. "Technological Advancements in Automated Crop Pest and Disease Detection: A Review & Ongoing Research." In *Proceedings of International Conference on Computing, Communication, Security and Intelligent Systems, IC3SIS 2022*. Institute of Electrical and Electronics Engineers Inc. https://doi.org/10.1109/IC3SIS54991.2022.9885605

Singh, Anil Kumar. 2022. "Smart Farming: Applications of IoT in Agriculture." *Handbook of Smart Materials, Technologies, and Devices: Applications of Industry 4.0: Volume 1-3* 2 (December): 1655–87. https://doi.org/10.1007/978-3-030-84205-5_114

Svetskiy, Arseniy Vladimirovich. 2022. "Application of Artificial Intelligence in Agriculture." *Сельское Хозяйство*, 3: 1–12. https://doi.org/10.7256/2453-8809.2022.3.39469

"Table of Advancements." n.d. https://www.jiva.ag/blog/top-13-innovations-in-agriculture-farming#:~:text=FarmAutomation&text=Farmersarealreadyusingdrones,droughtorother environmentalfactors

Talaviya, Tanha, Dhara Shah, Nivedita Patel, Hiteshri Yagnik, and Manan Shah. 2020. "Implementation of Artificial Intelligence in Agriculture for Optimisation of Irrigation and Application of Pesticides and Herbicides." *Artificial Intelligence in Agriculture* 4: 58–73. https://doi.org/10.1016/j.aiia.2020.04.002

Talero-Sarmiento, Leonardo Hernán, Diana T. Parra-Sanchez, and Henry Lamos Diaz. 2023. "Opportunities and Barriers of Smart Farming Adoption by Farmers Based on a Systematic Literature Review." (May): 53–64. https://doi.org/10.4995/inn2022.2022.15746

Tavakoli, H., J. Correa, S. Vogel, and R. Gebbers. 2022. "RapidMapper – a Mobile Multi-Sensor Platform for the Assessment of Soil Fertility in Precision Agriculture." *AgEng LAND. TECHNIK 2022.* (November): 351–58. https://doi.org/10.51202/9783181024065-351

Thilakarathne, Navod Neranjan, Hayati Yassin, Muhammad Saifullah Abu Bakar, and Pg Emerolylariffion Abas. 2021. "Internet of Things in Smart Agriculture: Challenges, Opportunities and Future Directions." In *2021 IEEE Asia-Pacific Conference on Computer Science and Data Engineering, CSDE 2021.* Institute of Electrical and Electronics Engineers Inc. https://doi.org/10.1109/CSDE53843.2021.9718402

Udayanga, Samitha, and B Kushan Aravinda Bellanthudawa. 2023. "A Case Study on Climate-Smart Agriculture, Community Farming, and Climate Change Adaptation in a Sri Lankan Case Study on Climate-Smart Agriculture, Community Farmi," February.

Vamadeva, Rubalavanyan, Nasser A. Saif Almuraqab, and Yassin M. Nour Khatib. 2023. "A Quantum Leap Towards More Effective and Efficient Smart Farming in Rural Areas Using IOT," (June): 1123–31. https://doi.org/10.46254/an13.20230332

Widianto, Mochammad Haldi, Mochamad Iqbal Ardimansyah, Husni Iskandar Pohan, and Davy Ronald Hermanus. 2022. "A Systematic Review of Current Trends in Artificial Intelligence for Smart Farming to Enhance Crop Yield." *Journal of Robotics and Control (JRC)* 3 (3): 269–78. https://doi.org/10.18196/jrc.v3i3.13760

"World Populaition Now vs 2050." n.d. https://www.aljazeera.com/news/2023/7/11/world-population-day-what-will-the-world-look-like-in-2050

Wu, Philip Fei, and Cevdet Bulut. 2022. "IoT Adoption in Agriculture: A Systematic Review." *Americas Conference on Information Systems* 14 (June): 1–10.

Yang, Jian, Amit Sharma, and Rajeev Kumar. 2021. "IoT-Based Framework for Smart Agriculture." *International Journal of Agricultural and Environmental Information Systems* 12 (2): 1–14. https://doi.org/10.4018/IJAEIS.20210401.oa1

Zhao, Junfang, Dongsheng Liu, and Ruixi Huang. 2023. "A Review of Climate-Smart Agriculture: Recent Advancements, Challenges, and Future Directions." *Sustainability (Switzerland).* MDPI. https://doi.org/10.3390/su15043404

Index

Page numerals in *italics* refer to figures and those in **bold** refer to tables.